INTERROGATING SOCIAL DEVELOPMENT

INTERROGATING SOCIAL DEVELOPMENT

Global Perspectives and Local Initiatives

Edited by

DEBAL K. SINGHAROY

MANOHAR
2010

First published 2010

ISBN 978-81-7304-871-5 (Hb)
ISBN 978-81-7304-876-0 (Pb)

Published by

Ajay Kumar Jain *for*
Manohar Publishers & Distributors
4753/23 Ansari Road, Daryaganj
New Delhi 110 002

Typeset at

Digigrafics
New Delhi 110 049

Printed at

Salasar Imaging Systems
Delhi 110 035

To my teacher
Professor Sharit Bhowmik
for all his ever friendly
guidance and encouragement

Contents

Preface

In recent years social development has emerged to be a major theme of discussion in policy planning, academic discourse and in collective activism in the wake of new policy initiatives by the state and supra state agencies at the top on the one hand and increasing pressure of the people from the below on the other. The process of globalization and economic liberalization have envisaged a paradigmatic shift in the social developmental perspectives of the state, international and national civil society establishments, corporate bodies and of local organizations operating at the grassroot level. As against the backdrop of such changes, varieties of new initiatives are initiated in all parts of India. This collection has tried to bring forth perceptive and critical understanding of these initiatives with the contribution from the scholars working in the field of social development.

The collection has come to a concrete shape with the contribution and cooperation of host of individuals and institutions. At the very outset I would like express my heartiest thank and gratitude to Professor T.K. Oommen, Professor S.L. Sharma, Professor Alka Dhameja, Professor H.N. Shankaranarayana, Dr. T.N. Sreedhara, Dr. Sujata Dutta Hazarika, Professor P.K. Biswas, Dr. Raj Kumar Khosla, Dr. Jagannath Ambagudia, Dr. Renu Addlakha, Dr. O.P. Mishra, Dr. Damayanti Mukhopadhyay, Dr. S.A.H. Moinuddin, Dr. Silima Nanda, Professor Sarjerao Salunkhe, Dr. Ritambhara Malaviya, Dr. Moumita Das, Ms. Suditi Naskar and Dr. Sutapa Bose for their valuable contribution.

I am thankful to Professor V.N. Rajasekharan Pillai, Vice-Chancellor Indira Gandhi National Open University, for his valuable leadership, encouragement and support to organize the International Conference on Social Development, Social Movements, and the Marginalized in Indira Gandhi National Open University, New Delhi in February 2008 with the co-sponsorship of the Research Committee 48: Social Movements, Collective Action and Social Change of International Sociological Association (ISA), Madrid, Indian Council of Social Sciences Research (ICSSR), New Delhi and United Nations Development Programme (UNDP), New Delhi. I am thankful to my university, IGNOU, to ISA, ICSSR and UNDP for their help and support. A large number of papers in this collection were initially presented in this conference and subsequently revised and modified. A few of papers were also specially invited to suit the thematic requirement of this collection. I am grateful to Professor Pillai for his unequivocal support for bringing out this collection.

I am thankful to Professor T.K. Oommen (India), Professor Partha Nath Mukherjee (India), Professor James Goodman (Australia), Tova Banski (Israel), Professor Benjamin Tejerina (Spain), Professor Peter Jay Mike (Canada), Dr. Tim Jordan (UK), Professor Sharit Bhowmik (India), Dr. Roger Spadling (UK) for their encouragement and constant support.

My sincere gratitudes are due to Professor Omprakash Mishra, Pro-Vice-Chancellor, Indira Gandhi National Open University and Professor Maitrayee Chaudhuri, Professor of Sociology, Jawaharlal Nehru University, New Delhi for their valued contribution in shaping this volume. I am also thankful to Prof. Pravin Sinclair, Pro-Vice-Chancellor, Professor Uma Kanjilal, Director, School of Social Sciences for their advice and guidance to bring out this collection in time.

I am also thankful Professor S.C. Garg, Professor Pandav Nayak, Professor Kapil Kumar, Professor Pardeep Sahni, Professor A.S. Narang, Professor Darvesh Gopal, Professor E. Vayunandan, Mr. Ajay Mahurkar of Indira Gandhi National Open University for their support and encouragement.

I am thankful to my department colleagues Professor Tribhuwan Kapur, Dr. B. Kiranmayi, Dr. Nita Mathur, Dr. R. Vashum, Dr. Archana Singh and Dr. Rabindra Kumar for their cooperation.

I am highly indebted to my wife Dr. Prava Debal for her observations and comments on my paper and timely supports. Despite her own professional commitments she has always taken an extra care to all academic initiatives. I am thankful to my daughter Purbali and son Aniruddha, for their cooperation and profound sense of tolerance.

Thanks are due to my office staff Mr. Shailendra Kumar Singh and Ms. Sonia Singh who have shown a good deal of dedication towards the completion of this work. Indeed it would have been impossible for me to organize this work without their support and help.

I am obliged to Mr. Ramesh Jain, Manohar Publishers to bring out this volume with utmost efficiency. I am also thankful to Mr. Siddharth Chowdhury for his cooperation.

DEBAL K. SINGHAROY

Introduction

DEBAL K. SINGHAROY

Contemporary world has borne witness to a paradoxical societal progression reflected in the unprecedented economic growth in many parts of the developing world (notwithstanding the very recent global economic slowdown) on the one hand and unabated continuation, reshaping and resurfacing of varieties of social, economic and political deprivations and exclusion on the other. The fast process of economic globalization, that has widely contributed to the extraordinary expansion of information and communication technologies, proliferation of knowledge economy, global and local connectivity, phenomenal economic growth and material prosperity, have seldom facilitated the eradication of poverty, livelihood insecurity, malnutrition, unemployment, illiteracy, ill-health, social inequalities, divides and exclusions and disempowerment of the largest segment of the population. It has been widely realized by now that economic development does not necessarily lead to social development; and that the growing imbalances not only threatens social cohesion but also cause retrogression to the development of a society as a whole. Hence formulation of perceptive policies and legal provisions are not sufficient and efficient enough to strike a balance between economic and social development until and unless these are commensurated by effective political will of the state and pressure from the below generated by the civil societies and people to implement the developmental mandates at the grassroots to ensure benefits of developments for each and every segment of the population. It is indeed, imperative on the part of the state to lay the foundation of a society with justice by ensuring educational development, livelihood, health, employment, security, social justice, dignity and freedom of all segments of the population. The citizens of the country, on the other hand, have the rights to development and justice. It is in this context that the perspective of social and human development has occupied the centrestage in the contemporary development discourse to espouse the ideals of 'development for all'.

Though the ideals of social and human development are of relatively recent origin, these have widely nurtured for long within the 'welfare' perspective of the state wherein the state have played crucial roles in meeting the basic goods and services related to education, health, housing, employment, income and livelihood security of the people. Though 'social welfare' is basically an European innovation, it has evolved over centuries to get to its current shape and to spread to other parts of the world. The concept of 'civil rights' has had also its origin within the welfare activity of the state starting in the eighteenth century through the articulation of civil rights of the citizens, i.e. freedom of speech, thought and religion, right to own property, right to equal justice before the law and such other social concerns. Significantly since nineteenth century there has been the articulation of 'political rights' of the citizens, i.e. rights to political participation, to vote, to hold political position, for democratic action; and then of the 'social rights' of the citizen since early twentieth century, e.g. right to economic and social security, through education, health care, housing, minimum wages and so on (Marshall, 1973). It is important that achievement of civil rights and political rights have paved the way for the emergence of social rights over the centuries. Moreover, the achievement of civil rights and political rights is the basis upon which social rights have been fought for and that none of these rights now can be taken for granted (Esping-Andersen, 1990). In this context it is important to mention that since last two centuries, the pursuits of liberty, equality, fraternity, justice and solidarity have been the cherished demands of most of the revolutionary, national liberation and labour movements (Frank and Fuentes, 1990). Hence the process of articulation of social rights is as much historically determined as much socially and politically. Thus contemporary ideal of social development as the evaluation and extension of civil, political and social rights is socially and politically constructed within the emerging nature of the state, civil society and the grassroot collective actions on the one hand, and the wider social processes of globalization on the other.

In the wake of globalization and adoption of Structural Adjustment Programme in most parts of the world, the developmental perspectives have undergone a phenomenal shift. This shift has been widely reflected in the emerging social, economic and political thoughts and developmental initiatives of the state, international and national civil societies and of grassroots organizations. The most conspicuous strategic shift has been those of from viewing development only on economic terms and as an end in itself to recognize it as the means to ensure livelihood security, equity, freedom and peace, increasing access to education, health care and employment opportunities, widening the scope of democratic practices, political participation, cultural freedom, and social choices of all segments of the society. In order to reconceptualize the changing social objectives of development there have been utmost urgency to put human agency at the centre stage of all activism; articulation of varieties of new initiatives from the above and recognition of the need of assertion of people from below.

Capital, infrastructure, organization of production (entrepreneurship), technology, social policies, institutions like market, as instruments, play decisive roles in development. Significantly these instruments are the product of a human being's own initiatives and are not independent determinants of development. In essence human beings are the embodiment of the capacity from within to produce those instruments for development. Developmental process releases, organizes and converts human energy into social capacity and material results that have a social purpose. Within this broad understanding, the perspective on social development shifts the focus from instruments to the creators of these instruments. Ideally 'social development should generate a framework around which all knowledge of the factors, instruments, conditions, agencies and process of development can be integrated (Sen, 1999). Human beings are brought in the centre-stage of development by emphasizing that 'human development is the end and economic growth is the means' (UNDP, 1996). Human development in essence is recognized to be a function of human awareness, aspiration, attitudes and values; and similar to all human creative processes human development is also a process of self-conception of human beings. Thus holistically human development does not grapple with the material dimension only. It also integrates with the developmental process—the dimensions of life and mind—including physical, genetic and biological determinants, social behaviour, skills, attitudes, customs, traditions, systems, formal organization, non-formal institutions, and cultural values—all of which interact and influence each other to impact the course of human development (Jacobs and Cleveland, 1999).

Though human development cannot be devoid of economic growth one must see beyond it. Amartya Sen largely points out: 'The end and means of development require examination and scrutiny for a fuller understanding of the development process; it is simply not adequate to take as our basic objective . . . just maximization of income or wealth. . . . Development has to be more concerned with enhancing the lives we lead and the freedom we enjoy' (Sen, 1999: 14). The broad perspective on social and human development addresses the issues of social, economic, political and cultural needs, well-being and engagements at the levels of individuals, groups and the society in diverse ways. It contributes effectively towards the process of increasing the assets and capabilities of individuals to improve their well-being; increasing the capacity of social groups to exercise agency, transform their relationships with other groups and participate in development processes; and increasing the ability of society to reconcile the interests of its constituents, govern it peacefully, and manage change. This also looks for transforming the institutional arrangements of society for 'greater inclusion, cohesion and accountability' with the goal to empower poor, vulnerable, marginalized women and men, with a view to promote equality of opportunity, to redress inequality and discriminatory practices based on caste, race, gender, ethnicity and class, to integrate the society both vertically and horizontally by distributing the benefits of development. Also it aims to promote equal access to opportunities to enable people to contribute to social and economic progress, to share its rewards, to enable people to work together, to address common needs, to overcome common constraints and consider diverse interests; to promote inclusive institutions, accountable and transparent institutions to respond to public interest through effective, efficient and fair manner and to economic growth for a better quality of life (World Bank, 2005).

The Social Development Summit, Copenhagen 1995 declared that economic and, social development are interdependent and mutually reinforcing components of sustainable development, which is the framework for our efforts to achieve a higher quality of life for all people. It emphasizes that social development is central to the needs and aspirations of people throughout the world and to the responsibilities of governments and all sectors of civil society. In view of the changing economic and political need of the globalized world the member states of the UN have formulated specific policies and strategies for social development.

The transformations of the world economy have profoundly altered the parameters of social development. Under the aegis of the Structural

Adjustment Programme and the Washington Consensus relationships between the state, market and civil society have got redefined and social developmental perspective has got implicitly market oriented. However, notwithstanding the declaration of the World Summit on Social Development in Copenhegan, 1995, Millennium Development Declaration 2000, World Commission on the Social Dimension of Globalization 2004 and reformulation social development policies at the national levels, and proliferations of the civil society initiatives through Non-Governmental Organizations at the grassroots social underdevelopment of vast segments of populations continue unabated. There have also been the manifestations of numerous discontents against globalization and the state failure to promote the social well-being of the marginalized.

'Developmental practices encounter near infinite variety and complexity of human beliefs, opinion, attitudes, values, behaviours, customs, prejudices, laws, social institutions and the most importantly social division, hierarchies and exclusions. Each of the social groups has specific sorts of developmental needs.' To be effective and efficient developmental practices need in-depth understanding of social complexities and adequate conceptualization of the ideals of social developmental praxis through proper contextualization and finally concerted efforts by the state, civil society and grassroots organization for the implementation of these praxis. However, the roles of the state towards such efforts have remained mostly ambiguous and its perspectives have been subject to diverse interpretations by the policy planners and the bureaucrats over time. Accordingly 'a good body of social developmental initiatives has mostly remained processes of trial and error experimentation with high failure rate and very uneven progress' (Jacobs and Cleveland, 1999). This has been further compounded with chaotic social transition reflected in the disjunction between economic prosperity and livelihood insecurity, increasing poverty, unemployment, global connectivity and local exclusion, and new process of economic and political structuration and tyranny of structure less identity.

In recent years the perspectives and practices of development have acquired several new dimensions. There have been articulations of new strategies and their experimentation both by the state and the civil societies. In India social developmental activism have been as diverse as have been the diverse cultural, geographic and political conditions of the society. A comprehensive understanding of these praxis encounters several interrelated questions as to what have been the relevance of dominant perspectives of social development in India? How has globalization affected the developmental perspective in India? What have been the roles of the state, corporate bodies and civil society in social development of the marginalized? What are the innovative social development practices initiated at the grassroot level? Have these new practices been able to alter the pre-existing state of social under development of the vast segments of the population? This collection of eighteen papers has addressed these questions based on research conducted in India. It is divided into four sections dealing with the emerging perspectives, state, civil society and corporate initiatives, nature of state and legal interventions, and emerging roles of ICTS and education in social development.

There are five papers in section one, critically examining the changing perspectives, strategies, practices of social development initiatives in the context of globalization. Besides dealing with these emerging perspectives, this section also discusses the crucial dimensions of civil society in social development in the globalized world. T.K. Oommen has delineated the three broad perspectives on development, namely the mainstream perspective on development (MPD), the alternative perspective on development (APD) and the post-development perspective (PDP) on development in his perceptive paper entitled: 'Social Development, Social Policy and Social Movement: The Interconnections'. After elaborating six important social and historical revolutions: (a) the revolt of the aristocracy against the clergy in Europe, (b) the revolt by the economic categories (the merchants, the capitalists, the entrepreneurs and the bourgeoisie) against the clergy and the aristocracy in Europe, (c) the proletarian revolution against the bourgeoisie for an appropriate share in the social product, (d) the revolt by the colonized peoples in Asia, Africa and the Americas, challenging the political dominance and economic exploitation by their colonial masters, (e) revolution in the Second World for the autonomization of the civil society and the market *vis-à-vis* the state through the twin ideas of *perestroika* and *glasnost* in Soviet Union, and (f) the ongoing global revolution initiated by the deprived and marginalized questioning the establishment, with a view to evolving a participatory society to improve the quality of life.

Within these revolutionary and the transformative dynamics of the society he locates the developmental perspectives practiced historically. He points out that the MPD has often conceptualized development with narrow economic framework as a single homogeneous process towards modernization. As against this backdrop the APD with the participatory, appropriate, people-centered, autonomous, holistic and ethno aspects of development has emerged as critique of mainstream perspective on development. This perspective has integrated civil society driven participatory, and people-oriented, and the anti-capitalism, green thinking, feminism, eco-feminism, new social movements within the development discourse. He also points out that many of the elements of ADP is integrated into the MDP and that APD has been increasingly incorporated into MPD. The shift of emphasis from economic to social development is an indication of this. To him the Human Development Perspective (HDP) of development is a cross-breed between MPD and APD. In recent decades there has been the emergence of the post-development perspective (PDP) that rejects development as conceptualized by MPD and APD. PDP advocates the death of development, indeed it is anti-development. The main target of attack by PDP is Western science. The main limitation of PDP to Oommen is that it puts a moratorium on human creativity; it ignores the capacity of MPD to adapt, denies the agency of South, and the relevance of APD and the sensibility of human development approach.

He brings out the relationship between developmental perspectives and social policy and the convergence of mainstream social development perspectives with the ideologies of the welfare and the socialist state. He has shown the shift in the unit of social policy from individual to collectivity and have pointed out the concomitant shift in the structure and source of deprivation, nature of social policy, and shift in the response patterns by the deprived to collective action. Turning to the marginalized groups he points out that there are multiple sources of deprivations; new consciousness, self-definitions and perceptions of these groups. Thus, the erstwhile stigmatized groups demand special considerations from the state and civil society, and in turn necessarily leads to a change in the definition of marginalized groups by the state, leading to an expansion of the constituency of the deprived. To him, within the contemporary democratic ethos and the collective mobilization, the marginalized are capable of putting considerable pressure on the state through frequent collective mobilizations.

The social developmental policies and strategies have been widely rearticulated in the wake of globalization. S.L. Sharma in his paper on 'Globalization and Social Transformation in India' seeks to examine transformative potential of globalization in India. He specifically analyses the possible roles and relationship of the structural adjustment of economy with the structural alterations in society and impacts of global market economy on the social development of the marginalization sections of society and of their traditional cultures. He has also examined whether globalization has ushered in some new trends of socio-cultural transformation which are different from those initiated by industrialization and modernization. This paper has delineated the trends of change in the socio-cultural landscape of India, particularly in the domains of social stratification, institutions, values and identities. It is concluded that globalization has resulted in transformative trends of change in Indian society, but not so much because of it as in spite of it.

Debal K. SinghaRoy in his paper 'Shifting Perspectives on Social Development: Changing Context and Emerging Challenges for India' examines the changing facets of social development perspectives on India and the implications of these changes on social and human development of the largest segment of population of the country. The paper underlines the implicit intertwining between perspectives on economic transformation and social development in India. It delineates that the social development perspective in India has undergone phenomenal changes in view of emerging technological, economic and political scenario in the country over the decades on the one hand, and the changing nature of commitments and obligations of the state towards the principles of several international declarations, conventions, summits and treaties and agreements on the other. To him, even though India's perspective on social development has been enshrined in the constitution, and strategies are articulated in the successive five-year plans, these have not been strictly implementated with strong political will of the state, as has been for economic liberalization and structural adjustment programme. These gaps in political commitments have contributed to generate a good deal of inconsistencies in patterns of economic development leading to the flux, fluidity and deformities in Indian society, and a space for discontents against the state on several counts. To him these inconsistencies have generated sustained social underdevelopment and a process of conflicting co-existence of several of the societal arrangements. Hence in the absence of proper political will for the rigorous implementation of transformative social policies, and emergence of conflicting-coexistence of several arrangements, social developmental initiatives only function as subservient to the global forces of neo-liberal economic order.

Civil society has emerged an inseparable partner of development. However, its relationships to the state, market and the people have been widely reformulated in contemporary world. Alka Dhameja in her paper 'Civil Societies: Issues and Challenges in the Context of Globalization' addresses the critical questions to establish the viability of positioning civil society as a distinct third sphere. She recognizes that the concept of civil society is not new; and it enjoyed high popularity in the eighteenth and nineteenth centuries in the Scottish, French and German writings. After examining the reasons for the invocation of civil society she elaborates that in western Europe, civil society has been heralded as a savior concept in the backdrop of retreat of the state and advance of the market. In the east, the rise of civil society is attributed to the fall of east European states. She avers that the reasons for emergence have shaped its nature and scope. In the present context, civil society has come to be regarded as an autonomous, integrated, uncoerced, just and righteous space between the state and market. This space comprises intermediary citizen institutions, which are independent of the state and market control, but at the same time constructively mediate between them through collective behaviour. Though the contemporary scholars treat the state as a political, the market as an economic and the civil society as a social and cultural domain, she recognizes that the perspectives on the nature of civil society today are quite diverse and debatable, especially in the absence of a consensus on its meaning and nature.

In her view, the state, civil society and market are autonomous, but not distinct spheres in themselves, as they have various intersections of serious consequence. She prefers to call civil society as a realm of discourse mainly because in her view the media have opened up a new platform for civil society that was not so conspicuous and accessible hitherto. Her realm of discourse dimension of civil society takes its cue from the writings of Immanuel Kant, Antonio Gramsci and Jurgen Habermas, and includes both formal and non-formal structures. She defines civil society as the realm of discourse comprising organizations, movements, non-formal and unstructured endeavours working as per the benchmarks of social justice, non-violence and reasoned discourse. She argues for keeping the three spheres in the 'checks and balances framework'. Bringing out the misgivings of civil society, she feels that it is not appropriate to adopt it as a panacea or a saviour concept. The reinforcement of civil society, as per Dhameja, has to be taken with a pinch of caution. It has to be accompanied by its systematic resurrection, which is based on intellectual introspection and empirical evidence.

What have been the main features of Indian civil society movement? H.N. Shankaranarayana and T.N. Sreedhara in their paper 'Growth and the Holistic Social Development: A Paradox of Civil Society Movement in India' examines the contributions of civil society initiatives in promoting inclusive, holistic social development. The study is based both on primary and secondary data collected through interviews and interactions with various civil society activists. Against the backdrop that the neo-liberal development project contributing to several contradictions, this paper critically evaluates the pros and cons of the mainstream development paradigm and tries to find out an alternate development paradigm that achieves the critical holism. The paper enquires into the nature of civil society interventions in not only promoting growth but also in furthering the cause of the holistic social development in the Indian context. To the scholars the post independent civil society movement in India either supplements neo-liberal development project (being the state sponsored cooperatives and the NGOs that are funded by the state and the national and international funding agencies), or critique it (evolving through meaningful social movement). If the former strand is used by the state to improve the delivery system of its various welfare promoting programmes, the other strand acts as 'whistle blower'. Here they emphasize the role of 'mission driven voluntarism' acting as powerful agents of alternative social change and social development. To them these varieties of civil society initiatives profoundly acts as catalyst to promote meaningful holistic, inclusive social development. They categorize that the Bhoodan Movement, Narmada Bachao Andolan (NBA), Chipko Movement and the movement led by Baba Amte to belong to this category.

Section two deals with the emerging nature of governance, a few state sponsored and legal initiatives and village panchayat activism on social development. Based on specific case studies it focuses on the issues of Tribals, Dalits, differently abled, and the sex workers.

Social undervelopment and conflict in the northern part of the country has been an immediate area of concern to the social scientists. Sujata D. Hazarika's paper on 'Social Development, Conflict and Participatory Governance in North-East India' aims to demystify the theory of cultural reproduction and integration which has aggravated the contradictions between the individual and state. She proposes that decentralization of governance and local level participation in democratic institution are the only viable means of establishing trust and peace in the region of north-east India. She explains that the growing conflict situation of Assam has led to mobilization of various movements in order to address this contradiction between the individual and the state. To her this complexity while at a manifest level presents itself as a contradiction of cultural reproduction, social integration and socialization of neglect, at a more pragmatic and latent level can be viewed as democratic response to the deficit of human development in the region. She brings out an interface of social movements in north-east with the lack of human development in the region.

Legal provisions play an important role for social development of the marginalized sections of the population. Though many of such legal provisions have remained in the rule book without making efforts to make them known to the intended beneficiaries, these provisions still hold the key for their empowerment. The Dalit forest right is one of such areas. P.K. Biswas in his paper on 'Dalits' Rights in Forests: Challenges and Opportunities' argues for the rights of Dalits in forest management. He highlights the fact that forest is an important resource for the rural poor for providing jobs, income and a variety of forest products, such as fuel, wood, fodder and timber to supplement their agriculture for sustainable livelihood; and that several legal provisions are made to provide them access to the forest. Apart from tribes, there are several other communities who depend on forest for subsistence. Biswas, however, points out that while several provisions are made for the tribes there is no such provisions for the rights of Dalits in the forest. This paper argues for the rights of Dalits in Forest Management as a tool for social development based on experiences of Madhya Pradesh.

All over India Panchayati Raj Institutions (PRIs) have emerged to be an effective vehicle to mobilize the marginalized sections of the rural population for their economic advancement and political empowerment. In the forest areas PRIs are integrated with the process of tribal development. Raj Kumar Khosla's paper 'Forest Rights and Tribal's Lives: An Analysis of Panchayati Raj Institutions in Koraput District of Orissa' elaborates the contexts of tribal peoples' dependency on forest in a backward scheduled area of Koraput district, Orissa,

India, and evaluates the role of PRIs in protecting the rights of the tribal people on forest. He elaborates that forest is an important source of livelihood for the weaker sections of the society, particularly the tribal people; that tribal communities have their symbiotic relationship with the forest; and India's rich forest resources were owned and managed by the local people, especially the tribal. It is however, pointed out that during the British rule, the tribal people lost their rights over forest resource. In the post-Independence period the state took it upon itself to protect the interest of the people and in the name of welfare it entered into all walks of life of people. In the process of the development, many industries and corporate sectors entered the tribal areas and gradually established their control over the resources. The tribal people, who conventionally depend on forest for their sustenance, now face the problem of poverty, indebtedness and ill-health. Even though under the 73rd Amendment Act, the rural communities were given the rights to manage their local resources, it excluded the tribal area which comes under the Fifth Schedule. The Government of India Panchayat (Extension to the Scheduled Area) Act, 1996 has enabled the tribal society to assume control over their own destiny to preserve and conserve their traditional rights over natural resources. As against this backdrop this paper examines the role of PRIs to protect the interest of the tribal's forest rights with a case study of Koraput district in Orissa, which falls under the Eastern Ghat hills, and is popularly known for its rolling mountains with rich forest coverage.

In the process of redefining roles of the state in social development, the relationship between the tribes and the state has undergone significant change. It has specific manifestations in various parts of the country. Jagannath Ambagudia in his paper 'Development or Destitution: Rethinking Tribal-State Relationship in Orissa' explores the changing relationship between the STs and the state in Orissa. Based on both primary and secondary sources of information it is argued that there has been a system of exploitative relationship between the state and the tribals in Orissa and that notwithstanding development and reservation policies, the state has emerged to be a invasive, predatory and dominating institution to legitimize its control over the customary rights of the tribals on land and other resources. The tribes in Orissa are a diverse community belonging to different ethnic, linguistic and religious groups with distinctive socio-economic and cultural characteristics and remain to be socially discriminated, economically exploited and politically marginalized. Their protest for the meaningful rights over their resources are met with continuous suppression of the state leading to the erosion of legitimacy and undermining the capacity of the state to rule.

Social development strategies for the differently able sections of the populations encounter numerous challenges. Gender is another core area of such challenges. Renu Addlakha in her paper on 'Engendering Disability in the Developmental Agenda in India' explores the situation of persons with disabilities in India with special reference to the plight of women with disabilities. Tracing the development of the disability movement in the country, it shows how the issue has moved from a marginal state-sponsored welfare programme to a social development issue highlighting the role of local and global factors in the process. Highlighting the role of legal measures in social development and the empowerment of the differently abled persons she points that the Persons with Disabilities Act, 1995 has transformed the political and public discourses on disability. The terms of the debate have moved now from segregation and exclusion to integration and inclusion, from charity and tokenism to human rights and entitlements. Globalization has given a fillip to this new identity politics based on a hitherto unacknowledged axis of oppression, namely disability. To her, although a rights-based approach has entered the disability rights movement in India, the specific concerns of women with disabilities have not yet found a place, neither in the government policies and programmes nor in the private or the voluntary sectors. As against this backdrop this paper also discusses the implications of the absence of a gender perspective in the disability movement and explores the lacunae in the laws, programmes and policies for the disabled from a gender sensitive perspective, and makes recommendations for gender mainstreaming at the levels of legal reform, policy planning and implementation.

Sex workers are one of the most vulnerable sections of Indian population. The state has evolved several strategies for their rescue and rehabilitation. O.P. Mishra, in his paper 'Rescue and Rehabilitation of Sex Workers: A Case Study of Delhi', highlights the intrinsic relationship between these two activities. To him the basic purpose of rescue is rehabilitation of the sex workers. While rescue is essentially a job of law enforcing agencies, rehabilitation lies with state and other NGOs. Locating the problem of the sex workers in the societal context, he points out that the very nature of the problem and its deep rooting in the social system, has always discouraged any systematic displacement/rescue of prostitutes from society. However, the growing menace of the problem from social point of view and concern by various non-government organizations and women rights activists, over a period of time, the issue of rescue and rehabilitation has assumed significance. Based on the experience of rescue operations carried out in GB Road brothel houses in New Delhi and interview of rescued victims in observation homes, he highlights the importance of law enforcing agencies in the whole process of rescue, and rehabilitation and explains how a meaningful strategy can prevent entry of innocent victims in this whole trade.

Section III deals with initiatives taken at the grassroots by Self-Help Groups (SHG), micro finance projects, corporate groups and cooperatives for social development of various segments of the population. It focuses on rural women and the cultivators and workers who form the overwhelming segments of the marginalized sections of society.

In recent years voluntary activisms at the micro level through SHGs has got momentum to be an alternative and effective tool for the empowerment of rural women in general of the marginalized groups in particular. Damayanti Mukhopadhyay and S.A.H. Moinuddin in their paper entitled 'Social Development and the Empowerment of Marginalized Women: A Study of SHGs' has examined the roles of the SHGs in the empowerment of women of the marginalized groups in West Bengal. To them social development is a process which results in the transformation of social structures in a manner which improves the capacity of social group to fulfil its aspirations and desires. Society develops by consciousness and social consciousness develops by its organization. It is delineated by these scholars that as long as the marginalized people do not become conscious of their own rights, speak for themselves, become socially and economically self-reliant; it would not be possible to free themselves from the shackles of age-old deprivation and subordination. The rural women are handicapped for various reasons which include their gender identity as women, as rural populace and as poor and backward. However, organizational initiatives have emerged to be an effective tool for the empowerment of women of the vulnerable groups. They focused on the 'Swarnjayanti Gram Swarozgar Yojana (SGSY)' launched in April 1999 which emphasizes on organization of poor through SHGs for training, and access to credit, technology, infrastructure and marketing. Based on fieldwork carried out in Paschim Medinipur district, which hosts nearly 20000 SHGs under SGSY programme, it looks into the functioning, issues of access to and utility of credits. It analyses the institutional and financial functioning of groups as well as their characteristics and describes the positive changes brought about by the SHGs among the women of the marginalized groups in particular and the group in general. These authors have examined the changes at the levels of awareness, feeling of empowerment, as well as in the financial ability of the rural women.

Micro credit is another aspect of contemporary developmental initiative. Silima Nanda in her paper 'Social Mobilization of the Marginal: A Case Study of Tribal Development Project' analyses the Wadi (orchard) project as an instrument of sustainable tribal development in the Dangs district of Gujarat. Based on data collected from a Comprehensive Tribal Development Project in Dangs district of Gujarat she elaborates various dimensions of an integrated package of livelihood programme in a tribal area. It includes income generating activity through horticulture programme, soil and water conservation, improved farming and forestry, health and women's development and micro-finance implemented by DHRUVA, covering 3483 families, on 3400 acres and across 88 villages. DHRUVA-BAIF started working in the Dangs district in the year 2001–2. This programme constitutes the foundation on which the organization has built its wide ranging development interventions. She has explained contributions of various institutions involved in this project. It is implemented with a grant from the Indo–German Bank; KFW through the Government of India and NABARD and RSVY Scheme of Government of India. NABARD is the nodal agency on behalf of the Government of India and the project executive agency is a sister agency (Voluntary Organization) of BAIF, DHRUVA. She delineates the innovative strategies employed in this project for income generation. Herein at the beneficiary level, which is mostly the tribes, one acre of plot is selected to plant fruit trees, namely mango and cashew. Inter-cropping of vegetables is also done in the plot, which gives an additional but frequent income. Such an arrangement helps in generating income flow periodically to the families; and gradually over the years, the families also have been diversifying into other enterprises like mango nursery, dairy with the help of credit from the mobilized savings of the SHGs. It is expected that in the days to come, the social mobilization of the tribals will be complete and successful and they will also start competing in the global markets.

India has a long tradition of cooperative movements. It has proved to be an effective tool to organize the vulnerable sections of the population for social development. Sarjerao Salunkhe in the paper on 'Co-operative Movement and Social Development of the Marginalized: A Case of Lift Irrigation' examines the impact of lift irrigation cooperatives on the socio-economic conditions of their beneficiaries and ecological conditions in the Warana River basin (which covers parts of Sangli and Kolhapur districts in Maharashtra) based on in-depth survey data from 635 beneficiaries of 14 lift irrigation cooperatives in 2002. The study reveals that the cooperative lift irrigation schemes have set in motion variety of changes which in turn have started transformation in the traditional asymmetrical relationships between groups based on ascriptive criteria, such as caste, religion, and communities and so on; and are also promoting non-exploitative and non-oppressive relationships among the numbers of the cooperatives. He effectively delineates the contribution of the lift irrigation cooperatives to elicit participation of the marginalized sections of the rural communities (i.e. lower strata of the village peasantry and socially underprivileged sections such as OBCs, SCs, NTs and minorities) in the process of development that have created space for them in the power structures of their management system. As the immediate impact the cooperative movement could be seen as a tool for promoting social development.

Economic liberalization has brought several challenges to the employment security and working conditions of the workers. There have been the articulation of the ideals of corporate social responsibility to provide adequate social security to the workers working in this sector. Ritambhara Malaviya in her paper on 'Role of Corporate and Community Partnership in Social Development' examines the interface between civil society and business organizations. To her, nation states are succumbing to the logic of free markets and the changed role of the state is reflected in the pressures over states to give up protectionism and turn into mere facilitators of trade; and globalization has created a global space of exploitation and has extended the reach of these gigantic monopolies into the domains of the local, destroying and further marginalizing the deprived and vulnerable. Yet globalization has failed to deliver the promised gains as is reflected in the phenomenal growth of inequality and marginalization of the underprivileged. The multinational cooperatives (MNCs) which expand into the developing countries, because of benefits like cheap labour, raw material and due to the lax implementation of labour and environmental standards in these countries, indulge into irresponsible and exploitative practices, contributing to further marginalization of the marginalized. Against this backdrop corporate social responsibility (CSR) has become a response by corporate houses to the rising expectations for the regulation of their behaviour. However, as the state is not expected to intervene or regulate the corporate behaviour, the corporate houses make voluntary social commitments through adoption of charters and codes of conduct and by undertaking certain welfare programmes. Business houses have also sought to co-opt the civil society in the process. Based on survey on the participation of civil society in corporate volunteering this paper evaluates the effectiveness of such efforts and critically examines the role of the state in this endeavour.

Global main streaming of the marginalized communities through trading of traditional plants has become a crucial and controversial issue in contemporary development discourse. Moumita Das in her paper 'Interactivity of Marginalized Indian Communities Subsisting on the Trade of Medicinal Plants with the Global Community' highlights some of these issues. Valuable medicinal plants growing in the hills and rural areas of India are an important source of subsistence for a considerable population of marginalized communities residing in these areas. The people from these communities usually collect and sell the collected medicinal plants in raw (unprocessed) form to the middlemen in the towns and cities. The raw material is ultimately brought and processed by the pharmaceutical companies, which derive huge profits from the products. The marginalized communities however, stand to gain no significant benefit from this. Economic globalization process has generated huge demand for the medicinal plants collected from the wild. This has put pressure on not only the ecosystems but also on the communities dependent on them for collection. This paper presents the current issues of the marginalized communities involved in the trade of medicinal plants, and explores the avenues of integrating them into the global mainstream for their sustainable development. It is concluded that interactivity of the marginalized communities in India with the global communities is possible only when these communities are first integrated into the national mainstream. As an important strategy, it is suggested that the marginalized communities involved in the collection of medicinal plants are required to be mobilized sufficiently to work through cooperatives at the grassroots level towards producing international quality medicinal plant-based products. The capacity building exercise of these communities needs to be seriously carried out to empower them and enable them to enter the global market with confidence.

The last section of this collection deals with the role of information and communication technology (ICT) and education in social development. Suditi Naskar in her paper 'Role of ICT in Social Development: A Critique' examines how the usage of ICT is increasingly being seen as a major tool for development. To her, in a huge country like India, this has deeper significances as the ICT enabled services can be used as an alternative to the government services where the latter cannot reach directly to the citizens. She recognizes that a striking majority of people are grossly under privileged without even basic access to modern technologies, and that India is a nation with worst kind of digital divide. This paper looks into these problems, seeks to present a critique of the ongoing projects and suggests an alternative. She suggests that ICT is just the tool and not the author. The chief responsibility of how a project works has to be shouldered by the ones who make decisions. The stakeholders need to be careful as there is immense scope of experimentation and research in ICT. She suggests that rigorous monitoring and evaluation are needed to be initiated at every stage if the benefits of ICT projects are worth the projects' costs—especially when they are aimed at social inclusion of the disadvantaged communities.

ICTs and knowledge economy are the co-constituents of globalization. None of these constituents can furnish without the process of lifelong learning. Sutapa Bose in her paper on 'ICT Mediated Lifelong Education for Alleviating Marginality in a Knowledge Society' explains the compelling need to eliminate the contemporary barriers in the building of an egalitarian knowledge society and the the changing concept of marginality in the context of a knowledge society. Inclusiveness is an important aspect of knowledge society, this is to be facilitated by the component of ICT aided life-long learning. She highlights that in a knowledge society, knowledge is the driving force of all the major social, cultural, economic and political activities.

Hence, investment in terms of intangible human capital namely knowledge, rather than land, labour and capital should gain importance. To her this necessitates the access to information, its processing, utilizing and sharing through a highly networked society.

The issues of social development are interlinked with the issues of marginalization, social exclusion, social conflicts and social movements. Hence many of the issues those have been raised and discussed in this collection have also been extended further in another two collections of this series entitled: Dissenting Voices and Transformative Actions: Social Movements in a Globalizing World, and Surviving Against Odds: The Marginalized in a Globalizing World.

REFERENCES

Esping-Andersen, Gøsta (1990), *The Three Worlds of Welfare Capitalism*, Cambridge: Polity Press.

Frank A.G. & M. Fuentes (1990), 'Civil Democracy: Social Movements in Recent World History', in S. Amin, G. Arrighi, A.G. Frank and Wallerstein (eds.), *Transforming the Revolution: Social Movements and the World-System*, New York: Monthly Review Press.

Jacobs, G. and H. Cleveland (1999), *Social Develepment Theory*, ICDP, www. Icdp.org.

Marshall, T.H. (1973), *Class Citizenship and Social Development*, Westport, CN: Greenwood.

Sen, A. (1999), *Development As Freedom*, New Delhi: Oxoford University Press.

UN (1995), *Declaration of the Social Development Summit*, Copenhegan: UNDP.

——— (1996), *Human Development Report*, New Delhi: Oxford University Press.

World Bank (2005), *Empowering People by Trasforming Institutions: Social Devlopment in World Bank Operations*, Washigntion D.C.: World Bank.

I. SOCIAL DEVELOPMENT: CHANGING CONTEXTS AND EMERGING PERSPECTIVES

CHAPTER 1

Social Development, Social Policy and Social Movement: The Interconnections

T.K. OOMMEN

There are at least three broad perspectives on development: the mainstream perspective on development (MPD), the alternative perspective on development (APD) and the post-development perspective (PDP). Roughly paralleling these, there are three models of social policies, the residual model (RM), the achievement-performance model (APM) and the institutional redistributive model (IRM). But these models of social policy crystallized as responses to social movements. What I propose to do is to trace the trajectory of interlinkages between development, policy and movement. But the nature of the phenomena under discussion vastly varied across the three worlds—First, Second and Third—before the launching of economic liberalization. Therefore, it is necessary to understand what historical processes created the three worlds, which in turn are also products of social movements.

I

Broadly speaking, so far, humanity has experienced six social revolutions, each of which may be conceptualized as a cluster of social movements and collective actions. First, the revolt of the aristocracy (those who claimed nobility based on birth) against the clergy (God's representatives on earth) which secularized the social order, separating the state and the church. The focus of this revolution was to arrive at a consensus regarding division of labour, resulting in assigning the secular realm exclusively to the state and confining the activity of the church to the spiritual realm. Such an arrangement also existed in ancient India as indicated in the distinct spheres of activities for the priest and the king. But this structural differentiation did not produce modernity due to the hierarchical social structure.

The second revolt was by the economic categories (the merchants, the capitalists, the entrepreneurs and the bourgeoisie) against the clergy and the aristocracy, thereby questioning the bases of status in society. Third, the proletarian revolution against the bourgeoisie for an appropriate share in the exchange value produced by them, so as to bring about distributive justice in the economic realm. Fourth, the revolt by the colonized peoples of Asia, Africa and the Americas, challenging the political dominance and economic exploitation by their colonial masters, in order to establish political equality between peoples, irrespective of race, creed or geographical origin.

The four revolts produced three worlds. The first two revolts, that is those of the aristocracy against the clergy, and that of the merchants against the aristocracy and the clergy, together constitute what many writers refer to as the 'bourgeois revolution'. This produced the First World, which crystallized in west Europe. The third revolt, that is, the revolt of the workers and the peasants produced the Second World and this occurred mainly in east Europe. The fourth revolt, namely the anti-colonial revolt, produced the Third World mainly confined to the erstwhile colonies of Latin America, Asia and Africa.

The three worlds produced different types of societies. Generally speaking, in the First World, the state, the market and the civil society emerged gradually and acquired autonomy. The situation in the Third World was a mixed one and even in democratic polities, the kind of balance which is believed to be desirable between the state, the market and the civil society is usually absent. As for the Second World, the story was entirely different. The state, the civil society and the market were fused into one. The state came to occupy the commanding position subordinating the market and civil society.

It is in this context that the fifth revolution occurred in the Second World. It was essentially an attempt at autonomization of the civil society and the market *vis-à-vis* the state launched through the twin ideas of *perestroika* and *glasnost* in Soviet Union resulting in the very demise of the socialist block. The sixth revolution, the ongoing one, has been initiated by the deprived and marginalized questioning those in the establishment, constituting the clergy, intelligentsia, aristocrats, capitalists, bureaucrats, entrepreneurs and technocrats, attempting to evolve a participatory society to improve the quality of life.

A few general points may be noted about the six revolutions as a prelude to our analysis. The first three revolutions occurred in particular polities or blocks of them, by and large confined to Europe in the beginning. The fourth revolution was necessarily confined to the ex-colonial countries, but there came about a substantial differentiation amongst these new polities after this revolution. While one set of ex-colonial countries (e.g. USA, Canada, Australia) got incorporated into the affluent First World, the polities of Asia, Africa and Latin America came to constitute the underprivileged and poverty-stricken 'Third World' in the wake of their political liberation from colonialism. The fifth revolution occurred in the ex-socialist countries of Soviet Union and east Europe leading to their democratization, as noted above.

The sixth revolution is truly global in its scale and scope in that although particular events may occur only in specific polities their reverberations are felt globally because of increased interdependence between polities and thanks to the impact of the satellite communication system. It may also be noted that while the first five revolutions were contentions about single dimensions, be it status, power, wealth, political freedom or sectoral autonomy, the sixth revolution is multidimensional in its thrust, in which the deprived are the victims of cumulative domination and inequality. Finally, while the first five revolutions have already terminated, the sixth is still going on. It is the womb out of which the notion of participatory development is emerging.

II

I began my talk by noting that there are three major perspectives of development. These perspectives crystallized in the First World and considerably influenced the Third World. But the Second World remained insulated from these thought processes because of the absence of democracy, till the structural adjustment programme (SAP) was launched in the 1990s.

The MPD often conceptualizes development as a single homogeneous process towards modernization, underestimating the potentials for diversity, complexity and adaptability. In fact, most studies in this tradition undertaken through sophisticated quantitative analyses conclude that growth positively prompts equality. On the other hand, dependency theory crystallized in Latin America, a part of the Third World, raised the issue of global inequality. But the fact is that inequality has been increasing even as rapid growth is taking place. How can one explain the gap between the theoretical claim of MPD and the empirical reality?

The narrow economic framework employed by MPD is consistent only when it leaves out social, cultural, political, psychological and environmental variables. In fact, development was initially understood as economic development. Sociology and social anthropology entered the arena of development studies to explain the factors which facilitated or hindered development and launched the notion of social development. Psychology provided insights about the variables which motivated or discouraged development. The concern of political science was to provide information regarding political factors influencing development. Finally, environmental concerns linked economic development and ecological depletion.

It is this moving away of development studies from economics, which heralded the beginning of the APD. The APD takes many banners—participatory, appropriate, people-centered, autonomous, holistic—development which erodes its coherence. But the APD is a critique of the mainstream perspective on development. It has two strands. First, an alternative approach to development wherein the goal is the same as that of MPD but the means differ—APD is participatory and people-oriented. Here the agency of development becomes crucial; a shift from state and/or market to civil society is emphasized. A visible manifestation of this shift of emphasis in the agency of development is found in the fact that in the past two decades the IMF and the World Bank channel more funds through non-governmental organizations (NGOs) than through governments. This also hints at the peaceful co-existence of the two perspectives, mainstream and alternative.

Secondly, an alternative goal of development is visualized through APD—people-centered development geared to the satisfaction of needs, which is endogenous, self-reliant and in harmony with the environment. In this rendition, the APD incarnates as anti-capitalism, green thinking, feminism, eco-feminism, new social movements, Buddhist economics and post-structuralist analysis of the development discourse. Alternative development then is development from below, that is, community centred and NGO initiated. APD generally refers to three spheres—agents (NGOs), methodology (participatory, self-reliant, endogenous) and objectives (geared to basic needs).

The hallmark of APD's methodology is participation, its epistemological root is local knowledge, and its implementation strategy is decentralization of economy and polity. But all these elements are being increasingly incorporated by MPD. The society-centred participatory development is now being co-opted even by neo-liberals under the pressure of social movements. What is labelled as indigenous knowledge is often insufficient, inadequate and even inappropriate. Therefore, we need to mutate the indigenous and the alien. It is the process of hybridization which renders the alien acceptable. Finally, decentralization is now widely endorsed by MPD. Even the World Bank advocates putting the people first!

The point I am making is that APD has been increasingly incorporated into MPD. Yesterday's alternatives are today's mainstream. Alternatives then only mean the latest. Institutionalization of dissent is a perennial possibility. New movements become old, and in turn solidify as institutions. Alternatives interrogate the maladies of mainstream; but they do not always provide an alternate goal. Both the mainstream and alternative perspectives pursue development, the quality of which is continuously bettered. The shift of emphasis from economic to social development is an indication of this.

However, APD assumed great importance as manifested in the following trends. First, the importance of environmental concerns and the sustainability of development has weakened MPD and given a boost to ecological economics. Secondly, the failure of several 'development decades' to achieve their goals unsettled MPD. Thirdly, the growing challenges to Bretton Woods institutions led to the question whether these criticisms are merely procedural and institutional (for more participation and democratization) or they involve fundamentally different principles. Finally, and most importantly, the enormous growth of NGOs in numbers and influence christened APD as a rival to MPD.

What I am suggesting is that there is a dialectical relationship between MPD and APD; they shape and influence reciprocally, giving birth to mutations such as human development perspective (HDP) which often becomes a cross-breed between MPD and APD. But the argument often takes the form of a simple binary opposition between the two. In order to emphasize the opposition between MPD and APD, the appeal of the mainstream perspective to various constituencies is underestimated. The fact is APD has been co-opted by MPD, which can be seen either as its castration or celebration depending upon one's perspective.

While both MPD and APD pursue development, even if of varying quality, the PDP rejects development as conceptualized by MPD and APD. PDP advocates the death of development; indeed it is anti-development. PDP emerged with a Western critique of modernity and techno-scientific progress such as critical theory, post-structuralism and green movements. APD rejects the idea of development equals modernization equals Westernization, which is often the refrain of MPD. APD refuses to be a mere endorser of the Western model of development; it rejects the notion of singular modernity. But it does not reject the notion of modernity as such; it pleads for multiple modernity, the non-West being creators of their versions of alternative modernity. But PDP rejects the very idea of modernity and hence development. Why?

According to PDP development is not required because poverty is not to be taken for granted; it is a culturally and historically variable notion. Subsistence economies which serve basic needs are not peopled by deprived people. They are defined as poor and deprived by Western theorists because they do not participate in the market economy. These people are first labeled as poor by Western theorists and then advised to develop. Development is not their felt-need, their natural aspiration. In the rendition of PDP poverty is first invented and development is then prescribed to eradicate poverty. Colonialism ended and development (modernization) took over and Coca-colonization, McDonaldization and Disneyfication came in. The dream of development is over. What is required is not more development but a different regime of truth and perception.

The main target of attack by PDP is Western science, particularly Newtonian Physics, Positivism, Cartesianism and Enlightenment thinking. But it forgets the fact that science has been continuously renewing itself through quantum physics, chaos theory and methodological anarchism. PDP ignores or is unaware of this new science. At any rate, in social science, which deals with the development discourse, positivism is no more the favoured paradigm. A development economist sensitive to the complex social reality cannot afford to ignore politics, society, culture, gender and ecology. Most concepts in currency in development studies—human development, institutional development, good governance, and accountability—are interdisciplinary.

The main limitation of PDP is that it puts a moratorium on human creativity; it ignores the capacity of MPD to adapt. PDP denies the agency of South, the importance of the dependency theory, the relevance of APD, and the sensibility of the human development approach. It is trapped by epistemological dualism, the very God that failed, according to its evaluation. It is not true that Westernization displaces everything through its version of development. Indeed PDP cannot account for Easternization, Japanization or a South Asian model of development. Polycentrism is denied, Eurocentrism is upheld, albeit unwittingly. It throws away the baby with the bathwater.

Let me now provide some proof as to how MPD constantly reinvents itself partly to reinforce its value-orientation and partly to respond to the criticism of PDP. As is well-known, the Structural Adjustment Programme (SAP) was launched on the basis of the Washington Consensus which advocated the retreat of the state from the arena of economic development and advocated market-driven development. By the mid-1990s, promises of the consensus—sustained growth, decrease in income disparity and poverty reduction—lay shattered in spite of all the compromises it made. It was realized that the trade-off between growth and equity is unrealizable and the two are in conflict; higher the rate of growth, steeper the inequality. This prompted the floating of a new approach, Washington Consensus Plus which started advocating good governance, development of human capital, gender equity and the like.

While retaining the goal of rapid growth, the spotlight was shifted to poverty reduction strategy (PRS); nay to make poverty history, to recall the seductive phrase floated by the Millennium Development Project. But the goal is to be formulated and pursued with the consultation of stakeholders—the marginalized and the NGOs. Here one can clearly see the impact of PDP and the social mobilization it initiates. But consultation was usually confined to well-resourced NGOs through whom the funds of the World Bank and similar other organizations were channelled rather than social movements which upheld the interests of the marginalized. Understandably those who led social movements on behalf of the marginalized did not fall prey because the effort of the MPD was essentially to castrate them of their protest potentialities.

At this juncture the MPD underwent a new *avatar* known as neo-structuralism, largely inspired by the successors of erstwhile dependency theorists of Latin America. The neo-structuralists proposed 'progressive' policies to bring about redistribution of income through strengthening human capital and productivity of the poor. For this higher spending on health, education, housing, and so on were recommended; indeed a re-incarnation of the social policy referred to as the institutional redistributive model. The neo-structuralists do not interfere in market forces but only attempt to make globalization palatable to the poor. Which is to say, neither the Washington Consensus Plus nor neo-structuralism fundamentally interrogate market-driven growth. They only attempt to mitigate poverty and moderate the income-widening core of it.

It is now widely known that the basic tendency of global market forces is to spawn poverty and inequality. In turn, this also engenders loss of control over common property resources traditionally enjoyed by local communities, the most telling instance of which is commercialization of water. The fundamental problem of capitalism is that it is a process of disembedding the market from its social ambience and rendering it the source that drives society. The welfare of the marginalized can be attended to only through re-embedding the market in society, to tame and subordinate it to the overarching goals of justice, equity and solidarity without ignoring national sovereignty. In this context social movements assume capital importance.

III

It is time that I bring in the interconnections between development perspectives and social policies. Under the residual model of social policy the state accepted very limited responsibility; it provided for the basic minimum needs of only the destitutes because the needs of the vulnerable groups were to be attended by family and kin, neighbourhood and community, religious organizations and charitable trusts. This approach to social policy co-existed with the early phase of MPD. By the mid-twentieth century the APM became popular in the capitalist societies of western Europe, as the state stepped in to provide for the basic needs of all citizens who belonged to the marginal groups. But the individual recipients were required to make a contribution in order to deserve state assistance. This approach and the later phase of MPD are organically related. In contrast, in the regime of the institutional re-distributive model (IRM) the state provides the citizens with all the basic needs irrespective of their contribution. APD and IRM functioned *in tandem*. This model of social policy, in effect, led to the convergence of the ideologies of the welfare state and the socialist state.

Notwithstanding the different value-orientations in the three social policy models, two things are common to them. First, the focus of attention in all the three models is the individual, and second, the emphasis is on meeting the material needs. But social policy has undergone profound changes in regard to these dimensions in recent times. The scope of social policy has enlarged to encapsulate the non-material needs and aspirations of the vulnerable groups. The unit of social policy today is as much a group as it is an individual. Presently I propose to trace the trajectory of this transformation.

Though social policy of one type or another is accepted by most contemporary politics, the Western capitalist states in which industrial revolution first occurred did not show any concern for the poor and the needy in the beginning as noted above. But thanks to the Fabian socialists who articulated their concern for distributive justice, the state gradually endorsed the ideology of welfarism. This process was at least partly accelerated because of the centrality given to distributive justice in the emerging socialist states. But within the European context the populations of state-societies, be they capitalist or socialist, were/are largely homogeneous, consisting of one physical type (race), one religion (Christians/Catholics/Protestants) and speakers of one language, constituted as they were on the maxim one nation, one state, barring a few exceptions. The needy citizens—the poor, the destitute, the physically disabled, the mentally challenged—and the well off ones were all drawn from the same people.

The scenario changed drastically when multiracial, polyethnic and/or multinational states emerged due to large-scale immigration, colonization and conquest. The marginalized groups in these state-societies were not simply the poor and the physically or mentally disabled but also the racially distinct (as in the case of the Native Americans and the Blacks in the US), culturally different (as in the case of different nationalities in the former USSR or the socially stigmatized (as in the case of the Scheduled Castes and Scheduled

Tribes in India). If the marginalized group, the traditional target of social policy in homogeneous societies, is an aggregate of individuals drawn from the same people, in heterogeneous societies the vulnerable group is an aggregation of different collectivities. Consequently, the primary source of deprivation, at any rate the cognition about it, shifts from individual biography to collective history. Understandably, the structure of deprivation provides the moment for collective action and the deprived collectivities often resort to it.

On the other hand, the state itself would have to respond to the situation by introducing innovations in social policy. Affirmative action in the US, nationalist policy in the erstwhile USSR, and protective discrimination in India afford examples of social policies to cope with the mobilizations of the deprived. But to the extent distributive justice and participatory development constitute important elements of state ideology, the situation gets further complicated. The people are no more mere targets to be developed through centralized planning; they are not clients of the state bureaucracy but are participants, at least by definition, in the very process of planning and development.

I have referred above to the shift in the unit of social policy from individual to collectivity as one moves from homogeneous to heterogeneous state-societies and have pointed to the concomitant shift in three contexts: (a) in the structure and source of deprivation, (b) in the nature of social policy, and (c) in the possibility of response patterns by the deprived who may resort to collective action. But the state-society still provides the frame of reference for policy formulation. I propose to show that gradually the definition of deprivation and the distribution of deprived have shifted from particular state-societies to whole blocks of them. This changed cognition is made possible because of a paradigm shift in social science. There are several elements/steps involved here.

First, the world has come to be conceptualized as one unit, thanks to the omnipresence and omnipotence of the capitalist system, popularized as the world system model, the forerunner of the Global Age. Second, notwithstanding the above, the differences in the levels of development and patterns of culture have led to cognizing the world as different, viz., the First, the Second, the Third as I have noted earlier. Third, once the world came to be viewed as one system, a new cognition crystallized: development or underdevelopment of blocks of state-societies was not simply a matter of production but was as much a matter of unequal exchange. The Third World, perching on the precarious periphery, is eternally disadvantaged, according to the refrain of dependency theory. In this rendition the vulnerable are not simply individuals and groups within state-societies but a whole set of state-societies, the Third World.

Even the world system model accounted only for the human world and ignored the non-human environment. The new paradigm of development focuses on participatory and endogenous development, which encapsulates the ecological perspective as an alternative to modernization. Authentic development implies quality of life and it is possible to achieve this only if development is sustainable, the pre-requisites being regulating the consumption of energy, avoiding ecological degradation and environmental pollution and arresting the rapid change of climate. The paradigm of limits to growth, initially enunciated by the Club of Rome and latterly articulated in the multiple incarnations of green movements all over the world, unfolds a new cognition about the concept of quality of life.

That is, invention and indiscriminate application of high technology create two new types of vulnerable groups, which are targets of social policy. First, high technology, due to its labour-displacing orientation, prevents the aspiring young from entry into the employment market while depriving the employed of their current employment, because they lacked the requisite new skills. Available evidence suggests that the victims in this context are mainly the less skilled, particularly the women. Second, the application of high technology leads to the dislodging of the peasantry and tribes from their traditional habitats and, in the absence of appropriate rehabilitation policies, makes them destitute. The burdens of my argument are to unfold a dilemma. The ongoing process of development paradoxically increases the size and variety of the deprived and the marginalized, the objects of social policy.

Even as we take cognizance of this phenomenon we should not be impervious to the importance of consciousness in the emergence of marginalized groups. First, there are multiple sources of deprivations and the saliency of the source varies from one category to another. A new source of deprivation may surface because of changed perception by a category.

Second, new consciousness is also a function of changing self-definitions and perceptions. Thus, the erstwhile stigmatized groups—unwed mothers, sex workers, same sex couples—who voluntarily retreat from mainstream society and may have remained invisible earlier, demand special considerations from the state and civil society. This in turn necessarily leads to a change in the definition of marginalized groups by the state, leading to an expansion of the constituency of the deprived.

Third, the contemporary democratic ethos and the collective mobilization, which it implies, can create subjectively deprived groups such as the rural elites, the new bourgeoisie emerging from the traditionally underprivileged groups or those from the traditionally privileged but currently experiencing a downward mobility. Given the arithmetic of adult franchise, they can put considerable pressure on a soft state through frequent violent collective mobilizations.

The point I want to underline is that the size, the context and the variety of those who are defined as marginalized are constantly increasing not simply because development is dysfunctional but also because new groups demand attention and consideration from the state and civil society. In turn, this often leads to a confluence of state action articulated through social policy measures and through people's action manifested in social movements. Therefore, the interconnections between social development, social policy and social movement assumes crucial significance.

Note: In the formulation of my argument in section II I have drawn heavily on Pieterse Jan Nederveen (2001), *Development Theory: Deconstructions/Reconstructions*, New Delhi: Vistaar Publications.

CHAPTER 2

Globalization and Social Transformation in India

S.L. SHARMA

An overarching trend of our times, globalization signifies a transformative force of enormous significance. It represents a force of reorganization of global economic order based on advocacy of open door economic policy between nations. Understandably, it has emerged as a powerful catalyst of economic transformation, particularly in the developing nations, entailing significant socio-cultural fallouts. While its importance as a catalyst of economic transformation in the developing countries has been widely acknowledged, its role in their socio-cultural transformation has not yet received intense scholarly attention. It is, therefore, time to undertake systematic studies of the socio-cultural impact of globalization in developing countries. A modest attempt in that direction is being made here with a focus on India, one of the major beneficiaries of globalization.

A look at the sociological discourse on globalization in India reveals that it has been concerned more with the cultural consequences of globalization than with its social outcomes. This is evident from the writings of Singh (2002) and Dhanagare (2003) among others. The social fallouts of globalization have received at best a cursory treatment. A question of seminal sociological significance to ask in this regard is: has globalization generated a trend of social transformation in India and, if so, what is its direction? This precisely is the question I seek to address in the present paper. In order to deal with this question in a systematic manner, I set for myself the following specific tasks: (i) to clarify the concept of globalization; (ii) to problematize the term social transformation and articulate it as a concept; (iii) to delineate the socio-cultural fallouts of globalization in India; and (iv) to appraise their transformational potential. The paper is accordingly organized into four parts, and in that order.

UNDERSTANDING GLOBALIZATION

There are many different interpretations of the term globalization, almost as many as its interpreters. This is hardly surprising in view of its multifaceted and dynamic character. However, it leaves a reader highly perplexed about the exact meaning of the term. In order to steer clear of the conceptual mess, I would like to unravel the meaning of globalization in a systematic manner. An analytical scrutiny of its various definitions reveals two distinguishable formulations under which these can be subsumed: (a) globalization as a process of unification of the world brought about by extraordinary advances in information and communication technology (ICT); and (b) globalization as a process of unification of the world by means of market integration across nations. A number of scholars have defined globalization as spatial and temporal compression of the world accelerated by recent advances in ICT. McLuhan was the first to conceive the idea of the 'global village' in the context of mounting significance of media in uniting the world. Startling advances in cyber technology have enabled mankind to conquer time and space. Accordingly, Robertson has defined globalization as a process that 'refers both to the compression of the world and the intensification of consciousness of the world as a whole' (1992). Similarly, Giddens interprets globalization as 'distanciation' which implies compression of time and space facilitating 'social action at a distance' (1990: 64). More pointedly, Waters defines globalization as 'a process in which the constraints of geography on social and cultural arrangements recede and people become aware that they are receding' (1995: 3). Viewed in this way, globalization, for all practical purposes, signifies emergence of a 'networked world', thanks to the rise of the worldwide web and other advances in ICT.

Turning to the other formulation, i.e. globalization as market integration, the following definition by the International Monetary Fund (IMF) may be cited as a representative one: 'Globalization is characterized by increases in flows of trade, capital, information as well as mobility of individuals across borders.' Similarly, Friedman and Kaplan (2002) have defined it as 'a process of integration of markets, finance and technology in a way that shrinks the world'. These and such other definitions thus project globalization as mobilization of capital, goods and services across borders without much restrictions.

The above delineated two constructs of globalization obviously differ in their points of emphasis, one stressing the communicative aspect while the other highlighting its economic dimension. Their differences of emphasis apart, the two need not be viewed as rival but as complementary constructs, only that they have to be reconciled in terms of primacy of the one over the other. In my view, globalization is primarily a process of economic reorganization of the world aided and accelerated as much by stunning advances in ICT as by sponsored liberalization of domestic economic policies. As a consequence, it also entails informational and cultural flows across borders.

In order to have a proper understanding of globalization, a few clarifications need to be made. First, that globalization in its present import is a new development, and not an age-old process. The earlier moves in the direction of effecting global unification such as those undertaken by world explorers, religious missionaries, and enterprising traders, followed by colonization and modernization, may aptly be viewed as precursors to globalization. While it is true that globalization is a cumulative consequence of all these moves, what distinguishes it, however, is the design of late capitalism to launch it as a global project. The idea of globalization actually gathered momentum following three developments of historic significance in the 1980s. These events include the collapse of the Soviet Union, the demolition of the Berlin Wall and the advent of the worldwide web. While the collapse of the Soviet Union and demolition of the Berlin Wall signified triumph of capitalism over socialism, the advent of the worldwide web paved the way to a networked world. It is the historic synchronization of these three dèvelopments which constructed the specific historical context from which the notion of globalization arose.

Secondly, globalization is not an innocent process of global unification. Instead, it is a transformative project of global capitalism to recast the world in its own mould. The reasons in support of my contention are: (a) that a call for globalization came around the 1980s from the global development agencies, including the World Bank and IMF. They urged the less developed nations to adopt the Structural Adjustment Programme (SAP) and open up their markets for integration with the global market; (b) globalization is commended as a new strategy of development for the developing nations, one that is claimed to be more effective than the earlier strategy which laid stress on capital, technology and expertise; (c) globalization is projected as a progressive policy *vis-à-vis* the policy of protective tariff followed earlier. The developing nations are accordingly advised to do away with restrictions on import and export and follow instead an open door economic policy. The credibility of these claims apart, there is more to the idea of globalization than what meets the eye. The fact of the matter is that globalization is a consequence of the development of productive forces of the leading industrialized nations necessitating search for markets in the developing nations to sell off their surplus produce (Castro, 1998). It is essentially *their need*, which is why, they are the powerful advocates of globalization. What is more, their pressure on the developing nations to abandon the policy of protective tariff is in contradiction of their own past policy of protective tariff which they themselves had used as a ladder to reach their present level of development, as documented by Chang (2003).

A third point is that globalization is not a process of free flow of trade, finance and services across the world, as it is generally projected to be. Instead, it is a hegemonically negotiated process of economic and cultural flows across borders. This is evident from the experience of the developing countries which for most part, have remained largely at the receiving end. Take, for example, the immigration laws of the advanced nations, including the USA and Britain. The laws have become more stringent in recent years restricting the entry of the people from the developing nations. It is the same story with the trade of certain commodities from the developing nations. Most important of all, it is evident from the parleys at the ministerial level meetings of the WTO held earlier at Doha and Concun and more recently at Hong Kong, where the leaders of the developed nations managed to manipulate reluctant consent of their counterparts from the developing nations on the question of phased withdrawal of farm subsidies, in spite of fierce protest from the latter. All this is understandable in view of the absence of level playing field between the developed and developing nations on account of their unequal levels of development.

Finally, globalization is not a fixed but an evolving reality. Its contours have changed significantly in the last few years. Launched as a hegemonic process of unilateral flow of trade and capital from the developed to the underdeveloped nations in the 1980s, globalization has now turned into a multilateral flow of investment and services from the developing to the developed world also. This is evident from the in-roads made into Europe and America by Chinese and Indian multinationals, besides software professionals in recent years. Furthermore, not limited to economic flows, globalization has as well accelerated a stream of cultural flows across the world. It has generated a matrix of growing intercultural contact and communication among diverse national cultures which have been brought face-to-face in the marketplace. It has thus created a scenario of cultural confluence as much as of economic interdependence.

DEFINING SOCIAL TRANSFORMATION

Few terms have gained as much currency in contemporary sociological parlance as social transformation. This is evident from its frequent use in prevailing sociological discourse as well as in recent writings. Its extant usage is understandable in view of the momentous changes taking place in society. However, the use pattern of the term reveals a tendency towards its indiscriminate use. Often than not, it is used in an interchangeable sense of social change. Its referents range from all kinds of passing changes to extraordinary ones. It has thus become a part of sociological vocabulary but not of sociological dictionary. Unlike other terms such as social evolution, progress, revolution and development, which figure in sociology texts as distinguishable forms of social change, the term social transformation has yet to acquire a technical connotation. There is, therefore, a need to articulate it as a sociological concept and indicate its *differentia specified*. This is precisely what I seek to do here.

The literal meaning of the term transformation is change from one form to another. It connotes a kind of change that transcends the original form of the object to which it is applied. In this sense, it signifies a systemic change rather than an incidental one. The term social refers to a system of social relationships, institutions, identities and values. Taken together, thus, social transformation literally means systemic change in the frame of social relationships, institutions, identities and values. To illustrate this, it is important to distinguish between two types of changes in society: transitory and transformative. In my view, transformative changes are distinguishable from transitory trends in terms of three parameters, that is, their profundity, magnitude and power of persistence. Profundity-wise, they are fundamental; magnitude-wise, they are phenomenal; and persistence-wise, they are relatively irreversible. To elaborate on the first, transformative change is that which represents a fundamental departure from the root, that is, from the original form of a social unit/system to which it pertains. Take, for instance, the trend of gay marriages. Given the original and the usual idea of marriage as a union of individuals of opposite sexes, gay marriage represents an instance of social transformation once it gains social acceptability. Moving on to the second distinguishing feature of transformative change, i.e. its phenomenal magnitude, social transformation is not a case of small but of substantial change. Proliferation of civil society groups such as social action forums, civil rights unions and social resistance movements in a communal society provides a telling illustration of this in that it is indicative of transformation of a communal society into a civil society. Coming to the third parameter, that is, irreversibility, a transformative change is that which is not likely to revert to its original point of departure. Rise of a new middle class cutting across caste lines in a caste ridden society is a graphic example of it.

Radical pace of change may as well be considered as a usual, though not a necessary feature of transformative change. Unlike gradual pace of change, as in the case of social evolution, social transformation is marked by a rapid pace of change. This means too tall a change in too short a time. A good example of it is the change in gender relations from a culture of hierarchy to that of equity. Even as radicalness is a usual feature of transformative change, it cannot be regarded as a parameter of social transformation for two reasons. One, that a systemic change does not necessarily take place as a sudden break with the past. There is generally a cumulative background to it. Two, radicality is more a distinctive feature of revolution which may or may not result in transformation. In the interest of conceptual precision, therefore, social transformation may better be viewed as a case of fundamental, phenomenal and irreversible change in a given social script.

In order to further clarify the notion of social transformation, it may be reiterated that for all practical purposes, it signifies a case of structural change. Structural change connotes a profound change in social institutions, relational frames, identities and values. To decode it, institutional innovations such as 'live-in' arrangement as an alternative to conventional marriage is a clear instance of profound change. In the domain of relational frames, a trend of change from asymmetrical to symmetrical relations as in the case of inter-caste relations, is certainly an indicator of structural transformation. In respect of identities, similarly, when in-born identities give way to achieved identities, this constitutes a case of transformative change. In the realm of values, a change from communitarian to individualistic values provides a telling illustration of social transformation.

A final point to note about the concept of social transformation is that it is a value-neutral category. This clarification is important in view of the fact that generally the victims of a given system raise a demand for transformation, implying thereby a change for the better. In my view social transformation is a fact, not a value. It is not a normative category for two reasons. One, because it stands for all kinds of structural shifts—upward as well as downward. For example, rise of a consumerist middle class in a society known for its culture of frugal living as a value is as much an instance of a transformative change as emergence of a civil society in a traditionally communal society. Social transformation is thus about all sorts of structural shifts regardless of their being desirable or otherwise. Two, that treating social transformation as a judgemental construct will render it indistinguishable from such other varieties of social change as progress and development which obviously are value laden.

SOCIO-CULTURAL FALLOUTS OF GLOBALIZATION

The era of globalization started in India in 1991 with the introduction of economic reforms comprising the trinity of liberalization, privatization and globalization, popularly known as LPG. While the three are interrelated, each carries its own specific connotation. Liberalization refers to the policy of liberation of economy from the shackles of state control, marking the end of the era of 'licence-quota-permit raj'. Privatization stands for the policy of allowing entry of private sector in all the fields of economy, including those earlier monopolized by the state such as power, transport, oil, gas, and so on, leading to the prevailing trend of disinvestment of public sector undertakings (PSUs). Globalization, as distinct from liberalization and privatization, signifies an open door economic policy for integrating domestic market with the world market. Among other things, it means allowing foreign multinationals to enter into Indian market as much as Indian multinationals to go global. There are three notable points about the onset of globalization in India. First, unlike many other nations, India opted for it more out of her domestic economic compulsions than out of volition. Given its increasing debt burden, fiscal deficit, poor state of balance of payment, high inflation and depletion of foreign reserves, the Indian State was left with no other option than accepting globalization. Secondly, unlike a number of other nations, the Indian State opted for globalization together with its two other accomplices that is, liberalization and privatization. Thirdly, unlike several other nations, including China, which settled for selective globalization, the Indian State went for it in a relatively big way.

Whatever be the background, globalization has done a miracle to the Indian economy. It has transformed the economy from a poor, backward and stagnant one to a buoyant, robust and fast growing one. This is evident from all accounts. Its rate of growth has surged from a low 3.5 per cent in pre-reforms period to a high 9.2 per cent in 2006-7 according to the Pre-Budget Economic Survey 2007-08. According to a World Bank Report (2005-6) India emerged as the twelfth richest nation of the world in 2005 based on its GDP, which grew at 13.4 per cent in dollars. Little wonder that India earned the enviable distinction of being the 'fastest growing free market economy' at the World Economic Forum's annual summit at Davos in 2006. Furthermore, according to Merrill Lynch Capgemini World Wealth Report 2006, the number of dollar millionaires in India grew by 19.3 per cent in 2005, this being the second fastest in the world. The Economic Survey (2006-7) reveals that India's foreign exchange reserves have reached a record $185.1 billion which has grown to $276 billion in 2007 (*Times of India*, 8 January 2008). This is a far cry from the pre-globalization era when India had to mortgage its gold reserves for getting foreign exchange. Similarly, the total foreign investment inflows into India have risen from almost zero in 1990 to $20 billion in 2005 and foreign remittances to over $24 billion. India is also now the sixth largest service exporter as well as a top destination for off-shoring according to a survey by A.T. Kearney in 2007. Above all, India became a trillion-dollar economy in April 2007 and thereby joined the elite club of eleven nations with such distinction. In view of these developments, the assessment of India in the Goldman Sachs BRIC report by Wilson and Purushothaman (2003) as an emerging global economic power along with Brazil, Russia and China sounds so prophetic. By all accounts, Indian economy is on the move on a fast track, thanks to globalization.

When economy is on the move, especially at this incredible pace, society, cannot remain unmoved. Globalization has set in motion a stream of changes in India's socio-cultural panorama as much as in Indian economy. These trends are noticeable in the domains of social stratification, institutions, values and identities. In the realm of social stratification, it has sprung up trends such as the following: widening disparities in the midst of growing prosperity, rise of a new middle class, marginalization of peasantry, growing caste polarization and Dalit assertion. Let us illustrate these before moving on to the trends in other domains.

Disparity in the Midst of Prosperity

It is obvious that globalization has generated an overall climate of prosperity in India. One has only to recall the depressing days of pre-globalization in order to appreciate the state of relative prosperity today. Globalization has, for sure, opened up opportunities galore for people with some measure of competence. Such opportunities were not available to them in the pre-globalization phase. Little wonder that many people of the lower classes have been able to make a grade to the lower middle classes as claimed by Friedman (2005). Similar sentiment is reflected in Das's book *India Unbound* (2002). It is developments such as these coupled with the story of the world class enterprise of Infosys in Bangalore that led Thomas Friedman, the *New York Times* columnist, to contend that the world is flattening, the global economic playing field is getting levelled and that many people in India and China have grown out of poverty, thanks to globalization (Friedman, 2005: 9).

While the above observation of Friedman is valid, it presents only one side of the coin. Globalization has no doubt enabled a wider population to see the benefits of economic growth, but it has made the super rich richer, leaving the poor largely unaffected. For the same reason, it has led to the widening and deepening of disparities. This is evident from almost all the available reports. For example, the rounds of National Sample Survey conducted in the mid-1990s point to deepening inequalities. Similarly, a report of the Department of Economic Affairs, UNO, points to rising economic disparities in India in the 1990s. Likewise, India's poverty ratio stands at a disgraceful 28 per cent (Aiyar, 2006). Most important of all, the Gini Coefficient, which is a measure of socio-economic disparities, has risen for India from 0.37 to 0.42 in 2007. What is more, according to the 'Wealth Report' published by Knight Frank in May, 2007 India is on the way to becoming a plutonomy, a society sharply stratified by a super wealthy top brand at one end and abject poor at the other, as reported in a leading national daily (*Times of India*, 2007).

On top of it, we have abundant observational evidence to see the widening gap between two Indias which I would like to call a *glittering* India and a *littering* India. The glittering India consists of the super rich while the littering India consists of the gutter poor. The glittering India belongs to the super earners and super consumers who enjoy lavish lifestyles, patronize mega malls, five star hotels, multiplexes and night parties. On the other hand, the littering India belongs to pavement dwellers, rag pickers, scavengers and sweepers, rickshaw pullers, brick kiln workers and undernourished millions. The story of two Indias may be an old one but what makes it more distressing in the era of globalization is an 'almost complete disconnect in between the 300 million, high flying Indians and the remaining 750 million of their countrymen, many of whom seldom get two square meals a day' (Malhotra, 2006). At any rate, the littering India remains unincorporated in globalized India. Nothing illustrates the existing scale of disparity in globalizing India better than the eloquent title of Loretta Schwartz's book *Starving in the Shadow of Plenty*.

Rise of a New Middle Class

One of the most visible consequences of globalization in India is the emergence of a new middle class. It is getting bigger, richer, younger, and spendthrift by the day. Its size has grown to an estimated 300 million, roughly 22 per cent as against 12 per cent elsewhere in the world. The new middle class is different from the traditional middle class in some significant respects, that is, in its composition, age group, income level, lifestyle and social outlook. It is composed of company executives, IT specialists, finance and management consultants, media professionals and the neo-rich, including the 'bullock capitalists' from the countryside to use Varma's phrase (2006). In terms of age composition, the new middle class is younger than its traditional counterpart which is understandable in view of the special value of its professional skills which are in big demand in the fast growing knowledge economy in the era of globalization. Not surprisingly, it is lauded by commentators like Varma (1998) for its buoyancy, energy, entrepreneurship and resilience. Its income levels have risen to an amazing high, thanks to the lucrative packages offered by transnational and private corporations, unthinkable in respect of traditional middle class. This has consequently enhanced its purchasing power as well as its spending proclivity. No wonder that the new middle class has emerged as a consumerist class which is willing to pay to live in style. More than its mode of living, the new middle class differs from the old in terms of its changing mores. Unlike the traditional middle class which distinguished itself by upholding the norms of conventional morality, the new middle class is seen as holding a brief for rethinking conventional morality. Well informed, alert and articulate, the new middle class is getting global in its world-view. Progressive on all these counts, it leaves something to be desired in respect of civic sensibility as it glosses over the larger public issues of poverty, inequality, corruption and oppression.

Marginalization of Peasantry

The effects of globalization are not confined to urban India. They are as well noticeable in the countryside. Globalization has brought the market forces to bear on agriculture in a big way. For the same reason, it has generated trends of corporatization of agriculture, crop diversification, monoculture, genetically modified crops and above all, creation of Special Economic Zones (SEZ). These trends coupled with the WTO-induced pressure to reduce farm subsidies have produced a new dynamic in agrarian structure, different from the one generated earlier by forces of modernization. If the thrust of modernization was on farm mechanization together with use of modern chemical inputs, the stress of globalization is on marketization strategies. In effect, globalization has accelerated a trend of de-peasantization of small and marginal farmers as well as immiseration of agricultural labour driving many of them away to cities. It has as well affected middle peasantry and big farmers in some very insidious ways. Sandwiched between rising costs of agricultural inputs and minimum support price fixed by the state, the middle peasantry has come under the terrible burden of indebtedness. This has led to alarming trend of increasing incidence of farmers' suicides in several states, such as Andhra Pradesh, Karnataka, Maharashtra and Punjab. A number of studies, including those conducted by the author (Kumar and Sharma, 1998 and 2006), have brought out the pre-eminent role of globalization in accelerating this trend. The latest shot has come in the form of the state policy of setting up SEZs, a move prompted by globalization, which has intensified farmer unrest and led to their vigorous protest against the state. Farmer mobilization in Singur and Nandigram provide solid evidence of it. While land acquisition by the state for purposes of promoting SEZs has caused widespread consternation among farmers in general, the trend of large-scale buying of rural land close to cities by private estate dealers and builders has as well brought fortunes to some farmers. A number of estate builders have entered into the fray to buy such land to construct malls and multiplexes and paid huge prices for it. This has come as a boon to some farmers, though their number is few and far between. By and large, globalization has led to the marginalization of the rural folk.

Dalit Assertion and Caste Polarization

Dalit mobilization is not a new phenomena. It dates back to the days of Mahatma Phule and Baba Saheb Ambedkar. Globalization has only intensified it and led to a renewed form of dalit assertion. It has produced this effect on account of its patronage to privatization on the one hand and its stress on disinvestment of PSUs, on the other. The contraction of that public sector has led to neutralization of reserved job opportunities made available to the Scheduled Castes (SC) and Scheduled Tribes (ST) in the public sector under the policy of reservations. Irked by this development, the leaders of the Scheduled Castes and Scheduled Tribes Federation as well as the youths of these groups have raised a demand for reservations in the private sector. This demand is being stoutly opposed by the leaders of industry and proprietors and managers of the corporate sector as well as non-SC students of professional courses. In effect, it has led to further unionization of dalits, on the one hand, and reaction formation among non-Dalits, on the other. The Dalit intellectuals have now begun to justify their demand for reservations in the private sector on the basis of systematic data rather than their general apprehensions. The following research-based observation by Thorat convincingly illustrates it: 'After July, 1990, the new measures have led to decline in the employment of SCs in government services and jobs. . . . Identical trends were observed in employment of SCs in public sector undertakings' (2001: 10). The leaders of private corporations are resisting this move by foregrounding the key importance of professional competence for organizational growth in this age of global competition. If Dalit youths are agitated about their shrinking job prospects in the wake of globalization, the non-Dalit professional students are militating against the move of reservation in private sector as it sets their careers at stake. Be that as it may, the point to note is that globalization has set the two against each other and thereby intensified the phenomenon of caste polarization.

IMPACT OF GLOBALIZATION ON BASIC SOCIAL INSTITUTIONS

Liberalizing Marriage Mores

Turning to the impact of globalization on basic social institutions, it will be apt to focus on marriage, family and gender. Let us take them one by one. Rise in the age at marriage is a notable consequence of globalization. The youth today, particularly those drawn into the corporate sector, have begun to accord precedence to career over marriage. This has become a source of anxiety to parents, especially those whose daughters of marriageable age shy away from marriage on account of their preoccupation with their careers. Globalization of the culture of dating is another remarkable trend that is catching up with youth in the metropolitan centres. This points to a trend of self-assertion by youth in matters of marriage. Equally important is the trend of commercialization of wedding arrangements which have been taken over by professional agencies leading to change of venue from homes to hotels and now to farm houses.

Globalization has also set in motion a move towards demerger of sex and marriage. This is evident from the increasing incidence of pre-marital and extra-marital sex, as reported by a number of surveys (Vieira, 1998; Bhandare, 2003; Wadhwa, 2004). This trend is of profound significance in the sense that it runs counter to the domain of marriage, that is, sex in wedlock only. There is now a tendency of ignoring the pre-marital affairs of the mate which earlier used to constitute an important consideration in mate selection. As with pre-marital affairs, so with extra-marital alliance: there seems to be growing a measure of tolerance of it as is evident from the emerging idea of 'office spouse'. There is thus a spouse at home and another at office/organization where one has now to spend a longer time. The office spouse is a colleague of the opposite sex with whom one develops intimacy and shares matters which one is traditionally supposed to share with one's life partner. Since the work scenario has changed in a manner that it has substantially cut down on one's family time, the couple hardly finds time for sharing and caring. The office spouse is thus a surrogate partner for fulfilling this need. It signifies more of a romantic relationship than a sexual one. The work organizations are reported to be acquiescent about it in the hope that it retains employees for a longer time at the workplace contributing to organizational growth. This should not be mistaken to mean decline of sexuality in wedlock. On the contrary, globalization has sparked off a culture of super sex in the wedlock. As in the boardroom, so in the bedroom, there is a growing passion for being innovative. Super sex is about getting better, aesthetic, fantastic and creative in sexual pleasure. Yet another development relates to the emergence of weekend unions, particularly in cases where the husband and the wife are working for two different organizations located at such a distance that it prevents the two from living together at one place. Most important of all is the rise of live-in unions, an institutional alternative to marriage. The trend of live-in unions first appeared in Sweden from where it has spread to other countries, including India, thanks to the forces of globalization. One result of these developments is that marriage is no longer a taken for granted institution. It now takes effort on the part of spouses to make marriages work. In view of the above, it will not be wrong to observe that conventional marriage is proving inadequate to handle the fancies being generated by the glamour shown in the media.

Changing Familial Relations

The pre-globalization era witnessed a sociological debate on the disintegrative impact of modernization on the joint family system. In present times, it seems that globalization has led to destabilization of the nuclear family as well. The increasing incidence of marital discord caused by the excessive demand of the corporate world over family time of its employees is proof enough of it. It is well known that in the era of globalization, commitment to career and consumerism has taken precedence over family obligations. This has led to several consequences, including its adverse effects on marital harmony, child care and care of aged parents. Little wonder that it has given rise to a trend of childless couples by choice and abandoning of aged parents, resulting in shrinking size of the family. The trend of decline in family size is not altogether new. It had started in the era of modernization itself which paved the way from 'double income single child' (DISC) preference to 'double income no child' (DINC) craze. The rise of globalization with and the resultant growth of corporates has only served to reinforce the ongoing shift from 'one child' concept to 'no child' preference. What distinguishes it is the new mode of justification. Earlier, it was a consequence of the lure of double income to provide for better parenting; now it is prompted by precedence to professional career over parental role. Though the number of couples opting to stay 'issueless' is quite small, it nevertheless is important enough to indicate that the thought has germinated and is likely to spread. This is no insignificant development in a society which values parenthood and frowns upon childless couples.

Another remarkable consequence of globalization is the altering conjugal power relations. Globalization has generated opportunities for women to enter high profile occupations and entrepreneurial positions. This has led to a new kind of power equation between the husband and the wife, with wife becoming more assertive and husband getting accommodative. The increasing incidence of husbands participating in household chores as well as wives' active say in decision-making is proof of this. The role of parents in the socialization of children is another dimension of family change. Fathers have begun to take on added responsibility in raising children which has made them more a friendly figure, unlike the earlier image of a patriarch. Mothers, on the other hand, have begun to assume the role of disciplinarians in their own ways. Both parents seem to be concerned more about the career of children than about their character. For the same reason, they are enrolling their children in additional skill building courses with a view to sharpening their intellect and honing their talents. This has brought the children under pressure to perform.

As such, along with the popular impression that globalization has led to parental neglect of children, it is also true that it has enhanced parental concern and quality of parenting. It is a different matter though that parental influence in respect of character training is somewhat on the decline. The media has emerged as an alternative agency of socialization with strong influence on the young generation. Accordingly peer culture, which is largely shaped by the media, seems to be exerting greater influence over the choices, preferences and value orientation of the youth. The mounting influence of the media, including television, computer and internet, which are an integral part of globalization, have also impacted parent-child relations. The traditional paradigm of parental authority and child obedience has begun to yield ground to the emerging pattern of child rights and parental obligations. As a result, what we have is a phenomenon of assertive child and accommodative parents. Parents today are faced with a dilemma about their cultural obligation to discipline and restrain the child and the limits set on it by the civil obligation to grant freedom of choice to the youth. This is more than just a case of generation gap. There are two ways to look at it: as a case of generation break and as a case of generation bridge. It signifies generation break in that the young generation today has begun to question the rationale of traditional norms in a manner as never before. Given the exposure of the young generation to global information about cultural diversities and more so about the emerging norms of civil society, its interrogation of traditional norms is almost belligerent. Hence a case of generation break. Viewed from the other perspective, it represents a case of generation bridge in the sense that the old generation is responding positively to the new situation. It is showing commendable accommodativeness in putting up with the emerging situation. Both ways of looking at the changing parent-child relations seem to be valid as they touch on two different but complementary facets of the same reality.

Yet another consequence of globalization for the family system is the emerging problem of abandoned aged parents. With their increasing concern for career and demanding corporate obligations, the young adults find it hard to take care even of their children, let alone their ageing parents. Add to it the prevailing ethos of pragmatism and privacy prompted by globalization which is taking a heavy toll on the bonds of affectivity for which the Indian family has been known worldwide. Globalization has thus led to the narrowing of the circle of family relations, resulting in many cases in the neglect of aged parents. The enormity of this problem can be gauged from the fact that the Indian state has had to come up with the Maintenance and Welfare of Parents and Senior Citizens Bill 2007 which was introduced in the 2007 Budget Session of Parliament and passed as an in 2007 itself. The purpose of the bill is to make it obligatory for children to care for their aged parents above 60 years. This only testifies to the fact that globalization impoverized greying parents, not only economically but also socially and culturally.

Upsurge of Culture of Consumerism

Globalization has impacted not only social institutions but also beliefs and values. This is evident from the outbreak of culture of consumerism, confounding moral ambiguity and appalling state of civility. Let us take them up one by one. Celebration of the culture of consumerism is one of the most visible consequences of globalization. This is evident from the proliferation of mega malls, marts, multiplexes and magnificent markets. This is also obvious from the emerging brand-conscious lifestyle, tastes, choices, and preferences. Above all, this is reflected in the growing mentality of acquisitiveness resulting in possessions far in excess of needs.

Culture of consumerism is not just about consuming more. It actually refers to a 'classy' lifestyle. The distinctive traits of such a lifestyle are concern for brand equity, craze for the latest, proliferation of wants over needs, and a tendency of exhibitionism. Brand equity serves as a measure of status. Accordingly, it is patronized as a status symbol. The connection between brand equity and globalization is clear from the manner in which multinationals and domestic companies invest in the projection of their brand equity for purposes of marketing.

Craze for the latest, another element of the culture of consumerism, implies an attitude of discarding the old and adopting the new, i.e. abandoning yesterday's buy in favour of today's fad. This desire for the latest is systematically kept up by organizations by continuously coming up with something 'new and different'. It is also sustained by stimulating a desire to stay ahead of others.

The third ingredient of the culture of consumerism signifies a crucial distinction between needs and wants. Needs represent necessities while wants represent desires. One may not need what one wants. This, in fact, is often the case and far more so in the era of globalization. Wants are manufactured desires, generated by advertisements patronized by the media. Little wonder that globalization has led to multiplication of wants over needs and a trend of unabashed consumerism. This development is at variance with the values of our culture which puts premium on curtailment of needs. Globalization has thus moved us from a state of simple living to that of high living and mindless consumerism. It calls for a revision of Descartes' classic dictum 'I think, therefore, I am' to 'I consume, therefore, I am', as cited in an editorial of a leading national daily (*Times of India*, 24 February 2007).

Conventional Morality Under Interrogation

Morality is extremely subjective. Built upon the notion of human good, it provides a normative framework for judging propriety of conduct pertaining to interpersonal relations including related to sex norms. Its defining feature is its stern applicability to self as much as to others. Hence, its primary dictum: do unto others what you want others to do unto you; don't do unto others what you want others not to do to you. Derived from this dictum are certain universal values such as truth, honesty, fidelity, integrity, incorruptibility, non-stealing and selflessness. Beyond such universal values which are usually incontrovertible, there are some relative values which are time-space specific. They vary from community to community. Take, for example, conduct such as kissing in public, dating and courtship. These are viewed as immoral in India but not in the West. However, even in India, compared to earlier times when they aroused a greater sense of moral indignation, today that is not so.

Proud of its glorious tradition of morality, Indian society today abounds in moral ambiguity. There is ample evidence of deviance from moral norms of truth, public probity, integrity, concern for others, pre-marital sex, etc. What is more, there is also emerging a tendency of open defiance of these norms in public. From *deviance* to open *defiance* is a notable trend. Conventional morality is increasingly coming under interrogation, and being confronted with 'alternative morality'. Globalization has ushered in a new era of alternative lifestyle (consumerist), alternative sex morality (liberalized) and alternative relational morality (pragmatic). Prompted by market-driven economy, such a morality is now viewed as 'progressive morality' (which is actually permissive morality). Mass media is glamourizing it in a big way. Leisure industry is marketing it vigorously. While conventional morality has not yet lost ground, alternative morality has yet to gain a firm foothold. As of now, the custodians of conventional morality view the present situation as a case of value decadence, while the protagonists of alternative morality look upon it as morality in quest of redefinition. Whatever it is, it certainly points to a state of moral flux, if not of breakdown of moral order.

Civil Values in Disarray

Civil values are different from moral values in that they pertain to the public domain unlike the latter which relate to the community domain. Public is a political category while community is a social entity. Accordingly, civil values represent the desirable conditions of public life such as liberty, equality, and secularity, etc., while moral values have to do with conceptions of human good. As with moral values, so with civil values: globalization has led to their impairment. This is evident from the disconcerting trend of fundamentalism, recurrent stream of communalism, rampant corruption, criminalization of politics, falling standards of public conduct, callousness towards the downtrodden, and diminishing concern for environment and ecology. Not generated by globalization, for sure, but globalization has certainly led to the aggravation of these trends by giving an upper hand to market over state, profit over people, economy over ecology, inequity over equity, meritocracy over compensatory justice, and 'haves' over 'have nots'.

These unwholesome developments have not gone unresisted. A number of civil and social resistance groups have come up in order to protest against these unwholesome trends. The role of civil rights unions, environment groups, social forums, anti-corruption councils, and, above all, anti-globalization movements are some of the instances in point. These are healthy signs, of course, as they point to the rise of civil society, but these developments are the unintended consequences of globalization.

Cultural Traditions and Identities Under Threat

Globalization is not just about economic flows; it is also about cultural flows. As a result, it has generated stirring effects on cultural traditions and identities across the globe, particularly in the non-Western parts of the world. Like elsewhere, in India too, there has appeared a debate about the repercussions of globalization on the cultural traditions and identities. Voicing a popular concern in this regard, Dhanagare has highlighted the 'pernicious effects' of globalization on local communities and cultures. In particular, he deplores the role of MNCs and media for exerting shattering impact on ethnic traditions and craftsmen. Without mincing words, he observes: 'local economies are being swallowed gradually by the global capitalism and traditional cultures are being displaced by the ever-expanding global market and consumer culture' (Dhanagare, 2003: 23). On the other side, there is Yogendra Singh who contends that globalization also accelerates the growth of cultural self-consciousness and cultural identities (Singh, 2000: 98). Admitting that 'the penetration of external market and capitalist interests may threaten local or regional cultures by new modes of appropriation and erosion of traditional cultural values' he argues that 'improvement and enlargement of the reach of communication may provide means to people to strengthen cultural identities' (2000: 96). 'In this sense' he adds 'the globalization process, instead of being a threat to such identities, has become a means for their construction' (Singh, 2000: 97).

For a systematic appraisal of the cultural consequences of globalization, I find Fukuyama's conceptual frame of 'globalized production of homogenization' (1992) and Appadurai's 'globalized production of differences' (1996) quite revealing. I would therefore like to build upon the same for analysing the Indian situation. For sure, globalization has resulted in 'globalized production of homogenization'. In the cultural field, this is evident from the upsurge of the following: culture of consumerism, commercialization and commodification of cultures, pop culture, and virtual culture. These may be regarded as cultural universals of globalization. As elsewhere, so in India: the culture of consumerism has made inroads into all local cultures, its greater visibility in new middle class notwithstanding. The proliferation of malls, marts and multiplexes, the easy availability of finances, the entry of big players in retail and rural marketing—these are all going to give a further fillip to the culture of consumerism. Its disruptive implications for the traditional cultures in a land known for its value of frugal living are too obvious to require any elaboration. Similarly, the trend of commercialization of cultural events and activities as also of commodification of cultural symbols cuts across cultural frontiers, thanks to the rise of global tourism. This has led to the trivialization of ethnic cultures as well as distortions in local cultures.

The universal spread of media-patronized pop culture is another force of homogenization. Known for its domination by American themes and concerns, it combines selective elements of British, African and some exotic cultures. McDonaldization, Coca-colization,

Valentinzation and Reggae mesmerization are some of its prominent markers among many others. Titillating in their appeal, it is known for luring people, especially youths, away from their cultural roots. More importantly, its polluting effects on classical as well as folk cultures are as much resented in India as in other parts of the world. Emergence of virtual culture is yet another manifestation of homogenization. Virtual culture is a product of the stunning advances in ICT. All productions of electronic media, including films, television programmes and Internet communication are parts of the stream of cultural productions. The stupendous growth of cultural productions constitute a distinguishing mark of the age of globalization. If the era of modernization was an era of mass-scale material productions, the era of globalization is an era of mass-scale cultural productions. These cultural productions have generated a virtual culture which consists of animated signs, manufactured images and make-beliefs. Such is the mounting significance of virtual culture in the age of cyber technology that it has acquired an autonomy of its own. For all practical purposes, it is independent of existential culture. Its autonomy can be gauged from the quality of its role in the socialization of the young generation. Virtual culture indeed has emerged as a powerful agency of socialization, one that is more powerful in shaping the perceptions, choices and preferences of the youth than existential culture and its agencies like the family and the school. Even as virtual culture is largely illusory in its content, it is vital in its impact on the young generation. And this is so all the world over.

The above outlined forces of globalized production of homogenization have led to erosion of certain aspects of local cultures. The invasion of culture of consumerism has adversely affected traditional lifestyles and tastes, customary practices, sanctity of rituals and even the normative order. Similarly, commercialization and commodification of culture has turned local and ethnic cultures into a marketable commodity and thereby robbed them of their symbolic value. In much the same way, pop culture has not only marginalized classical and folk cultural traditions of arts and aesthetics but also led to their obliteration on account of mixings and blendings. Above all, the rise of virtual culture has served to erode the very foundations of existential local cultures. For all these reasons, globalization has in some ways created a threatening situation for cultural diversities and distinctions. Little wonder that there is a threat perception in local cultural circles where it is feared that MNCs-led globalization is destroying their traditional cultures and identities.

There is, however, another side of the repercussions of globalization on traditional cultures. This relates to what Appadurai calls 'globalized production of differences' (1996). Paradoxical though it may appear, globalization has as well triggered off certain trends which are indicative of upsurge of cultural distinctions and identities. Prominent among them are enhanced salience of ethnic pride and products, identity assertion by diverse cultural communities, rise of fundamentalism and resurgence of diasporic cultures. Like modernization, globalization has resulted in sharpening of ethnic consciousness as well as craze for ethnic things. The upsurge of ethnic consciousness is a case of ethnic backlash against the homogenizing forces of globalization. But the craze for ethnic things, including food, art and crafts, is generated by globalization in order to cash in on them. Advertently or inadvertently, in both the cases the net result is the upsurge of ethnic pride. Another fallout of globalization is the trend of identity assertion by diverse cultural groups. Faced with the challenge of hegemonic homogenization thrown up by globalization, local, regional and national cultures have responded by motivated articulation or reinvention of their respective identities. This is evident from the trend of assertive celebration of religious festivals and regional fairs, be it Durga Puja in West Bengal, Ganesh Utsava in Maharashtra, or Gur Purab processions in Punjab (Sharma, 1990). Such celebrations serve as measures of identity reaffirmation by local and regional cultures. In organizing such celebrations, interestingly enough, the local cultural groups enthusiastically use all the new means and resources of globalization to reiterate their respective cultural identity. Thus, there is as much evidence of appropriation of globalization by ethnicity as of ethnic specialties by globalization.

Aside from the activization of ethnicity, globalization has also precipitated ethnic fundamentalism, especially religious fundamentalism. The spurt in ethno-nationalism as well as fundamentalism, both in India and abroad is proof enough of it. Academic indictment of Huntington's thesis of clash of civilizations (1996) notwithstanding, the incidents of 9/11 and its sequels in Iraq and Iran provide telling illustrations of it. Similarly, the recurrent events of terrorist attacks in India bear further testimony to this.

Finally, globalization has led to the activization of diasporic cultures. Not a new phenomenon, diasporic cultures have gained salience in the wake of globalization. This is so partly because of enhanced incidence of 'translocation' of cultures on account of accelerated migration of people due to globalization and partly because of emergence of transnational networks between diasporic groups of the same nationality. Globalization has generated a scenario of face-to-face contact of diverse national cultures in an alien setting. In a situation such as this, every diasporic culture shows a proclivity to retain its identity *vis-à-vis* others. As a matter of fact in such a setting culture serves as an identity resource for its people to maintain their identity as well as their integrity. This is reflected abundantly in the diasporic literature. Furthermore, the development of transnational networks between diasporic groups of the same 'homeland' has led to further strengthening of their cultural integrity across nations. This fact has been brought out by recent diasporic research (Bhat, 2005).

At this point it will be in order to appraise the above alluded to debate about the cultural fallouts of globalization. Let us take the homogenization thesis first. On the face of it, the homogenization thesis seems to be credible in view of the near universal spread of the culture of consumerism, mass-mediated pop culture and virtual culture. On closer examination, however, these trends do not make for convergence of cultures, nor for uniform global culture, or neutralization of cultural diversities and distinctions. Therefore, the homogenization thesis is untenable. On the other hand, the thesis of globalized production differences', though largely valid, is also not wholly true. Notwithstanding the evidence of backlash of ethnic or local cultures, their identity assertion and the salience of diasporic cultures, the fact remains that they are no longer the same authentic cultures as before; they represent reinvented versions, and they have lost some of their integrity under the spell of globalization. Thus, because of globalized production of differences, globalization has made a difference to their authentic forms. In view of the substantial evidence of identity consciousness of local, regional and national cultures, the popular threat perception seems to be a case more of panic reaction than rational contention. All the same, a dispassionate look at the situation suggests that traditional cultures are not going to remain the same any longer.

THEORETICAL INFERENCES

Having deciphered the trends of change in the Indian sociocultural panorama under the impact of globalization, it will be in order to bring out their theoretical implications. To this end, the following three questions are of core sociological significance:

(i) Has the structural adjustment of economy led to structural shifts in society?
(ii) Has the upsurge of global market economy insinuated marginalization of traditional cultures?
(iii) Has globalization ushered in some new trends of sociocultural transformation which are different from these unleashed by industrialization and modernization?

The theoretical significance of these questions lies in the fact that they address the seminal sociological issue of interrelations among economy, society and culture.

To take up the first question, it is evident from the above analysis that globalization has led to a measure of mobilization in the realm of social institutions and role-relationships. In some ways it has generated structural shifts as well, such as the rise of a new middle class, marginalization of peasantry and proliferation of civil society groups. However, it has not been able to make a dent into, let alone displace, the basic social structure of India which consists of the caste system. If anything, it has only served to reinforce the caste structure as is evident from the vigorous Dalit mobilizations for reservation. For sure, the recent caste-based student mobilizations, both of the Dalits and forward castes, have been precipitated by the impact of globalization on the policy of reservations. However, these moblizations are indicative of the power of structural diversities to assert themselves in the face of globalization. Similarly various other primal groups, including ethnic and communal, have been negotiating with the forces of globalization in their own respective ways, thus influencing the course of globalization in India. From all this it is clear that the impact of globalization on Indian social diversities is not unilateral. It is indeed dialectical as the socio-cultural diversities have as well been impinging on globalization here and influencing its character.

Turning to the impact of globalization on traditional cultures, it is evident from the preceding section that globalization has introduced some elements of the so-called global culture in India, such as the culture of consumerism, pop culture and virtual culture. It has thereby generated a semblance of cultural transformation entailing a threat of annihilation of the identities and distinctions of traditional and local cultures. A deeper probe, however, reveals that the traditional and local cultures have not taken it lying down. There is ample evidence of backlash in the form of re-invocation of ethnic pride and reiteration of cultural identities and distinctions. More important than that, there is also noticeable substantial evidence of the traditional cultures usurping the material and communicative resources of globalization for proclaiming their identities and distinctions. On net balance, then, we find considerable evidence of cultural transformation. Stated in theoretical terms, globalization provides a site for the contest of economy and culture. As a form of economic reorganization, globalization has generated some measure of cultural change in India. At the same time, cultural systems have as well shown a great deal of vibrancy and agility to keep their identities intact in spite of the bulldozing effect of globalization. The upshot of it all is that like the relationship between globalization and social structure, the relationship between economic globalization and culture is also not unilateral, but dialectical.

Coming to the third question, it may be observed with some measure of theoretical reflection that globalization has generated limited sociocultural transformation which is distinctive of it. Two of them are particularly notable: one relates to the locus of change and the other to its direction. It is well known that the era of industrialization heralded changes in the forces of production and the relations of production, resulting in the emergence of capitalism and capitalist class structure. Unlike that, the era of globalization is marked by changes in the larger frame of social relations, that is, in the mode of how people relate to one another beyond the frame of class relations. A discerning mind can see it that in the wake of globalization people have begun to relate themselves more in the frame of egalitarian relations than in the inegalitarian relations of class structure. Globalization has opened up opportunities for all to make a grade and be counted on his/her merit. To recall Friedman's phrase, it has led to the emergence of a 'flat world'. This obviously points to a new direction of change—from hierarchical to egalitarian, puritanical to liberal, and oppressive to emancipatory. A recall of the trends of change in the wake of globalization, as discussed in the preceding section, clearly indicates this direction. No matter which sphere of social structure we take, be it gender system, kinship system, caste system or ethnic communities, the trend of change is in the direction of egalitarian, liberal and emancipatory impulse. This renders the impact of globalization distinguishable from that of industrialization which patronized a structure of unequal socio-economic relations in the singular frame of class structure.

Let me hasten to add here lest I am accused of taking a contradictory and an untenable stand that I am aware of the fact that globalization in its elemental form represents a project of hegemonic homogenization of the world. Therefore, it is not so much because of its intent that globalization has turned out to be an emancipatory force, but in spite of its intent. Actually, this is due to the emergence of certain ideological developments which coincided with the course of globalizaton, including the movements for gender justice, compensatory justice to the underprivileged, human rights, and social resistance movements, that globalization has paved the way to libertarian trends. Many of these trends indeed emerged in the era of modernization. Globalization has only served to accelerate them. Thus, globalization has not produced the transformative trends all by itself, or independent of other factors and forces, but in conjunction with them.

REFERENCES

Aiyar, Swaminathan S. Anklesaria (2006), 'End of Poverty?', *Sunday Times of India*, New Delhi, 17 December.

Appadurai, Arjun (1996), *Modernity at Large: Cultural Discontents of Globalization*, Minneapolis: University of Minnesota Press.

Bhandare, Namita (2003), 'Classified Information', *Hindustan Times*, 4 December.

Bhat, Chandrashekhar (2005), 'Indian Diaspora and Transnational Networks: The Emergence of Global Networking Among the Telugus', Presented at the International Seminar on Indian Diaspora, Vallab Vidya Nagar: Sardar Patel University, 4-5 January.

Castro, Fidel (1998), *On Imperialist Globalization*, New Delhi: Leftword Books.

Chang, H.J. (2003), *Kicking Away the Ladder: Development History*, London: Anthem.

Das, Gurcharan (2002), *India Unbound: From Independence to the Global Information Age*, London: Profile Books Ltd.

Dhanagare, D.N. (2003), 'Globalization: Towards an Alternative View', *Sociological Bulletin*, 52 (1), March.

Friedman, Thomas L. (2005), *World is Flat: A Brief History of the 21st Century*, New York: Farrar, Strauss and Giroux.

Friedman, T. and B Kaplan (2002), 'States of Discord', *Foreign Policy*, March-April, pp. 64-70.

Fukuyama, F. (1992.), *The End of History and the Last Man*, New York: Free Press.

Giddens, Anthony (1990), *The Consequence of Modernity*, Cambridge: Polity.

Huntington, S.P. (1996), *The Clash of Civilizations and the Making of World Order*, New York: Simon & Schuster.

Kearney, A.T. (2007), Microsoft Case Studies. http://www.microsoft.com/casestudies.

Kumar, Pramod and S.L. Sharma (1998), *Suicides in Rural Punjab*, Chandigarh: Institute for Development and Communication.

Lall, Rashmee Roshan (2007), 'India's Super Rich are Getting Richer', *Times of India*, Chandigarh, 10 May.

Malhotra, Inder (2006), 'India's Economic Paradox: High Growth, Growing Disparities', *The Tribune*, 20 October.

Robertson, Ronald (1992), *Globalization: Social Theory and Global Culture*, London: Sage.

Sharma, S.L. (2003), 'Globalization and its Socio-Cultural Dimensions', in Paramjit S. Judge et al. (eds.), *Development, Gender and Diaspora: Context of Globalization*, Jaipur and New Delhi: Rawat Publications.

——— (1990), 'Salience of Ethnicity in Modernization: Evidence From India', *Sociological Bulletin* 39 (1 & 2), March-September.

Singh, Y. (2000), *Culture Change in India: Identity and Globalization*, Jaipur and New Delhi: Rawat Publications.

Thorat, S. (2001), 'New Economic Policy and its Impact on Employment and Poverty of the Scheduled Castes', presented at the National Seminar on Liberalization, Dalits and the State, Chandigarh: Panjab University, Department of Sociology.

Varma, Pawan K. (1998), *The Great Indian Middle Class*, New Delhi: Viking.

Vieira, Walter E. (1998), 'Changing Marriage Mores', *Business World*, 22 July and August.

Wadhwa, Soma (2004), 'Sex Survey: Fleshed Out', *Outlook*, 2 December.

Waters, Malcolm (1995), *Globalization*, London: Routledge.

Wilson, Dominic and Roopa Purushothaman (2003), 'Dreaming with BRICs: The Path to 2050', www2.goldmansachs.com/insight/research/reports/99.pdf

CHAPTER 3

Shifting Perspectives on Social Development: Changing Context and Emerging Challenges for India

DEBAL K. SINGHAROY

The perspectives on economic transformation and social development have remained implicitly intertwined in India even though these have undergone phenomenal changes in view of the emerging technological, economic and the political scenario in the country on the one hand, and the changing nature of commitments and obligations of the state towards the principles of several international declarations, conventions, summits and treaties and agreements of UNO, and its organs like the United Nations Development Programme (UNDP), WTO, World Bank and International Monetary Fund (IMF) and other agencies on the other. India's perspective on social development has been enshrined in the constitution both as citizens' rights and obligations of the state to protect and promote those rights by ensuring social welfare, equity and justice for all citizens. In the successive five-year plans strategies have been articulated for furthering the process of economic growth and social development. However, the constitutional commitments for social development have not been supplemented by strict implementation of these commitments through a strong political will of the state, as has been for economic liberalization and the structural adjustment programme. These gaps in political commitments have not only generated host of inconsistencies between the emerging patterns of economic development on the one hand and of social development on the other, but also have also contributed to further the flux, fluidity and deformities in Indian society. As against this backdrop, this paper aims to examine the changing facets of social development perspectives in India and the implications of these changes on social and human development of the largest segments in the population in the country.

THE SHIFTING PERSPECTIVE AND CHANGING CONTEXT: GLOBALIZATION, ECONOMY AND WORK PARTICIPATION

For centuries, all over the world development has been equated with economic growth. This growth perspective has been widely nurtured as panacea to all social ills, and accordingly has got a place of paramount significance within the developmental discourses of capitalism, economic modernization and globalization. However, with the increasing disjunction between economic growth and social development, that ensures livelihood security, employment, education, health, clothing, shelter and basic civic rights for all sections of the population, collective endeavour to redefine the course of development has emerged to be a reality. The facts that social development is an inalienable part of economic development, that economic development is relational and not autonomous of social development and that economic development is a means to social and human development have got wide recognition in recent years. Human well-being is now posited at the centrestage of all developments (Haq, 1997; Sen, 1999; UN, 1948 and 1986; UNDP, 1990 and 1991). Sen (1999) has viewed development 'as a process of expanding real freedoms that people enjoy' by contrasting the conventional (narrow) view of development that identifies development with growth of GDP, rise in personal income, industrialization, technological advancement and social modernization. Hence,

> viewing development in terms of expanding substantive freedoms directs attention to the ends that make development important, rather than merely to some of the means that, *inter alia* play a prominent part in the process. . . . Development requires the removal of major sources of unfreedom: Poverty as well as tyranny, poor economic opportunities as well as systematic social deprivation, neglect of public facilities as well as intolerance or over activity of repressive states.

The lack of substantive freedom to him, is linked directly to economic poverty that in turn deprives people from satisfying their hunger, minimum nutritional requirements, remedies for illness, adequate clothing, shelter, clean water, sanitary facilities, and so on. Development, as a process of enhancing freedom, is again dependant on the free agency of people. 'Not only is free agency itself a constitutive part of development, it also contributes to the strengthening of free agencies of other kind. . . .' The relation between individual freedom and the achievement of social development goes well beyond the constitutive connection (Sen, 1999: 1-5).

This approach to development is located within the social, economic and political interconnections of the society wherein a variety of institutions like market, administration, legislature, political parties, NGOs, judiciary and community in general contribute to the development process precisely through their effects on enhancing and sustaining individual capability and freedom. Though development can't be seen in isolation from the dynamics of market, it need not be privileged over other institutional arrangements of the society. Herein the human development approach to development calls for 'an integrated understanding of the respective roles of these institutions and their interconnections (Sen, 1999: 297).

Market, however, has emerged to be the powerful institution to engineer the process of development in contemporary world along with the failure of the controlled and centralised regime of the state. In recent decades most of the world economics including the erstwhile communist countries who experienced an alternative economic system between 1917 and 1990 in one form or the other, have embraced the decentralized market mechanism and open trade policy as against centralized planning (World Bank, 1996). This shift in many ways has altered the perspectives on social development globally and locally. The operational dynamics of market and their interface with the developmental dynamics have now posited to be interlinked with the processes of globalization, emergence of new economic order and work participation.

Since the mid-1980s all nation states have been experiencing new waves of shifts in their pre-organized social and economic foundations that are widely caused by globalization. New technological innovations, especially the Information and Communication Technologies (ICTs), ideas of economic liberalization, state, market and civil society partnership are the integral parts of globalization. Indeed globalization has emerged to be a plural phenomena that includes the processes of economic integration, exchange of goods and services, and mobility of resources and adaptation to the structural adjustment programme of the IMF and the World Bank, transnational cultural flows and communication to territorialize culture (viz., Americanization, hybridization, etc., cf. Barber, 1992; Appadurai, 1996), *planetarization* of ecology (Meadows, 1972), and cultural extension and technological connectivity. Ideologically many scholars have seen globalization as an expression of capitalist ideology (Ferguson, 1992) and new relationships of power. It also inculcates global interdependency and global social awareness (Robertson, 1992). Globalization, however, takes place in different socio-historical contexts, which provide very different meanings and implications in various parts of the world. It is posited in composite economic, technological, socio-cultural and political connectivity, 'with multiple tendencies to a worldwide reach and connectedness of social phenomena or to a world-encompassing awareness among social actors' (Therborn, 2000: 154).

Fast expansion of ICTs and the forces of knowledge economy are inseparable constituents of globalization with enduring impact to the process of social development. In recent decades the processes of generation, dissemination and exploitation of knowledge as commodity has occupied the central place in emerging free-market modern economies (Machlup, 1962; Drucker, 1968; Romer, 1995). Now knowledge has become a public good (Foray and Lundvall, 1996; Lundvall and Johnson, 1994), and economically 'it is also linked to the expansion and rejuvenation of global capitalism' (Castells, 1997: 17-19). It has become a new source of power and domination by acquiring commodity value after entering the labour market (Lash, 1999; Jessop, 2003). The emergence of knowledge economy depicts the failure of the welfare state economy and the triumph of market economy (Giddens, 2001), and shaping up of the Schumpeterian 'post-national work frame regime' to promote entrepreneurship for a knowledge-driven flexible economy. In this framework knowledge as an applied tool is converted into monopoly capital by embedding it through the Intellectual Property Rights (IPR), General Agreements on Trade in Services (GATS), and so on in enhancing social inequality and polarization within and across national societies (Jessop, 2003).

Knowledge workers are the pivotal force in a knowledge economy. They can get access to work and social position in knowledge society through formal education and training that controls access to opportunity and advancement. Learning accordingly becomes a lifelong process to transform knowledge into application in knowledge society (Drucker, 1968). As knowledge is the capital in the knowledge economy it needs a distinctive process to accumulate and trade this capital and a relevant social development strategy for social stability. The process of globalization which has expanded the philosophy of economic liberalization and free trade that are implicitly and explicitly liked to the processes of economic development through expansion of knowledge economy.

The composite forces of globalization, ICTs and the knowledge economy have placed the thrust for social development and social transformation at crossroads by inducing new momentum in the social dynamics bringing forth several old social concerns in the new context. They have also provided new developmental perspectives to address old social issues. Though the interdependency of social concerns has been widely recognized (Robertson, 1992), market-driven interventions have emerged to be the key strategies in addressing these concerns. In this context, it is important to examine emerging dimensions of the social and economic development perspectives across the globe and the intertwining between the new social and economic initiatives.

DEVELOPMENTAL PERSPECTIVES ON THE MOVE

The United Nations has from its very inception regarded social development as a moral obligation of its member states, to evolve social and legal frameworks and conditions for ensuring equality, fraternity and justice to all citizens. The Universal Declaration of Human Rights 1948, International Covenant on Economic, Social and Cultural Rights 1966, United Nation Resolution of Right to Development 1986, and the subsequent regulations widely depict these concerns. However, in the wake of globalization and expansion of economic liberalization, the relevance of market dynamics has been integrated to the framework of social development. This has been widely reflected in the Washington Consensus 1990, UNDP's framework on human development since the 1990s, Resolution of the Social Development Summit, Copenhagen 1995, and the formulation of the Millennium Development Goal by the UNDP in 2000, adoption of the Structural Adjustment Programme (SAP), General Agreements on Trades and Tariffs (GATT) and in the GATS, and in the directives of the World Bank.

After Second World War the United Nations began to consider social rights in conjunction with basic political and civil rights (Faist, 2009). For example, the Universal Declaration of Human Rights 1948 recognized that:

> All human beings are born free and equal in dignity and rights . . . everyone, as a member of society, has the right to social security and is entitled to realization . . . of the economic, social and cultural rights indispensable for his dignity and the free development of his personality;

and that

> Everyone has the right to a standard of living adequate for the health and well-being of himself and of his family, including food, clothing, and housing and medical care and necessary social services, and the right to security in the event of unemployment, sickness, disability, widowhood, old age or other lack of livelihood in circumstances beyond his control. (UN, 1948)

The International Covenant on Economic, Social and Cultural Rights 1966 also recognized

> the right of every one to an adequate standard of living for himself and for his family, including adequate food, clothing and housing, and to the continuous improvement of living conditions.

Both these declarations have recognized education as the corner stone of development of human personality and accordingly realized that everyone has the right to education and recommended that elementary and primary education shall be free and compulsory. These universal rights are again reframed and re-emphasized in the Right to Development formulated by the United Nation General Assembly in its resolution 41/128 of 4 December 1986. The resolution resolved that

> the human person is the central subject of development and should be the active participant and beneficiary of the right to development. . . . The States have the right and the duty to formulate appropriate national development policy that aim at the constant improvement of the well-being of the entire population. (UN, 1986)

Significantly these proclamations for social rights, which are essentially moral in nature, have got widely represented in the successive Human Development Reports of the UNDP since 1990. In these reports the UNDP has posited human development as a

> process of enlarging people's choices to live a long and healthy life . . . to be educated and to have access to resources needed for a decent standard of living by creating conducive environment for people . . . to develop their full potential and to have a reasonable chance of leading productive and creative lives in accord with their needs and interests. (UNDP, 1990: 1-3)

The UNDP has also firmly recognized the adverse impact of gender, racial, ethnic and economic divides and disparities on the people (UNDP, 1994: 1-12); and unequivocally advocated that human development is to be gendered and that 'if not engendered, it is endangered' (UNDP, 1995: 1-12). It also emphasizes that the developmental perspective is to be inclusive in order to integrate ethnic, religious, linguistic and multicultural diversity with the philosophy of cultural freedom, democracy and equitable growth (UNDP, 2004). The UNDP strongly advocates for the human approach to development as against the economic growth approach. Through this approach the UNDP has expressed its firm commitment 'to redress all evils of manifestation of jobless, ruthless, voiceless, rootless and futureless growth' by strengthening the scope of equity, enhancing of human capabilities, ensuring good governance and functioning of active civil society (UNDP, 1996: 1-7).

In the fast changing world this approach emphasizes on the effective measures for reducing the gap in consumption (UNDP, 1998), developing a common vision and a common purpose—to secure well-being and dignity for all (UNDP, 2000); converting new technology to be the harbinger of greater social freedoms, increased knowledge and more productive livelihoods (UNDP, 2001); providing a new thrust in the UN Millennium Declaration that aims to eradicate poverty, promote human dignity and equality and achieve peace, democracy and environmental sustainability by 2015 or earlier by its member states (UNDP, 2003). The UNDP looks for the sustenance of national resources and environments that supports our livelihoods (UNDP, 2006), stands for concerted efforts by the state, civil society and international bodies to meet the challenge of climate change (UNDP, 2007, 2008) which is the most crucial problem encountered by living beings on the earth.

As indicated, the UNDP has formulated the perspectives on human development in the backdrop of economic globalization, initiation of SAP by the World Bank and the IMF and the Washington Consensus (1990) that stipulated strict state policies for adhering to fiscal discipline; redirection of public expenditure priorities toward fields offering both high economic returns and the potential to improve income distribution, such as primary health care, primary education, and infrastructure; tax reform (to lower marginal rates and broaden the tax base); interest rate liberalization; a competitive exchange rate;

trade liberalization; liberalization of inflows of foreign direct investment; privatization; deregulation (to abolish barriers to entry and exit) and secure property rights (www.cid.harvard.edu).

The emerging perspective on social and human development most significantly has an inbuilt linkage with economic liberalization. The UNDP has been underlining from the very inception of shaping the Human Development Report in 1990 the need to develop strong linkages between economic growth and human development, the need for the involvement and cooption of the civil society and integration of the market dynamics with the processes of human development. It propagates that 'human development requires economic growth—for without it, no sustained improvement in human well-being is possible.' Hence the UNDP emphasizes on the strategies for mobilizing and developing human capacities and investing to expand and diversify the economic base (UNDP, 1991: 1-9).

The UNDP has been advocating the expansion of the philosophy of free market as the means to achieve human well-being in the globalized world (UNDP, 1992: 1-9) by expanding the process of globalization, especially global markets, global technology, global ideas and global solidarity (UNDP, 1999) and fair trade across the globe (UNDP, 2007). It aims to ensure human security and sustainable human development through partnership between state, markets and civil society (UNDP, 1993, 1997, 2002, 2006, 2008). Indeed this perspective has been explicit in the resolution of the Social Development Summit and the GATT and GATS.

The World Summit for Social Development (1995), Copenhagen, recognized several opportunities and challenges to the philosophy of human development within the processes of expansion of free trade, ICTs and globalization. It observed:

> Globalization, which is a consequence of increased human mobility, enhanced communications, greatly increased trade and capital flows, and technological developments, opens new opportunities for sustained economic growth and development of the world economy, particularly in developing countries.

The summit also recognized that the global transformations of the world economy are profoundly changing the parameters of social development in all countries. Accordingly it committed itself to

> promote and implement policies to create supportive external economic environment through, *inter alia*, cooperation in the formulation and

implementation of macroeconomic policies, trade liberalisation, . . . for sustainable development, enhance financial stability, and more equitable access of developing countries to global markets. . . .

The heads of state and government who were present in the Social Development Summit recognized that 'empowerment of the poor, women and the disadvantaged is the cornerstone of sustained social development and social justice; and this is to be achieved through sustained economic growth within the environment of open market philosophy, democratic institutional arrangements and civil society activism'. Hence a paradigm shift in the development strategy was envisaged in the Social Development Summit. The shifting perspective on development has also envisaged

state's partnership with free and representative organizations of civil society, and strengthening of the abilities and opportunities of civil society and local communities to develop their own organizations, resources and activities.

It has committed to promote

dynamic, open and free markets, while recognizing the need to intervene in markets, to the extent necessary, to prevent or counteract market failure, promote stability and long-term investments, ensure fair competition and ethical conduct, and harmonize economic and social development. . . .
(UNDP, 1995)

In another international commitment (commitment 3) they promised to 'foster international cooperation in macroeconomic policies, liberalisation of trade and investment so as to promote sustained economic growth and the creation of employment, and exchange experiences on successful policies and programmes aimed at increasing employment and reducing unemployment'.

This summit also committed (commitment 7) to 'implement at the national level structural adjustment policies, which should include social development goals, and effective development strategies that establish a more favourable climate for trade and investment. . . .'(UN, 1995).

The World Bank has also been constantly emphasizing on the increasing roles of the civil societies and the market in social development. To the World Bank,

The world is changing, and with it our ideas about the state's role in economic and social development. . . . The global integration of economies and the spread of democracy have narrowed the scope for arbitrary and capricious behaviour. . . . Technological change has opened new opportunities for unbundling services and allowing a larger role for markets. These changes have meant new and different roles for government who is no longer as sole provider but as facilitator and regulator.

The World Development Report provides a broad framework for addressing the issue of the state's effectiveness worldwide.

> Getting societies to accept a redefinition of the state's responsibilities will be one part of the solution. This will include strategic selection of the collective actions that states will try to promote, coupled with greater efforts to take the burden off the state, by involving citizens and communities in the delivery of core collective goods. . . . And it means making the state more responsive to people's needs, bringing government closer to the people through broader participation and decentralization. (World Bank, 1997: 3)

As the above-mentioned reports of the UN bodies have emphasized, in one form or the other, on the growing need of adhering to the principle of free market to ensure social and human development, it is imperative on our part to delineate some of the guiding principles of trade related issues of globalized free market.

GATT, GATS and Trade Related Aspects of Intellectual Property Right (TRIPS) are integral components of the free market philosophy. Under the principles of the GATT of the WTO, all member countries will provide equal market access and national treatment to all WTO members and guarantee equal conditions for foreign exporters and importers of services and investors in the sectors to do business. Ideas and knowledge emerging out of research, innovation, invention, and application of advanced technology are important parts of trade. The WTO agreement on TRIPS aims to grant the creators 'the right to prevent others from using their inventions, designs or other creations and to use that right to negotiate payment in return for other using them'. Under the GATS trading is extended from banking, telecommunications, tourism, professional services to health care, education and energy and to social sectors. It has been stipulated that the Most Favoured Nation (MFN) treatment and equal opportunity be given to service providers from all WTO members; that government would make and modify all relevant laws and regulations governing public services accordingly; and that progressive liberalization of the services sector is a goal of GATS, which is to be achieved through negotiations (WTO, 2001). All these changes in social and economic perspectives of the supra-state bodies have implicit and explicit bearings on the social development policies in the globalized world general and for India in particular.

CHANGING DEVELOPMENT POLICIES IN INDIA: FROM STATE TO MARKET DRIVE

India has well articulated her broad perspective on social development as the rights of the citizens in the Fundamental Rights, and as the moral obligation of the state in the Directive Principles in the State Policy of the Constitution.

The Fundamental Rights embodied in the Indian Constitution guarantees that all Indian citizens can and will lead their life in peace, enjoy civil liberties, such as equality before the law, freedom of speech and expression, freedom of association and peaceful assembly, freedom of religion, and the right to constitutional remedies. In addition, the Fundamental Rights have also been used to prohibit discrimination on the grounds of religion, race, caste, sex, or place of birth; forbid trafficking in human beings and also forced labour. The Fundamental Rights also aim to protect the cultural and educational rights of religious and linguistic minorities.

The Directive Principles of State Policy suggest the moral obligations of the state to 'strive to promote the welfare of the people by securing and protecting as effectively as it may a social order in which justice, social, economic and political, shall inform all the institutions of the national life'. It states that the state shall, in particular, direct its policy towards securing equally among citizens, adequate means of livelihood, equal pay for equal work; health and strength of workers and the tender age of children; protection against exploitation and against moral and material abandonment. The constitution has also advocated for equal justice and free legal aid, promotion of local self-government, right to work and to education, provision for free and compulsory education for children, promotion of educational and economic interests of Scheduled Castes (SCs), Scheduled Tribes (STs) and other weaker sections and raising the level of nutrition and the standard of living and to improve public health (Constitution of India, Part IV).

These have got re-emphasized in several constitutional amendments, enactment of new laws and formulation of new social welfare policies and have got strategized in the successive five-year plans.

Immediately after Independence, to restructure the society and to accelerate the process of economic growth India initiated programmes of radical land reform, community development and state-sponsored heavy industrialization in the 1950s. It also introduced new technology for Green Revolution in agriculture in the late 1960s and 1970s. Herein initiation of social welfare activities has remained predominantly the obligation of the state, and economic protectionism was the state philosophy to promote economic self-sufficiency and social stability. Drawing its perspective from the Directive Principle of State Policy, the state envisaged through centralized planning: 'to initiate a process of development which will raise living standards and open out to the people new opportunities for a richer and more varied life' (First Five Year Plan, 1951-6), and 'sought to rebuild rural India, to lay the foundations of industrial progress, and to secure to the greatest extent feasible opportunities for weaker and under-privileged sections of our people and the balanced development of all parts of the country' (Second Five Year Plan, 1956-61).

In the 1960s the focus of development planning was on the distribution and social justice. Thus the Third Five Year Plan envisioned that 'economic activity must be so organized that the tests of production and growth and those of equitable distribution are equally met'. It explicitly talked about the foundation of a socialist pattern of society (Third Five Year Plan, 1961-6).

In the 1970s and 1980s the Indian development planning emphasized on equity, social justice and self-reliance. During this period, the plan was to align the tempo of economic activity with the basic goal of 'a rapid increase in the standard of living of the people, through measures which also promote equality and social justice' (Fourth Five Year Plan, 1969-74). Emphasis was placed on the common man, the weaker sections and the less privileged. In view of imbalanced economic development and proliferation of social unrests and radical movements in several parts of the country, the second phase of land reform was initiated in the early 1970s. Therein objectives in view were removal of poverty and achievement of self-reliance (Fifth Five Year Plan, 1974-9), removal of unemployment and inequalities (Sixth Five Year Plan, 1980-5), building 'a new India free from the fear of want and exploitation to move forward at a still faster pace on the road to progress, prosperity, social justice and self-reliance' (Seventh Five Year Plan, 1985-9).

India experienced in the late 1980 and early 1990 a host of political unrests and changes in the political and economic climate. Phenomenal reorientation was made in the planning perspective during this period. Since early 1990 the focus has been on participation of people, civil society and private partners in achieving the objectives of development. The planning process was very categorical 'to undertake re-examination and reorientation of the role of the Government as well as the process of planning'. It planned 'to work out the ways and means of involving people in the developmental task and . . . empowerment of women and socially disadvantaged, promoting people's participation in bodies like Panchayti Raj institutions, co-operatives and self-help groups . . . ' (Eighth Five Year Plan, 1992-7). It also proposed to

> usher in a new era of (economic) growth with social justice and participation in which not only the Governments at the Centre and the States, but the people at large, particularly the poor . . . public and private sectors and all tiers of government will be vital of ensuring growth with justice and equity. (Ninth Five Year Plan, 1997-2002)

In the new millennium the development perspective has been oriented towards human well-being and inclusive growth. Significantly the planning process now aims to

> represent a visible shift in the focus of development planning from the mere expansion of production of goods and services, and the consequent growth of per capita income, to planning for enhancement of human well being. . . . The notion of human well-being itself is more broadly conceived to include not only consumption of goods and services in general but more specifically to ensure that the basic material requirements of all sections of the population, especially those below the poverty line, are met and that they have access to basic social services such as health and education. (Tenth Five Year Plan, 2002-7)

Now in view of impressive economic growth on the one hand and a glaring socio-economic disparity on the other, the Eleventh Plan aims to:

> build on our strengths to trigger a development process which ensures broad-based improvement in the quality of life of the people, especially the poor, SCs/STs, Other Backward Castes (OBCs), minorities and women. . . .

Significantly this developmental process is to be initiated in an environment in which the society is much more integrated into the global knowledge economy.

In the changing economic climate it has been emphasized that:

> The growth is to be achieved in an environment in which economy is much

more integrated into global economy, an integration that has yielded many benefits, but also poses many challenges. (Eleventh Five Year Plan, 2007: 2)

The developmental perspective of India has undergone a phenomenal shift in recent years, paving the way for its integration with the global economy. The process of this integration with the global economic order has invited a paradigmatic shift in the social development process since the 1990s. The 'growth and stability' based development policy of early Independent India got reoriented to incorporate the philosophy of 'social justice' in the 1970s and 'empowerment' and 'people's participation' in the 1980s. This again got reoriented in the 1990s to integrate itself with the perspective of human development and inclusive growth through state and market partnership. The social development strategy in India which was mostly state driven based on socialist and mixed economic perspective, has largely emerged to be market driven ever since the 1990s. India accepted the policy of economic liberalization and the SAP in 1990. This has paved the way for expansion of privatization of trade in economic and social services. With continued economic liberalization India has emerged to be a favourable destination for foreign direct investment (FDI). As per the global survey of corporate investment plans carried out by KPMG International, released in June 2008, India will see the largest overall growth in its share of foreign investment, and it is likely to become the world leader for investment in manufacturing. Its share of international corporate investment is likely to increase from 8 to 18 per cent over the next five years. It will help India to rise to the fourth from the seventh position in the investment league table, pushing Germany, France and the UK behind. In spite of the global meltdown, in fiscal year 2007–8, about US $32.4 billion as foreign investment had poured into India. The country posted a 45 per cent growth in FDI over the previous year, with US $23.3 billion between April and December 2008. The FDI inflows between April and November 2008 stood at US $19.79 billion (www.ibef.org).

Globalization however has not produced the required balance between social development and economic growth. Notwithstanding the fast economic transition from agriculture to non-agricultural and knowledge-driven service economy, a vast part of India has been reeling under the pressure of persistent poverty, livelihood insecurity, mass illiteracy, lack of skill, traditional bondage and domination, social exclusion, increasing quantum of displacement and migration, discontent and resurgence of protest of vast segments of population at the grassroots against new forms of hegemony and domination. Moreover, these have produced varieties of deformities, disparities, flux and fluidity in societies by developing a substantive mismatch between economic development on the one hand, and social and human development on the other. Paradoxically again, while globalization has (propagated) the philosophy of liberal democracy, social equity and equal opportunity, it has in essence furthered the expansion of the pre-existing patterns of social and economic inequalities.

DEVELOPMENT AT CROSSROADS: DEVELOPMENT, DEFORMITIES, FLUX AND FLUIDITY

The developmental processes initiated by globalization and economic liberalism have furthered and at times introduced new inconsistencies and deformities in society. While the new initiatives have helped stimulate the process of economic growth of the country, and specifically economic prosperity of a limited section of the population, issues of social inequality and persistent social and human under-development have remained intertwined with a vast section of the population. Within the emerging developmental processes societies in India encounter a host of inconsistencies in all prominent areas of socio-economic transition and project a dismal performance key areas of social and human development.

INCONSISTENCIES IN SOCIO-ECONOMIC TRANSITION IN INDIA

Increased Productivity vis-à-vis *Sustained Hunger and Downward Mobility in Agriculture:* India has seen phenomenal increase in agricultural production since the 1970s. The average per hectare yield has increased from less than 10 quintals in the 1960s to over 24 quintals in many parts of the country (CMIE, 2004). However, this growth has not been able to ensure food security of the rural poor. According to the latest NSSO report, the proportion of rural population unable to access the required 2400 calories a day has climbed from 75 per cent in 1994-5 to a record 87 per cent by 2004-5. In the urban areas too, the nutrition norms are lower at 2100 calories a day, the proportion of undernourished rose from 57 to 65 per cent (NSSO-2005). According to the Global Hunger Index, India ranks 94 among 119 countries of the world with 230 million rural people being undernourished—the highest for any country in the world. More than 27 per cent of the world's undernourished people live in India, and 20 per cent of India's population is undernourished. Significantly inflation in food prices rose from 5 to 11 per cent during July 2008 and January 2009, even though the general inflation rate was reported to have come down significantly. Again this economic growth has not been able to provide social security to the farmers. According to a report farmer's suicide in the country has taken a total of 1,82,936 lives since 1997. In 2006 alone 17,062 farmers committed suicide (Sainath 2009) because of increasing burden of indebtedness, repeated crop failure, food insecurity and social and political apathy on the farmer's issue. The farmers' suicide constitutes more than 15 per cent of the total suicide in the country (National Crime Bureau, 2008).

Along the line, the processes of marginalization and casualization of workforce in agriculture have also been very sharp. Persistent landlessness (11 per cent of rural household), predominantly marginal and semi-marginal landholding (among 77 per cent of rural households), downward mobility of cultivators as agricultural labourers (from 51 to 25 per cent), increase in the category of agricultural wage labourer (from 29 to 33 per cent), sharp increase of marginal (not getting more than 180 days work in a year) workers (from 4 to 11 per cent) during the period 1981 to 2001, continuous decline in real wage and earning, non-recognition of their work, livelihood insecurity and stigmatized existence widely characterize the state of work participation in Indian agriculture.

Increasing Contrast between Economic Growth and Social Vulnerability: In recent years, India has recorded a high and fast rate of economic growth of 8.4 per cent per annum (2007-8). However, the vulnerable segments of population who can't afford to spend more than Rs.14.6 for daily consumption constitute 77 per cent of the population. The report of the National Commission for Enterprises in the Unorganized Sector, Government of India, shows that 92 per cent of the Indian workforce is employed in the unorganized sector and 77 per cent of this population does not have even Rs.20 a day for consumption. Again 87.8 per cent of SCs and STs, 79.9 per cent of OBCs, 84.5 per cent of Muslims and 54.8 per cent of the general category of workers working in the unorganized sector are economically poor and vulnerable (GOI, 2007). In terms of share of income or expenditure the poorest 20 per cent of the India has access over only

8 per cent of the total income or expenditure and the richest 20 per cent over 45.3 per cent of the same (UNDP, 2008).

According to the Human Development Report of 2009 India ranks 134 among 182 countries in terms of her attainment of human development index. India stands far below Sri Lanka, Bhutan and Maldives, and marginally above Pakistan, Bangladesh and Nepal.

Poor State of Child Health and Nutrition: While examining the area of child health and nutrition one easily finds that more than 43 per cent of children below 5 years are underweight, 51 per cent are under-height, 30 per cent are with low birth weight in India (UNDP, 2008). More than 70 per cent of children of this age group suffer from anaemia, and 80 per cent do not get vitamin supplement. Malnutrition accounts for nearly 50 per cent of the child deaths in India as every third adult (15-49 years) is reported to be thin. More than 1.5 million rural children are at risk of becoming malnourished (World Report on Hunger, 2008). The UNICEF reveals that one million infants in India die every year and 40 per cent of them die in the first week after birth. According to the NSSO report (2007) between 1998-9 and 2005-6, the number of children suffering from nutrition has gone up from 15.5 per cent to 19.1 per cent and the number of children under five with anaemia has risen from 74.2 per cent to 79.2 per cent.

India's performance in the area of health care is again very dismal. Only 43 per cent of the Indian population use improved sanitation, 14 per cent population is unable to get access to safe water sources. The percentage of women with chronic energy deficiency is 40 per cent. However, India has only 60 physicians for per one lakh population. India's public expenditure on health constitutes only 0.9 per cent of the GDP. There are enormous disparities in the maternal and child health care. For example, 84 per cent of the birth of the poorest 20 per cent of India are not attended by skilled health personnel. Similarly incidences of infant mortality, under-height and under-weight are substantially higher among the poorest segment than those of the richest.

Burden of Literacy: Even after 62 years of Independence and notwithstanding constitutional directives, India is yet to achieve full literacy. The adult (15 years and above) literacy rate in India is 61 per cent, and the adult literacy rates for male and female are 73.4 and

47.8 per cent. The combined gross enrolment ratio for primary, secondary and tertiary education is 63.8 per cent. India's expenditure on education has always remained very low at around 3.8 per cent of the GDP. It altogether forms 10.7 per cent of the total government expenditure (2000-4). India spent only 0.8 per cent of the GDP in research and development as against around 3 per cent in the developed countries. India has only 119 researchers in research and development for per million population. The gross enrolment ratio in higher education (percentage of the 18-23 age group enrolled in higher education institution) is only 11 per cent as against 25 per cent in many of the developing countries (Planning Commission, 2008).

Curse of Child Labour and Child Marriage: India has enacted progressive laws to ban child labour and child marriage. However, the practice of both the institutions is rampant. According to the UNICEF report 'State of the World's Children 2009', 40 per cent of the world's child marriages take place in India and that 45 per cent of women married before they turned 18 years and 78,000 women die during childbirth every year. Due to persistent livelihood insecurity the prevalence of child labour has emerged to be a reality in India, howsoever disgraceful and inhuman this practice may be. Though the government estimate (Census 2001) shows 12.6 million, child labourers the NGO unofficial figures vary between 60 to 100 million (www.savechildren.in). There is a strong relationship between poverty, illiteracy and the increasing incidences of child labour in India.

Changing Work Participation, Sustained Poverty and Unemployment: The economic scenario of rural India is experiencing a steady shift. More than 78 per cent of the workforce of the country was engaged in agricultural activities in the early 1980s. Work participation in agriculture declined to 52 per cent in 2008. Around 45 per cent of the rural population are engaged in non-farm activities in rural areas as subsidiary sources of their occupation. As the land-man ratio has declined to .79 hectare per household (2003), vast sections of the rural population either migrate out of the village or look for alternative avenues of livelihood security outside agriculture.

According to the NSSO though the proportion of population living below the poverty line in India has declined to 28.6 per cent, the absolute number of population belonging to this category has substantively increased, with more than 330 million living below poverty line. The UNDP (2008) shows that 34.3 per cent of the Indian population earns less than a US$1 per day and cumulatively 80.4 per cent earn less than US$2 a day.

Unemployment rate in India has gone up despite phenomenal economic growth during the period 1993-4 to 2004. During the reference period, unemployment rate for males increased from 5.6 to 9.0 per cent in rural areas and from 6.7 to 8.1 per cent in urban areas. In the financial year 2004-5 unemployment grew at the rate of 8.3 per cent and the GDP growth rate was hovering around 8 per cent.

Growing Slums and Urbanization: The extent of urbanization in India has substantially increased with a decadal growth rate of around 31 per cent during 1981-2001. Now 285 million (27.8 per cent) of Indian population live in urban areas. Simultaneously India's slum-dwelling population has been more than doubled, rising from 27.9 million in 1981 to 61.8 million in 2001. They altogether form 22.6 per cent of the total urban areas reported as slums in 2001. The growth of slums is widely recognized as the natural extension of poverty, declining land-man ratio, resourcelessness, and unemployment and livelihood insecurity in the rural areas.

Shortage of Housing: With the population explosion and increasing power of urbanization India encounters enormous shortage of housing. According to an official estimate, provided by National Building Organisation (NBO), a total of 19.4 million housing shortage (6.6 million in urban and 12.8 million in rural areas) was reported in 1998. Significantly over 90 per cent of this shortage is for the poor and low income category. The unofficial estimate of housing shortage is currently pegged at over 40 million dwelling units (Karnad, 2003).

Growing Unemployment among Educated Youth: The youth (15-29 years) form 29 per cent of India's population and there has been substantial improvement in the level of education among them. However, the rate of unemployment is substantially high with 13 per cent in the rural and 9.1 per cent in the urban areas. Significantly this unemployment rate is very high among the educated female population of this age group with 26.7 per cent among rural females and 20.8 per cent among urban females (NSSO, 2005). Even though there has been phenomenal proliferation of the service sector with 39 per cent of the workforce being employed here, the newly literate youth are yet to get fully integrated with this economy. Indeed the mismatch between acquired qualifications and the job market requirement is very high in rural areas.

Increasing Access to ICTs and Digital Divides: Over the decades the usage of ICTs has increased phenomenally in India. In 2005 around 4.5 per cent of the people had access to telephone mainlines and 5.5 per cent could access internet in India. However, notwithstanding such increase, vast sections of the urban poor, slum dwellers, workers in the unorganized sector, agricultural labourers, tenants, poor peasants and artisans in the rural areas are far from being fully integrated into the digital culture. The increasing access over mobile telephone however has introduced the fast flow of information and communication among cross-sections of the population and has altered many of the societal and livelihood options.

Industrialization and Livelihood Insecurity: Despite high growth rate in industrial production in recent years (9.4 per cent pre-slow down), India has not been able to replace the traditional patterns of work participation and societal needs. Industry absorbs only 11 per cent of the total labour force of the country. In the wake of economic liberalization and GATT agreements there has been renewed interests among the big industrial houses and multinational companies towards industrialization and formation of Special Economic Zones. Large sections of Indian labour forces that are either illiterate or semi-literate, find it difficult to get integrated with the industrialization and emerging new avenues of employment. In view of their available skill, capacity, traditional and cultural resources, a large section of them still consider agriculture as the source of livelihood security. Herein the attempt for forceful acquisition of agricultural land by the state has met with organized peoples' resistance against industrialization. The proliferation of agitation of agriculturalists in various parts of the country against acquisition of land for industrial purposes depicts the underlying contradiction between traditional bases of economic, social and cultural security and the market forces of globalization.

Economic Development and Gender Discrimination: India has been experiencing declining female sex ratio over the decades. We now have 933 females per 100 males. The child sex ratio has declined from 962 in 1981 to a shocking 927 in the year 2001. Significantly, sex ratios are sharply adverse in the economically developed areas of the country in comparison to the other areas. For example, Punjab had only 798 girls, Haryana 819, Delhi 868 and Gujarat 883 girls per 1,000 boys in the 2001 Census. This points to the traditional preference for male child, high incidences of female illiteracy, practice of child marriage, early marriage, and dowry, sustained low status of women (in terms of poor access to productive resources, health, education, capacity building opportunities, lack or negligible participation in the decision-making processes) and predominance of patriarchal values, which all contribute to unfavourable sex ratio. The phenomena of female infanticide and foeticide also contribute to the declining sex ratio. According to the UNICEF 50 million girls and women are missing from India's population as a result of systemic gender crimination in Indian society.

The emerging mismatch between fast economic growth and sustained social underdevelopment has aggravated the state of poverty, hunger, unemployment, ill-health, drudgery, hardship and overall human deprivation for millions. These have contributed substantially to the increasing social instability in Indian society, that are reflected in increasing incidences of violence, crime, delinquency and corruption in society.

Criminalization and Corruption has taken a deep root in the country. These are as rampant in local officialdom as in the high corridors of power. A report prepared by the National Social Watch Coalition (2006) reveals that as many as 518 out of 3,182 candidates who contested for the 14th Lok Sabha election had criminal backgrounds. Again 120 Members of Parliament, which is about one-fourth of the total elected in the 14th Lok Sabha, have been chargesheeted in criminal cases. In the 15th Lok Sabha (2009–14) 150 (28.14 per cent) out of the 533 Members of Parliament (whose affidavits were available) have criminal charges against them (www.adrindia.org). India ranks among the thirty most corrupt nations in the Corruption Perceptions Index (CPI) in 2002. According to a report released by the Transparency International (TI) in 2008, India turned out to be the 22nd most corrupt country in the world (www.india.com, 20 September 2008).

Violence and Extremision have also increased in India from 18 per cent of the total crime in 2003 to 19.4 per cent of the total crime in 2004. In 2007 there were 971 cases of Naxalite extremism covering 156 backward districts of 13 states. A large part of the country including north-east India, Jammu & Kashmir has been subject to extremist violence. Over 47,500 died in terrorist violence between 1994-2007. Over 4,700 died in Naxalite violence during 2002-7 (Mohan, R. 2008). One-third of the country is now under the influence of Naxalite extremism. The state also recognizes that Maoist violence as an outcome of poverty in some regions of the country. Prime Minister Manmohan Singh states 'Maoist violence needs to be tackled holistically. The focus should be to end the alienation of tribal people. But observance of law of the land would be a pre-condition to any social and economic development (*Times of India*, 30 October 2009).

Along with the penetration of the ICTs there has been increasing incidences of *cyber crime* as well with 165 cyber crimes in per one lakh of crimes. About 68 per cent of the cyber crimes are committed by the young population in the 18-30 age group.

Dowry death, rape and female foeticides have taken endemic form in society. The National Crime Bureau of the Government of India reports that 6,787 dowry death cases were registered in India in 2005. Incidents of dowry deaths during the year 2005 (6,787) increased significantly by 46.0 per cent over the 1995 level (4,648). Rape cases have increased from one case a day in 1971 to 53 cases a day. Female foeticide has emerged to be a serious concern in India. According to a recent report by an Indo-Canadian Team more than 50,000 (half million) female foeticides are committed in India per annum (www.IndianExpress.com, 6 January 2006) and as indicated earlier such incidences are higher in the developed regions of the country. The incidences of crime against children, SCs, STs and other vulnerable sections have also increased in recent years.

India lives in paradoxical platform. Contemporary disjunction between economic growth and social development has furthered those paradoxes and contributed to emerging social instability and perversion in many areas of social and economic lives. Significantly, a large section of population who belongs to the bottom of the social and economic hierarchy of the society mostly representing the ST, SC, OBC, religious minorities and other marginalized sections has emerged to be highly vulnerable in the wake of furthering these paradoxes and increasing social instability. The shift in the developmental perspective has largely accelerated these processes by making vast areas of social service and obligations commoditized and market oriented.

MARKET, STATE AND SOCIAL SERVICE: EMERGING CONTRADICTIONS—HIGHER EDUCATION AS AN EXAMPLE

For long the ideals of social and human development have remained as moral standards for the Indian state without being strictly implemented. A visible gap existed between the constitutional mandates and policy formulation relating to social development on the one hand and those of political commitment of the state for implementation of the same on the other. Within the welfare perspective, the state has remained to be the key provider of social services in all the sectors including education, health and related services. However, with the state failure on the one hand and the initiation of market-driven development perspective on the other, private partners have emerged to make services like education and health tradable commodities which are the key social services to be made available by the state for the common people. Besides introducing diverse practices by the public and private providers, it has also introduced hierarchy in social services. Access to quality social services are often restricted to the limited few who have favourable purchasing power in the market. The market is more committed to earning profit by generating demands for their service than to providing social service as social commitment. The lack of commitment in social services by the market forces only widens the scope of such concerns (Chanda, 2002). Private providers seldom provide quality health or educational services to the poor and the needy on a regular basis unless they are conditioned by the state to do so, which is a rare possibility in the changing context.

Education has always remained an invasive instrument for bringing about social, economic and political inclusion and a durable integration of people, particularly those excluded from the mainstream of society (GOI, 2001: 48). The proliferation of the knowledge economy has enhanced the potential of education to be a source of mobility and effective means of integration with the global economy (UNESCO, 2001). Educational institutions have always provided the required national role and social services to meet the emerging challenges. However, with privatization and education being converted to a tradable commodity under GATS, there has been a lack of interest in treating education as a social service for the nation. With corporatization of higher education the capacity of the state has been restricted to providing a social and national perspective to the market-oriented education providers. Herein the interests of the corporate houses appear to be more ensured (Edsalt, 2000; Frase and O'Sullivan, 2003) than those of the nation and the society. With the introduction of GATS there has been a perceptive change in the attitude of the state towards higher education. Besides treating the national and foreign education providers equally (under the Most Favoured Nation Treatment of the GATS), market dynamics also govern the perspective of the state on higher education. There has been a categorical statement on the part of the government 'that the universities must make greater efforts to supplement resources from the government'. Now there has been the added emphasis on private fund in higher education. The Tenth Five Year Plan Approach Paper of the Government of India suggests that universities must make efforts to supplement resources from government by way of (a) hiking student fee, (b) introducing students' loan, (c) increasing the role of the private sector, (e) introducing self-financing courses (Government of India, 2001a).

All these developments need to be seen against the backdrop of integrating the higher educational institutions with the global market economy through GATS and the WTO. This has got rooted in the political system through the plea for privatization of higher education as propagated by the Birla Ambani Report (2001). The report has proposed 'to provide and support the private sector in the establishment of high quality secondary education facilities' and to enforce strictly 'users pay principle for higher education supported by loan schemes as well as financial grants for economically and socially backward sections of society'. The introduction of the Private University Bill in the parliament is another step forward in this direction.

There is no denial to the fact that the 'let the users pay' philosophy may work well for the economically affluent or elite sections of the society. This approach however adversely affects the students of the marginalized groups of the same society. The philosophy of equity in and access to higher education as emphasized by the National Policy on Education 1986 is now sidelined in the wake of implementation of SAP.

In recent decades in order to make higher education accessible to the cross-sections of the population and also to meet the growing need of life-long learning the Open and Distance Learning (ODL) systems were promoted in the country. Significantly the open system of education is established in this country with the mandate to provide quality education to the disadvantaged sections of the population. More than 25 per cent of the students in higher education belong to the open education system today. However, over the years it has emerged to an effective tool for commoditization of higher education in the process of developing private-public partnership in the open universities. The open university system is now experiencing a shift from supply-driven to a demand-driven education (Latchmen and Hanna, 2002). It is now experiencing growing hegemony of the corporate world and the bureaucrat over academics, a top-down approach, commodification of the educational function of the university (Noble, 1997), triumph of ideologies of market forces and 'technicization of education' (Harris, 1987), increase in the Fordist trend (of industrialization of education) and an urge for 'quick fix' academic courses to trade through available materials (Evans and King, 1991). The state has also increasingly used the open universities as mainstream educational endeavours to serve its political purposes and in the process this system has lost its innocence and academic sensibility (Tait, 1994). The open universities in India are at crossroads in the process of developing public-private partnership, getting governmental aids, developing academic content and modes of delivery. The space created by the committed academics of the open education system to cater to the educational needs of the disadvantaged segments of the student population has now widely been encroached by the market-driven expansion of the ODL.

STATE, MARKET AND CIVIL SOCIETY

In the emerging social development discourse civil society has emerged to be a key player 'to take the burden off the state' (World Bank, 1997: 3) and to ensure empowerment of the marginalized in society (UN, 1995). Civil society has long been playing a pivotal role in influencing the state's policy on social welfare, articulating views on current issues, serving as a voice in constructive debates, providing forums for exchange of new ideas and information and initiating social movements by way of creating new norms, identities, institutions (Cohen and Arato, 1994). In Putnam's argument higher levels of civil involvement gives rise to higher quantum of 'social capital' which in turn makes possible for more civic involvement (Putnam, 1993). Civil society, however is posited in between the state and the market continuum. 'The civil society is, together with state and market, one of the three *spheres* that interface in the making of the democratic societies. It is the sphere in which social movements become organized (UNDP, 1993:1). Globalization and increasing expansion of the ICTs have enabled the civil societies to undertake new roles, expand local boundaries, to influence the decision-making processes at the national and global levels, to mobilize concerned groups and most importantly to develop interface among the structural elements of the society in new ways (Scott, 2001; Smythe and Smith, 2003). However, in the changing world, the increasing significance of the civil society in state functioning has been attributed to the crises in the states on the one hand and that of the market triumph on the other. At times the state is also beset by legitimization deficit that destroys the conditions of its own stability, paving the way for the civil society (Chandhoke, 1995).

In the developmental activism India witnesses the process of NGOfication of civil societies. There is no denying the fact that a small section of NGOs have done substantive work for the social development and empowerment of the marginalized groups, opting for various innovative alternative channels of development. However, a good section of the NGOs have emerged to be the 'states in disguise' as many of the civil society activisms have got co-opted by the state. A large section of the NGOs also sustain themselves by producing stereotypes, contributing to the prevailing power structure and inculcating the culture of 'target group' of beneficiaries who are passive recipients of benefits of various development schemes.

In the globalized world the local and the national civil society work in collaboration with the global civil society and within the framework of state and the market partnership to implement the social safety net of the Washington Consensus 1990, Social Development Summit 1995. Thus the structure of the contemporary civil society has been envisioned to privilege stability over change. In the given arrangement the civil societies function more as pro-market and pro-state agents than as change agents for the people. In this process of co-option, the civil society has largely engaged to be ineffective in organizing social movements to resist the combined hegemony of the state and the market on the people.

GLOBALIZATION, SOCIAL TRANSFORMATION AND MULTIPLE DISORIENTATIONS

The journey of globalization is accompanied by innovations in technology (especially ICTs) and neo-liberal economic policies. Introduction of new innovation, technology and economic policies has always generated imbalanced development in society. The observation that technology (material culture) changes at a faster rate than social institutions, values, beliefs, attitudes and traditions (non-material culture) and that unequal pace of change between these cultures creates 'cultural lag' (Ogburn, 1937) still holds good in many parts of the world. This unequal rate change creates disharmony and maladjustment between the various elements of society. New discoveries also encroach into social lives in the form of increased turnover rates. They demand a new level of adaptability and set the stage for the potentially devastating social illness—'future shock' with dizzying disorientation in social life (Toffler, 1970: 161). Revolution in the ICTs has led to serious political and social discontinuities with the past in the advanced industrial societies (Drucker, 1968). However, this revolution, that has brought the 'third wave' of change, has replaced 'first wave' and the 'second wave' of changes brought in by the agricultural and industrial revolutions, respectively. 'Even though the third wave has begun to surge across the earth, transforming everything it touched, in many countries the simultaneous impact of first and the second waves along with third waves of change, are moving at different rates of speed and with different degrees of force behind them'. Their changes have brought in our lives 'new family styles, ways of working, loving and living; new economy, new political conflicts' (Toffler, 1980: 25-30). Now there are new and unprecedented momentums for social mobility of people, information and objects that have no clear point of departure, or arrival, leading to de-territorialization of society. These processes are essentially transforming the 'social as society' into the 'social as mobility'; constructing network flows and fluids of uneven and unpredictable mobility of people (Urry, 2000). Thus social network involves half-flow and half-being (Castells, 1996) and is now organized across time and space with a profound process of sociocultural disembededness (Giddens, 1991).

In India globalization has injected new varieties of tension, crises and deformities in society. It has generated contradictions between prevailing established societal norms and the new ideals; between socio-political perspectives on inclusion and exclusion, between traditional framework of continuity and the constitutional and legislative mandates for change. Significantly in the organization of production the introduction of advanced and state of the art information technologies have neither made the traditional agricultural economy and even the household industry obsolete, nor are these being replaced by advanced industrialization and knowledge economy. Thus even though the third wave of electronic age has radically affected social and economic lives in India, the first and the second waves of revolution continue to exercise their influence in all realms of life. All these have contributed towards the conflicting co-existence of disoriented elements of part agrarian, part developed, part industrial, part urban, part modern and part elements of knowledge society. In this transitional phase the society has emerged to be part secular and part primordial, part localized, part global, part knowledge based and part primitive, part integrated and part isolated, part capitalist and part feudal, part rooted and part mobile, part secured and part fragile, part homologous and heterogeneous, part orthodox and part heterodox. These disorientations and deformities have been accentuated since the new social processes generated by the forces of globalization are yet to get fully integrated or adapted to the pre-existing societal arrangements. Much of the social underdevelopment is being sustained by the processes of social deformities in India, making the social and the economic order to be 'half raw' and 'half cooked'. Again, the society has remained consolidated, rooted and contextualized with sustained social under development for the majority at one end, while it has been experiencing, mobility, and faster social and economic well-being for a limited section of the population on the other.

Significantly in the midst of such anomalous transition, many of the old institutions and processes have remained rooted therein to play significant roles in providing added complexities to the problems of persisting social underdevelopment. The ideals of secularism, institutionalization of norms and values and, social equity very often get blurred by caste, religion, and ethnic feudal and patriarchic social practices. Many of the problems related to social underdevelopment have remained linked to the issues of traditional societal and hegemonic political arrangements that relegate vast sections of the population at the social margin.

The pre-existing social and political arrangements operate both as cause and function of social underdevelopment in India by contributing to promote the vicious circle of poverty, illiteracy, livelihood insecurity, unemployment and ill-health. This vicious circle has again been strengthened through the long-standing gap between constitutional mandates on social development on one hand and lack of political commitment to execute those mandates on the other. The routinized bureaucratic developmental ritualism has indeed proven to be too inadequate to break pre-existing institutional managements and the vicious circle that sustain social underdevelopment. Here again with the growing emphasis on the market-driven development perspective, the prevailing gap between the constitutional mandate and the political will of the state to implement that mandate has been widened.

The problem of mass illiteracy, unemployment, poverty, and casualization and marginalization of workforce lack of skill and motivation for upward social mobility are largely linked to several old institutional arrangements including the practices of child marriage, child labour and lack of capacity building opportunities in the rural areas. Even though the constitutional and legislative mandates have abolished child marriage and child labour, the practice of such institutions continues unabated due to the lack of political will of the state to implement these mandates. Again there has been lack of pressure from below due to lack of awareness and organizational ability at the grassroots.

The positive co-relationships between child marriage, early child birth, illiteracy, and poverty are well established in India. These are also linked to futureless growth. Child marriages contribute to early child birth. In a situation of sustained poverty and lack of educational and skill development and proper capacity building opportunities, a large number of children, especially from the poor socio-economic background, are pushed to join the labour force. Once adults, but without adequate educational background, they remain permanently attached to the unorganized sector of economic activities, both in the rural and urban areas. Consequently they have remained attached to the inhuman cycle of livelihood insecurity, employment uncertainty, labour market segregation, un/underemployment, poverty, illiteracy, ill-health and socio-political apathy. As the positive correlationship between lower social status and socio-economic deprivations are well established in India vast section of population from the ST, SC, OBC, religious minorities and women are pushed to remain integrated with these cycles. As the efforts of the state have been unable to break these cycles and many of the pre-existing institutional arrangements, they are pushed to survive as cheap pools of labour force to help sustain the expansion of the global market forces.

Illiteracy as a curse blocks the scope and opportunities for human development and relational social mobility. Millions of human potential go untapped due to inadequate opportunities for education. The political elites of the country have taken 62 years to consider the bill in the parliament for free and compulsory education at the primary level. One is not so sure that the political will of the state would ensure quality education for sections of population at least at the primary level. Lack of access of quality education at an early stage of life not only breeds human deprivations, but also contributes to persistent inequality and social discontents.

India has witnessed various types of people's movement for social reforms and social development at all phases of history. The ideals for the abolition of practice of sati (bride burning), ideals of women's education, abolition of child labour, bonded and force labour, widow remarriage, abolition of untouchability, articulation of the national policy for positive discrimination for the SC, ST and OBC are consolidated through long drawn people's movement. In the wake of increasing awareness and pressure from below, many of the social ideals and perceived standards have taken shape of legal rights (viz., political representation of women and the marginalized in the statutory bodies at different levels, right to livelihood, right to information, right to basic education, and so on). However, the lack of political will in implementing constitutional mandates and legal rights has generated a space for discontents against the state on several counts. This discontent is manifested in the form of peasant, worker, Dalit, tribal, ethnic minority, women's, human rights and environmentalist, pro-agriculturalists anti-globalization, and several other movements. These movements now question the moral authority of the state to rule as the state has miserably failed to ensure even the elementary forms of social development for a vast segment of its population. These have also generated unprecedented pressure from below on the state functionaries.

CONCLUSION

Over the decades India has shifted her strategic orientations for social development from centralized planning to maket determinism. In the wake of globalization and adaptation to the SAP the public-private partnership has emeged to be a dominant strategy for the delivery of education, health, employment and social security to the people. Besides, the social safety-net strategy of the Washington consensus has also emerged to be a guiding principle of the contemporary social development initiative of the state. Notwithstanding the increasing publicity of the concept of corporate social responsibility, the national and transational corporations have little interests to transform the pre-existing arrangements and the state of social underdevelopment. They seek market stability, disciplined and cheap pool of labour to further their economic and political interests. Here state provides the stability by creating favourable business environment, by enacting new legislation, by providing infrastructure, by acquiring land and by prescribing code of conducts of the labour union and such provision that promote neo-liberal economic interest as per SAP. The incidences of forceful acquisition of land for the national and multinational corporations in Singur and Nandigram in West Bengal, Kalinganagar in Orissa, Hyderabad in Andhra Pradesh and in many parts of the country only show the eagerness of the state to adhere to the philosophy of neo-liberal economic order. Such eagerness is seldom reflected in adhering to the constitutional mandates for social development of the marginalized segment of the population, even though India has well-established network of bureaucracy and state machinery.

The process of implementation of social development measures needs a radical zeal to transform several of the pre-existing arrangements. It also invites a transformation in the attitudes and functioning of the prime institutions through which developmental initiatives are channellized. In the absence of proper political will for radical transformation and the emergence of conflicting-coexistence of several arrangements, social developmental initiatives only function as subservient to the global forces of the neo-liberal economic order in contemporary India. Herein the state is as much required to rededicate itself to minimize the gap between constitutional and legislative mandates and their implementation as much to adhere to the peoples will since all these mandates have emerged out of long drawn peoples movement in pre-Independent and post-Independent India. The state is as much required to fulfil the intransational/global commitments and obligations as much to the local need to ensure *roti* (food), *kapda* (clothe), *aur makan* (and shelter), to arrange *bijli* (electricity), *sadak* (road), *pani* (water), to protect *jal* (water body), *jamin* (land), *jangal* (forest), to protect *mati* (cultivable land) for *manush* (common man), promote *siksha* (education), *svasthya* (health) and *roji* (employment) for each and everyone in the country. As the approach to human development recognizes the human population as the real asset of the state and nation, it is rather imperative for the state to design a holistic perspective with implicit and explicit political commitment to integrate and not alienate, all sections of the population with the state by making social development as a tool for such integration. Development, besides ensuring livelihood security and enlarging choices should upheld human dignity of each and every member of the society. This can be achieved by making the state politically committed to the mandate for social development as enshrined in the Constitution: Every member of the society has the right to make the state to fulfil its political commitment.

REFERENCES

Ambani, M. and K. Birla (2001), *Report on A Policy Framework for Reform: Policy Framework for Private Investment in Education, Health and Rural Development*, New Delhi, PM's Council on Trade and Industry, Government of India.

Appadurai, A. (1996), *Modernity at Large: Cultural Dimensions of Globalization*, Minneapolis: University of Minnesota Press.

Balakrishanan, N. (2001), 'Information and Communication Technologies and the Digital Divide in the Third World Countries', *Current Science*, vol. 81, no. 8: 966-72.

Barbar, B.R. (1992), 'Jihad versus McWorld', *The Allantic*, 269.

Bartelson, J. (2000), 'Three Concepts of Globalisation', *International Sociology*, vol. 15, No. 2: 180–96.

Bell, D. (1976), *Coming of Post-Industrial Society: A Venture in Social Forecasting*, Harmondsworth: Penguin.

Beteille, A. (2000), *Antinomies of Society: Essays on Ideologies and Institutions*, New Delhi: Oxford Univeristy Press.

Blaney, D.L. and M.K. Pasha (1993), 'Civil Society and Democracy in the Third World: Ambiguities and Historical Possibilities', *Studies in Comparative International Development*, vol. 28, no. 1: 3-24.

Boshier, R and C.N. Onn (2000), 'Distance Constructions of Web Learning and Education', *Journal of Distance Education*, vol. 15, no. 2: 1-16.

Byres, T.J. (1981), 'New Technology, Class Formation and Class Action in the Indian Countryside', *The Journal of Peasant Studies,* vol. 8, no. 4, 405-54.

Castells, M. (1997), *The Information Age: Economy, Society and Culture*, vol. II, *The Power of Identity*, Malden: Blackwell Publishers.

Chanda, R. (2002), 'GATS and Its Implications for Developing Countries: Key Issues Concerns', Department of Economic and Social Affairs, World Bank: Washington.

Chandhoke, N. (1995), *State and Civil Society: Exploration in Political Theory*, New Delhi: Sage.

CMIE (2004), *Economic Intelligence Service*, Mumbai: CMIE.

Cohan, J.L. and A. Arato (1994), *Civil Society and Political Theory*, MIT Press: London.

Drucker, P.F. (1968), *The Age of Discontinuity: Guidelines to our Changing Society*, London: Heinemann.

Edsalt, S. (2000), 'GATS to Impact Public Education NSW Teachers Federation', *Education on Live*, August 2000.

Edwards, M. (2000), *NGO Rights and Responsibilities*, London: The Foreign Policy Centre.

Evans, T. and B. King (eds.) (1991), *Beyond The Text: Contemporary Writings on Distance Education*, Greelong: Deakin University Press.

Ferguson, M. (1992), 'The Methodology about Globalisation', *European Journal of Communication*, vol. 7, no. 1: 69–93.

Foray, D., Lundvall, B.-Å. (1996), 'The Knowledge-based Economy: From the Economics of Knowledge to the Learning Economy', in D. Forary, B.-Å Lundwall (eds.), *Empoyment and Growth in the Knowledge-based Economy*, Paris: OECD Documents.

Frase, P. and B. O'Sullivan (2003), 'The Future of Education under the WTO', www.Campusdemoeracy.org/wtoed.html.

Galtung, J. (1979), *Development and Technology: Towards a Technology of Staff Reliance,* New York: UN.

Giddens, A. (1991), *Modernity and Self-identity*, Cambridge: Polity Press.

——— (ed) (2001), *The Global Third Way Debate*, Cambridge: Polity.

Government of India (1951, *First Five Year Plan 1951-56*, New Delhi: Planning Commission.

——— (1956), *Second Five Year Plan 1956-60*, New Delhi: Planning Commission.

——— (1961), *Third Five Year Plan 1961-66*, New Delhi: Planning Commission.

——— (1969), *Fourth Five Year Plan 1969-74*, New Delhi: Planning Commission.

——— (1971), *Census of India*, New Delhi: Ministry of Information and Broadcasting.

——— (1974), *Fifth Five Year Plan 1974-79*, New Delhi: Planning Commission.

——— (1980), *Sixth Five Year Plan 1980-85*, New Delhi: Planning Commission.

——— (1981), *Census of India*, New Delhi: Ministry of Information and Broadcasting.

——— (1982), *The Constitution of India*, New Delhi: The Government of India Press.

——— (1985), *Seventh Five Year Plan 1985-89*, New Delhi: Planning Commission.

——— (1986), *The National Policy on Education*, New Delhi: Ministry of Education.

——— (1991), *Census of India*, New Delhi: Ministry of Information and Broadcasting.

——— (1992), *Eight Five Year Plan 1922-97*, New Delhi: Planning Commission.

——— (1997), *Ninth Five Year Plan 1997-2002*, New Delhi: Planning Commission.

——— (1998), Higher Education of India: Vision and Action: Country Paper of UNESCO World Conference on Higher Education in 21st Century, Paris, 5-9 October 1998.

——— (2001), *Census of India*, New Delhi: Ministry of Information and Broadcasting.

——— (2001), The National Human Development Report. New Delhi: Oxford University Press.

——— (2002), *Tenth Five Year Plan 2002-07*, New Delhi: Planning Commission.

——— (2007), *Eleventh Five Year Plan 2007-12*, New Delhi: Planning Commission.

Gill, S.S. (2003), 'Globalization: Higher Education will Suffer', *The Tribune*, 20 July.

Gramsci, A. (1998), *Selections from the Prison Notebooks* (rpt.), Chennai: Orient Longman.

Gultung, J. (1979), *Development and Technology: Towards a Technology of Self-reliance*, New York: UN.

Gupta, D. (1999), 'Civil Society or the State/What Happened to the Citizenship', in R. Guha and J. Parry (eds.), *Institutions and Inequalities: Essays in Honour of Andre Betelle*, New Delhi: Oxford University Press.

Harris, D. (1987), 'Openness and Closure in Distance Education', London: Flamer.

Haq, M.U. (1997), *Human Development in South Asia*, New Delhi: Oxford University Press.

International Food Policy Research Institute (2008), *The 2008 Global Hunger Index*, http://www.ifpri.org/publiction/challenge-hunger-

Jarvis, P. (1993), 'Paradoxes of Learning: On Becoming an Individual in Society', Jossey-Bass, San Francisco, CA.

Jessop, B. (2003), 'The Future of State in an Era of Globalisation', *International Politics and Society*, 3.

Karnad, R.S. (2003), Housing Finance Mechanisms in India, United Nations Human Settlement Programme. www.unhabitat.org.

Kumar, K. (1993), 'Civil Society: An Inquiry into the Usefulness of an Historical Term', *British Journal of Sociology*, vol. GG, no. 3, 375-95.

Letchmen, C. and D.E. Hanna (2002), 'Leadership for Open and Distance Learning', *Open Learning*, vol. 17, no. 3: 203-15.

Lundvall, B.-Å., B. Johnson (1994), 'The Learning Economy', *Journal of Industry Studies*, vol. 1, no. 2, pp. 23-42.

Machlup, Fritz (1962), 'The Production and Distribution of Knowledge in the United States', Princeton, NJ: Princeton University Press.

Meadows, D.H. (ed.) (1972), *The Limits to Growth*, New York: Pan University.

Mohun, R. (2008), *India Worst Victim of Terror*, Boloji.com www.boloji.com.

Naisbitt, J. (1986), *Reinventing the Corporation: Transferming your Job and your Company for the New Information Society*, London: Nicholas.

National Crime Bureau (2008), *Crime in India*, New Delhi: Ministry of Home Affairs, Government of India.

National Social Watch Coalition (2006), *India: Citizens Report on Governance and Development*, New Delhi: NSWC www.infibeam.com.

Night, J. (2002), 'Trade in Higher Education Services : The Implications of GATS', in Observatory on Borderless Higher Education, Report March.

Noble. D.F. (2001), *Digital Diploma Mills: The Automation of Higher Education*, New York: Monthly Review Press.

NSSO (2002), *Report of National Sample Survey: Household Consumer Expenditure and Employment-Unemployment Situation in India*, NSS 58th Round, New Delhi: Ministry of Statistics and Programme Implementation.

——— (2003), *Report of National Sample Survey: Land Holding in India*, NSS 59th Round, New Delhi: Ministry of Statistics and Programme Implementation.

——— (2005), *Report of National Sample Survey: Level and Pattern of Consumers Expenditure, 2004-2005*, NSS 62nd Round, New Delhi: Ministry of Statistics and Programme Implementation.

——— (2005), Employment and Unemployment Situation in India 2004-05, 60th Round Survey, New Delhi: Government of India.

Observer Statistical Handbook *2005 India 2005*, New Delhi: Rupa.

Ogburn, W.F. (1937), *Social Change*, Chicago, Illinois: University of Chicago Press.

Peters, O. (2002), '*Distance Education in Transition: New Trends and Challenges*, Biblio and Kg. and Informations System Der University. Oldenburg, Germany, Bildioteksund Informations system der Universitst Oldenburg.

Putnam, R. (1993), *Making Democracy Work: Civic Traditions in Modern Italy*, Princeton: Princeton University Press.

Robertson, R. (ed.) (1992), *Globalisation, Social Theory and Global Culture*, London: Sage.

Romer, P. (1995), 'Beyond the Knowledge Worker', *Worldlink*, January/February 1995.

Sainath, P. (2009), 'Farmer's Suicide', *India Together*, 6 November.

Sen, A. (1999), *Development as Freedom*, New Delhi: Oxford University Press.

Sengupta, A. (2008), Report on the Conditions of Work and Promotion of Livelihoods in the Unorganised Sector, New Delhi: National Commission for Enterprises in the Unorganised Sector, Government of India.

Scott, M. (2001), 'Danger-Landmines', NGO-Government Collaboration in the Ottawa Process', *Global Citizen Action*.

SinghaRoy, D.K. (2001), 'Critical Issues in Grassroots Mobilizations and Collective Action', in D.K. SinghaRoy (ed.), *Social Development and Empowerment of the Marginalized Groups: Perspectives and Strategies*, New Delhi: Sage.

Smith, P.J. and E. Symthe (1999), 'Globalisation, Citizenship and Technology: The MAI Meets the Internet', *Canadian Foreign Policy*, 7(2): 83-105.

Smythe, E and P.J. Smith (2003), NGOs, Technology and the Changing Face of Trade Politics', in K.L. Brock (ed.), *Delicate Dances: Public Policy and the Non Profit Sector*, London: McGill-Queen's University Press.

Tait, A. (1994), 'The End of Innocence: Critical Approaches to Open and Distance Learning', *Open Learning: The Journal of Open and Distance Learning*, vol. 9, no. 3: 27–36.

Transparency International (2008), *The Global Coalition against Corruption*, www.transparency.org

Taylor, C. (1990), 'Modes of Civil Society', *Public Culture*, vol. 3, no. 1: 95-118.

Therborn, G. (2000), 'Globalization: Dimensions, Historical Waves, Regional Effects, Normative Governance', *International Sociology*, 15(2); 151-79.

Toffler, Alvin (1970), *Future Shock*, London: The Bodley Head.

——— (1980), *The Third Wave*, London: Collins.

Tonnies, F. (1957), *Community and Society*, East Lansing: Michigan State University Press.

UN (1948), *Universal Declaration of Human Rights*, Washington, United Nations.

——— (1966), *International Covenant on Economic, Social and Cultural Rights*, United Nations, Washington.

——— (1980), Rights to Development (Resolution 41/128), United Nation, Washington.

——— (1995), *Declaration of the Social Development Summit, Copenhagen*, New York: UN.

——— (2008), Missing Girl Child in India, Department of Economic and Social Affairs, http:esaconf.un.org/wb/default/

UNDP (1990), (1991), (1992), (1993), (1994), (1995), (1996), (1997), (1998), (1999), (2000), (2001), (2002), (2003), (2004), (2005),

(2006), (2007), (2008), *Human Development Report*, New Delhi: Oxford University Press.

UNDP (1993), *UNDP and Civil Society*, New York: UNDP.

UNESCO (2001), *Monitoring Report on Education for All*, Paris, UNESCO.

——— (1998), World Conference on Higher Education in 21st Century, Paris, 5-9 October.

UNICEF (2008), India: The big Picture www.unicef.org/infobycountry/india_background.html

——— (2009), *The State of the World's Children-2009*, UNICEF.

Urry, John (2000), 'Mobile Sociology', *British Journal Sociloyg*, vol. 51, no. 1: 185-203.

Webster, F. (1995), *Theories of Information Society*, London: Routledge.

White, L.A. (1949), *The Science of Culture*, New York: Farrar, Strans and Cudahy.

World Bank (1997), (1998), (1999), (2000), (2001), (2003), (2005), (2008), *World Development Report*, New Delhi: Oxford University Press.

WTO (2001), *The Fourth WTO Ministerial Conference* held in Doha, Qatar, from 9 to 14 November, www.wto.org

CHAPTER 4

Defining Civil Society: Issues and Challenges in the Context of Globalization

ALKA DHAMEJA

INTRODUCTION

The concept of civil society is not new. It has only resurfaced after lying dormant for more than a century. The term civil society enjoyed high popularity in the eighteenth and nineteenth centuries in the Scottish, French and German writings before falling into disuse. The concept of civil society remained inactive till the 1960s, as the focus on state-centric approach dominated Liberal and Marxist writings. It was restored when scholars turned their attention to the self-organization potential of the community, and the limitations of state-based theories. A serious revival was witnessed with the resuscitation of Antonio Gramsci's work in the 1960s. The period after that also saw the emergence of Pluralist, Communitarian and Post-Modern writings that focused on the bargaining potential and pertinence of interest associations, pressure groups, grassroots activity and local narratives.

The reasons for invocation of civil society have varied from region to region and shaped its present contours. In western Europe, civil society has been heralded as a custodian concept in the backdrop of retreat of the state and advance of the market. It has also come to be seen as a panacea for the ills of market in this part of the globe. In the East, the rise of civil society is attributed to the fall of east

*Sincere acknowledgements are due to Saugato Sen, Faculty of Economics, School of Social Sciences, IGNOU for his invaluable comments and suggestions. Any errors and omissions are however completely and solely mine.

European states. The collapse of erstwhile socialist societies in eastern Europe has been projected as a victory of civil society against the excesses of the state. The velvet revolutions of the 1980s in these countries have paved the way for civil society, which did not have a place in the Stalinist states. In the southern part of the world, especially in the Third World countries, civil society has come to be seen as a solution to the skirmishes ensuing from the transition from the state- to market-driven economies. A fundamental change in the state's commitment to welfare and social security is visible. There is a general disenchantment of people with governmental policies and the notion of participation, and we find a surge in the NGOs, social movements, global civil society organizations (GCSOs), as well as private and corporate initiatives. Moreover, international agencies including the World Bank have initiated the adoption of civil society as a 'saviour' concept by funding the myriad NGOs working in the developing countries.

In the present liberalization and globalization context, civil society has come to be regarded as an autonomous, integrated, uncoerced, just and righteous space or sphere between the state and market. This space, as per the present definition is essentially non-state and non-market. It comprises intermediary citizen institutions which are independent of the state and market control, but at the same time constructively mediate between them through collective behaviour. The present-day meaning of civil society draws deeply from the classical literature on the subject, but at the same time, also differs significantly from it. The classical thinkers used the term civil society very differently from how it is viewed in the modern-day context. A peep into the evolution of civil society shows how it was examined in relation to the natural society, commercial society, political society and community in general. The present trifurcation of state-civil society-market has superseded the Hegelian trifurcation of family-civil society-state. This three-folding considers civil society as the distinct third realm of society. Contemporary scholars have somehow begun to treat the state as political domain, the market as economic domain and civil society as social and cultural domain.

As a third sphere, the civil society is supposed to consist of NGOs, non-market associations, voluntary association, community-based organizations, self-helf groups, grassroots support organizations, social movements and other non-state and non-commercial endeavours. The perspectives on the nature of civil society today are quite diverse and debatable in the absence of a consensus on its meaning and nature. Civil society has become a wide and encircling concept, examined differently by what have been described as the 'various philosophical vantage viewpoints'. We are trying to look at civil society beyond its present definition of non-state and non-market sphere or a mediating sphere between the state and market. Wikipedia describes civil society as a society composed of voluntary civic and social organizations and institutions, which form the basis of a functioning society, as opposed to the force-backed structures of the state and commercial institutions. So what is a civil society? Why is civil society the new buzzword? Is it a solution to the ills of the state and market? Is our understanding of civil society merely limited to NGOs and social movements? This chapter aims to address these critical questions to establish the viability of positioning civil society as a distinct third sphere. The object is to look at the relationship of civil society with the state and market, and analyse its objectives to ascertain whether it can be regarded as an all-virtue separate sphere, to the extent that it could check the excesses of the state and market. The society-state-market association is age-old. The three sectors have functioned more or less separate step with each other. So, why should civil society be treated as a third sphere in the present context? Can we actually do so? What is then our definition of civil society? In order to find answers to these questions, we will examine the relationship between the civil society state and market; and also identify certain goals and objectives of civil society to determine its interactions wtih other spheres.

CIVIL SOCIETY AND THE STATE

Civil society is generally considered to be autonomous of the state realm. The first query that needs to be addressed is: Can civil society lie completely outside the state? If the answer is in the affirmative, then anything and everything that is not the state or opposed to the state would come under the domain of civil society. Khilnani (2006) has observed that if civil society is defined in opposition to the state, then it is difficult to provide a positive definition of civil society because it is a question of listing everything that has been left over, after limiting the sphere of the state. For classical scholars, the state and civil society were never completely separate entities. The imprecision in the relationship between the state and civil society, in fact, has emanated from civil society-state interaction, propagated by them. Thomas Hobbes, John Locke and Jean Jacques Rousseau used political society and state coterminously. For Locke, civil society was a civilized form of political order. Georg Hegel developed the notion of civil society as a domain separate, but parallel to the state. His civil society was a moment between the family and state, where family was a natural unit, and civil society a sphere of bifurcation comprising the pursuit of particularistic individual interests as well as universal collective interests. State, in his view, was the higher institutional order and ultimate arbiter of morality, which gave civil society its necessary moral direction.

Karl Marx felt that Hegel's elevation of the state to a moral pedestal for ensuring the common good among competing interests was idealistic. In his view it was not possible under capitalism, as true civil society could only flourish in a classless society. Gramsci felt that civil society fulfilled a political function and political could not be confined to the state alone. His civil society was an arena for political struggle and transformative politics (Mackenzie, 2005). For Gramsci, both the state and civil society were a part of the superstructure. He believed that civil society existed as a kind of intermediary linked both with the economic structure as well as the state. Baron de Montesquieu talked of civil society being involved in educating citizens, facilitating communication and making government more effective. From the Montesquieu tradition, we have got the conception of civil society which has a life outside the political structure, but at the same time, is also engaged, with politics (see Elliot, 2003). Alexis de Tocquieville also viewed civil society as a sphere of autonomously created associations as well as intermediate institutions in which civic interests were formed and self-government was learned and exercised (Goodin and Pettit, 2007).

Modern-day scholars, however, believe in a pointed separation between the civil society and state. In a bid to do so, they tend to disregard the role of the 'political' in civil society. It is felt that the state stifles all civil society protests in the name of political unity, since its real agenda is homogenization (see Gupta, 1999). Scholars like Robert Putnam, Jurgen Habermas and Andre Beteille have kept the state distinct from civil society in their writings. Beteille (2002, 2003) has argued that the well-being of modern institutions can be guaranteed only if civil society is understood as comprising truly autonomous bodies. In his view, village councils with women and Dalits at the centre is an indigenous institutional innovation. Putnam

(*Bowling Alone*, 2000) has projected the state and society as pitted against each other in opposition. He has talked of the state as a passive agency, which is acted upon by civil society.

In the present scenario, we find that many autonomous civil society organization vie for a political space in the state realm. Thus, the separation is not so pointed in practice. There are many organizations that look for a space in the political domain. The Jharkhand movement and Dravida Kazhagam movement have been very much a part of the political field. The new movements with their formal or quasi-formal structures, do at times aim to transform governmental policy agendas. Then there are trade unions which are aligned to political parties. Do we exclude these organizations from civil society? Chandhoke (1995) observes that a sharp separation of civil society from the state does not make for an easy relationship, as it may overlook the state's agenda for civil society. The sphere of civil society can be colonized by the legitimizing strategies of the state. Criticizing Liberal and Marxist oversight on the issue, she observes that just as the attention paid to the state has failed to account for civil society, the focus on civil society could fail to comprehend its complex relationship with the state.

The relationship between the state and civil society is thus of coexistence rather than one of straight opposition in the sense of one homogeneous entity confronting another. If is felt that if civil society is where the rights of individuals receive primacy over all else, then it cannot be external to the state, standing against it or trying to curtail its powers (see Mahajan, 2003). We may find it necessary to keep civil society institutions autonomous and independent of the state control, but this autonomy has to be matched with equivalent responsibility. It is this interdependence between the state and civil society that needs to be kept in view. In developing nations like India, civil society cannot function in a vacuum. The heterogeneity of the country sometimes makes if necessary for the state to intervene wherever the civil society oversteps its mandate or wherever the state needs to take forward its mandate. The dichotomous nature of functioning between the civil society and state is thus difficult to maintain. In east Europe, as Walzer (2003) points out, the civil society project can only be described in terms of all the other projects. There is a need to decentralize the state, so that citizens could be given more opportunities to take up responsibility; and to socialize the economy so as to promote its diversity.

So, where does this debate lead us? In India, post-Independence planning efforts have tilted more towards devolution and decentralization. Various grassroots organizations and local self-help groups have proliferated the rural areas. Panchayati Raj's institutional set-up across the country is a formidable example of the state's proximity to civil society. It is at the local level that the state must function in close association with the grassroots groups, village associations and village level workers. The Bhagidari programme of the Delhi government is another example of the state working in close partnership with the Resident Welfare Associations in the urban milieu. Many more civil society organizations (CSO) can be seen working along with the governmental agencies in the areas that were hitherto strictly in the state domain. There is thus a need to move beyond the state *versus* society dualism to grasp their intertwined dynamic processes. The developments in the areas of state-society synergy, embeddedness of the state, and interaction between citizens and public officials are quite apparent. Joel Migdal (2001) observes that in order to avoid conflicts, social organizations must coexist with the state in a symbiotic manner. The state is hemmed in and even transformed by internal social forces, just as the society is transformed by the state. Neither states nor societies are fixed entities; they both structure goals, constituencies, rules and social control in their process of interaction.

CIVIL SOCIETY AND MARKET

Another point to ponder over is the association between civil society and market. We have to see whether market mechanisms are a part of civil society. Can civil society function as a sphere that is separate from the market? Classic Liberals have regarded markets as crucial institutions of the civil society and neo-liberals too tend to see productive and commercial associations as part of civil society. It was Adam Smith who first articulated the classical bourgeois understanding of civil society as a market-organized sphere of necessity, driven by the self-interested motion of individual proprietors. Smith insisted that economic realm also produced a realm of human interaction, which was not governed by need. Smith's *Wealth of Nations* speaks of commercial society as a social, economic and moral order, all at the same time (see Khilnani, op. cit.). For Hegel and Marx too, civil society was driven by private economic interests. Marx felt that the private dimension of civil society had a tendency to overpower the public aspect.

This very vision of the market has somehow been kept out of the folds of civil society in the current definition of the term. Cohen and Arato (1994), observe that in today's context, the ethos of the market does not constitute civil society. Underlining the dangers of markets, they separate them from the civil society and state, and call civil society the third realm. Scholte (2000) also calls the civil society a non-commercial realm. In his view too, the market is out of the boundary of civil society. The pertinent questions in this regard are: Can all non-commercial activities be kept outside the civil society? and what exactly then is the market?

A market is the sphere where individuals, firms and institutions do commerce, i.e. exchange goods and services for profit. But does this exchange take place outside the civil society? Citizens are the stakeholders in market, as they invest in its firms. Besides, they are the consumers who actively participate in the market process. Some of them are a part of the supply side of the market in their capacity of manufacturers and distributors. Then there are market-based professional and trade associations that facilitate the structures and processes of commerce. So do we exclude these associations from civil society?

We cannot overlook the fact that the legal and political framework for functioning of civil society is determined by the state as well as the market at times. There are organizations such as Federation of Indian Chambers of Commerce and Industry (FICCI) that promote the cause of market by ensuring that the market institutions adhere to the laws of the state. They are part of civil society even as they encourage market-friendly environment and initiatives. Similarly, market-state endeavours have overwhelmed the economy in the recent past with many public sector enterprises divesting and opening up to private entrepreneurs. The civil society-market ventures and hybrid organizations too cannot be completely ruled out; a trend in this direction is visible in many Latin American countries in the form of Public-Private-People Partnerships within the good governance framework, which talks of synergy among all actors in society. In countries like Italy, Sweden and Holland, as Taylor (2003) points out, many trade unions and employers' associations are being integrated into state or governmental planning.

The role of media, which falls under the realm of civil society, could also be a point of discussion on market-society interface. Majority of the media in India is in the private sector, yet their role in building opinions on relevant issues in civil society, as we will examine later in this chapter, cannot be underplayed. It has to be seen how the market beneficially associates with the state as well as the civil society in the near future. Civil society certainly has a crucial role in making market socially responsible. It needs to be kept in view that the state and market associations draw on and are responsive to the same citizens. Civil society draws strength from the legal framework provided by the state, and collaborates with the market to empower itself. The state and market, on the other hand, need the civil society for infrastructure support. Markets also need the state for ensuring stable conditions for their operation. They need contracts that are enforceable through an effective administrative and judicial mechanism. The convergence between NGOs and informal profit-oriented enterprises, as Fisher (1998) observes, offers some promise for building a different model of society, since profits generated within this new non-profit-for profit nexus are invested in public as well as private goods and services.

Civil society thus has a tough task keeping itself distant yet associated with the state and market. The civil society should be strong enough to counterbalance the state and should also be able to ensure that the state fulfils its role of a keeper of peace and arbitrator of conflicts. In the same way, the civil society has to facilitate the market process and make sure that it takes the principles of fairness and justice into purview. The domain of civil society is determined by the processes of the state and market, and in turn, it has the potential to influence these processes constructively. Civil society cannot therefore be treated as merely a third sphere that comprises all non-state and non-market activities. We would not like to call it only a mediating sphere or space between the state and market either, as the state and market too are mediating spheres. The state mediates between the civil society and market, and the market between the civil society and state. Thus, the state, civil society and market, distinct spheres in themselves, have various intersections of economic, political, social and cultural consequence. They are autonomous but not isolated or insulated spheres. They need each other for their sustenance even though it is difficult to determine the boundaries of interaction between these spheres. The contemporary third space connotation takes this very essence away from the civil society. It makes it a vacuous space that includes all that is non-state and non-market. This, in fact, limits the domain of civil society, as very few activities could then ideally fall under it.

It is interesting to note that the classical thinkers also talked of three realms, but these existed within the civil society and not outside it. These realms are visible in the writings of Adam Ferguson who talked of civil society as an ethical and cultural realm. With Smith and Hegel, civil society was a realm of competing material or commercial interests, while Tocquieville regarded civil society as a realm of communal self-organization and public debate. Encompassing the cultural, material and social dimensions, the civil society for these thinkers was a complementary sphere to the state and political society. The present-day description somehow fails to comprehend the pertinence of these three dimensions within the very fold of civil society.

CIVIL SOCIETY: GOALS AND OBJECTIVES

Another ponderable over here could be, can the civil society be treated as an all-virtue sphere, for it to perform its arrogated guardian role against the excesses of the state and market?

To address the query, let us delineate the major identifiable objectives of civil society. These could be:

1. Empowering the disadvantaged, by eliminating social, caste and religious inequalities
2. Checking atrocities and violations of human rights
3. Creating bonding, networks and collective consciousness
4. Demanding accountability and transparency from the state and market; and
5. Providing a viable forum for the exchange of ideas and information amongst its organizations.

As far as the *first* objective of empowering the disadvantaged is concerned, the state too aims to do just that. The corporate social responsibility of the market sector is also in line with this objective. The functions of the state in terms of its social legislation, anti-poverty programmes, reservation of seats for the disadvantaged, and invocations of relevant constitutional provisions are pursued to meet this aim. Again, just as the state and market, civil society too seems to vacillate at times on this count. There are many CSOs that are not even accessible to all castes and sections to be able to fulfil this objective, especially the ones which are based on single-caste or religion like Catholic Mahajana Sabha, Kannada Chaluviligar, and Lachchit Sena. The Amarnath Yatra Sangharsh Samiti and the Hindu Jan Jagaran Manch may think of themselves as CSOs, but their fundamentalist position and *modus operandi* may refrain us from doing so.

With respect to the *second* objective of checking atrocities and violation of human rights, the track record of civil society is as controversial as the state's. The notion 'civil' excludes those that act primarily outside the law. Violent protests, vandalism, hooliganism practised by associational groups cannot be considered as acts of a civil society. Thus, if religious and caste-based organizations indulge in activities that transgress this notion of 'civil', they need to be banished from the purview of civil society. Kandhamal in Orrisa has seen a spate of violence being inflicted on Christians by the Bajrang Dal and Vishwa Hindu Parishad activists. Mumbai in Maharashtra has been a witness to persistent attacks on migrants from different states, having or seeking jobs in the city, by the Maharashtra Navnirman Sena. These are instances of violence generated by some sections of the civil society itself. These cases need to be analysed to arrest the excessive eulogizing of civil society as a saviour concept.

Civil society movements that emerge in reaction to oppressions of the state, it is felt, may themselves be oppressive in nature. In India, the turmoil in Kashmir and north-east is regarded as a reaction to the state's repressive policies. The anti-state movements in these areas have assumed separatist tendencies. The counteracting steps taken by the state have also led to problematic situations. Salwa Judum, or peace mission, for instance, was initiated in 2005 by the Chhattisgarh government in India as an anti-Naxalite vigilante group. Even though it has been projected as frontline of defence against Naxalites, gross violations of human rights, lack of accountability, excessive corruption, forcible induction of tribals and displacement of people are the charges levelled against it. Civil society cannot check the violation of rights if it is not itself able to uphold the principles of equality and justice. When we examine civil society as a diverse and isolated category from the state and market, we tend to disregard the tensions that may exist within its actors like the voluntary groups, and protest movements.

The *third* objective of creating bonding and networks is also debatable. Putnam's views on the social capital concept show how dense networks in civil society can produce a sense of self, solidarity, public spirit, collective consciousness, trust, democratic ambience, and cooperation. Putnam has used the social capital model to depict different levels of economic performance in northern and southern parts of Italy. He has shown that the regions of Italy which have both flourished economically and suffered less corruption are those that have fostered social capital formation.

James Samuel Coleman (*Equality of Educational Opportunity*, 1966 and *Individual Interests and Collective Action*, 1986) is one of the earliest users of the term social capital. His views have, however, differed from Putnam's. Coleman's concept of social capital, as observed by some scholars, has suggested that it is a property, not of individuals but of social relations and contexts. Coleman's civil society is a fragmented, divided and hierarchically structured realm. He has pointed out that outside a specific context, norms and values may or may not translate themselves into social capital. This is in contrast to Putnam's views on social capital as being historically inherited. Putnam has not considered the role of the state and relationships of power in his deployment of the concept of social capital (see Elliot, op. cit.; Sobhan, 1998, and Chandhoke, 2004). It means that all associations and movements, based on thick bonds and trust, need not always produce social capital in a society. Sudha Pai and Neerja Jayal raise certain points that could be considered here: Is sociability a basic requirement of the civil society? Can social capital be constructed? Do mere thick unbreakable bonds between members of associations make for civil society? Or how do people build trust and reciprocity in associational life, or when do the arenas of collective life exhibit mistrust? If one goes by the general definition of social capital, the civil society, which values equality, justice and fairness, should gradually lead to the creation of social capital, but it is not always so in reality. The use of social capital as synonymous with civic networks by Putnam, it is felt, is problematic, because communal organizations based on a single religious group can also be seen to foster strong trust among their members (see Chandhoke, 2004). However, such organizations are frequently associated with the occurrence of communal violence.

The World Bank also views social capital as an acontextual and ahistorical realm (Bhattacharya et al., 2004). If social capital gives legitimacy and entry to organizations in the civil society, then the Shiv Sena and Rashtriya Swayamsevak Sangh also contribute towards the formation of social capital in disaster situations. The fluidity of associations gives considerable scope for political manoeuvring that could reshape the boundaries and concerns of the community identity. The problem with this kind of formulation, observes Chandhoke, is that it fails to distinguish civil society from counter-civil society movements such as religious fundamentalism. Society, in this perspective, is collapsed into civil society. In the absence of a tight conceptualization, she feels, civil society has become a residual category (see Chandhoke, 1995 and 2004, op. cit.).

In India, as (Mahajan, op. cit.) points out, where the task of ensuring inter-group and intra-group equality still remains unfulfilled, empowering all types of social and religious institutions tends to hinder the realization of equality, and the groups and institutions that do not operate on the principle of equality get indirectly legitimized. In the words of Andre Beteille (op. cit.), the modern institutions should be open to all citizens and not controlled by religious authorities. He thinks mediating institutions, which include schools, universities, and professional bodies, have to be different from those based on kinship, caste and religion. However, can we then presume that all single religion or caste organizations will be inegalitarian, intolerant and unjust? Many Church-based organizations, Gurdwara committees, Buddhist trusts, Krishna Samitis, Dalit Sammelans and Jain Muths, are doing a lot of humanitarian work. Many a time, funding for crisis situations also comes from these types of associations. It is thus difficult to infer that these could be kept out of purview of civil society

The *fourth* objective of demanding accountability and transparency from the state and market is what the civil society appears to be striving for. However, foreign funding of some of the organizations, mainly NGOs, and also the cooption of CSOs and social movements by the state could be regarded as bottlenecks in the realization of this goal. Many allege that the NGOs serve the interests of their fund donors rather than the citizenry of their respective countries. The Narmada Bachaao Andolan has been labelled by the critics as a movement which is funded and supported by the big foreign NGOs, and therefore working in their interest. This type of criticism has been levelled against many NGOs and movements by those who regard environmentalists to be anti-development. It is actually the way a social movement is perceived by the state that determines its nature and complexion. It is not necessary, as many scholars believe, that a social movement would oppose unresponsive governments or even automatically lead to social change.

Thus, both the CSOs and social movements, though functionally autonomous from the state, can somehow survive only within the framework provided by the state. The organizations and movements that maintain a distance from their own states are many a time the ones that are funded by foreign states. Another viewpoint is that the support of bilateral and multilateral aid agencies to civil society, through the NGO network, is nothing short of double standards. For instance, Jenkins (2006) feels that the World Bank's support to indigenous African political tradition is a kind of backdoor attempt to transform African societies. The blueprint from which aid agencies like the United States Aid Programme (USAID) use the term governance, as a euphemism for politics, underplays the contingencies which influence the formation of opposition movements and exercise of the state power.

Chandhoke (2004, op. cit.) observes that if the state must roll back from social and market sectors in the name of furthering democracy, something has to take its place. This something, she says, is conceptualized by donor agencies as civil society, which they fill up with NGOs or the voluntary sector. We thus need to seriously address the increasing labelling of the civil society as NGOs and vice versa. Whaites (2002) points out that the combination of donor, NGO and UN interest provides the background to what has been described as the 'civil society grab'. The query that assumes significance over here is: Do NGOs that sub-contract for the state and the foreign agencies make for civil society? As Eade (2002) suggests, it has to be seen as to how the NGOs separate beneficial from non-beneficial civil society, how do they maintain autonomy and accountability, and what type of self-regulation do they follow. There are hardly any research studies that analyse the nature of membership of NGOs. Adequate information is not available on the power relationship, transparency of accounts, openness of activities, participation levels and funding systems of these organizations. Many feel that rural cooperatives and groups can use resources more judiciously. Their participation standards are more democratic and functioning more accountable. But again, not much concrete empirical data is available to authenticate these conjectures. This limits the understanding of a broad process of interaction among different types of CSOs and social movements, and their capacity to ensure state and market accountability.

A few cases in point indicate that even the indigenous NGOs could be manoeuvred in favour of the state agendas. For instance in India, as Baviskar (2005) mentions, the Maharashtra government persuaded social activist Anna Hazare to replicate his Ralegaon Siddhi experiment in all parts of the state by providing him with the necessary infrastructure and financial support. But, since the state government had its own agenda, the experiment encountered problems under the state patronage and was eventually abandoned. However, there is also a positive side to the picture. Many well-meaning organizations and movements have been able to transform the state's policies in citizens' interest. In fact, in India, the proclamation of Emergency in 1975 is considered the threshold period for civil society initiatives. This was the time when state institutions collapsed and could not protect the rights of the citizens. Emergency spurred the civil society, as democracy, citizenship and constitutional protection of fundamental rights became pertinent issues of public debate. (Tandon and Mohanty, 2002). Many instances corroborate this observation. We have seen success stories in movements such as Chipko, Silent Valley and consumer protection, and endeavours like Citizens' Charters, and Self-Employed Women Association (SEWA). The goal of new social movements is a reformed state in which they can play a major role. They also recognize new categories of oppressed, namely, women, dalits, tribals and disabled. These social movements ensure accountability by allowing individuals to air grievances and put forth their concerns that may otherwise go unheeded.

Sometimes, it is seen that NGOs can also generate large-scale awareness and metamorphose into social movements. Tarun Bharat Sangh, an NGO based in Rajasthan, is spearheading a water conservation or *Jal Bhagidari* movement in the country. Mazdoor Kisan Shakti Sangathan (MKSS), through its *jan sunwai* meetings in Rajasthan, has paved the way for the Right to Information (RTI) movement, culminating in the passing of RTI Act in the year 2005. In Andhra Pradesh, Shah and Ambasta (2008) point out, the MKSS is doing substantial work in the social audit area of National Rural Employment Gaurantee Act (NREGA) by filing of applications for NREGA records under the RTI Act. Citizens are becoming aware of their rights and duties. Singur in West Bengal is an example of a political party-led movement against the Special Economic Zones (SEZs). It would be difficult though to call it a people's movement, as its context remains somewhat unclear. Nevertheless, it has been able to provide a voice to the protest of the farmers in the area; a trend now visible in many other parts of the country.

The *fifth* objective pertains to providing a platform to citizens' voices, which is being met through different types of media. It is through the new trends in the media (Web blogs, social network or other internet groups, investigative journalism, citizen journalism, sting operations) that people are realizing their potential role in airing concerns and grievances on critical socio-economic issues. The role of the media in facilitating the deliverance of justice in cases such as Priyadarshini Mattoo, Jessica Lal, Nitish Katara and Sanjeev Nanda, has reposed the trust of the aggrieved in governance processes. The media have opened up a new realm of discourse for civil society that did not exist hitherto. These opportunities could not have been possibly visualized by the classical theorists. However, their writings had substantial analyses on the issues of culture, use of reason, ethics, and universalism for us to arrive at a wider definition of civil society, which these thinkers did not specify as such, but surely implied.

It is thus clear that the functions and objectives of civil society are not clearly distinct from the state and market, and do not lend it an isolated third sphere character. Even the virtues that we anoint civil society with are not always apparent in its actors. In theory, all the three spheres are striving to achieve equality, justice and democracy, but at the implementation level, most often they all falter, including the civil society. The tendency of civil society to degenerate, unless controlled, was recognized by classical theorists. For the State of Nature proponents (Hobbes, Locke and Rousseau), the state was needed to control the savageness of society, protect private property and grant individual freedom. Hegel believed that the state's institutional mediations were essential to ensure ethical freedom. Adam Smith, on the other hand, believed in the propriety of 'censorious gaze'. In his opinion the self-regulating element in the society was enough to tame it. It was, in his opinion possible as market transactions presupposed the existence of disciplined, predictable and socialized behaviour. Thus, unless the 'non-civil' elements, or if may call them pathologies of civil society, are identified and plugged, it is difficult to arrogate the role of a 'rescuer' to civil society that can guard against violations by the state and market. We must, therefore, identify the benchmarks for gauging the virtues of civil society. These could be social justice (equality and fairness), non-violence (tolerance and democratic participation); and rational discourse (debate and dialogue). We do not want to indiscriminately exclude organizations based on class, caste, region or religion from the arena of civil society, as it is not always true that they violate the benchmarks we have identified. Sometimes, even the multi-religious modern institutions could be seen breaching these benchmarks. We need to banish only those organizations and movements that indulge in and propagate injustice, violence and intolerance from the domain of civil society.

TOWARDS A DEFINITION OF CIVIL SOCIETY

The identified benchmarks compel us to look for a definition of civil society that describes it more comprehensively than a mere non-state or non-market realm. We would thus like to call it a realm of discourse. By this definition, we go beyond the two more conspicuous actors of civil society, namely the NGOs and social movements, and analyse civil society as a more encompassing sphere. We describe it as a realm of discourse in order to include in its domain the public opinion that gets created outside the formal structures of organizations and movements. It does not mean that the formal organizations do not produce any realm of discourse or are not based on it. The media also consists of formal organizations, but many components of the media facilitate formation of opinions through unstructured, but rational discourse. Many underprivileged, isolated and victimized voices may find amplification through the media, underlying their significant role in the realm of discourse. NGOs and social movements also engage in negotiation and bargaining on the basis of reasoned discourse. Their object to bring about changes in socio-economic concerns, governmental policy and attitudes emanates from a systematic discourse on why and how the change should take place. We therefore include both formal and non-formal structures in the realm of discourse.

The discourse on issues of social relevance shared by the people on the internet, radio, television, newspapers, conferences, seminars, coffee houses, as well as circulation of information through books, reviews, journals and magazines have become essential to the survival of civil society. These processes and forums become spaces where citizens get information and engage in exchange of ideas. They also build a basis for public spiritedness, effective governance and economic growth. Those registering their views or discourse may or may not be a part of the organizational structure of the different media and other organizations. Street plays by volunteers, awareness and information campaigns, and folklore are also different types of media, and an integral part of the realm of discourse. The 'Teach India' and 'Teach for India' campaigns of the Times of India Group are a manifestation of the realm of discourse. Though initiated by a formal organization, it is creating small pockets of non-structured spaces for imparting knowledge and skills. Putnam has made use of newspapers as effective components in the creation of social capital. Rudolph and Rudolph (2003) demonstrate how Gandhi made an effective use of travelling theatre, oral tales and prayer meetings to communicate with a rural, religious and predominantly illiterate audience during India's freedom struggle.

The realm of discourse dimension of civil society also takes its cue from the writings of Immanuel Kant, Gramsci and Jurgen Habermas. For Kant, the sphere of the 'public' was the sphere of reason, exchange of opinions and free discussion. The greatest contribution of Gramsci has been his belief that a society was not a matter only of legal rights guaranteed by the state or of economic interests driven by the market, but of intellectual and cultural organizations that created non-violent modes of hegemony, and gave citizens the protective shield of associational life. This interpretation of civil society is very significant in the present context, since it arrogates a non-structural dimension to the civil society, as against the strictly institutional or structural one. Beteille (2000) observes that for Gramsci, civil society was a sphere of ideas, beliefs, values, customs and habits that acted on the state and the market and were, in turn, acted upon by them in complex ways at different levels. The state and market contributed something, but not everything towards the cohesion and dynamics of societies.

Habermas has written extensively on the public sphere in his book *Transformation of the Public Sphere* (1962). He has outlined the emergence of a new sphere between private life and public authority during the eighteenth century. For him, the society can be seen in terms of 'life world' and 'system', and 'public' and 'private' are both a part of life world and system. His public sphere is a site where the dialectic between public and private is negotiated through discourse based on reasoned arguments, a theatre where public goals are debated and deliberated to reach a common understanding. It is also a place where scrutiny over the state is exercised by private individuals (see: Goodin and Pettit op.cit. and Fraser, op. cit.). Neera Chandhoke

(1995, op. cit.) also uses civil society and public sphere interchangeably. For her, civil society is the public sphere that is accessible to all and liberates the individuals from entrenched social hierarchies.

Fraser (op. cit.) feels that there is a need for 'subaltern counter-publics', a conglomeration of many discursive arenas, where members of subordinate groups invent and circulate 'counterdiscourses'. This is important, he thinks, to expand the discursive space, even if these groups exhibit anti-democratic and anti-egalitarian tendencies.Thus, we may not overplay the virtousity of civil society even when we define it as a realm of discourse. The informative and analytical role of the media as a pertinent component of the realm of discourse needs to be examined carefully. The gluttony of the media to increase its viewership and stakeholders at all costs, and its tendency towards sensationalism and trivialization needs to be kept in control. The 'reality' shows on television have come in for a lot of flak. Even while the television soaps, project social and economic realities, they do tend to reinforce certain stereotypes that need to be abandoned. The mediascape, for instance in India, does seem to give its subscribers a sense of collective identity and participation in public affairs. Nevertheless, at the same time, it reduces the discussion of vital issues to simple caricature, leaving people in the community interconnected, but dangerously uninformed (see *The Hindu*, 23 March 2003). It is also felt that cyber-savvy global activists have become a substitute for people's participation and empowerment as civil society is being created through the social networking sites on the internet. Bruhns and Gosenwinkel (2005) comment that the word community no longer implies a mere geographical construct, but it is a virtual space of shared and moral affinities that express the ethics of self-governance. Civil Society Network (CiSo Net) in Europe is a manifestation of this process.

Chandhoke (2003, op. cit.) observes that it needs to be kept in mind that civil society is not an institution; it is rather a process whereby inhabitants of civil society constantly monitor both the state and the monopoly of power within the civil society. Civil society does not automatically lead to democratic participation. It merely provides the sphere, institutions, and modes for political reflections and positions, to engage with each other. The contemporary invocation of civil society, she feels, needs to be mulled over, as it perfectly fits into a minimalist version of democracy.

The meaning and composition of civil society, therefore, needs to be critically reviewed. An alternative paradigm or model, which looks into the synergies arising out of the emerging relations between the state, private sector, and civil society must thus be put to practical use (see Rahman, 2000). David Easton, has observed that the conceptualization of the state might lead to conceptual morass. In the same vein, it is possible that conceptualization of civil society will do just that. Any definition of civil society would have to be adaptable in the view of changing circumstances and perceptions. We would simply like to call civil society a realm of discourse. This realm could be a third realm other than the state and market, but certainly not a non-state and non-market realm or sphere. While operating within a 'checks and balances' framework. It is a sphere which also includes the pockets and spaces of civil society present under the state and market spheres. We thus, define civil society as 'realm of discourse' encompassing several structured and unstructured pockets of dialogue and debate, functionally autonomous from the state and market spheres, but constantly interacting with them in order to pursue their objectives on the bases of justice, non-violence and reasoned discourse.

CONCLUSION

The globalization scenario has opened up new avenues for the growth of civil society. The new developments in the form of World Civil Society Forum, World Social Forum and Asian Social Forum are trying to build the capacity of civil society, expand its involvement, enhance its diversity, and increase its vigilance potential. They are putting forward various issues of concern such as caste, class, gender, liberalization, displacement, war, religious fundamentalism, environment, capacity building and labour, primarily from a people's perspective, which is indeed a healthy sign. Despite the fact that some of these concerns do develop biased or partisan undertones over time, the fact that mobilization of common people is taking place around these issues is a step in the right direction.

In the contemporary context of market dominance and state minimalism, the civil society has assumed many catalytic and facilitative tasks that it needs to achieve along with the state and market. In this chapter, we have defined civil society as the realm of discourse, as we believe that different types of media and their role in expanding the domain of civil society need to be extensively studied. It can help us understand civil society beyond its ascribed meaning of social organizations and movements or an insulated third sphere.

We also feel that it is not appropriate to adopt civil society as a panacea or a saviour concept. By this, we presume the other two spheres to be the perpetrators of rights and justice. The social science literature is replete with what we may call 'taming of the shrew' instances. States have been eulogized and then termed monstrous by scholars and researchers. Markets have had their share of adulation and then pushed aside by chants of 'bringing the state back in'. Now civil society is being projected as a tamer of both the state and market. We have to be very sceptical of such revivals. The reinforcement of civil society has to be taken with a pinch of caution. It has to be accompanied by its systematic resurrection, which is based on intellectual introspection and empirical evidence. Theory determines practice; in turn practice too should ideally translate into modified theory. We have to thus be very clear about the meaning and domain of civil society as they underline its major constraints as well as its basic evaluative benchmarks.

REFERENCES

Baker, Gideon (2002), *Civil Society and Democratic Theory: Alternative Voices*, London: Routledge.

Baogang, He (2002), 'Civil Society and Democracy' in April Carter and Geoffrey Stokes (eds.), *Democratic Theory Today*, Cambridge: Polity.

Barber, R. (1996), 'Three Challenges to Reinventing Democracy' in Paul Hirst and Sunil Khilnani (eds.), *Reinventing Democracy*, Oxford: Blackwell.

Bardhan, Pranab (1999), 'The State against Society: The Great Divide in Indian Social Science Discourse' in Sugata Bose and Ayesha Jalal (eds.), *Nationalism, Democracy and Development: State and Politics in India*, New Delhi: Oxford University Press.

Baviskar, B.S. (2005), 'Non-governmental Organizations and Civil Society in India' in N. Jayaram (ed.), *On Civil Society: Issues and Perspectives*, New Delhi: Sage.

Beteille, Andre (2000), *Antinomies of Society: Essays on Ideologies and Institutions*, New Delhi: Oxford University Press.

——— (2002), 'Village Republics', *The Hindu*, 3 September.

——— (2003), 'Civil Society and its Institutions' in Carolyn M. Elliot (ed.), *Civil Society and Democracy: A Reader*, New Delhi: Oxford University Press.

Bhattacharya, Dwaipayan, Neerja Gopal Jayal, Bishnu N. Mahapatra and

Sudha Pai (eds.) (2004), *Interrogating Social Capital: The Indian Experience*, New Delhi: Sage.

Bottomore, Tom and Patrick Goode (eds.) (1983), *Readings in Marxist Sociology*, London: Oxford.

Box, Richard C. (2005), *Critical Social Theory in Public Administration*, New Delhi: Prentice Hall of India.

Brathwaite, John and Heather Strang (2001), 'Introduction: Restorative Justice and Civil Society' in Heather Strang and John Brathwaite (eds.), *Restorative Justice and Civil Society*, Cambridge: Cambridge University Press.

Bruhns, Hinnerk and Dieter Gosewinkel (eds.) (2005), *Europe and the Other Non-European Concepts of Civil Society*, CiSo Net Perspectives: WZB, Berlin.

Callahan, David (1998), 'What is Global Civil Society', *Features*, vol. 3, no. 1 (January-February), www.uia.be/node/135

Callahan, James J. (2002), *Article and Web Alert*, New Delhi: The American Centre.

Chandhoke, Neera (1995), *State and Civil Society: Explorations in Political Theory*, New Delhi: Sage.

——— (2002), 'Civil Society Hijacked' in *The Hindu*, 16 January.

——— (2003), 'The "Civil" and the "Political" in Civil Society', in Carolyn M. Elliot.

——— (2004), *The Conceits of Civil Society,* New Delhi: Oxford University Press.

Chatterjee, Partha (2003), 'Beyond the Nation? Or Within?' in Carolyn M. Elliot.

Cohen, Jean L. and Andrew Arato (1994), *Civil Society and Political Theory,* London: MIT Press.

Eade, Deborah (2000), 'The Discourse of Civil Society' in Deborah Eade (Series Editor), *Development, NGOs and Civil Society*, London: Oxfam.

Elliot, Carolyn M. (2003), 'Civil Society and Democracy' in Carolyn M. Elliot.

Fisher, Julie (1998), *Non-Governments: NGOs and Political Development of the Third World*, West Harford, U.S.: Kumarian.

Fraser, Nancy (2003), 'Rethinking of the Public Sphere' in Carolyn M. Elliot.

Gellner, Ernest (1994), *Conditions of Liberty: Civil Society and its Rivals*, London: Hamilton.

Goodin, Robert E., Philip Pettit and Thomas Pogge (eds.) (2007), *A Companion to Contemporary Political Philosophy*, England: Blackwell.

Gupta, Dipankar (1999), 'Civil Society or the State: What Happened to Citizenship' in Ramachandra Guha and Jonathan Parry (eds.), *Institutions and Inequalities: Essays in Honour of Andre Beteille*, New Delhi: Oxford University Press.

Hindess, Barry, Nikolas Rose and Claus Offe (2000), 'Modern Regimes of Governance' in Richard V. Ericson and Nico Stehr (eds.), *Governing Modern Societies*, Toronto: University of Toronto Press.

Hoffman, Stefan-Ludwig (2005), 'Civil Society and Democracy in Nineteenth Century Europe; Entanglements, Variations, Conflicts', Discussion Paper: WZB, Berlin.

Hirst, Paul (1994), *Associative Democracy: New Forms of Economic and Social Governance*, Cambridge: Polity Press.

Human Development in South Asia (1999), *The Crisis of Governance*, New Delhi: Oxford University Press.

Jenkins, J. Craig (2005), 'Introduction' in Thomas Janoski et. al (eds.) *Handbook of Political Sociology: States, Civil Societies and Globalization,* Cambridge: Cambridge University Press.

Jenkins, J. Craig and William Form (2005), 'Social Movements and Social Change' in Thomas Janoski et al. (eds.), *Handbook of Political Sociology: States, Civil Societies and Globalization.*

Jayaram, N. (ed.) (2005), *On Civil Society: Issues and Perspectives*, New Delhi: Sage.

Karlson, Nils (2002), *The State of State: Invisible Hands in Politics and Civil Society*, New Jersey: Transaction.

Kaviraj, Sudipta (2006), 'In Search of Civil Society' in Sudipta Kaviraj and Sunil Khilnani (eds.), *Civil Society: History and Possibilities*, New Delhi: Cambridge University Press.

Khilnani, Sunil (2001), 'The Development of Civil Society' in Sudipta Kaviraj and Sunil Khilnani (eds.).

Mackenzie, Lane (ed.) (2005), *Political Concepts: A Reader and Guide*, Edinburgh: Edinburgh University Press.

Mahajan, Gurpreet (2003), 'Civil Society and its Avtars' in Carolyn M. Elliot, op. cit.

Migdal, Joel S. (2001), *State in Society: Studying How States and Societies Transform and Constitute One Another*, Cambridge: Cambridge University Press.

Pearce, Jenny (2000), 'Introduction' in Deborah Eade.

Putnam, Robert (2000), *Bowling Alone,* New York: Simon and Schuster.

Rahman, Atiur, Sayed Naimul Wadood and Mohammed Abu Eusuf (2000), 'Civil Society and Governance' in Hasnat Abdul Hye (ed.), *Governance: South Asian Perspectives*, New Delhi: Manohar.

Robinson, Mark (2003), 'Civil Society and Ideological Contestation in India' in Carolyn M. Elliot.

Rudolph, Susanne and Lloyd L. Rudolph (2003), 'The Coffee House and the Ashram: Gandhi, Civil Society and Public Spheres' in Carolyn M. Elliot.

Schechter, Michael G. (1999), 'Globalization and Civil Society' in Michael G. Schechter (ed.), *The Revival of Civil Society: Global and Comparative*

Perspective (International Political Economy Series), London: Macmillan.

Scholte, Jan Aart (2000), 'Global Civil Society' in Ngaire Woods (ed.), *The Political Economy of Globalization*, New York: Palgrave.

Self, Peter (1985), *Political Theories of Modern Government: Its Role and Reform*, London: George Allen and Unwin.

Shah, Mihir and Pramathesh Ambasta (2008), 'NREGA: Andhra Pradesh Shows the Way' in *The Hindu*, 8 September.

Sobhan, Rehman (1998), 'State, Society and Economic Performance' in Rehman Sobhan (ed.), *Towards a Theory of Governance and Development: Learning from East Asia*, Dhaka: University Press.

Subramanian, A.K. Venkat, (2001), 'Towards People's Politics' in *The Hindu*, 8 May.

Tandon, Rajesh and Ranjita Mohanty (2002), *Civil Society and Governance*, New Delhi: Society for Participatory Research in Asia, Samskriti, New Delhi.

Taylor, Charles (2003), 'Conceptualizing Civil Society' in Carolyn M. Elliot (ed.).

The Hindu, 6 August 2002; 14 December 2002; 9 January 2003; 3 April 2005.

Urry, John (1981), *The Anatomy of Capitalist Societies: The Economy, Civil Society and the State*, London: Macmillan.

Varshney, Ashutosh (2003), 'Ethnic Conflict and Civil Society' in Carolyn M. Elliot.

Viswanath, Kalpana (2003), 'Despair and Hope' in *The Hindu*, 9 March.

Walzer, Michael (2003), 'The Idea of Civil Society: A Path to Social Reconstruction' in Carolyn M. Elliot.

Whaites, Alan (2000), 'Lets Get Civil Society Straight: NGOs, the State and Political Theory' in Deborah Eade.

Whitehead, Laurence (2003), 'Bowling in the Bronx' in Carolyn M. Elliot.

Zoninsein, Jones (1999), 'Global Civil Society and Theories of International Political Economy' in Michael G. Schechter.

WEBSITES

Brien, Rory O. (1999), 'Philosophical History of the Idea of Civil Society', www.web.net/~robrien/papers/civhist.html

Ehrenberg, John (1998), 'Beyond Civil Society', *New Politics*, vol. 6, no. 4 (New Series). www.wpunj.edu/-newpol/issue24/ehrenb24.html

Gellner, Ernest (2005), 'Conditions of Liberty: Civil Society and its Rivals', http: members.tripod.com/gellnerpage/liberty/html

http://www.undp.org.lb/partners/civil.html

CHAPTER 5

Growth and the Holistic Social Development: A Paradox of Civil Society Movement in India

H.A. SHANKARANARAYANA
T.N. SREEDHARA

INTRODUCTION

The drift, in the course of the human civilization, in new millennium is evident in the fact that the neo-liberal development project is appearing to create a situation of 'Man *versus* Nature'. In fact, the UN Agenda 21 in the 1970s, while highlighting the problems of 'Myth of Development', highlighted the significance of development at the local level and the preservation of indigenous cultures and values in promoting sustainable development. To avoid 'The Tragedy of Commons', it is not only imperative that we have to critically evaluate the pros and cons of the mainstream development paradigm but also to find an alternate development paradigm that achieves the Critical Holism.

The paper is an attempt to enquire into the nature of civil society interventions in not only promoting growth but also in furthering the cause of the holistic social development in the Indian context. India, being one of the forerunners of the neo-liberal development project in the world, can be a kaleidoscope of the human civilization as it accounts for 18 per cent of the global population with just fewer than 2.5 per cent of the global resources. As such it provides an ideal canvas to examine efficacy of the contemporary mainstream development project that is growth oriented in all its manifestations and ramifications.

The post-independent civil society movement in India is not a homogenized and monolithic movement. We can broadly discern two main strands. One that is tangent to neo-liberal development project, the other that is critiquing it. If the former strand is used by the state to improve the delivery system of its various welfare programmes, the other strand acts as whistle blower. The paper makes an attempt to make a comparative study the contributions of civil society initiatives belonging to these two strands and underscores the necessity of achieving synergy and convergence between these two strands of civil society initiatives in promoting inclusive, holistic social development.

CIVIL SOCIETY—A CONCEPT

We are witnessing epoch-making changes in the contemporary global society and these changes are being engineered by the new information technology. In fact, the global society is in transition today and it has not only made hitherto believed values, institutions and ideologies irrelevant but has also created a sense of vacuum and uncertainly regarding the future. In the realm of management of global resources the efficacy of the state and the market is being questioned and the rigorous search for an alternative institutional mechanism is on. It is in this backdrop that the 'civil society' as a concept assumes significance. The civil society could be broadly defined as a space between the state and the market covering the wide range of voluntary initiatives. It is a converging sector in the sense that it tries to bring together the objectives and ideals of the diametrically opposite institutions, that is, the state and the market.

As a concept the civil society is polymorphous and hence, elusive and ambiguous. The conceptual elusiveness has provided scope for its varied interpretations in such a way that some even doubt the relevance of searching for a conceptual framework for the third sector. The more amorphous the concept, the more appealing it might become as a concept and consequently more elusive. In this context Neera Chandoke observes that

> We have also witnessed its almost uncritical celebration, so much so that it has become a somewhat consensual concept. And when a variety of dissimilar groups such as international funding agencies, non-governmental organizations and institutions of the state on the one hand and left liberals, trade unions and social movements, on the other, subscribe equally to the validity of the concept, it is time to worry. For if groups who should otherwise be disagreeing on the concept come to agree on it, it means that the concept has been

flattened to such an alarming extent that it has lost its credibility. (Neera Chandhoke, 2003)

In fact, civil society as a concept has multiple dimensions belonging to social, political, religious and cultural realms and in a normative sense signifies an ideal society. So an attempt to search for a conceptual framework of 'civil society' in the Indian context is a challenging task as it encompasses a number of concepts. 'There is conspicuous absence of self-reflectivity in the scenario of third sector in India and an effort to evolve third sector perspective relevant, comprehensive and specific to the Indian context invariably involves a discussion of civil society in India within which a perspective of third sector has to be situated' (T.N. Sreedhara and Rajarama Tolpady, 2003). Therefore, it is a matter of necessity that we have to use the terms 'Civil Society' and 'Third Sector' interchangeably. Since we do not have a systematic and reliable knowledge about this arena even regarding the basic information like their number, size, their domain, source of funding, the legal and institutional framework within which they work, their policy framework, etc., the third sector has remained an unexplored social landscape in India.

INDIAN CIVIL SOCIETY—A PERSPECTIVE

Theorizing civil society in the Indian context, therefore, is a very daunting effort. Here religious, social, cultural, political and economic factors play a vital role in determining the civil society initiatives. In India the religious and cultural factors appear to dominate in this arena. The Indian society is multi-religious and multi-cultural and not a homogeneous entity. Unlike the European experience where Judeo-Christian values dominate, in India we have different religions emphasizing diverse values. In fact, all these values are bound to influence the civil society initiatives in India. For example, Hinduism, which is a dominant religion of India, highlights the role of individualism. It highlights individualism and individual initiative in its stress on personal spiritual devotion as the path toward inner peace and salvation. This is not conducive to institution building. Also, Hinduism as a religion is not a monolithic institutional structure. It is polymorphous giving scope to diverse initiatives in the third sector. Christianity is conducive for institution building. As such we have witnessed many civil society initiatives coming from the Christian missionaries. Islam as a religion is not rigidly modular as most of the other religions are and it highlights the effective integration between politics and religion. Therefore, Islamic civil society initiatives are more coordinated and properly structured. Buddhism and Jainism as religions are also individualistic but have an orientation for building institutions. However, they too have a higher degree of integration with the temporal than the real. India is a land that influences and has been influenced by these religions and in this scenario civil society, as a conceptual framework, should be understood in a convergence spectrum.

The civil society as a concept has also been greatly influenced by the process of colonization in India. The legal framework and the political movements that evolved during the colonial period have had their impact on the development of civil society movements in India. The secular ideals, the ideals of Western liberalism, democracy, human rights and modernism have greatly influenced the civil society movement in India. This is one of the important reasons why India has a highly vibrant and heterogeneous civil society movement.

The emphasis on the role of NGOs by the multilateral funding agencies and international donors also has greatly contributed to the growth of civil society movement in many countries including India. These institutions and organizations, having greater adherence to the principle of governance, are promising better delivery systems than the state. This is encouraging the development of many grassroots organizations. Most of these initiatives are aimed at either supplementing the state or enhancing the efficiency of the state. Therefore, the foundation, evolution and the development of civil society in India could be traced to the native cultural traditions, ethos and the value systems and also to the integrative impact of Indian society with the Western world.

Till the advent of European colonization the civil society initiative in India was largely motivated by the religious ethos and sentiments. Later the 'secularized' third sector initiatives gathered momentum due to the Western influence in India. The initiatives of the Brahmo Samaj, the Arya Samaj and Ramakrishna Mission were essentially secular in nature. Later, during the nationalist movement the Gandhian tradition further strengthened the secular third sector movement in India. This tradition highlighted the concept of voluntary sharing through trusteeship, decentralization of economic power and economy based on need rather than greed.

In the post-independent period it was soon realized that the meaningful development strategy must synergize the state, the market and the voluntary sector in the process of development. Therefore, the importance of voluntary civil society initiatives was highlighted in all the five-year plans. The report of the steering committee on voluntary sector in the Tenth Plan observed:

> Voluntary Organizations play a vital role in the shaping and implementation of participatory democracy. Their credibility lies in the responsible and constructive role they play in society. They have been contributing immensely for quite some time towards various development programmes. They work at grassroots level even in remote areas and, therefore, their reach is much wider. They are closer to ground realities and know the needs of the communities. Their approach with the target group is direct, emphatic and therefore they are able to draw more contextualized plans of action. They also manage to develop intimate contacts with the people and develop confidence among them. (Report of the Steering Committee on Voluntary Sector in the Tenth Plan 2002-7)

Though the civil society is evolving in its conceptual and institutional framework in recent years in India, as an idea it could be traced even in the writings of the ancient India. For instance, we can trace in Kautilya's *Arthashastra* the ideas regarding profit, cooperation and voluntarism. However, it should be noted that these notions are not similar as they connoted different meanings in different contexts in India. Therefore, one cannot place these notions parallel to contemporary perspectives of civil society.

INDIAN CIVIL SOCIETY—A CONVERGENT CONCEPT

In the Indian context we cannot choose any single frame to discuss the civil society as a concept. As Anheier observes,

> While civil society is a somewhat contested concept, definitions typically vary in the emphasis that they put on some characteristics of civil society over others. Some definitions primarily focus on aspects of state power, politics and individual freedom, and others more on economic functions and notions of social capital and cohesion. . . . The prevailing modern view sees civil society as a sphere located between state and market—a buffer zone strong enough to keep both state and market in check, thereby preventing each from becoming too powerful and dominating. . . . Some analysts adopt an abstract, systemic view and see civil society as a macro-sociological attribute of societies, particularly in the way that state and society relate to each other.

Others take on a more individualistic orientation and emphasize the notions of individual agency, citizenship, values and participation, using econometric and social network approach in analysing civil society.

There is also an institutional approach to studying civil society by looking at the size, scope and structure of organizations and associations, and the functions that they perform. . . . As a concept, civil society is essentially an intellectual product of the eighteenth-century Europe, when citizens sought to define their place in society independently of the aristocratic state and when, simultaneously, the certainty of a status-based social order began to suffer irreversible decline. The early theorists of civil society welcomed these changes. For Adam Smith, trade and commerce among private citizens created not only wealth but also invisible connections among people: the bonds of trust and social capital in today's terminology. Others such as John Locke and Alexis de Tocqueville saw civil society less in relation to the market but more in political terms and emphasized the importance of democratic association in everyday life as a base of a functioning polity (Helmut K. Anheier, 2004).

We might have to integrate all these simultaneously to arrive at a broader conceptual framework of civil society. It is in this sense the civil society, as a concept, is a convergent and a positive concept. A democratic perspective is membership in terms of pressure groups. A Marxist perspective is in terms of membership to worker's organizations. Similarly a liberal perception of the third sector is located in the market arena where individuals come together autonomously based on the principle of freedom of association and they adhere to the rules of the market. Here the basis of association is contract rather than membership. There are also associations with what could be termed as conservative values seeking to preserve, protect and flourish the nationalist values.

All of this is to say that participation in a civil society movement represents not just a tool for solving social problems or a set of organizations, but rather a way of involving in the world. This way of involving carries with it a set of values, interests, behaviours, and even a language. This is why the diverse value commitments, processes, operating styles, and modes of participation of third sector organizations are vital to their existence and not just secondary to some other overarching goal to which they are 'really' directed. At the mainstay of the argument, then, lies the unique character of civil society. It provides an alternative to the ways in which economic and political frameworks structure our world. It is a vital alternative, because it allows for a realm of free socially connected action in the public realm.

But it is susceptible to intrusion by both the state and the market. The success and power of either of those other spheres can begin to overwhelm the rather fragile construction of the third sector organization. In the contemporary world that is dominated by the neo-liberal ideology the market forces place increasing pressure on the third sector to respond to social problems in a fragmented bottomline-driven way. This mercerization process threatens to impose its own frame of reference, substituting the singular idea of return on investment for the rich pluralism of material, associative, aesthetic, and moral ends of civil society. This tilt towards the private dimension, reinforced by a growing emphasis on rights at the expense of civic obligation, threatens to destabilize civil society's delicate balance between individualist and communal purposes. In this sense it is an inductive concept, giving rise to myriad possibilities, yet reflecting the ideas of convergence.

Most of the existing connotations imply that the civil society is divergent in nature rather than convergent; exclusive rather than inclusive. For example, American scholars and activists use the term non-profit sector that is based on the principle of exclusion in the sense that it excludes the active market activities and activities related to profit. Even the term third sector used by researchers and scholars associated with International Society for Third Sector Research (ISTR) is not a convergent concept as it implies a watertight compartmentalization of society into different sectors and the third sector is exclusive from the other two sectors, that is, state and the market. Also the term third sector implicitly recognizes the dominance of the first two sectors, that is, the market and the state. Such a conceptual framework is pessimistic for it envisages a future scenario in which the third sector would remain the 'Third' eternally, being always subordinate to the first two sectors. Even the term independent sector is not suitable because first, it is exclusive in nature and second, in an oriental society like ours the social fabric is so well knit in terms of its religion and culture that this transcends the idea of an independent sector. It should be stressed here that none of the above terminologies are universal and permanent for they are evolved under certain historical and cultural contexts and these contexts, in turn, are evolving continuously. Different societies might adopt different vocabularies that are embedded in their culture at different times.

Given the complexity of the Indian society, understanding civil society as a concept is not easy. The complexity arises due to the social structure, size and diversity. Indian society and its rural economy are submerged in social relations. Primarily, the people are not driven to safeguard their interest in terms of acquiring material goods. They primarily act to project and safeguard their social standing, social claims and social assets. They value the material goods so far as they serve their ends. Neither the production function nor the distribution function could be linked to economic motives *per se*, independent of social motives. The dominant religion of Indian society, Hinduism, is highly nebulous. Added to this, the Indian society is multi-religious and multi-cultural. The Indian Constitution, which provides the institutional and legal framework of the society, recognizes not only this diversity but also accommodates a secular democratic society. The Constitution, in its legal framework, provides the basis for unifying the divergent socio-economic forces within the Indian society. Viewed from this perspective, the third sector could be visualized as a convergent area. It is the convergence of diverse ideologies—religious, political, economic and social—the commonalities are the promotion of welfare of the society at large through promotion of equality, ensuring social justice and sustainability. In this sense the Indian civil society is all encompassing in nature. Politically, there may be organizations committed to the leftist, centrist or rightist ideologies. There may be organizations which are represented by either a majority or a minority religion, economically there may be either non-profit and not-for profit organizations. Culturally, there may be organizations which are caste, clan or sect based. It should be noted in this context that the Indian civil society is not a hybrid of other forms but convergence of them.

A number of reasons could be given for emphasizing the convergent pragmatics of civil society. The civil society is a convergent area or concept due to the qualitative changes the global society is undergoing and also due to the role played by information technology. The booming Internet activity has virtually eliminated any distance. This has resulted in effective dissemination of information and exchange of ideas globally. This, in turn, has resulted in effective networking and the growth of virtual communities based on common concerns. With the collapse of the state-dominated systems of Soviet Union and eastern Europe and the consequent fall of the Berlin Wall, the old international order based on Cold War has become a thing of the past. Now, there is a growing suspicion about the immutable nature of any ideology. There is growing awareness that contemporary global problems like poverty, inequality, and environmental degradation could be addressed as global common concerns rather than in terms of watertight compartmentalized ideologies. Therefore we find that the anti-WTO movements, an environmental protection movements, and anti-poverty movements are gaining momentum globally in an ideologically convergent format. The volunteers belonging to all ideological shades are proactively initiating these movements. Thus we find that in the global context the civil society is a vast terrain of ideological convergence. This convergence terrain is now acting as an effective antidote to the ills of the unipolar world.

> What is important, according to this definition, at a trans-national level is the existence of a global public sphere—a global space where non-instrumental communication can take place, inhabited by trans-national advocacy networks like Green Peace or Amnesty International, global social movements like the protestors in Seattle, Prague and Geneva, international media through which their campaigns can be brought to global attention, new global 'civic religions' like human rights or environmentalism. (Mary Kaldor, 2003)

In the Indian context the civil society, if conceived as a convergent area, becomes an inclusive movement having no indomitable claims of supremacy of one segment of 'civil' society over the other in social dynamics. Only a convergent approach could help in initiating such a social dynamics in a society complex as ours and could bring about a meaningful, qualitative socio-economic change. It is an area with common priorities, agenda, legitimacy and values. Voluntarism is a distinctive perspective on the totality of this activity.

Indian civil society as a concept transcends the idea of non-profit organizations or non-governmental organization, as it popularly perceived in the West. Such a conceptual framework presupposes the existence of a vibrant market economy. Even today the notion of natural origins of the market principle is attributed to Adam Smith's famous statement of man's 'propensity to barter, truck and exchange one thing for another' and the division of labour in society was dependent upon the existence of market. But as Polanyi asserts, 'Division of labor, a phenomenon as old as society, springs from differences inherent in the facts of sex, geography, and individual endowment; and alleged propensity of man to barter, truck, and exchange is almost entirely apocryphal' (Karl Polanyi 2002). As Polanyi points out the market system violently distorts our views of man and society, and these distorted views were proving one of the main obstacles to the solution of the problems of our civilization

(Karl Polanyi, 1947). Polanyi carefully records as to how in the nineteenth-century European economy was created as an autonomous sphere, disjointed from the rest of the society. He emphasizes that the national market did not appear as the gradual and spontaneous emancipation of the economic sphere from government control. On the contrary the market was the result of a conscious and often violent intervention by the government. So according to Polanyi the price-making market is 'unnatural' and 'exceptional'.

The American concept of the third sector is essentially market based. So the concept is not suitable to explain the non-market or outside-the-market activities conducted in many communities in India. American researchers have largely driven the growth of scholarly interest in the third sector over the past thirty years. Economists in the United States have shaped the theory of development, focusing on non-profit organizations, particularly those listed in the US tax code as charities. In this process of theory of development, they have worked within the neoclassical paradigm, privileging markets. Non-profit organizations are explained as responses to various sorts of market failures. Although these theories claim universal application, for the most part they unconsciously reflect the cultural and institutional environment of the United States and assume that it applies everywhere (Voluntas, 2005).

The rural economy in India, at the grassroots level, is not an 'acquisitive society'. Polanyi observes: Even economic relationships are deeply embedded in social relationship.

> The maintenance of social ties, on the other hand, is crucial. First, because by disregarding the accepted code of honor, or generosity, the individual cuts himself off from the community and becomes an outcast; second, because, in the long run, all social obligations are reciprocal, and their fulfillment serves also the individual's give-and-take interest best. Such a situation must exert a continuous pressure on the individual to eliminate economic self-interest from his consciousness to the point of making him unable, in many cases (but by no means in all), even to comprehend the implications of his own actions in terms of such an interest. (Karl Polanyi, 2002).

In a rural economy the main driving force behind economic activity is reciprocity and redistribution and as such, a non-market society, 'the absence of motive of gain; the absence of the principle of labouring for remuneration; the absence of the principle of least effort; and, especially, the absence of any separate and distinct institution based on economic motives' (Karl Polanyi, 2002), are general characteristics of this economy at the grassroots even today. In this environment the production and distribution are ensured through reciprocity and redistribution that are essentially non-market in nature. 'The reciprocity works mainly with regard to the sexual organization of society, that is family and kinship; redistribution is mainly effective in respect to all those who are under a common chief and is, therefore, of a territorial character' (Karl Polanyi, 2002). In fact, the transaction cost in such a society would be less, for 'reciprocity and redistribution are able to ensure the working of an economic system without the help of written records and elaborate administration only because the organization of the societies in question meets the requirements of such solution with the help of patterns such as symmetry and centricity' (Karl Polanyi, 2002).

India is not a monolithic, homogeneous market economy. It includes the wide spectrum of religious and cultural life of society and some have emerged from the traditions of ancient society. The others emerging in the medieval period were rooted in socio-cultural movements. As such Indian society is also marked by plurality of economies as observed by Polanyi—a market economy, a non-market or redistributive economy, and a non-monetary or reciprocal economy. A particular organizational form highlights each of these economies. The firm marks the market economy. The redistributive economy is dominated by the state. The household or family dominates the non-monetary or reciprocal economy. Within this model, the third sector with its core values of altruism, charity and voluntarism exists as a convergent entity among the three main economies. Therefore in the Indian context the third sector as a concept should be viewed in an integrative, holistic and converging perspective. Otherwise we might miss out the social, political, cultural, religious and economic facets of Indian society. Precisely due to this reason, the European terminology, 'social economy' is also not suitable for highlighting the Indian third sector scenario. No doubt, it is a much broader conceptual connotation than the US non-profit sector. Yet it would not entirely reflect the Indian societal context, which is wide and complex. We have a rich network of organizations rooted in caste and religion based on the basic philosophy of altruism and the principle of voluntarism and these unique organizations would be found both in rural and urban areas. The Indian experience therefore would provide new theoretical insights into an understanding of the third sector as a concept. The civil society in the Indian context is a complex dynamic element, an element that is outside the purview of state, that is voluntary in nature and self-preserving as an organization, providing a productive dialectical relationship between the state and the market. As a normative concept it includes the following features: voluntary, religious, cultural, political, social, secular, not-for profit, formal, informal, private, government-initiated or sponsored. Thus the civil society in India is created out of a rich mosaic oozing out diversity.

It could be viewed as a belief system which espouses a kind of ideal society that we all want to live in, in an atmosphere of trust and tolerance. Therefore, the idea of civil society as a concept becomes a moral statement about the 'good' society. It symbolizes a sum total of organically related entities that are vested with the responsibility of achieving civility through voluntary initiatives. It is an arena for social action which aims at providing an enabling environment in society. It is a concept which has emanated in a particular historic epoch, which reiterates the importance of human rights and individual rights in relation to the state and the market. The civil society in the Indian context could be viewed as a social movement which highlights the decentralization of economic and political power. The market-driven liberalism, on the other hand, invariably leads to the opposite due to the presence of market externalities. In this sense, the civil society in the Indian social context is an anti-thesis to atomized liberalism that is being highlighted by the prevailing international neo-liberalism. Essentially, it is an effective antidote to any form of hegemony either of state or of an ideology.

CIVIL SOCIETY AND HOLISTIC DEVELOPMENT

If the market is based on the exchange relationship, the state is dependent on authority. The relationship in the market arena emanates from the process of exchange and is difficult to define. In a broad sense, the process of exchange embraces all forms of social behaviour. In the framework of market, the exchange is confined only to *quid pro quo* transactions. In the realm of state the basis of relationship is authority and it is even more difficult to comprehend. This is because authority can be found in every form of social organization, whether it is a command organization, a commercial organization or a voluntary organization. However, generally the state is identified with commands and these commands are enforceable, not due to contractual obligations but due to legal compulsions. We have to understand the nature and structure of the third sector in a society with reference to the exchange that is characterized in that society's market and authority of the government.

In the market the exchange takes place on the free rational choice of an individual consumer. As these choices are hedonistic, the market relationship is voluntary but self-seeking and is based on the principle of *quid pro quo*. It is in this context that we have to make a distinction between market-based individual rationality and collective rationality. The market economics emphasizes that under perfect competitive conditions the individual rationality and collective rationality will converge. But the market is seldom perfect and individual rationality and collective rationality need not always converge. So, we require an institutional mechanism to bring about such a convergence. The state intervention is justified on the ground that, the state will achieve the objectives of collective rationality by using its coercive legislative powers. The uniqueness of the third sector is that it is aimed at achieving the same objective, without invoking the coercive powers. Theoretically the third sector provides a framework for the convergence of the individual and the collective rationalities. The civil society activists identify themselves with a collective interest and this becomes the basis of relationship between an individual and the organization.

The distinctiveness of civil society is that it enjoys a higher degree of autonomy than the organizations that belong either to the state or market. It is characterized by lower degrees of means, rationality and formality and a higher degree of solidarity and direct exchange than other forms of organizations that operate in the realm of the state and the market. The rationale for civil society is analysed from the perspective of functions and contributions to resource allocation and social welfare. There are two broad orientations. The first is the American micro-economic school. This school explains the emergence of civil society in terms of the state and the market failure and as an institutional mechanism to reduce the transaction costs.

The second functional approach to civil society is neo-corporatist. According to this approach civil society is a buffer zone between the state and the market and this buffer zone mitigates social tensions and political conflicts. These organizations dwell in those areas or segments of society where the state is not conveniently positioned to perform and deliver or the state would allow the private for-profit organizations to operate. The civil society organizations might perform certain functions that will recompense the members who might have lost certain benefits that they would have got from their families. This organization might help in integrating these members into the societal fold, which the families might have failed to in achieving.

The civil society is less subject to market and political pressures. Consequently the means of economic rationality is not a dominant element in decision making as it is in the realm of market and public bureaucracy. As such it has partial access to corrective mechanisms when compared to the public sector in terms of ballot box and for profit sector in terms of the market. Some welfare organizations continue to operate unchallenged despite serious shortcomings and failures. The civil society managers find it easier to deviate from their objectives, as the means-rational considerations are less important. This built-in feature of a civil society organization is a source of strength and weakness at the same time. It makes civil society suitable entities for 'functional dilettantism', a 'mellow weakness' that could be misused by the vested interests to create an illusion that 'at least something is being done' (Seibel, 1989).

The civil society though distinct from the government and the market organizations, is yet by no means independent of these two. The interdependency arises, not due to the fact that the civil society organizations are dependent on subsidies and other financial transfers but because there is a greater degree of overlapping in the area of policy formulations. The state finds it increasingly difficult to formulate policies at all levels, on its own. Civil society managers serve as a 'consulting institutional think-tank' for political bodies in policy formulations. This precisely explains why the third sector, despite continuing to be relatively insignificant economically, has achieved a visible prominent status (Gronbjerg, 1987).

The contemporary development paradigm in India is dichotomized between the urban and rural interests, and this dichotomy is reflected in the Indian civil society movement. The Gandhian thinking that is closer to Indian villagers, their faith, traditions and culture, influences one strand of civil society movement. Gandhi wanted to preserve village India. He wanted to liberate village India from the colonial yoke and develop it as an economically self-sufficient unit with its members having neither the necessity to exploit each other nor any one else. He visualized a moral democracy for village India. He wrote in *Young India*:

Industrialization is, I am afraid, going to be a curse for mankind. Exploitation of one nation by another cannot go on for all time. Industrialism depends entirely on your capacity to exploit, on foreign markets being open to you, and on the absence of competitors. . . . In fact, India, when it begins to exploit other nations—as it must if it becomes industrialized—will be a curse for another nation, a menace to the world. Anyway why should I think of industrializing India to exploit other nations? (*Young India*, 12 November 1931)

Highlighting the significance of village economy Gandhi wrote in *Harijan*:

I have been saying that if untouchability stays, Hinduism goes; even so I would say that if the village perishes India will perish too. It will no more be India. Her mission in the world will get lost. The revival of the village is possible only when it is no more exploited. Industrialization on a mass scale will necessarily lead to passive or active exploitation of the villagers, as the problems of competition and marketing come in. Therefore, we have to concentrate on the village being self-contained, manufacturing mainly for use. Provided this character of the village industry is maintained, there would be no objection to villages using even modern machines and tools that they can make and can afford to use. Only they should not be used as a means of exploitation of others. (*Harijan*, 29 August 1936)

Gandhian thinking is more relevant today than at any other time in India before because the dynamics of globalization is creating the same impact on village India as Gandhi prognosticated. Claiming himself as a socialist, Gandhi highlighted the concept of trusteeship that seeks to destroy capitalism and not the capitalist through non-violent means. In *Young India* he declared:

When the people adopt it (non-violence) as a principle of conduct, class war becomes impossibility. . . . By the non-violent method we seek not to destroy the capitalist, we seek to destroy capitalism. We invite the capitalist to regard himself as a trustee for those on whom he depends for the making, the retention and the increase of his capital. . . . Immediately the worker realizes his strength, he is in a position to become a co-sharer of the capitalist instead of remaining his slave. If he aims at becoming the sole owner, he will most likely be killing the goose that lays the golden eggs. Inequalities in intelligence and even opportunity will last till the end of time. A man living on the banks of a river has any day more opportunity of growing crops than one living in an arid desert. But if inequalities stare us in the face, the essential equality too is not to be missed. Everyman has an equal right for the necessities of life even as birds and beasts have. (*Young India*, 24 March 1931)

This Gandhian ideology influences one strand of civil society movement in India. Many voluntary initiatives in this strand are mission-driven initiatives by the development volunteers or third sector managers. If the development volunteers, due to their sheer commitment to a cause, initiate an activity and this, in turn, leads to an establishment of an organization or a movement then these are Mission Driven Movements and Organizations (MDMOs). The initiative of voluntarism in these types of organizations will be with the development volunteer and the development volunteer, who acts as a manager of that organization or the movement, mobilizes beneficiaries. The major resource of these types of organizations is the spirit of voluntarism and a commitment to a cause by the development volunteer who acts as the manager. In subsequent stages the other resources, both tangible and intangible, will start flowing to these organizations. The organizations belonging to this type conform to the ideals of empowering, enabling and sustainable values as this forms the bedrock of the organizations. Historically, many voluntary initiatives are of this type and they have brought about fundamental social changes in the society. For example, the Indian nationalist movement belongs to this category. In post-Independent India, there are many movements that can be traced to this category of third sector initiative. Almost all of these are influenced by the Gandhian development paradigm.

The Gandhian ideal of rural democracy and economic self-reliance, going under the name *sarvodaya*, is fundamentally opposed to the contemporary dynamics of globalization that is based on the neo-liberal ideology. Gandhi described it as follows:

Independence must begin at the bottom. Thus every village will be a republic or panchayat having full powers. It follows, therefore, that every village has to be self-sustained and capable of managing its affairs even to the extent of defending itself against the whole. This does not exclude dependence on and willing help from neighbors or from the world. It will be free and voluntary play of mutual forces. Such a society is necessarily highly cultured, in which every man and woman knows what he or she wants, and, what is more, knows that no one should want anything that others cannot have with equal labor. In this structure composed of innumerable villages, there will be ever-widening, never-ascending circles. Life will not be a pyramid with the apex sustained by the bottom. But it will be an oceanic circle whose center will be the individual always ready to perish for the village, the latter ready to for the circle of villages, till at last the whole becomes one life composed of individuals, never aggressive in their arrogance but ever humble, sharing the majesty of the oceanic circle of which they are integral parts. In this, there is no room for machines that would displace human labor and concentrate power in a few hands. Labor has its unique place in a cultural human family. Every machine that helps every individual has a place. (Kunal Roy Chowdhuri, 1993).

Sarvodaya as a concept aims to improve the material standard of living of the people without compromising the spiritual values of life of the people and thus attempts to integrate the values of ethics and economics. The cardinal principles of *sarvodaya* are *swadeshi*, bread-labour, non-possession, trusteeship, non-exploitation, and equality. If *swadeshi* underscores the ability of a community to support itself without undue dependence on others, then bread-labour emphasizes the participation by individuals in work to produce the necessaries of life. The principle of non-possession is akin to the Marxian principle of 'each according to his ability and need'. The principle of trusteeship entails that those who own and use resources look after them for the benefit of the community. The principles of non-exploitation and equality entail not taking advantage of others and providing equal opportunities for all. The concept of *sarvodaya* emphasizes the importance of education as a tool for enhancing social consciousness namely to ensure that they are aware of wider obligations and connections, and see themselves as part of and serving something greater. The basic organizing unit at a political level is the principle of village self-rule. Appropriate technology is chosen to maintain the principle of system including equity and useful work.

Sarvodaya has been one of the most inspiring ideologies that has spurred the voluntary movement in post-independent India. Acharya Vinoba Bhave, who was a close follower of M.K. Gandhi, spearheaded the *Bhoodan* (donate land) movement. This involved landowners voluntarily donating land to the communities. The land in turn would be used for development and made cultivable so that the poor communities could benefit from it. Vinoba believed in establishing the independent power of the people as a power opposed to the power of violence. Closely connected to the Bhoodan movement there were other movements like *Gramdan* (gifting of village), *Sampatti-dan* (gift of wealth), *Shramadan* (gift of labour), *Shanti*

Sena (army for peace), *Sarvodaya Patra* (the pot where every household gives daily a handful of grain) and *Jeevandan* (gift of life). The Bhoodan movement was remarkable in that it signified a change in the attitude of the land owning donors. The gifting of land signified the desire for social change on the part of the landowners. The religious idea of charity triggered a voluntary movement of the kind of Bhoodan movement in India and the entire movement was mission driven and not agenda driven or sponsored by anyone.

It should be noted here that the movement did not represent just the economic life. It represented the moral regeneration of the people and the desire to reconstruct the society on a new basis. It aimed at making morality the guiding principle of social life, and to make economics subservient to the moral values of society. Sarvodaya workers went to villages and worked there to foster self-reliance among the people. They constructed houses, schools, installed energy systems and educated the farmers on soil conservation techniques. These actions helped in awakening individuals and groups to their own potential for compassion, sharing and cooperative endeavour.

Baba Amte, another volunteer influenced by the Gandhian ideology believed that an ideal society rests on two pillars: one, the pillar of mutual recognition of rights and, the other, the pillar of mutual cooperation for the common good. He premised that in a society, the dignity of every human being must be respected and this can happen when every individual in the society is self-supporting. He declared:

> I believe as a society we have to evolve, through experimentation, a system that combines the principles of individual freedom and common ownership. And this is what we have tried, basically with success, in all our projects, involving leprosy patients, tribal people and the so-called 'disabled' persons. Consider the honeybee. Its treasure is nectar, obtained even from the chilly plant. It is not at the cost of the flower. In fact, its act of extracting honey contributes to the progress of the flowers. You need not learn from Khalil Gibran, Marx or Gorbachev, not even from Gandhiji. Choose instead to learn your lesson from the honeybees as your silent partners: they will show you how to develop without destroying.

Baba Amte nurtured his *Anandawan* as a model of the India of his dreams.

Another important voluntary movement that was initiated in India inspired by Gandhi is the Chipko movement. This is the movement of volunteers hugging the trees so that they may not be axed. Sundarlal

Bahuguna spearheaded this movement. Located in the Himalayan region of Uttaranchal, Chipko started with a slogan, 'what do the forests bear?—Soil, water, and pure air'. This was a slogan pitted against the government refrain, 'What do the forests bear?—Raisin, timber and foreign exchange'. The protest against the felling of trees continued for eight years. In 1981, the Government of India banned the felling of trees.

Bahuguna joined the campaign opposing the construction of Tehri dam in the late 1980s. In 1995 he ended his 45-day fast when the government promised to review the Tehri dam project. As the promise was not kept, in the following year he committed himself to another fast. He ended his fast after 74 days when the prime minister gave a personal undertaking to conduct a thorough review largely on Bahuguna's terms. Meanwhile the Chipko movement has taken the shape of a movement to protect the Himalayas. Bahuguna raised his concern about the receding glaciers of Himalayas and the danger it posed to the river Ganges. He warned the government that the people in the Himalayas were facing a crisis of survival due to suicidal activities being carried out in the name of development. The monstrous Tehri dam was the symbol of this. He urged the government to adopt a long-term policy to protect the dying Himalayas. In this context he strongly opposes the interlinking of rivers. Bahuguna warns that the interlinking of rivers means building of big dams everywhere and it would lead to the killing of the rivers.

Yet another movement that is influenced by Gandhian thinking is the Narmada Bachao Andolan (NBA). This is a movement against the building of a big dam across the river Narmada and is an important voluntary movement that is being spearheaded by Medha Patkar. She is mobilizing tribal people, farmers, environmentalists, and human rights activists against the Sardar Sarovar Dam being built across the Narmada River, in Gujarat, India. As a movement it is concerned with the issues of resettlement and rehabilitation of the people who are displaced due to the construction of the dam and other larger issues like development and environment.

NBA's singular achievement is that it has brought to the forefront the issue of development by questioning the relevance of a neo-liberal paradigm of development in a developing country like India. It initiated the quest for an appropriate development model. The movement in the process of addressing the issues of resettlement and rehabilitation realized that the very basis of the dam projects is flawed;

the very model of development they represent is a Himalayan blunder. Medha Patkar has started questioning the relevance of these projects undertaken in the name of development as these projects involve huge social costs and cannot be incorporated even in the most scientific cost-benefit analysis.

Medha Patkar, in this context, underscores the significance of a bottom-up approach to development. The plans according to her must emerge from a real democratic participatory polity. Only then the process of development will reflect the perceptions and perspectives of the people with right kinds of priorities. She emphasizes the development activity which must be based on natural and human resources and decentralized planning. Tackling the criticism that she is against development, she says:

> We've made it very clear that we are not against development per se, if that is defined as a change that is desirable and acceptable within our value framework. Our framework is not an individualist one. It is the framework of the Indian constitution, values of equity and justice. Sustainability has to mean justice to the population beyond one generation. That can come only if the priorities are set right. Our priority is the basic need fulfillment of every individual and that cannot happen unless the planning process is really democratic. Equitable and sustainable development presumes that the natural resources will be used. But in the choice of technologies and the priorities of goals and objectives, the preference should be given to the most needy sections, not to those who already have. . . . Our view of development is supportive of labor-intensive technologies that would not create unemployment, but would create livelihood opportunities for people when the resources are used. We are for technology that will not spoil, pollute, and destroy our natural resources, which still are rich enough and still in the hands of rural communities, which are simple-living, non-consumerist communities. The choice of technology is invariably related to the kind of living standard and lifestyle one visualizes as a part of development. Simple living, which would bring in more equity and justice across the world, among countries and within countries, is what we value. Technologies can bring some comforts, but we shouldn't go to the other extreme of not using the human body and human power. (Robert Jensen, 2004)

Like the Gandhian thinking, the Nehruvian ideas of development influenced another strand of third sector management in India. Though Gandhi and Nehru worked closely during the nationalist movement and had for each other strong affection and regard, they differed radically in their objectives and programmes for change. By temperament, Nehru was closer to the cities of the world than the villages of India. Nehru was more inclined to modernization of rural India through mechanization of agriculture. He favoured promoting rapid urban industrial growth in India and acknowledged the antagonism between Gandhi's ideas and his own, and stated:

> The Khadi movement, hand-spinning and hand-weaving, which is Gandhiji's special favourite, is an intensification of individualism in production, and is thus a throw-back to the pre-industrial age. As a solution of any vital present-day problem it cannot be taken seriously, and it produces a mentality which may become an obstacle to growth in the right direction. . . . Gandhiji has said repeatedly that he is not against machinery as such; he seems to think that is out place in India today. But can we wind up the basic industries, such as iron and steel, or even the lighter ones that already exist? It is obvious that we cannot do so. If we have railways, bridges, transport facilities, etc., we must either produce them ourselves or depend on others. If we want to have the means of defense we must not only have the basic industries but a highly developed industrial system. No country today is really independent or capable of resisting aggression unless it is industrially developed. (Jawaharlal Nehru, 1958)

Many voluntary initiatives were undertaken in the post-independent India influenced by Nehruvian thinking. Many initiatives were state sponsored or sponsored by funding organizations or donors. Many initiatives were part of the planning process. The Community Development Programme and Indian cooperative movement belonged to this category. In the post-1990s many voluntary initiatives were started that could be identified within the Nehruvian thinking framework. Most of these were Agenda Driven Organizations and Movements (ADOMs). The dominant voluntary initiatives in India today are agenda driven voluntary initiatives only.

It is necessary to make a comparative analysis of MDMOs and ADOMs to know the impact these organizations make in terms of bringing about a meaningful social change. Most ADOMs operate as per the parameters set either by the donor agencies or organizations or the government. The Indian five-year plan adheres to the Nehruvian model of development. This model was reformulated in the 1990s to further the objectives of globalization. To improve the delivery system and mechanism of mobilizing additional resources for development, the Government of India is encouraging the active participation of NGOs and other voluntary organizations funded and supported by international organizations and donor agencies. Most of these agencies do not challenge the development paradigm sponsored by the neo-liberal ideology. In these cases the donors set the agenda and it is accepted by the voluntary organizations and, consequently, they work in the fringes to mitigate the problems of globalization. As most of these organizations are started with the intention of getting funds, their primary consideration would be to get funds than to set the agenda for themselves with a missionary zeal. As agenda-driven organizations, their capacity to bring about fundamental social change is very limited. Though many of the organizations even within this group apparently criticize the dynamics of the neo-liberal ideology-sponsored globalization process, they cannot fundamentally challenge them the way the MDMOs do. In the post-globalization period many of the third sector initiatives belong to this category and consequently their managerial ideology is not fundamentally different from the neo-liberal ideology. Many organizations that are receiving funds from international donor agencies and from the government belong to this group. In fact, it is this group that is constituted by myriad organizations based on religion, caste, language and region. There are also organizations based on corporate philanthropy and cooperative organizations. These are both formal and informal and include both urban and rural. The styles of management in these types of organizations vary depending on the background of those who initiated the organization. The style ranges from the native traditional to modern corporate. Lack of uniform managerial practice is one of the dominant features in ADOMs.

The fact that the third sector conceptually constitutes a terrain between the state and the market should not make us to believe that this terrain is uniform and homogeneous and that the managerial philosophy is distinct from that of the state and the market. In India this sector is so heterogeneous that many organizations working within this sector are not only at variance with others but also sometimes even antagonistic. If the mission-driven organizations are committed to Gandhian ideology, the agenda-driven organizations, by and large, further the cause of neo-liberal ideology. The roots of this dichotomy could be found in the ideological divergence between the Gandhian and Nehruvian models of development. In the Gandhian paradigm of development, the people are at the centre of the development. The eco-system is a resource that should be conserved and used in a regenerative fashion. The production of physical capital must be done in such a way that it should not destroy the natural capital of the society. It can happen if the material requirements of the humans are subservient to the regenerative capacity of nature. This paradigm emphasizes that the people at the local level must have effective control over their resources and it can happen only when governance is decentralized.

The neo-liberal model, on the other hand, believes that the eco-system is a passive resource and it should be harnessed to satisfy the material needs of the society. No doubt it recognizes the fact that the resources are limited but it believes that new technologies will not only result in efficient and optimal utilization of existing resources but will also result in the invention and innovation of new resources. This could be achieved in a liberated competitive market environment. Pruning of state bureaucracy and minimization of state intervention will go a long way in creating such an environment. In this context the role of the third sector is emphasized to complement the efforts of the state and the market. It is widely believed that the delivery system of the third sector organizations are far more efficient than the state and the market, and the delivery agendas are determined by the donors and the third sector organizations are called upon to meet those agendas.

It is necessary that the policy makers, activists, researchers and academicians distinguish between these two types of third sector organizations and create the right environment for the flourishing of the meaningful third sector management practices that will further the cause of genuine voluntarism. The problem of management in a fund-driven third sector organization is that there may not be an urge for change for the managers. The managers might find only limited opportunities for the creative expression of their urge to relate to socially marginalized groups. Donor agencies might give little attention to the urge for voluntarism of a manager and rather give importance to their organizational agendas and programmmes. But the problem of development is so complex that it cannot be addressed effectively without nurturing voluntarism among managers and employees within the organization. Large-scale social change cannot be brought about through isolated initiatives of voluntary organizations without a commitment to genuine voluntarism and a broad consensus regarding common good.

Indian voluntarism is rooted in its culture. The Indian culture essentially nourishes the value of non-accumulation or not keeping anything more than that is necessary for one's minimal needs. Again, in the Indian cultural context the process of giving and receiving takes place on the same plane, that is, the process of giving is based on the willingness to receive. As such, the act of giving is accompanied by the enculturation or assimilation of humility and duty towards the receivers. If the receivers are merely viewed as resource-scarce beneficiaries rather than equal participants in the development process, then the act of giving will be considered paternalistic. Hence, it becomes a source of external resource and skill. Many donor agencies and international development organizations not only fail to understand this, but they also fail to recognize the resource richness of the economically poor people. These organizations do not view the assimilation of knowledge from the poor as a rich resource in their management decisions. Consequently they fail to tap the rich indigenous reserve of technical, institutional and social knowledge of the poor. It is necessary for the managers of these organizations to understand the dilemmas of the poor for whom compliance and conformity to a given social order seemed virtually the only choice. Creating an enabling environment is one of the difficult challenges faced by these organizations.

There are tens of thousands of marginalized people having a strong urge to take initiatives and to achieve excellence in skills that may be needed in society. Their condition and background may not permit them to become entrepreneurs. The civil society organizations do not consider fostering or nurturing such initiative as part of their major role. The non-utilization of this potential energy by mainstream organizations could create frustration on both sides. If the stifling, non-cooperative bureaucracy frustrates these organizations, the marginalized feel frustrated due to the non-responsive attitude of the organizations in harnessing their initiatives properly. This situation is due to the absence of organizational or societal support that helps in pursuing the search for socially useful innovations. Therefore, there is an urgent need to bring about an effective convergence between the creative aspirations of the marginalized and the managerial objectives of the civil society organizations. Only then, the society can witness meaningful social change through a new institution-building capacity, in an enabling environment.

The success of the civil society movement in India must be viewed more in terms of creating proper environment for voluntarism that would lead to meaningful social change. The role of civil society organizations is significant in that it will fill the void that is being created by the state and the market. Unfortunately, the donor agencies have a tendency to give more prominence to voluntary organizations than the zeal of voluntarism of the managers. Such an overriding importance to the organizational aspect than voluntarism of the civil society activists (development volunteers) would only undermine the corrective dynamics in the realm of the state and the market. The people with an urban background manage most of these donor agency sponsored organizations. These people might suppress the spirit of voluntarism among the local people and consequently, fail to nourish their creativity by superimposing their own agendas or the agendas of the donor agencies. As a result, the process of social change becomes more of a function that is engineering by exogenous factors than due to the dynamics of the endogenous factor of voluntarism. A proactive activist must take care to discredit the values that generate helplessness and nourish the creativity of locally and indigenously anchored disadvantaged because it is the source of genuine voluntarism that contributes to meaningful social change.

Meaningful social change is that sustainable process which would widen the canvas of decision making and enabling environment of the locally disadvantaged. This sustainable process must not only enhance the accessibility of the resources of the people but also their capacity to convert these resources into investment with an assurance of future returns. If the process of social change is to be meaningful it must be experienced simultaneously both by the activists and the people who are involved in it. Otherwise there will be a cleavage between the managers of these organizations and the people as 'beneficiaries' and the people may resent the paternalistic attitude of the developmental organizations, as they are not recognized as equal partners possessing any potential wealth in terms of their cultural and moral knowledge and wisdom. Involving the local people in their development endeavour as equals, building upon their cultural roots of voluntarism, and respecting their mores and values would go a long way in changing the situation. The civil society activists have to understand that by acknowledging social initiatives and knowledge of the local people and identifying its scientific merit, they can revive the spirit of experimentation in the local people. The process of institution building entails the dispensation of external leadership and recognition of the fact that there exists an opposing relationship between status and skills. The civil society movement in India has not adopted the lobbying and pressure building tactics to achieve the local agendas. It should be noted that the state and the market perform better if they are under constant insurgent vigil of the third sector organizations. The civil society organizations will have to work in such a way that there is proper coordination between local action and lobbying at the macro level. The civil society activists must blend themselves with grassroot activists, organizations, and professionals to strengthen social change at the local level by augmenting local ideas and innovations into global thinking, and introducing the global arena for local development volunteers to testify their hypothesis.

CIVIL SOCIETY AND THE CHALLENGES OF HOLISTIC SOCIAL MANAGEMENT IN INDIA

Since the 1990s there has been a remarkable growth of civil society initiatives in India and these initiatives, as has been identified so far, derive their inspiration from different ideological sources. These initiatives and organizations operate under a wide variety of legal and institutional frameworks. They are supposed to represent the renewed expression of civil society against the backdrop of negative fallouts of globalization and the consequent crisis in the welfare state.

The significance of the civil society in India, as elsewhere, is in that it is broadly supplanting the socio-economic roles of modern welfare state. It is involved in the allocation of resources through the production of quasi-public goods and is assuming the redistribution role through the provision of these goods to the deprived section of the society, almost free of cost. The neo-liberal economic policies of the Indian state in the post-globalization era have increased the problem of poverty and unemployment. The state, as a logical corollary of neo-liberal policy, is constrained to reduce its budgetary deficits and to keep these deficits at a low level. The state has apparently lost its way in effective implementation of traditional social policies and there is a need for a new institutional mechanism to put in place a more vibrant integrative social policy. It is in this backdrop that the question about the role of the civil society is being debated and there are no definite answers. If some feel that civil society is an ideal institutional response to the state and the market failure, others fear that it will only further the dynamics of globalization with all its negative ramifications. The global economy now is undergoing a great transition and the human civilization is witnessing drastic changes in its entire spectrum. Globally, the process of redefinition of relationships among institutions is taking place and the emergence of civil society to mitigate the adverse effects of the state and the market failure is a part of that ongoing process. The civil society, probably, is a new institutional mechanism to achieve the objective of the perfect market and the modern welfare state based on the criteria of both efficiency and equity. In this sense the civil society is a realm that tries to converge the objective of opposite poles, that is, the state and the market.

The emergence of new enterprise always is in response to the needs of the emerging new circumstances. The civil society as an enterprise has emerged to fill the vacuum created by the inadequacies of the private market and the state in providing a satisfactory solution to the contemporary global problems. The civil society entrepreneurship is expressed in terms of new types of services offered by these organizations to the needy people. The inability of the state in India to augment welfare measures to the people has resulted in the emergence of a civil society enterprise and the state is looking upon this enterprise to achieve its welfare objectives. These organizations are providing the kind of services that are better suited to the needs of the poor, whether it is in the field of micro finance, sustainable agricultural practices, empowerment, protection of old women and children, aid to the physically challenged and protection of the environment.

The methods of organization and production of civil society are different from the traditional private market and the state. If the actors in the realm of private market or state constitute more or less a homogeneous group, in the realm of civil society we can observe the most heterogeneous groups. Government bureaucrats, local representatives, salaried workers, voluntary workers, beneficiaries, donors are often partners in the same productive endeavour. As a multi-stakeholder organization, the third sector provides an alliance of interested parties to compete more effectively with the private market organizations.

The most distinguishing feature of the civil society is the mobilization of a new factor of production called the voluntary labour. This not only reduces the transaction cost in the production process but also ensures better quality of products, as there will be greater degree of involvement of the voluntary labour in the production process. The combination of paid and voluntary labour in the production process is a significant innovation of their sector as an enterprise.

Unlike the previous forms of enterprises the civil society as an enterprise is socially embedded. The socially embedded nature of these enterprises is discernible in the following elements. First, serving the members of the community is the overriding priority of these enterprises, not profit generation. Second, the resource base of civil society is generally non-commercial and sometimes non-monetary. This will ensure greater benefits to the community in general, and the target group in particular, and such benefits provide the rationale for subsidy support to the civil society enterprises. The non-monetary resources in the form of voluntary labour or donations generate significant goodwill on which these enterprises depend, due to their role in providing services. Finally, these organizations are distinguished by the democratic decision-making process. They are founded on the participatory principle and the power of participation of members is not linked to the amount of capital contributed by them.

The civil society organizations are newly emerging entities in an institutional and competitive arena, and this arena is rapidly changing. The activists who run these organizations have to face many challenges and difficulties. These organizations are relatively new in their conception and structure. Unlike already well-established forms of organizations, these organizations are still in an evolving state. Proprietorship, partnership, joint stock and even state enterprises are well structured and have their own organized legal and institutional framework. As such, the procedures of operation and the nature of working of these organizations are known. The civil society organizations, on the other hand, are not well structured either organizationally or legally. The managers of these organizations have to face problems right from the stage of inception. Once it is established, the managers have to provide legitimacy to these organizations. As the legal framework of the third sector is amorphous, providing legitimacy to these organizations and setting the standard parameters of governance are the most difficult tasks for the managers of these organizations. Then the managers have other challenges like getting the appropriate social mission and imparting high degree of efficiency to the organization. They also have to manage the organization's key assets and committed volunteers and employees. The civil society organizations are converging in the sense that they try to converge the positive factors of two diametrically opposite organizational forms, that is, the state and the market. The convergent nature of civil society is reinforced by many factors.

The civil society organization is essentially an (private) organization devoted to achieving some social good. It has to mobilize both commercial and non-commercial resources. The commercial resources might originate from both private and public customers and founders, and non-commercial resources include donations and voluntary contribution of labour. This organization provides private goods with positive externalities or a redistributive component. Second, the third sector organization is wedded to the promotion of social good. But the concept of social good is ambiguous and amorphous. Civil society provides those goods that are characterized by individual demand associated with a perceived social utility. As such, the definition of social good is related to a specific institutional context in both time and space. Third, a civil society organization works with multi-faceted objectives. It has to satisfy the donors and funding agencies through its mission. Also, it has to satisfy its stakeholders through its effective delivery system. Therefore the manager of this organization must strike an ideal balance between advocacy and fund-raising and management of quality and customer satisfaction. This requires a high degree of operational efficiency in management. The third sector by its very nature requires adequate management practices that are typically oriented toward effectiveness and efficiency. Finally, civil society organizations are multi-stakeholder organizations. Their successful working depends upon the vibrant participation of workers, volunteers and customers. Consequently, the embedded goals of these organizations may become even more confused by the need to combine different interests and balancing them in the ongoing management activities. These factors contribute to the convergent nature of the third sector and create problems not only in terms of giving legitimacy to the organizations but also to its activists. The socio-economic and political environment might enable the passive acceptance of the emergence of the third sector, while those that have emerged must have a clear focus on their management strategies.

The challenges of Indian civil society could be both exogenous and endogenous. If these organizations are confronted with problems in the realm of finance and legal framework they are outside of the organization and consequently constitute exogenous challenges. All the activists of the civil society organization in cohesion could address these challenges by constituting a common front. As these are not the internal matters of organizations they cannot control them.

However, they can face the challenge through influence and lobbying. Endogenous challenges relate to factors like the ability of civil society activists to enhance legitimization and operational efficiency of these organizations. It is necessary that the activists must identify the core areas of intervention and locate the specific nature of the organizations that they manage. If they fail to do so then the very legitimacy of the organization will be at stake. Therefore, the civil society activists will have to face daunting challenges in managing their organizations. Unfortunately the existing management literature does not throw adequate light in terms of solving these problems. The contemporary literature on non-profit organizations addresses these issues only marginally. The principal reason is that this literature is largely concerned with the problems of traditional non-profit organizations, and is mainly concerned with North America. These organizations are, on average, larger and they rely more heavily on traditional management techniques, supplemented by fund-raising and volunteer management. The predominant view of the non-profit organization is that, 'it is a donative form, and when it evolves into an entrepreneurial form, the common view is that the risks outnumber the advantages' (Hansmann, 1980).

CONCLUSION

In India the civil society organizations are emerging organizations and their activities have certain commonalities with the activities of many existing service providers. As such they have to not only compete with these organizations but also strive to acquire legitimization and institutional recognition. The civil society in India at this stage of development is trying to gain recognition as a collective entity and in that process is facing the following challenges:

- The social nature of civil society as an institution in India is not yet established. The existing legal and institutional framework is not conducive for this sector to get a clear definitional framework. Whenever an emerging institution is properly recognized in a particular legal and institutional framework, the performance of such an institution has improved considerably. In this regard, the Indian third sector has a long way to go.
- The civil society can effectively compete with the public and private sector organizations only when they provide quality

service on a sustained basis. The nature of goods and services rendered by civil society in India is such that it requires constant investment in quality. Though these organizations could be benefited by their closeness to customers and local communities, yet they cannot ignore the imperatives of providing high quality services and it requires constant investment.

- People with special skills and expertise and motivated commitment to the vision and mission are required to manage and administer these organizations. In this sense these organizations heavily rely not only on human capital but also on social capital. If expertise and skill constitute human capital, motivation of employees determines social capital. Larger resources are to be diverted for the development of the much needed human resource for these organizations. The civil society organizations must sponsor specific graduate and postgraduate programmes in these areas. These organizations must devise training programmes for its staff to impart work skills in this area.
- Civil society, as a modern emerging concept in India, is in the early stages of its evolution. In the early stages, all organizations strive hard to attract people with the competencies and the skills they require. These skills are needed not only from the point of view of efficiency and productivity, but also to acquire legitimacy and institutional recognition for these emerging organizations.
- One of the distinguishing features of civil society organizations is that they are capital light. This feature is particularly true to those organizations that are working in rural areas of India. The nature of activity of these organizations is such that in most cases they don't require huge capital. But given the nature and extent of poverty, the Indian civil society organizations are finding it difficult to mobilize even the moderate quantum of capital to initiate an activity. Self-financing a project is a difficult task in India as most of the beneficiaries are so poor that they lack even the critical minimum financial resources required to start the project. As civil society is an emerging organizational pattern, institutional financial support is difficult to come by. This is due to the fact that the funding agencies find it difficult to analyse and interpret these organizations. Well-developed financial institutional support is an important prerequisite for the growth of third sector organizations in India.

- The development of network-based relations of support among civil society organizations is needed for sustained development of civil society movement in India. This networking must happen not only at the local level but also at the global level. No doubt, small-scale operations would enable third sector organizations to keep in closer contact with the stakeholders. But that would limit the capacity of an organization to reap the benefits arising from the scale of economies. This, in turn, might inhibit the capacity of an organization to undertake new ventures or to be proactive in executing its organizational strategies. The civil society organizations can reap the advantages of scale of economies arising in the form of better resources, knowledge sharing, additional resources for innovation and development, if they create a second and third level of complementary organizations. Through these strategies they can reap the advantages of scale of economies, without losing the benefits of small size of operation. But this becomes possible only if third sector organizations network properly at both the local and the global levels.
- The civil society organizations in India are required to establish a dependable governance structure. Such a structure must recognize that different stakeholders have varied interests and consequently they are required to preserve their locally embedded democratic structures. Some times local institutional environment might come in the way of establishment of adequate governance structures. It is necessary for these organizations to have a distinct identity as they are working to promote social welfare. They have to preserve their social identity embedded in positive externalities. The philosophical foundations of civil society, the nature of stakeholders and their socio-cultural antecedents impose serious limitations on the extent to which the civil society activists can emulate the leadership style and the management principles prevalent in traditional public and private sectors. Therefore, these activists are required to maintain a different management principle and leadership style emphasizing identification of the vision and mission of the organization and in ensuring an active participation of all concerned in achieving it. The overriding objective of the activists of civil society organizations in India, at this stage of evolution, is to establish legitimacy of these organizations both within and without.

REFERENCES

Amte, Baba, http://mss.niya.org/people/baba6_amte.php

Anheir, Helmut K. (2004), 'Civil Society—Measurement, Evaluation, Policy', CIVICUS, London: Earthscan.

Chandhoke, Neera (2003), 'A Critique of the Notion of Civil Society as the "Third Sphere"', in Rajesh Tandon and Ranjitha Mohanty (eds.), *Does Civil Society Matter? Governance in Contemporary India*, New Delhi: Sage.

Chowdhuri, Kunal Roy (1993), 'Gandhi's Theory of Sarvodaya Socialism', *Gandhi Marg*, vol. 12 (1).

Dadrawala, N.H. (1998), *Philanthropy*, September-October issue.

Deccan Herald, 6 November 2005.

Gandhi, M.K (1931), *Young India*, 12 November.

——— (1931), *Young India*, 24 November.

——— (1936), *Harijan*, 29 August.

Hansmann, H.B. (1980), 'The Role of Nonprofit Enterprise', *Yale Law Journal*, 89, pp. 835-98.

Nehru, Jawaharlal (1958), *An Autobiography*, London: The Bodley Head.

Polanyi, Karl (2002), 'The Great Transformation', in Nicole Wodsey Biggart (ed.), *Readings in Economic Sociology*, Oxford: Blackwell Publishers.

——— (1947), 'On Belief in Economic Determinism', *Sociological Review*, vol. XXXII, section one.

PRIA: Management of Voluntary Organizations, New Delhi.

Jensen, Robert (2004), 'Citizens of the Empire: The Struggle to Claim Our Humanity' (City Lights, 2004). www.nowar.collective.com

Sreedhara, T.N. and Rajarama Tolpady (2003), 'Towards an Understanding of Third Sector', Third Sector Research Resource Centre, University of Mysore, Mysore.

II. STATE AND LEGAL INTERVENTIONS

CHAPTER 6

Social Development, Conflict and Participatory Governance in North-East India

SUJATA DUTTA HAZARIKA

Theories of social movements are closely connected with the general problems of social development. The 'new social movements' approach (Habermas) treats social movements as both symptoms of, and solutions to, the contradictions inherent in the modern super-bureaucratic society. Social movements articulate the tension between the expanding spheres of human autonomy and growing regulation inherent in the logic of post-industrial development. This contradiction is reflected in new conflicts which, according to Habermas, 'no longer arise in the areas of material reproduction; they are no longer channeled through parties and organisations. . . . Rather, the new conflicts arise in areas of cultural reproduction, social integration and socialisation' (Habermas, 1981: 34). The main feature of social movements, according to 'new social movement' theorists is their anti-state, anti-apparatus turn of mind and action. New social movements, in contrast to old social movements, are produced by new contradictions of society, contradictions between individual and state.

The growing conflict situation in Assam has led to mobilization of various movements in order to address this contradiction between the individual and the state. This complexity while at a manifest level presents itself as a contradiction of cultural reproduction, social integration and socialization of neglect, at a more pragmatic and latent level it can be viewed as democratic response to the deficit of human development in the region. This paper aims to demystify the neglect theory of cultural reproduction and integration which has aggravated the contradictions between the individual and state and proposes decentralization of governance and local level participation in democratic institutions as the only viable means of establishing trust and peace in the region.

Good governance is necessary not only to bring about changes in allocation and alignment of powers and resources within government and the wider society, but also to address root causes of conflict and create an environment for sustainable peace building. In the north-east, decentralization can clearly become one of the significant keys for sustainable peace building given that that major responsibility for local development and community welfare now lies with local governments and autonomous councils. If handled well, decentralization can support peace building by encouraging transparent and accountable actions by key actors, building local participation in public decision-making processes, empowering communities and increasing their sense of security. It encourages social cohesion by strengthening both vertical and horizontal relationships. Making local administrations more efficient and effective enhances their credibility in the eyes of the community. But if handled badly and without proper accountability mechanisms, this reallocation of power and resources can reproduce power struggles leading to renewed violence and trauma. Reforms can reinforce unequal power structures, enable elite capture of resources and perpetrate differential treatment for different groups, particularly related to religion and ethnicity. While lack of transparency encourages rumour-mongering, lack of accountability quickly leads to perceptions of corruption and injustice.

All these risks are exacerbated when, as in the case of Assam, local governments are characterized by an inadequate policy framework for decentralization and post-conflict recovery, poor capacities for peace building and local development, lack of meaningful community participation and ineffective mobilization of resources.The purpose of this paper is to undertake a scoping exercise to provide recommendations on strategic options for strengthening local democratic governance and peace building in the conflict-affected regions in Assam.

This paper is indebted to the project 'Participation of Women in Local Self Governance in Assam' which was carried out in three districts of Assam namely, Sonitpur, Cachar and Nalbari. The districts were selected on the basis of dynamics ranging from economic backwardness to insurgency, from cross-cultural and linguistic homogeneity to patriarchal social relations. The project, which evaluated the efficacy and functioning of the Panchayati Raj Institutions in Assam especially after the 73rd/74th Amendment of the Constitution, had clearly identified Panchayati Raj Institutions in India as the most viable and effective means of grassroot participation in governance. This paper uses the same argument in the context of Assam, a state in north-east India marred by insurgency and conflict within its multi-ethnic myriad and proposes decentralization and effective implementation of PRI as the most visible means to ensure participatory governance, sustainable peace and human development in the region. This paper focuses on the linkages between governance, peace building and decentralization as the central theme, with a particular interest in the capacities of local institutions, players and systems to make these linkages. It proposes Peace Through Development (PTD) as a viable approach to be taken by local institutions, players and systems to make these linkages, and assesses the capacity and willingness of governance institutions to address conflict prevention and peace-building in Assam through improved governance, identifying the specific governance areas that could contribute to peace-building based on stated needs and priorities of civil society representatives.

BACKGROUND

INTRODUCTION

Almost all the states of north-east India have, at some time or the other, experienced political mobilization and organized violence against migrants (anti-outsider movements), leading to victimization and expulsion of communities of migrant origin. At times there have even been ethnic cleansing of the non-indigenous groups. This 'identity politics', which became the defining theme of post-colonial north-east Indian political agenda, laid exclusive claim to a land that had emerged as a shared homeland since the earliest times. The anti-outsider politics came sharply into focus by the 'son of the soil' agitation in Assam (the Assam Movement, 1979-85), which became a point of reference for many of the subsequent nativist movements in the rest of the north-eastern region. These tensions, overtly organized against illegal immigrants, also spilled over to affect some Indian citizens because the categories were never clearly defined and perhaps intentionally left hazy. The victims soon came to include tribals and descendants of migrants in the various states of north-east

India. What began as ethnic strife between 'indigenous' and 'foreign' groups turned into ethnic clashes between populations that had essentially become local to the area. There are three key grievances that led to the push for secession or movements for political autonomy in the north-east. First, a refusal to recognize the distinctive ethnic and cultural traditions of the region. Second, the exploitation of its resources without due compensation or development. Third, the dismantling of local land rights. As a consequence, in all seven states there is some type of militant movement; and unrest—and repression—is widespread. (See Tables 6.1 and 6.2 for details.)

TABLE 6.1: FATALITIES IN INSURGENCIES AND TERRORIST CONFLICTS IN INDIA'S NORTH-EAST, 1992-2001

		Assam	Manipur	Meghalaya	Mizoram	Nagaland	Tripura	Arunachal Pradesh	Total	
1992	C	80	84	0	0	34	59	0	257	492
	SF	34	30	0	0	33	18	0	115	
	M	19	51	0	0	29	21	0	120	
1993	C	74	266	0	0	62	148	1	551	913
	SF	24	91	0	0	43	28	2	188	
	M	33	66	0	0	68	7	0	174	
1994	C	173	189	4	0	110	206	3	685	1058
	SF	35	98	0	0	26	22	0	181	
	M	63	63	0	0	56	10	0	192	
1995	C	170	183	7	0	80	178	3	621	1071
	SF	73	64	0	0	25	34	0	196	
	M	27	74	0	0	108	45	0	254	
1996	C	302	117	3	0	144	140	4	710	1235
	SF	87	65	4	4	48	31	1	240	
	M	62	93	0	0	112	18	0	285	
1997	C	285	233	3	0	104	205	9	839	1680
	SF	85	111	0	0	38	50	1	285	
	M	167	151	1	0	218	19	0	556	
1998	C	531	87	5	0	26	214	2	865	1431
	SF	72	62	14	0	14	25	2	189	
	M	180	95	1	0	72	26	3	377	
1999	C	214	89	5	2	26	240	2	578	1216
	SF	77	64	17	5	4	41	0	208	
	M	212	78	0	0	118	22	0	430	

2000	C	366	93	12	4	13	453	7	907	1701
	SF	65	51	7	4	4	16	3	162	
	M	327	102	17	1	84	45	24	585	
2001	C	264	70	24	0	25	239	40	662	1380
	SF	59	25	8	0	2	31	12	137	
	M	283	161	8	0	76	42	11	581	
Total	C	2,459	1,411	63	6	624	2,082	72	6,717	12,181
	SF	611	661	50	16	237	297	21	1,892	
	M	1,373	934	27	1	941	255	41	3,572	
CT State-wise		4,443	3,006	140	23	1,802	2,633	134	12,181	

Note: CT: Cumulative Total (All Categories); M: Militants; SF: Security Force Personnel; C: Civilians.

TABLE 6.2: VIOLENCE AND VICTIMS IN ASSAM BY ETHNIC GROUPS

State	Year	Causes	No. of Displaced Persons	Ethnic Groups
Assam	1947	Partition/Riots	53,000	Muslims
	1961-7	Prevention of Infiltration from Pakistan (PIP) Scheme	1,92,097	Muslims
	1960	Asamiya Language Movement	Unknown	Hindu Bengalis
	1972	AASU (Asamiya Language Movement)	Unknown	Hindu Bengalis
	1980	Assam Movement (Lok Sabha Elections), Nellie Massacre	1,200-3,000	Na-Asamiya Muslims
	1984	Choulkhowa Chapori (Darrang), Silapathar (Lakhimpur), Gohpur (Darrang)	Unknown	Bengali Hindus, Ex-refugee/ displaced East Pakistan, ethnic Nepalis
	1991-3	Bodoland Movement	60,000	Bengalis
	1994 (July)	Massacres at Kokrajhar, Barpeta, Bongaigaon	1,000 persons (60 villages)	Na-Asamiya Muslim peasants
	1995 (Oct.)	Massacre at relief camp at Bansbari in Barpeta	70,000	Na-Asamiya Muslims, Hindu Bengalis, Santhals, Nepalis

1996 (May-June)	Ethnic Cleansing (Bodoland Movement)	2,50,000	Ethnic Santhals, Bodos, Nepalis
1998	Ethnic Cleansing (Bodoland Movement)	82,000	Santhals, Bengalis, Bodos, Nepalis

Source: Lopita Nath, *Migrants in Flight.*

A substantial proportion of the current proliferation of armed groups representing various tribal and ethnic identities in the north-east is the result of the demonstration effect of the 'success' of other such groups in the past. Such 'success' is not necessarily measured in terms of any political gains but, increasingly, in terms of the financial gains of widespread criminal operations that are undertaken by all militant groups in the north-east (as in other theatres of conflict in India). The collusive character of many of the terrorist movements in the region, in terms of their linkages with overground organizations, legitimate businesses, the state bureaucracy and the political leadership enormously reduces the actual risks of militant activity and also provides secondary incentives for the creation and operation of armed gangs.

According to Dr Ajay Sahni from the Institute for Conflict Management the internal conflicts in India's north-east are overwhelmingly conceptualized within the framework of unique ethnic identities that are threatened by, and in confrontation with, the nationalist state, which is often seen as a representative of an inchoate cultural 'mainstream'. While some of the conflicts in the region certainly fit into this general framework of interpretation, very few, if any, are completely explained by it. Others, moreover, are entirely unrelated to this reductionist scheme of 'freedom struggles' by ethnic minorities against the 'homogenizing state'. Indeed, even where militant groups direct their rhetoric and their violence against the symbols of the state, the underlying motives and ideologies are more correctly interpreted in terms of conflicting tribal identities and histories of internecine warfare based entirely on tribal, sub-tribal, or tribal-outsider rivalries and corresponding competition over limited resources, especially land. It is, consequently, appropriate to analyse and assess conflicts in the north-east in terms of three basic 'fault lines': tribal groups *vs.* the state, tribal *vs.* tribal (internecine), tribal *vs.* non-tribal.

HUMAN DEVELOPMENT

The basic purpose of development is to enlarge people's choices. In principle, these choices can be infinite and can change over time. People often value achievements that do not show up at all, or not immediately, in income or growth figures: greater access to knowledge, better nutrition and health services, more secure livelihoods, security against crime and physical violence, satisfying leisure hours, political and cultural freedoms and sense of participation in community activities. The objective of development is to create an enabling environment for people to enjoy long, healthy and creative lives.

Mahbub ul Haq, Founder, Human Development Report

In Assam the key obstacles to human development, poverty reduction and achieving the Millennium Development Goals (MDGs) (details of MDG are available at http://www.undp.org/mdg/.) are the general ambience of dissent among the contending ethnicities and the resulting voices of autonomy and secession through insurgency, counter-insurgency and ethnic conflict. The most basic conditions for human development in order for choices to be available and opportunities in life to be accessible is a peaceful environment where one can lead a long and healthy life, choose to be knowledgeable, have access to the resources needed for a decent standard of living and be able to participate in the life of the community.

According to India's National Human Development Report 2001 (NHDR), which is the latest in a series of publications linked to, but independent of the annual global Human Development Report issued by the United Nations Development Program (UNDP), (While India's NHDR derives its conceptual moorings and methodology from the UNDP's Human Development Reports, it incorporates ideas from elsewhere, including the Reports on Human Development in South Asia published by the Human Development Centre, Islamabad) the relative rankings of the states on the Human Poverty Index stayed unchanged over the 1980s and 1990s, with HPI in Bihar, Arunachal Pradesh, Assam and Uttar Pradesh ranging between 55-60 per cent while the better-off states like Kerala, Punjab and Himachal Pradesh had a HPI of 32-5 per cent. Most of conflict-affected districts in Assam had poverty rates double and GDP growth less than the national average, according to the same report.

The NHDR authors note that there is no direct relationship between the economic attainments of a society and the quality of life of an individual, and an even less direct connection between economic development and social development, or the distribution of benefits between various regions of the country and different social groups. But in the case of Assam the overall presence of violence presupposes a fallen standard of HDI even if we choose to emphasize on a paradigm shift—that material attainments or means of development need to be substituted by a concern for 'outcomes that are either desirable in themselves or desirable because of their role in supporting better opportunities for people'.

This paper emphasizes the NHDR report and reiterates the governance approach to human development, adopting the UNDP's concept of governance. Further, it views governance as a continuous interplay between (a) institutions, (b) the delivery mechanism and (c) the supportive and subordinate framework of rules, procedures and legislation. This conception of governance, sanitized of political content, instead of offering a framework for governance in any holistic sense, merely suggests small structural and procedural changes at the national level. It proposes an alternative model of governance in which the institutions of decentralized governance—Panchayats (statutory, democratically-elected, self-governing local authorities in rural areas) and civil society actors—are seen to have a central role. However, no correlation is made between decentralization and its impact on human development.

DEMOCRATIC INSTITUTIONS *VIS-À-VIS* TRADITIONAL GOVERNANCE

North-east India consists of seven states of the Indian Union, viz., Assam, Arunachal Pradesh, Manipur, Meghalaya, Mizoram, Nagaland and Tripura, covering 8 per cent of the total geographical area and 3.78 per cent of the total population of the country. A large part of the north-east is governed by the Fifth and Sixth Schedules of the Constitution of India. The Panchayats (Extension to the Schedule Areas) Act, 1996 extends the 73rd Amendment to the Fifth Schedule areas. Three states, viz., Mizoram, Nagaland and Meghalaya, which are covered by the Sixth Schedule, are exempted from the purview of the 73rd Amendment. The Sixth Schedule envisages the establishment of autonomous district councils. These councils have been given legislative, administrative and judicial powers. No law of the centre or the state in respect of the legislative powers conferred on the Autonomous District Councils could be extended to those areas without the councils' prior approval. The councils are responsible for looking after the social, economic and minor criminal and civil matters of the tribal people. More specifically these councils are empowered to make laws with respect to: (a) land; (b) forest; (c) water course; (d) shifting cultivation; (e) establishment of village and town and its administration; (f) appointment of, or succession to chiefs or headmen; (g) inheritance of property; (e) marriage and divorce and matters relating to any other social customs. The district councils are also empowered to constitute village councils and also village courts. While the Autonomous District Councils have the advantage of legislative powers the PRIs are exempted from it. Moreover the Autonomous District Councils do not make provisions for reservation for women and backward classes. Thus in north-east India we find two simultaneous democratic institutions at work, a modern democratic system *vis-à-vis* a traditional system among the hill tribes. The traditional system has never recognized the rights of women as primary decision makers in matters of community concerns like inter-ethnic conflicts, crisis management, and social sanctions. Of Assam's 23 districts only 2 (N.C. Hills and Karbi Anglong), fall under the Sixth Schedule Areas; the other 21 districts fall under the modern democratic institution of Panchayati raj.

The call for autonomy and the formation of autonomous councils was shaped by the Indian example of granting territorial autonomy to resurgent minority peoples in north-east India. However, autonomy does not seem to be a feasible solution to end ethnic conflicts when the claimed territory is shared with other ethnic groups and in-migration leads to numerical minoritization and the areas dominated are not contiguous, as in the case with Bodos. The mismatch between demographic reality and the vision of territorial autonomy is the main reason for the relative intractability of the Bodo conflict. The territorial area of Bodo Autonomous Council (BAC) and Bodo Territorial Council (BTC) has less than 50 per cent of tribal population, which also includes other tribals such as Rabhas, Mechas, Miris, Hojais, Deoris, Saraniyas. There are also non-tribals such as Koch Rajbanshis, Scheduled Castes, Caste Hindus, and Muslims (original and immigrants), Santhals, Mundas, Nepalis, Biharis, Marwaris who form a substantial portion of the population. The Census of India 1991 showed that this area had an approximate tribal population of 34.41 per cent which had been reduced to below 30.5 per cent in 2001. It has about 2,494 villages of which 300 villages are completely tribal, 821 are tribal dominated villages (more than 50 per cent tribal population), leaving 1,313 villages where tribal population is less than 50 per cent (Nunthara, 2006). Barpujari (1998) wrote

> It is in vain to expect that the grant in autonomy will keep the unity and intergrity of the state. What is the guarantee that the Karbi's and the Bodo's (Even accorded full autonomy) will not clamour for full-fledged statehood? How can the Union and state government resist legitimate and forceful claims of Koch Rajbanshis and Tai ahoms . . . will the tea tribes and Muslim immigrants remain silent spectators for long?

Keeping the different ramifications of autonomous councils in mind, it has been suggested that the political aspirations of the homogeneous tribal groups could be appropriated by amendments to the Sixth Schedule and the 73rd Amendment provisions for devolution of power at the local level and bringing the entire issue of local governance within the ambit of Panchayati Raj Institutions.

PANCHAYATI RAJ AND ASSAM

This section begins with the details of the Panchayat system and its operations in order to get a perspective of good governance that can successfully address issues of human develoment and sustainable peace in Assam. Tenth Schedule of the Indian Constitution defines the functional items for which states may devolve responsibility to the Panchayats. While states vary in the extent to which they devolve policy powers to Gram Panchayats, most Gram Panchayats have responsibilities of civic administration in the village together with limited independent taxation powers. On an average roughly 10 per cent of a GP's revenue comes from its own revenues, the remainder consisting of transfers from higher levels of government. While the ambit of GP's policy influence varies across Indian states, they perform two distinct policy tasks. The first is beneficiary selection for central and state welfare schemes. These are low spillover public goods because the benefits are likely to accrue to individual households. These include a variety of transfer programmes such as schemes that provide beneficiary households with funds to acquire housing, water supply and private electricity. Eligibility for these schemes is usually limited to households below the official poverty line, with a minimum fraction of beneficiaries to be SC/STs. Thus an important part of the panchayat's job is also to identify households which are 'below the poverty line' (BPL households). Possession of a BPL card makes the household eligible for an array of government schemes ranging from subsidized food through the public distribution system to free hospitalization. The GP in collaboration with the state government officials is supposed to identify via a census households with income below the poverty line and prepare the list of BPL households. This list and subsequent selection of beneficiary households under different schemes (from among BPL households) are supposed to be ratified in Gram Sabha meetings. Since all BPL households are eligible for a BPL card, the procedure makes the allocation of BPL cards highly political where the success or failure in targeting needy households is a key issue.

The second area of GP policy activism is the construction and maintanence of village public goods such as streetlights, roads and drains. These are 'high spillover public goods' since the benefits accrue more broadly across members of the village. The GP decides the distribution of these public goods and the quality of provision both within the village and across villages within a GP.

Two important institutional features of the GP which are specific to decentralization in India are political reservation and village meetings (Gram Sabhas). The 73rd /74th Constitutional Amendments mandated political reservation in favour of SC/ST and women, and required that the extent of such reservation in a state reflect the SC/ST population share in that state. It also required that no GP reserve for the same group for two consecutive election. The most viable methodology for conflict resolution embedded in the panchayat system is that of the panchayat legislation requiring the *Pradhan* or elected panchayat leader to consult with villagers and ward members before deciding the choice of beneficiaries and allocation of public goods. These are done via village meetings (Gram Sabha) called by elected local government to discuss resource allocation in the village.

The other most vital area for grassroot-level intervention for peacebuilding in Assam can be the Gram Sabha which is the lynchpin of the Panchayat system. Citizen participation at the village level can improve workings of democracy primarily by improving the flow of information into the political process beyond that available through electing representatives.

In the case of Assam, PRI not only has the potential to improve information flows and structure democratic institutions to ensure fair and efficient allocation of funds but also to facilitate arbitration between conflicting parties in the presence of a governing body whose membership is determined by a legitimate, universal and constitutional mandate that cuts across ethnicity and community. According to a study by Besley, Rohini Pande and Rao on 500 villages in the four south Indian states of Andhra Pradesh, Karnataka, Kerala and Tamil Nadu, the main ways in which Gram Sabhas can improve the workings of the government is firstly relative to elected representatives. These meetings can better reflect citizens' preferences on issues such as how to target resources to the most needy groups. Moreover by providing a forum for monitoring the actions of elected representatives they may reduce agency problems in politics and the extent of corruption.

According to an article by Gulshan Sachdeva titled 'Demystifying Northeast' (*Dialogue*, vol. 7, no. 3, January-March 2006), besides certain areas of may be political or psychological neglect the facts about devolution and transfer of resources from the centre to the north-east reveal an entirely different story. Between 1990-1 and 2002-3, the region received about Rs. 1,08,504 crore. Assam received about Rs. 43,000 crore from the centre, Arunachal and Manipur received about Rs. 9,900 and Rs. 11,500 crore, respectively. Meghalaya received about Rs. 9,000 crore and Tripura's share was about Rs. 14,000 crore. Similarly, the figures for the same period for Nagaland and Mizoram were about Rs. 12,000 and Rs. 9,000 crore, respectively. These are gross figures. A portion of that money is also given back to the central government as repayment on loans and interest payments. Still, the cumulative net devolution from the centre to the north-east for the period between 1990-1 and 2002-3 is about Rs. 92,000 crore. Only grant portion to the region during these 13 years has about Rs. 65,000 crore. So the lack of development could not be because of shortage of funds (see Table 6.3 for delaits). In fact, as economist and Congress leader Jairam Ramesh has argued, this kind of public expenditure has become very much part of the problem of the north-east.

If lack of devolution of funds for development and infrastructural growth through effective democratic structures is seen as one of the primary sources of conflict in this region, it can be easily argued that PRI has all the institutional safeguards, at least theoretically, to deal with effective fund allocation and distribution of resources ensuring universality and legitimacy. Permeation of central fundings into the

TABLE 6.3: DEVOLUTION AND TRANSFER OF RESOURCES FROM THE CENTRE TO NER (1990-1 TO 2002-3)

	1990-1	1991-2	1992-3	1993-4	1994-5	1995-6	1996-7	1997-8	1998-9	1999-2000	2000-1	2001-2	2002-3	1990-2003
Arunachal Pradesh														
Gross Devolution	351	415.5	472.3	485.2	553.5	702.9	780.5	822.1	907	954.3	1,049	1,246.9	1,172.6	9,912.85
Net Devolution	329.2	385.8	452.9	459.8	543.8	675.9	748.1	782.9	859.4	899.4	985.48	1,173.5	1,095.6	9,391.83
Assam														
Gross Devolution	1,955.9	1,873.13	1,874.2	2,756.5	2,512.1	3,002.8	3,211.5	3,734	3,522.4	4,261.6	4,047.2	4,781.2	5,541.5	43,073.8
Net Devolution	1,399.4	1,256.8	1,236.8	2,046.8	1,730.5	2,298.5	2,416.4	2,789.3	2,910	3,076.4	3,207.1	3,679.6	4,383.8	32,431.32
Manipur														
Gross Devolution	413.8	430.8	494.3	604.5	541.2	641.9	768	919.5	981	1,080.1	1,198.3	1,753.2	1,648.7	11,475.32
Net Devolution	388.6	393	418.7	513.6	575.7	613.4	714.3	804.8	849.6	1,012	1,063	1,342.1	1,274.8	9,964.59
Meghalaya														
Gross Devolution	326.1	359.3	388.4	529.3	472.9	571.6	634.15	632.8	741.8	807.6	971.2	1,177.6	1,281.1	8,893.79
Net Devolution	307.2	330.5	363.8	423.6	441.3	537.1	595.99	590.6	694.5	752.9	911.17	1,109	1,210.2	8,267.75

(*Contd.*)

TABLE 6.3 (*Contd.*)

	1990-1	1991-2	1992-3	1993-4	1994-5	1995-6	1996-7	1997-8	1998-9	1999-2000	2000-1	2001-2	2002-3	1990-2003
Mizoram														
Gross Devolution	355.3	380.3	400.2	487.3	519.1	607	644.3	700.8	726.5	951.4	1,084.5	1,096.4	1,003.5	8,956.62
Net Devolution	191.1	366.7	384	471.2	500.3	588.3	621.4	673	694.5	913.5	1,046.7	1,051.9	951.13	8,453.85
Nagaland														
Gross Devolution	446.07	509.88	659.09	712.5	596.44	754.9	835.33	955	1170.5	1,245.7	1,394	1,569.9	1,598.6	12,447.78
Net Devolution	402.06	438.8	444.1	585.8	560.9	725.86	796.6	912.2	940.2	1,140.7	1,331	1,402.9	1,502.7	11,183.83
Tripura														
Gross Devolution	519.5	551.8	592.8	614.3	709.6	883.8	987.8	1,065.4	1,260.4	1,419.3	1,499.5	1,748.2	1,892	13,744.32
Net Devolution	477.98	506.2	540.6	563.2	656.1	833.9	932.7	1,001.1	1,183.3	1,325	1,392.1	1,627.4	1,756.7	12,796.27
NER total														
Gross Devolution	4,367.7	4,520.7	4,881.3	6,189.6	5,904.8	7,164.9	7,861.6	8,829.6	9,309.6	10,720	11,244	13,373	14,138	1,08,504.5
Net Devolution	3,495.5	3,677.8	3,840.9	5,064	5,008.6	6,272.9	6,825.5	7,553.9	8,131.5	9,119.9	9,936.5	11,386	12,175	92,489.44

Source: Author's calculations based on Reserve Bank of India and CMIE data.

grassroots can be effectively ensured by structures in the PRI, through both distributive justice and equitable distribution of resources. If well intended, decentralization of governance through democratic institutions like PRIs can ensure constitutional homogeneity and equality within the multi-ethnic myriad of tribal and non-tribal identities in Assam. Considering this fact we have to now protect and nurture this institution by cleansing it of the discrepancies that plague the system. Both policy tasks undertaken by the Panchayat through reservation of socially deprived categories like SC/ST and women are effective means of ensuring distributive justice that can permeate the grassroot at large without triggering sensitive sentiments of ethnicity and identity.

The feature of constitutional universality in democratic governance provides Panchayat institutions a powerful weapon to mediate in sectoral crisis. Although knowing that the scars of identity formation experienced by Assam have larger political issues that need to be resolved like state border concerns, land ownership and immigration, but as the first step to intervene in the present conflict situation would be to strengthen local governance through Panchayat. It is a viable means for the Indian state to establish its credibility and regain the trust of the common people. The 2001 panchayat election in Assam implemented 73rd/74th Amendment for the first time in Assam and saw increased participation but unfortunately functionally at least most categories seem to be mere filling up of numbers of the reserved seats. The study highlights the fact that the elected members (both men and women in the areas where the study was conducted) has had very little or no knowledge whatsoever of either 73rd Amendment or 33 per cent reservation as a mandatory inclusion in the Panchayati Raj Act. This is a result of the ignorance at every level about the Panchayat Act, and the resulting duties and functions of the institution as a whole.

TOWARDS GOOD GOVERNANCE: PERSPECTIVES OF PANCHAYAT IN ASSAM

Ensuring peace and human development is, in a larger perspective, dependent on each other and a synthesis of both is an essential prerequisite for economic growth. At the same time unless we try to ensure a sustainable and durable economic growth both peace and human development will elude us. Based on the study conducted we have ascertained the primary impediments to the realization of the full potentials of the Panchayat system in Assam. These include as bureaucratic red-tapism, fund transfer through Directorate of Rural Development, Assam (DRDA), which is extremely cumbersome and time consumimg, lack of tranparency in fund transfer and percolation of incentives to BPL households, benefits of schemes most often do not filter down to those who actually need them but get diverted to those with connections, highhandedness and condescending attitude of Block Development Officers (BDO) in their dealings with women members, and party affiliation of candidates which today is an important criteria, so much so that powerful parties sideline deserving candidates who are either independent or belong to other parties. Besides these factors, indifference of mainstream politics towards the marginalized section not only impedes political participation of women but more generally of the whole community.

Major government policies for overall development and capacity building of common people at the grassroots, like micro credit, literacy, infrastructural development, reproductive health care, and so on have more or less suffered due to lack of sensitization of these development programmes. In this context it is worth mentioning that though women put in equal and more often extra hours of work there exists gross disparities in remunerations. In case of tea gardens, women, in spite of the provision for equal wage for equal work, were discriminated in work allocation. Heavier and thus more paying work were not given to women, on the pretext of her physical limitations. In plucking too the permitted weight of the tea leaf to be plucked by women was less than that allowed to men, inspite of the fact that women are considered quality pluckers than men. The discriminations were carried out more commonly at the latent rather than the manifest level.

The paper strongly recommends effective implementation of the 73rd Amendment to increase women's participation in the local governance, with the objective of autonomous participation rather than numerical participation. This alone can change governance at the local level because women bring their experience of governance of civic society into governance of the state. In this way, they make the state sensitive to issues of poverty, inequality and gender injustice. Every issue of governance taken up by women is ideally influenced by two sources of self-perception. First, their own sense of shared experience and second, from attitudes and imagery imposed on them by men. It appears that gender can supersede class and party lines. Women can open up the possibility for politics to have not only new faces but a new quality.

However, increasing the representation of women alone may not automatically lead to a more gendered analysis of the issues confronting local government. Nor will it necessarily raise the profile of women's needs and interests in the policy agenda, given that elected women often act as proxies for men's views at the councils, being advised by their male relatives. In spite of this there is always the possibility that a small minority of women who are in politics because of their own leadership qualities or feminist consciousness may exhibit different priorities and values someday.

Some of the ways in which women, through PRI, can change governance are evident in the issues they would choose to tackle (as was evident in the course of our work), e.g. water, alcohol abuse, education, health and domestic violence. Women also express different values. They value proximity, whether it be to a drinking water source, a fuel source, a creche, a health centre, a court of justice or an office of administration. The enormous expansion of women's representation in decentralized government structures most of the time highlights the advantages of proximity, namely the redress of grievance and (most important of all) the ability to mobilize struggle at the local level where it is most meaningful. Thus women can help to radicalize local government towards the building of a peaceful society. But this can only happen if steps are taken to ensure that basic awareness is generated to improve the quality of life of women in particular by eradicating poverty, illiteracy, entrenched socio-cultural values and patriarchal ideologies through sensitization and capacity building. PRI and its democratic spirit will always be out of common people's grasp unless civil society ensures equal access to resources irrespective of sex. This will only be possible when there are other such accompanying constitutional rights to ensure this. On the other hand, these measures cannot be effectively achieved without proper functioning of the local self-government. We are thus faced with a situation where the number game in the politics of democracy is not subsumed to the democratic spirit of the panchayat system. Democratic autonomy of women is only possible by developing social capital and human resource at the same time. Proxy representation many a times has proved that reservation is not an end in itself but a means to an end which is to ensure participation of women. Women who need to be brought forward are not those who are puppets and mouthpieces of powerful and unscrupulous male influences but those who are themselves capable of making a difference to the lives of other women like them. The tussle between muscle and money power also makes it difficult for honest and dedicated leaders and participants, both male and female, to come forward to ensure effective functioning of the Panchayat system.

Thus the obstacles to the realization of PRI's transformative potential are many, especially for Assam given its political instability, identity movements and a multi-ethnic paradigm susceptible to ideologies of dissent and conflict. There continues to be a resistance to the real devolution of power and funds from centres of (male) power to the periphery. Women as we have seen still face considerable handicaps to their involvement in politics; for example, inadequate education, the burden of reproductive and productive roles, a lack of self-confidence and the opposition of entrenched cultural and religious views. Urvashi Butalia in her article 'Confrontation and Negotiation: Women's Movement Response to Violence Against Women' [Karin Kapadia (ed.), *The Violence of Development: Politics of Identity, Gender and Social Inequalities in India*, Delhi: Kali for Women, 2002], articulated the understanding of violence by women's group as:

> We started with the basic insight that violence is inherent in all social structures of society like class, caste, religion, ethnicity, etc., and in the way that state controls people. However within all those general structures of violence, women suffer violence in a gender specific way and Patriarchal violence permeates and promotes other forms of violence.

Given that women have always been the first victims of a violent society, a transformative feminist politics in India is only possible when politics directly and frontally engages in caste discrimination, communalism, class-based inequalities and state repression, which are the basic structures that create a subordinated and tyrannized identity for women. In Assam the transformative potential of the 73rd Amendment for feminist politics has to be fully exploited in order for women to evolve as the most important actor in peacemaking. Prof. Sajal Nag in his article 'His Master's Voice: Women, Peacemaking and Genderization of Politics' writes:

> In an otherwise doomed situation in India, women in North East India have played a very important role as peacemakers . . . not just between families,

clans, and tribes but underground insurgents called national workers and Government of India as a unique and unparalleled instance in entire South Asia.

Experiences of Naga Mothers Association (the only group in South Asia to have participated in a ceasefire negotiation), the Mothers Union Tura (Meghalaya), Meira Peibes of Manipur, Naga Women's Union of Manipur and Mizo Women's Federation are indicative of the evolving of feminization of the civic space beyond ethnic identity and imposed subjectivity for women in societies marked by extreme militarism and insurgency. The peace building activities of Naga women's groups have produced a social consciousness in Naga society that upholds womanhood, human values and rights, recognizng peace as the prerequisite for any human development. It validates women as making a difference, especially in reaching out to bitterly divided Naga armed factions and fostering reconciliation and healing. It has persuaded the top leaders of the armed groups to recognize women as significant resource for peacebuilding and legitimized their identity as stake holders in a plural peace process. According to Prof. Anuradha Dutta the Bodo women, in spite of being victims of violence once, are working for sustainable peace today.

These women in particular were strong supporters of the movement for identity in the Bodoland areas organised by the students under the leadership of Upendra Brahma. The Bodo women organized under the banner of the All Assam Tribal Women's Welfare Federation (AATWWF) joined the movement for the adoption of the Roman Script way back in 1974. Later when the Bodo movement established a military wing to conduct an armed struggle it trained the womenfolk in arms and from 1989 onwards, some women did join the arms wing. The AATWWF was not in favour of this decision. And in 1993 the AATWWF changed its nomenclature to All Bodo Women's Welfare Federation (ABWWF). Since ABSU could not reach the nooks and corners of the Bodoland, they took the help of women group to mobilise people in support of the movement. These women's organization explained the programme of the ABSU to the people from time to time, convincing people about their demands and taught people to remain alert about army and police raids. They approached people to help the ABSU with food and shelter. Thus this group of women activists had unique characteristics. They as victims also protested against frequent police and army raids in the villages and arrest of innocent people. The Bodo women group has had a very good networking in every nook and corner of the different Bodo dominated areas.

The Bodo women despite being so active in the Bodo movement have not been a part of the formal peace process. Post-reconciliation also, the ABWWF has failed in finding for itself a political space. In the election to the BTC, the Bodoland People's Progressive Front (BPPF) which was formed in April 2005 was divided in May. One faction comprised the BLT leaders and surrendered cadres, while the All Bodo Students' Union (ABSU) which took the lead in the formation of the BPPF comprised the other faction. In Kokrajhar, several leaders of the disbanded militant outfit filed nominations against the BPPF president Rabiram Narzary. The BTC chief Hangrama Mahillary supported former comrade Manoj Kumar Brahma. Though initially the ABWWF, a key player in Bodo politics, lent its support to the new party BPPF, it withdrew from the party as not a single woman candidate was nominated. The influential women's body extended support to the former BLT leader instead, who stood as a rebel candidate against the official BPPF candidates.

If we see the lack of effective political leadership of women in the Bodo movement as a crisis of participation and motivation we will overlook the latent structure and the fruitless effort in fighting an institutional governance where women's political potentials have never been recognized traditionally. Being ethnically bound these women have never been exposed to the constitutional universality of democratic governance of decentralization as in the Panchayati Raj Institutions. The true potential of womens's political participation can be explored when fearless and sensitized women like them are provided with specific kinds of institutional support which go beyond technical training. They need support to build solidarity amongst women, through strengthening links between women's organizations and elected bodies. They need information about innovative organizations which enhance women's lives such as health providers and credit institutions. It is also necessary to strengthen women's sense of common identity by articulating the elements of a feminist consciousness and presenting it as the special quality of women's leadership. There has been insufficient elaboration of what that leadership has to offer which distinguishes it from men's leadership and which commends it as something special. Such an elaboration through feminist discourse and action is essential for this revolution to deliver the promise it holds for peace making.

On the basis of our work we have chalked out possible areas of intervention where self-help groups, NGOs, and government institutions could intervene to generate political awareness of citizenship rights and the democratic electoral process of the Panchayati Raj system:

1. Any plan of intervention should highlight the following seven categories:
   A. Gaon Sabha mobilization through street plays and theatre
   B. Communication workshops
   C. Media workshops
   D. Block elected women's representative forums (BEWRF)
   E. Leadership workshops for women
   F. Public opinion building and awareness generation on PRI
   G. Participation in national-level alliances and Networking
2. Training on the Panchayati Raj system, its functions and modules of activity have to be organized for everyone—general public and elected members. Issues that need to be sensitized are:
   A. Complete right over the subjects mentioned in the Eleventh Schedule
   B. Compulsory elections
   C. Immediate transfer of power
   D. Quorum in Gaon Sabha meeting should not be substituted with quorum of Panchayat meetings
3. Accessibility of information networks on health service providers and credit institutions.
4. Strengthening links between women's groups and elected bodies through effective networking, in order to smoothly facilitate lobbying to accrue to panchayats.
5. Capacity building of women through awareness and sensitization of vital issues without depending solely on reservation.
6. Formation of SHG groups, which aim at savings and thrift, to collectively raise economic concerns before the Panchayat effectively.
7. Most important is infrastructural development, like ensuring basic facilities of health, sanitation, education for women and other weaker sections that cut across ethnicity, tribe, caste and religion, in order to boost confidence and morale. In case of women infrastructural support can combat the burden of entrenched cultural and socio-religious values which has for generations subjected them to a dual structure of exploitation, in the domestic domain and as part of a wider male-centric value system.

8. Forming women's organizations or other such groups as supervisory bodies for
   - ensuring that the women are not marginalized in the revenue and expenditure committee structures that will emerge to manage the development in these bodies;
   - ensuring the devolution of project design and monitoring powers from central government to the elected bodies, so that the people can develop their own policies, reflecting the views of their own representatives rather than those of the central government, and be held accountable for them;
   - strengthening the identity and feminist consciousness of women representatives, for example, by leadership training;
   - building global coalitions through the activist as distinct from the academic mode. This includes bringing women into political structures and supporting the backward and forward linkages of women's presence in politics, linking household and family priorities with macro-planning processes;
   - pressing for South Asian regional economic cooperation amongst women to be based on regional support to empowering women's role in local and national governance;
   - campaigns and training programmes to prepare women both as electors and elected; and
   - urging multi- and bi-lateral agencies to revise their own patriarchal structures.

PROPOSED STRATEGIC FRAMEWORK: PEACE THROUGH HUMAN DEVELOPMENT

PRIs and decentralization of rural governance in Assam can be seen as the most viable means for sustainable peace in Assam, provided we can use it to build a strategic framework for peace through development (PTD) which encourages conflict sensitivity in development. The paper highlights the undeniable fact that with better access to the knowledge of the Panchayat Act, its rights and duties, training and capacity building of men and women alike, the institution alone can facilitate rural upliftment and bring the marginalized rural society closer to mainstream development. In the specific context of Assam economic deprivation and a grueling human development crisis manifest in cultural alienation, persecution complex and an identity crisis, leading to conflict.

It is proposed that the strategic framework provided by the PTD approach be channellized through the participatory governance embedded in PRI focusing on the building of partnerships on long-term development, governance and peace building among government actors, local civil society groups and the public. The key strategic approaches recommended for incorporation in the design of PTD as a programme in rural Assam are:

(a) *Government leadership:* Government ownership is vital for the success of the programme. The programme strategy is based on strengthening existing government mechanisms and the application of existing regulations.
(b) *Area-based approach:* Within the context of decentralization in Assam, PTD can be an area-based programme focused on the districts. An area-based approach allows capacity building and the experience of hands-on delivery to be combined within an existing institutional framework targeted at areas with significant conflict risk. PTD can initially work in selected core districts in which it will provide comprehensive support. The selection of districts can be based on selected criteria and will be approved by a national committee. The provincial level will be supported in its mandated role of managing cross-district initiatives, oversight of district PTD performance and establishing and monitoring minimum service standards.
(c) *Multi-stakeholder processes and collective benefits:* Effective multi-stakeholder processes are of great importance in rebuilding trust and confidence in conflict and post-conflict contexts. PTD can achieve this through effective programme mechanisms, management arrangements and assistance aimed at strengthening processes and the skills of those involved. The effectiveness and performance of multi-stakeholder processes will be monitored and reviewed by those involved. PTD will link multi-stakeholder processes with the delivery of collective benefits for the community that can strengthen social cohesion.
(d) *Building capacities for peace and development:* The emphasis of the programme will be on capacities for building long-term peace and development. Capacity building should be demand driven with careful identification of needs and formulation of capacity building responses. Capacity has been defined as 'the ability of an individual, organization or a system to perform

functions and meet objectives effectively and efficiently'. Capacity-building therefore concerns support to achieve performance and produce outcomes focusing on three interrelated levels:

(a) the systems level, which sets the policy, legal and regulatory framework that includes management and accountability systems, resource allocation and broad system-level processes such as planning and evaluation;
(b) the organization (unit) level including its core business and strategy; culture, organizational structures and competencies; internal management processes and procedures; its human, financial and information resources; and its infrastructure;
(c) the individual level including general and specific skills such as initiative, judgement, values, professional competencies, motivations and work attitudes. Capacity building to support decentralization highlights the need to build the capacity of a variety of stakeholders including government, non-government organizations and local communities. It includes four key stages: (i) comprehensive identification and formulation of capacity building needs within the context of regional autonomy, (ii) formulating priorities for capacity building initiatives, (iii) determining comprehensive plans for capacity building and (iv) allocation of technical and financial resources for capacity building plans including donor and government sources.The programme can focus on developing sustainable mechanisms for capacity development through the local and national institutions responsible for supervision and capacity building support.

The essential capacities for long-term peace have been identified through the PDA as those relating to governance and social cohesion. Social cohesion refers to the cross-cutting social and economic relations within society, including trusts, intergroup associations, networks of communication and cultural patterns of interaction which that bond a society together, promote harmony, a sense of community, and a degree of commitment to promoting the common good. The concept of social cohesion emphasizes the importance of horizontal equity between groups and places with the responsibility for minimizing disparities, avoiding polarization and facilitating balanced development.

(a) *Capacities for local governance:* PTD will support the executive and legislative arms of local governments (Panchayats), civil society and the community through enhanced public awareness and participatory planning mechanisms to strengthen the capacities for local democratic governance to promote peace and human development. Although the rule of law and the role of the judicial arms of government are essential, there are limitations to the extent that work can be done within the context of PTD as a decentralized programme. For example, AFSPA in Assam.

(b) *Capacities for social cohesion:* Social segregation and prejudice need to be overcome in the promotion of peaceful and equitable development. PTD will strengthen the capacities of government and civil society to promote social integration and harmony. The PDA when implemented in conflict-torn countries like Indonesia has shown that opportunities for strengthening inter-community networks and relations exist and are a priority in these provinces. PTD will focus its support to organizations and networks that promote social cohesion through meeting priority development needs across community divisions. In particular there is scope to address the issues of currently or previously displaced people which, in some areas, is the main barrier to sustainable peace. In all cases there is a need to analyse the issues at the local level, link them to the broader environment and create conditions within which local solutions can be found or advocacy activities supported to resolution at a higher level.

In India for local government to be both representative and accountable, both in form and practice, the PTD approach through PRI needs to be sensitive to the fact that governments generally create institutions that are upwardly accountable to the central state. For reaping the theoretical benefits of community participation, however, accountability needs also to be downward towards the local population. Elected local representatives are not always downwardly accountable. If candidates can only be chosen by political parties, they may be more accountable to the parties than to the local populations that elect them (Hesseling, n.d.: 17; Ribot, 1999).

Further, even when independent candidates are admitted to local elections, there are many ways in which local elite or political parties are able to capture the electoral process, bringing the local accountability of leaders into question. Nonetheless, elected representatives are one important building block in the construction of accountable local government. Crook and Manor (Parker, 1995: 27) indicate that locally elected representatives can make the central government more responsive to local needs. In order for PRI to effectively facilitate PTD it will require power, downward accountability, and durable institutional forms.

It is thus proposed, as Hadi does in his study of Indonesia, that we accommodate a possible shift from Integrated Rural Development (IRD) to Integral Local Development (ILD) through representation, entrustment and accountability which is possible by moving away from forms of PTD orchestrated from the outside or 'above' (joint management, stakeholder approaches, participatory rural appraisal, etc. (World Bank, 1996; Chambers, 1983) to forms that are built into local government. PTD can merge with decentralization and democratization to become one—participation through rural democracy. ILD, rural or otherwise, is an appropriate and timely approach that is based on allowing rural communities to integrate across community differences through decisions made by locally accountable local authorities—representative bodies who are downwardly accountable to the local population. It is integral rather than integrated since it depends on authority that is integral to the community, rather than being the product of outside agency, integrated before delivery. It is also integral because in this model of rural development, ecology and environment are not separate from other matters of local government; rather they are part of a more organic or integral whole. That whole is the realm of decision making under the jurisdiction of locally accountable authorities. It is integral since all sources of community revenues (taxes, stamp fees, central government grants, loans, financial development assistance) are pooled and are allocated not according to their origins, but according to the needs and aspirations of the community as expressed through locally accountable representative government. ILD is the creation of a domain of local autonomy in which local representatives can act on the integrity of local resources and local needs and desires. IRD is based on providing an array of interventions at multiple levels supporting the productivity of the farm household and the development of agrarian economies and thus the approach became cumbersome quite quickly, leading to large, costly, top-down projects, given the name 'Christmas tree projects' since there were always more components that could be hung on the IRD frame to assure success. It was the mechanism of integration that was wrong. IRD is based on a farm-systems model of local needs, usually designed in far away places to be flown in and set up around rural communities who had little influence on the process. While participatory approaches to rural development as in the Panchayat system have improved the situation, mostly by soliciting local input into decision-making processes, they still have not systematically increased local control by representative local authorities. ILD, on the other hand, integrates through local representative bodies. This is its principal difference from the IRD approach.

Finally, PTD through PRI, unlike other participatory approaches to development has avoided the state and tried to approach development by avoiding state and going directly to the people, can avoid certain impending risks involved in state alienation. While the ideal of many practitioners of state alienation has been greater inclusion and justice, the choice of this approach is part of a larger global narrative that pits people against government rather than seeing government as an effective partner in development.

The growing conflict situation of Assam has led to mobilization of various movements in order to address this contradiction between the individual and the state. This complexity while at a manifest level presents itself as a contradiction of cultural reproduction, social integration and socialization of neglect, at a more pragmatic and latent level it can be viewed as a democratic response to the human development deficit in the region. It is the call of the hour to demystify the neglect theory of cultural reproduction and integration and abhor the Indian example of granting territorial autonomy to resurgent minority groups. This has not only aggravated ethnic conflict and competition for limited resources, both political and social, but has also led to increasing contradictions between the individual and state. In a situation where people face great economic hardships through loss of livelihoods and withdrawal of investment funds from the region as a result of economic crisis and conflicts, reliance on government is even higher and community self-reliance is very low. Years of so-called 'bottom-up' planning have resulted in few real welfare gains for communities or specific groups. Poor coordination between district and provincial governments results in duplication of development programmes within villages or very poorly targeted support that does not match community needs. Women's status has not improved and educated young people are unable to find employment. The presence of internally displaced persons remains a challenge for social cohesion and human development (especially in health, education and economic empowerment). The lack of coordination among village, sub-district, district and provincial levels of government means that problems emerging at the village level hardly even reach the district, let alone the provincial government. Vice versa, policies at the provincial and district levels hardly reach people in villages (particularly women and poor). The solutions to inherent problems range from extreme inhumanity of anti-insurgency acts like Arm Forces Special Act (AFSPA) and suspension of democratic rights to soft-peddling by granting autonomous councils or promises to solve almost nothing. Decentralization of governance and local-level participation through democratic constitutional measures like PRIs can facilitate a PTD, which appears a viable means of establishing trust and good governance in the region.

ACKNOWLEDGEMENT

This paper is indebted to the project 'Participation of Women in Local Self Governance in Assam'.

REFERENCES

Adamolekun, Ladipo (1991), 'Promoting African Decentralization', *Public Administration and Development*, vol. 11, pp. 285-91.

Agrawal, Arun (1997), 'Community in Conservation: Beyond Enchantment and Disenchantment', Conservation and Development Forum Working Paper No. 1, University of Florida, Gainesville (18 March draft).

Agrawal, Arun and Jesse C. Ribot (1999), 'Accountability in Decentralization: A Framework with South Asian and West African Cases', *Journal of Developing Areas*, vol. 33, pp. 473-502.

Allen, Chris (1997), 'Who Needs Civil Society?', *Review of African Political Economy*, no. 73, pp. 329-37.

Baland, J. (1996), *Halting Degradation of Natural Resources: Is There a Role for Rural Communities?*, Oxford: Clarendon Press.

Berry, Sara (1989), 'Social Institutions and Access to Resources', *Africa*, 59(1).

Bhagwati, J.N. (1982), 'Directly Unproductive, Profit-seeking (DUP) Activities', *Journal of Political Economy*, vol. 90, no. 5, pp. 988-1002.

Blaikie, P. (1985), *The Political Economy of Soil Erosion in the Third World*, London: Longman.

Blair, H. (2000), 'Participation and Accountability at the Periphery: Democratic Local Governance in Six Countries', *World Development*, 28(1), pp. 21-39.

——— (1998), 'Spreading Power to the Periphery: An Assessment of Democratic Local Governance', Program and Operations Assessment Report No. 21, Washington, D.C.: USAID.

GTZ, USAID, Ministry of Home Affairs and Bappenas (2001), 'Capacity Building for Local Governance: A Framework for Government Action and Donor Support', see http://www.gtzsfdm.or.id/cb_nat_fr_work.htm for further details.

Bordieu, P. (1977), *Outline of a Theory of Practice*, Cambridge: Cambridge University Press.

Cernia, M. (ed.) (1985), *Putting People First: Sociological Variables in Rural Development*, New York: Oxford University Press.

Chambers, R. (1983), *Rural Development: Putting the Last First*, Essex: Longman Scientific & Technical.

Dahl, R.A. 1993 [1961], 'Who Governs?' in Philip Green (ed.), *Democracy*, Atlantic Highlands, NJ: Humanities Press, ch. 13, pp. 104-19.

Dutta, Hazarika, S. (2007), 'Examining Autonomy and 73rd Amendment in Assam' in Paula Bannerjee and Samir Das (eds.), *Autonomy Beyond Kant and Hermeneutics*, New Delhi: Anthem Press.

Echeverri-Gent, J. (1992), 'Public Participation and Poverty Alleviation: The Experience of Reform Communists in India's West Bengal', *World Development*, 20, no. 10 (October 1992), pp. 1401-22.

Granovetter, M. (1985), 'Economic Action and Social Structure: The Problem of Embeddedness', *American Journal of Sociology*, vol. 91, no. 3, pp. 481-510.

Hadi, S. (2005), 'Enhancing Local Governance through Decentralization Policy in Managing Conflict-Affected Regions in Indonesia', presented at the International Conference on Engaging Communities; UNDESA/UNCRD Workshop on Decentralization: Poverty Reduction, Empowerment and Participation, Brisbane, Australia, 14-17 August, http://unpan1.un.org/intradoc/groups/public/documents/UN/UNPAN020695.pdf

Mawhood, P. (1982-3), 'The Place of Traditional Political Authority in African Pluralism', *Civilisations*, vol. XXXII, no. 2, 1982; vol. XXXIII, no. 1, 1983, pp. 209-37.

Manor, James (1999), *The Political Economy of Democratic Decentralization*, Washington, D.C.: World Bank.

Mazonde, Isaac Ncube (1996), 'The Basarwa of Botswana: Leadership, Legitimacy and Participation in Development Sites', *Cultural Survival Quarterly*, Fall.

Mehta, A.S. (1996), 'Micro Politics of Voluntary Action: An Anatomy of Change in Two Villages', *Cultural Survival Quarterly*, Fall.

Mkandawire, T. (1995), 'Beyond Crisis: Toward Democratic Developmental States in Africa', paper presented at CODESRIA's Eighth General Assembly, Crises, Conflicts and Transformations: Responses and Perspectives, 26 June-2 July.

Oyugi, W.O. (2000), 'Decentralization for Good Governance and Development', *Regional Development Dialogue*, 21(1) Spring, pp. 3-22.

Ribot, J.C. (1999a), 'Integral Local Development: Authority, Accountability and Entrustment in Natural Resource Management', Working Paper of the Africa Region RPTES Program, The World Bank, April 1999.

Sen, Amartya (1981), *Poverty and Famines: An Essay on Entitlement and Deprivation*, Oxford: Clarendon Press.

Shiva, V. (1989), *Staying Alive*, Atlantic Highlands, NJ: Zed Books.

World Bank (2000), *Entering the 21st Century: World Development Report 1999/2000*, Oxford: Oxford University Press.

——— (1996), *The World Bank Participation Sourcebook*, Washington, D.C.: The World Bank.

CHAPTER 7

Dalits' Rights in Forests: Challenges and Opportunities

P.K. BISWAS

INTRODUCTION

India is a developing country the majority of whose population live in rural areas. Since Independence there has been considerable activity in the field of economic development. A vast amount of money has been spent by the government and various international donor agencies for the upliftment of the poor. Yet the level of development remains alarmingly low. There is still much poverty, malnutrition, unemployment, under-employment. This is more true for the rural poor among whom Dalits constitute a significant proportion. The Dalits largely depend on natural resources for their livelihoods. *Jal, jungle, jameen* (water, forest, land) are the key resources for their survival.

The forests support development of Dalits and sustain their economic, environmental and social well-being. Development is not merely in terms of economic growth (GNP/GDP) but essentially social development, with emphasis on equitable distribution, freedom of expression and qualitative aspect of life. The contribution of forest is immense in terms of ecological conservation and economic sustenance of the poor rural communities in general and Dalits specifically.

ROLE OF FORESTS IN THE DEVELOPMENT OF DALITS

It is a fact that a large number of Dalits live in the forest fringe areas. They have been co-existing with mutual benefit to each other since time immemorial. In times of distress the forest is the last resort for them. Even in areas where forests do not exist, Dalits continue to periodically visit the distant forests to procure their traditional requirements. Apart from this, some financial benefits accrue to them from the collection and sale of Non-Timber Forest Products (NTFP). Forests are their economic resource base and occupy a central position in their economy.

For several rural communities living in or near forests, about 30 per cent of their diet is derived from forest resources (i.e. wild vegetables, tubers, fruits, nuts, bamboo shoots, small animals). Medicinal plants are important in the primary health care system. The rural communities have developed interesting and often sophisticated knowledge system of ethno-medicine and use of a vast variety of plants for medicinal purposes (NFAP, 1999).

It is a recognized fact that forests essentially provide three different kinds of benefits: *job and incomes*, often needed to supplement inadequate returns from agriculture; *produce* such as fuelwood, fodder and poles for building homes; and less directly but just as importantly a range of *environmental benefits* without which other activities, such as agriculture, might be impossible (FAO, 1979).

Forest is the second largest land use after agriculture and it is a source of goods and services used by the Dalits. In remote forest fringe villages about 300 million rural people depend on the forests for their subsistence and livelihood and about 70 per cent of them depend on fuelwood to meet their domestic energy needs (Biswas, 2000). Tribals and other less favourably placed groups like Dalits depend on the forests and wastelands which are suitable for fuel and fodder trees and various kinds of scrubs and grasses (Chowdhry, 1983). Without doubt forests play a significant role in the development and sustenance of rural communities and Dalits whose existence depends on a close and ecologically sustainable relationship with the forests they inhabit (Biswas, 1988).

The agricultural sector, which is important for the survival of Dalits, depends almost entirely on livestock for the energy needed for various farm operations. The economics of maintaining cattle, sheep, goats is largely dependent on forests as a source of fodder, be it leaf or fruit or fodder.

Wood (timber) is also required for making various types of ploughs and agricultural implements, each with a different life span. The bullock-cart is the main means of transport in the rural sector. According to one estimate, there are about 13 million bullock-carts in the country, which accounts for an investment of about Rs. 3,000 crore. About 2 crore people find direct or indirect employment in the bullock-cart transportation system.

The Dalits living in the forest fringe areas also require small timber for the construction of houses. Timber, bamboo, grass, creepers and barks are useful for this purpose. Forests offer scope for the development of cottage industries for Dalits. Many trees provide of raw materials such as *tassar* for silk production, fodder for rearing milch cattle, *pattal* (leaf-plate) making, basket weaving, oil and paper making, and others economic activities.

As mentioned before, the potential of NTFP for poverty alleviation among Dalits is tremendous. These people collect various kinds of forest products throughout the year to sustain their employment and supplement their income. Activities related to NTFPs provide employment during slack periods in the agricultural cycle and provide a buffer against risk and household emergencies. These constitute a part of the household activities where old women and children also contribute and in several cases can be the main source of income. Therefore, the life of Dalits is profoundly affected by whatever happens to the forests.

DALITS AND MANAGEMENT OF FOREST

Management means the organization and control of an enterprise or undertaking. Forest management from this point of view broadly refers to the organization and control of access to and utilization of trees, woodlots, plantations and natural forest and associated resources including benefits derived from them. It involves professional foresters, institutions like village-level organizations, NGOs, the tribals and Dalits.

In the context of forest management, we have to understand the legal status of forest as a resource for the Dalits. Forest has essentially been state property. The high profile of the state in the forestry sector, and in particular its control over reserved forests, dates back to the colonial period. The Indian Forest Act, 1865 was the first attempt at establishing monopoly holding rights by the state and these were formalized and made explicit in the subsequent Acts of 1878 and 1927. Under these, the state was allowed to demarcate valuable tracts of forests and its exclusive exploitation.

The inhabitants of these areas—mostly the indigenous people and dalits—were deemed to derive their customary usage of the forest and its products not from a right of ownership but from a limited and contingent privilege. The state, in this framework, was thus able to assert its rights to absolute ownership, and this was done through the reservation of certain forest areas.

Therefore, in this context, it is essential to understand the meaning of property. 'Property is a right to a benefit stream that is only as secure as the duty of all others to respect the conditions that protect that stream. When one has a right, one has the expectations in both the law and in practice that their claims will be respected by those with duty' (Bromley and Cernea, 1989). Hence it is the use of land or some other resource in relation to others that is the central theme in property definition. The bare fact of ownership, then, is not as critical as the relationship with, and the expectation of, others who are associated with it. The right to use or not to use a property, or resource, implies inclusion and exclusion, i.e. rights of access. As evident, resources are a fundamental aspect of property use and property rights.

The forest area is shrinking considerably causing further poverty and misery for the Dalits. While the scale of deforestation has in the recent period emerged as a matter of widespread national concern, the substantive measures that have been initiated for reversing this trend have been limited in scope and efficacy.

The Debate on Property Rights in Forest

In recent times, there is a considerable debate as to whether forest area has to be managed as state property or as private property or as property of local communities which includes tribals and Dalits.

(a) Argument for Management of Forest as State Property

The case for state ownership or, at least, state management of forests is hinged on a number of factors. Firstly forest management is associated with a wide range of externalities that impinge on the economy, not just on proximate producers but also the economy as a whole, as with the relationship between forest cover and climate. In general, it can be said that forests provide, if maintained, external benefits to the rest of the eco-system. Any loss in the value of the benefit—function of the rate of depletion—would therefore tend to exceed, often substantially, the loss in intertemporal benefits experienced by the person or institution controlling the actual forest resource. Secondly, it can be argued that the management of forests requires a level of professional training and scientific competence that lies outside the capacities of potential private owners or Dalits and other communities. Thirdly, the time horizon for forest management and the spatial requirements for an efficient, conjoint exploitation of the resource through harvesting and replanting favour state ownership and investment. Private rights would either be too fragmented and hence inefficient or else would need to be too large, thereby running counter to the general policy regarding land ceilings. Fourthly, the ecological variety of Indian forests is only likely to be preserved in the context of state management. Private entrepreneurs would tend to replace diverse stock by fast growing varieties. Fifthly, state ownership allows for major economies of scale and a longer-term planning framework. Lastly, state ownership ultimately allows for a wider and more just distribution of revenues derived from forest products through the overall structure of government spending. Although this effect could be achieved through the taxation of private returns, this would imply major revision of the basis of public finance in the country, let alone a more satisfactory control over 'leakages'.

Although each of these arguments contains attractive features and, in summation, would appear to offer a strong case for state ownership, that case remains strongly dependent on the degree to which these attributes can be fulfilled and sustained. After all, state ownership is largely argued for as a more efficient outcome, rather than in terms of any supposedly ethical superiority to private ownership. In this regard, all available evidence points unequivocally to the fact that state ownership has been unable to sustain the basis of India's forest resources. While some would argue that this has been because of the weakness in the construct of state ownership, consolidation of state monopoly would appear to run into difficult, probably insoluble problems.

To that extent, the very same issue that necessarily predominates any discussion of the demand for forest products by rural communities, comes to the fore in the general discussion of the relative virtues of state ownership. For, although it could be argued that both in terms of research and actual management practice, the forest department's monopoly has yielded poor and very limited results, the nub of the question of state ownership remains the degree to which the necessary conditions for an efficient utilization of exclusive rights can be consistently met.

(b) Argument for Management of Forest as Private Property

If state control over forests has proven to be an inefficient means for their management, let alone retention, attention needs to be given to the processes by which a set of different economic signals get transmitted to potential exploiters of the resources. This requires above all a radical approach to the system of property rights itself. As the aim of any reform must be to harmonize to the greatest extent possible the social and private rates of return from forestry activity where time-preferences are the key issue, this implies a more graded and subtle use of controls and contingent rights. In the era of globalization, one argument would be to say that private property rights and a market in land and trees would be the most simple and efficient outcome. There is plentiful evidence from Europe and elsewhere that forests can be maintained in a private ownership context and that the privatization of rewards ensures the satisfactory enforcement of rights. The state, precisely because of its amorphous and disparate nature, is inherently a weak vessel for the physical, let alone psychological enforcement of exclusive control.

This argument runs into a number of problems in the Indian context. Firstly, private management of trees has customarily been associated with plantation or specialized husbandry. Secondly, given the political difficulties of establishing properties outside the usual land reform parameters, there are problems associated with the wrapping of rights. Forest management clearly has considerable potential for scale of economies and, given the ecology of most remaining Indian forests, the working areas is relatively large. Thirdly, there remains the problem of the forest-dependent communities. They lack, in general, both capital and expertise and, for privatization. Even if forestland was sold or leased to outside agencies, this would still raise the problem of what to do with forest-dependent communities. Both practical and ethical considerations strongly suggest that the *latter must be actively included in any reform of the current system.*

(c) Argument for Management of Forest as Common Property for Dalits

As evident in the argument above, it seems desirable that there should be reform in the property rights in favour of rural communities, especially Dalits. Let's examine this in the context of Madhya Pradesh, which has the largest forest area, and also a substantial population of Dalits and tribals.

Context of Dalits Livelihoods in Madhya Pradesh

Most of the Dalits are mainly dependent on agriculture for their livelihoods. However, traditionally they are deprived of ownership of lands. In MP, though Dalits constitute 12.6 per cent of the total population they have operational landholding of only 8.1 per cent (NCAS and Ekta Parishad, 2002). Coupled with denial of access to natural resources this make their lives more miserable. Dalits have been depending on forests for their livelihoods. Forests supplement their income from agriculture. In fact, during the time of drought and distress forest is the last succor for them. In addition to it, the common pool resources such as village common lands, tank/water bodies, wastelands (under Panchayats) and the lands that are assigned to Dalits by the government are all under direct/indirect control and possession of the landed elites of the villages. Therefore, non-access to both on-farm and non-farm activities makes them more vulnerable in the context of livelihoods.

As per the data available for main workforce, there are 21.06 lakh Dalits in the primary sector (74.62 per cent), 3.86 lakh in the secondary sector (13.67 per cent) and 3.28 lakh in tertiary sector (11.62 per cent). Among them, the proportion of landless agricultural labourers is 40.46 per cent and proportion of cultivators is 32.38 per cent (The Bhopal Document, 2002). In this context, it is obvious how adversely Dalits are affected for livelihoods.

One of the major concerns for us is how to secure employment for Dalits. It is reported that agriculture, which used to be the major employment generator, has now stopped absorbing people. The annual growth rate in this sector has declined from 1.51 per cent in the 1983-94 period to –0.34 per cent in 1994-2000. Another indicator of the worsening employment scenario in rural areas is the declining share of self-employment in the total rural employment, from 58.9 per cent in 1977-8 to 52.9 per cent in 1999-2000 (Barik et al., 2004).

In the prevailing scenario, it is increasingly being argued that natural resource management would facilitate more job opportunities for Dalits and ensure livelihood security. Interestingly, the S.P. Gupta

Special Group set-up by the government so that in the Tenth Plan we should target our focus on forests, agroforestry, medicinal plants and bamboo development for more job opportunity in the rural sector (see Figure 7.1).

It has been reported that Sal leaf generates 2.5 million jobs in Orissa alone. It has high capacity for employment because India has several Sal forests. Similarly bamboo generates 10 million jobs currently. It can generate 8.6 million jobs if bamboo plantations are undertaken and high value artisanal and other products are marketed (Barik et al., 2004). However, the bottlenecks are legal hurdles and inappropriate definition of property rights.

This is substantiated by the fact that though MP has substantial forest area (almost one-fourth of the country), the plight of Dalits living near forests has not been mitigated. Consider the demographic features of MP given in Box 7.1.

It is evident from Table 7.1 that despite good forest resources, development of Dalits is inadequate and further loss of forest and denial of access to natural resources would impoverish their conditions.

For livelihood support system, forest resource is critical. Most of the Dalits have livestock and they depend on the forests for various products to supplement their income from agriculture. Most of the

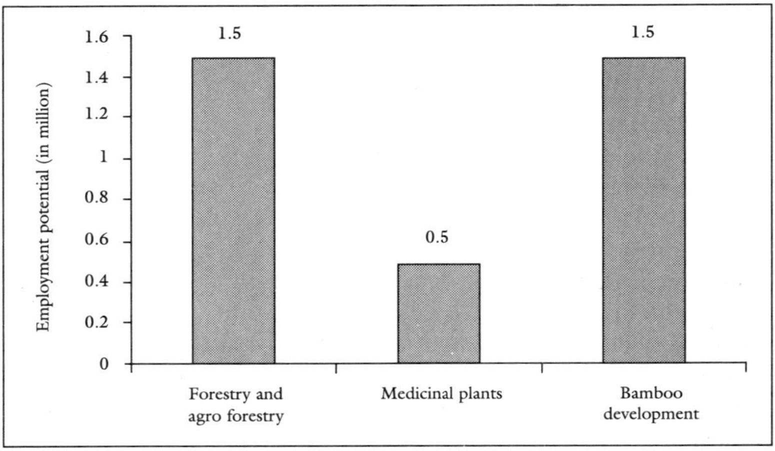

Source: Special Group on Targeting Ten Million Employment Opportunities Per Year, Planning Commission.

FIGURE 7.1: THE EMPLOYMENT POTENTIAL

BOX 7.1: DEMOGRAPHIC PROFILE OF MP

Total Population of MP	:	603.85 lakh
Villages	:	51,806
Rural Population	:	73 per cent
Forest Area	:	30.9 per cent
Forest Fringe Villages	:	20,000 approximately
Dalit Population	:	12.6 per cent (Dalits and tribals together 35.3 per cent)
Population Below Poverty Line	:	37.43 per cent
Cattle Population	:	303 lakh
Forest-dependent Livestock	:	105 lakh

Source: Third Human Development Report, Government of MP, 2002 and Census of India, 2001.

TABLE 7.1: DALITS, FOREST AND DEVELOPMENT INDEX IN SELECTED DISTRICTS OF MP

District	Dalit Population (in %)	Forest Area (in %)	Total Employment in Farm Sector (in %)	Rural Employment in Non-farm Sector (in %)	Agriculture Labour (in %)	HDI Rank
Chhatarpur	23.7	25.0	75.34	15.4	20.4	43
Panna	20.4	42.0	78.94	15.8	23.8	41
Satna	17.8	27.0	65.98	23.7	31.8	38
Sheopur	16.6	43.0	81.15	11.0	27.4	33
Shivpuri	19.4	32.0	82.90	9.2	17.7	40

Source: Third Human Development Report, Madhya Pradesh, 2002.

Notes: 1. Districts were selected on the basis of percentage of Dalit population (more than state average of 12.6 per cent) and forest area (25 per cent and above).

2. HDI: Human Development Index (MP has 45 districts).

cultivated land is rainfed. There is large-scale migration from western MP, and other areas. Forest has the potential to reduce poverty but if we consider the development indices in selected areas of MP the picture is dismal.

Forest Policy Initiatives

From the foregoing discussions it is evident that there has to be reform of property rights in forest management for poverty alleviation among the Dalits. Sustainable forest management is key to the sustainable development of Dalits. It is obvious that answer to India's immediate problem of poverty lies in access to the biomass available in nature for such people.

Even in the age of liberalization and globalization it has to be understood that there can be no financial assets if there are no ecological assets. Sustainable development is increasingly linked to environmental conservation. There has to be a harmonious balance between conservation of forests and development of Dalits through livelihood security.

In this context, it is important to note that the National Forest Policy 1988 recognized that 'the life of tribals and other communities living within and near forests, revolves around forests. The rights and concessions enjoyed by them should be fully protected. Their domestic requirements of fuelwood, fodder, minor forest produce and construction timber should be the first charge on forest products' (NFP, 1988). Conservation and Dalit livelihoods are integral parts of sustainable development from this point of view.

The NFP 1988 has been further strengthened by the 1 June 1990 circular of the Ministry of Environment and Forests, Government of India and subsequent circulars of February 2000 and December 2002. They have highlighted both the need and process for involving village communities and voluntary agencies in the protection, development and management of forests.

JOINT FOREST MANAGEMENT

These processes facilitated the formation of village-level committees known as village forest committees, forest protection committees or Van Samrakshan Samitis (VSS). This strategy is known as Joint Forest Management (JFM) where government and people are partners in forest conservation, protection and development. According to the Ministry of Environment and Forests, Government of India, by March 2002, 27 Indian states had adopted JFM as the main strategy. There are about 63,000 village forest protection committees which are implementing JFM in 14 million hectares of forest area (GOI, 2002). JFM programme has led to several positive impacts:

- Rehabilitation and improvement in the conditions of forests
- Increase in livelihood options
- Reduction in encroachments

- Involvement of NGOs
- Change in attitude and relationships

On the basis of these findings, one is inclined to argue that the JFM movement needs to be strengthened and more rights be granted to the rural communities, specially the Dalits who are more oppressed and vulnerable.

In keeping with the philosophy of decentralized governance, people's involvement in decision-making process and consequent empowerment is crucial. Therefore, tenurial rights for Dalits must be secured. The following factors may be considered for effective local management control systems. The main institutional issues are:

- The provision for secure tenure rights to Dalits.
- The development of systems of regulation and enforcement based on local decision making.

There is a greater need to formalize community-based management systems both at the local and state levels. The culture of rural people and dynamics of social processes have to be understood properly. Sociological insights, perceptions and knowledge are, therefore, instrumental and essential for bringing reform in properly rights for sustainable development of Dalits.

CONCLUSION

Sustainable forest management is key to sustainable livelihood of Dalits. There has to be a harmonious balance between conservation of forests and development of Dalits through livelihood security. Forestry is no more a technical subject dealing with trees only. It is socio-technical and now a synthesis of wide-ranging and diverse subjects. Silvicultural practices and forest management have to be integrated with subjects like sociology, anthropology, economics, law, environmental science, remote sensing, system science, computer science, cartography, business administration, communication, tribal art, culture, museum, parks of wildlife management, hydrology and plant and animal genetics, as we are dealing with a whole complex ecosystem which is trying to address the poverty of this country. The holistic view is but essential. A sustainable alliance has to be forged among government organizations, non-government organizations and local-level organizations. There has to be an effective partnership among all the stakeholders for capacity building, monitoring and evaluation of JFM to achieve the ultimate goal of planning and development, i.e. self-reliance. And Gandhiji's *Gram Swaraj* may become a reality.

However, it is clear that forest productivity will ensure equity and livelihood for the Dalits. The livelihoods of Dalits must be integrated with the rehabilitation of forests, with the active involvement of them in the form of village forest committees/forest protection committees. Once they are involved, the forest resource cycle will be completed. The schematic diagram in Figure 7.2 depicts the real scenario.

It is important to empower communities to take decisions on the management of forests. There has to be a legal sanctity to village forest/forest protection committees. It is imperative to have a memorandum of understanding signed between communities and the government. In forestry, unlike agriculture, the gestation period is long. Only NTFP-based activities would provide livelihood options. The JFM experience is only a decade old, but on the basis of this it is strongly recommended that JFM should move towards community forest management (CFM), implying more legitimacy and power to the communities. The National Forest Policy, which essentially pleads for community empowerment, needs to be backed up by appropriate acts and legislations. There is an urgent need to amend various forest laws and acts to facilitate the process of CFM. This needs to be harnessed properly for environmental stability and ensuring livelihoods for Dalits. There is need for CFM, to ensure livelihoods of Dalits, and forest conservation to go hand in hand. We need to strengthen and sustain these for a bright future of both.

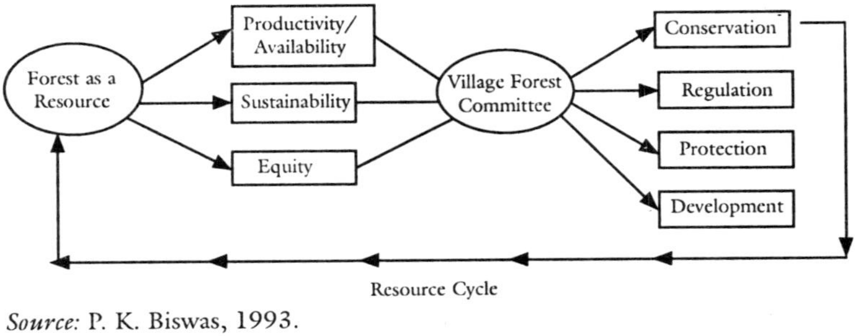

Source: P. K. Biswas, 1993.

FIGURE 7.2: FOREST RESOURCE CYCLE

REFERENCES

Barik, Satya Sundar et al. (2004), 'Jobs', *Down to Earth*, 30 November 2004.

Biswas, P.K. (1988), 'Sociological Issues in Forestry', *Indian Journal of Social Sciences*, vol. 1, no. 2.

——— (1993), 'Forestry-based Sustainable Development: The Social Dimensions', *Indian Journal of Public Administration*, vol. XXXIX, no. 3.

——— (2000), 'Joint Forest Management for Sustainable Rural Development', IIFM, Bhopal, Mimeographed.

Bromley, D.W. and M.M. Cernea (1989), 'The Management of Common Property Natural Resources: Some Conceptual and Operational Fallacies', World Bank Discussion Paper 57, Washington D.C.

Centre for People's Forestry (2004), Concept Note for National Conference on Dalit Concerns in Forestry, Hyderabad.

Chowdhry, Kamla (1983), 'Social Forestry and the Rural Poor', Discussion Paper Series No. 10, Ford Foundation, New Delhi.

FAO (1979), 'Forestry for Local Community Development', FAO Forestry Paper No. 7, Rome.

Gopal, Ashok (ed.) (2002), *Land for Life: Promise and Performance of Land Reforms in Madhya Pradesh*, National Centre for Advocacy Studies, Pune, and Ekta Parishad, Bhopal.

Govternment of India (1988), National Forest Policy, New Delhi.

——— (1999), 'National Forestry Action Programme—India', Ministry of Environment and Forests, New Delhi.

——— (2002), 'Joint Forest Management: A Decade of Partnership', Joint Forest Management Monitoring Cell, Ministry of Environment and Forests, New Delhi.

Govternment of Madhya Pradesh (2002), *Third Human Development Report*, Bhopal.

——— (2002), 'The Bhopal Document: Charting a New Course for Dalits for the 21st Century', Bhopal.

CHAPTER 8

Forest Rights and Tribal Lives: An Analysis of Panchayati Raj Institutions in Koraput District of Orissa

RAJ KUMAR KHOSLA

India is a land of strong population heterogeneity in which the tribals are an important intrinsic group. A tribe or an ethnic community is defined as a group of families that have a general name, whose members speak a common dialect, reside in a common territory and who have well-developed reciprocal exchange. Since time immemorial, forest is the habitat of the tribal people and they are still living in close proximity to the forests. In addition to the usual rights and privileges of all Indian citizens, the tribal groups have been provided with protective measures under various constitutional provisions and policies to make them developed socially, economically, politically and educationally. Their welfare is being treated as an integral part of the country's developmental plans. However, the tribal groups remain a backward segment of the society, in spite of various welfare measures implemented for socio-economic progress. Despite protective laws and legislations formulated by the Government of India, the tribals are being exploited in all spheres. Their natural homeland, livelihood and socio-economic status are more vulnerable then those of other sections of population. Their ranking on several human developmental indices leaves little doubt about their unenviable position.

Emphasizing the tribals' dependence on forest, the study was especially undertaken to assess major forest policies in aimed at conserving forest resources being enforced in the Koraput district of Orissa. Secondly, the study focused on examining the role of the

Gram Panchayat in preserving and protecting forest resource under the Panchayat (Extension to the Scheduled Areas) (PESA) Act. There is serious concern regarding the fast decreasing forest areas in different part of the country. The major part of deforestation is caused due to large-scale commercialization of forest resources and various development projects like setting up of industries, construction of roads and railways and other public uses. The Koraput district, which falls in the Eastern Ghat hills, is no exception. The Government of India enacted the PESA Act, 1996, in the Fifth Scheduled Area to preserve, protect and manage the resources without undermining the tradition and culture of the tribal societies. Following the guidelines of the Central Act the State Confirmatory Act came into existence in 1997.

FOREST AND TRIBAL LIFE

Historically, the tribals of India have adopted the nature as their habitat. Their subsistence pattern, economic and social institutions, beliefs and practices have been closely linked with the environment (Sarkar and Dasgupta, 2000: 103). The relationship between the tribals and forest has often been called symbiotic. The tribals depend on the forest and the forest in its turn depends on them for its preservation and continuity. The social, religious and economic systems of the tribals revolve around the forest. Tribals still like to live in their original natural abode consisting of hills, forests, rivers and soil, practice their traditional way of living, their rituals, customs, dance, music and the traditional belief system. A set of religious myths and social customs were built around the forest to ensure that the economically important trees were protected, human needs were met and the species that were more commonly available were equitably distributed. Given the extent of their dependence, it is not surprising that they built a system that treated forests as a renewable resource (Vidyarthi and Rai, 1985: 25).

Forest is the way of life for the tribal people. Millions of tribal communities depend on the forest products for food, which includes fruits, plants, flowers, etc. Shifting cultivation is a major source of sustenance of the tribal people. It is also referred to as *Jhum* or slash and burn cultivation. In Andhra Pradesh and Orissa, it is known as *Podu* cultivation (Deeney and Fernandes, 1992: 50). Many tribes in south and central India, Chhota Nagpur and Bengal, slopes of the

Himalaya and especially north-east India practice shifting cultivation.

The health care pattern among the tribals is very much connected with the forests. The tribals traditionally depend on forests for medicinal plants for the treatment of diseases (Chaudhuri, 1997: 242), despite a well-advanced health care system in the country. The tribals collect the roots, branches, leaves and bark of various trees and plants for medicinal purposes.

Forest is the base of tribal economy. The tribal people collect the Non-Timber Forest Produce (NTFP) to meet their household expenditure. NTFP also provides employment to them, particularly to the womenfolk of the tribal society. The sociocultural system of the tribals too is linked with the forest. Their traditional beliefs and practices have helped in the preservation of their age-old culture and along with it the conservation of ecology of this country (Sarkar and Dasgupta, op. cit.: 134). The concept of sacred groves—a belief in which the tribals regard different the deities represent various elements of nature such as sun, rain, fire, and so on, who all reside in these sacred groves—is believed to have played a big role in forest protection.

CONSTITUTION AND TRIBALS' FOREST RIGHT

The fundamental philosophy of the Constitution of India is grounded on the notion of egalitarianism, social justice and empowerment. In the political sphere, the state adopted 'universal adult franchise' allowing common people to participate in the political process that forms the government at various levels. The institution of Panchayati Raj was created with a view to extending the decision-making process to the grassroots level. In this perspective, the 73rd Amendment has testified the efforts. The Constitution (73rd Amendment) Act, 1992 came into existence to promote people's participation and strengthen the democratic process at the grassroots level of the Indian polity. The 73rd Act vested Panchayati Raj Institutions (PRI) with subjects such as social forestry and minor forest produce, which were earlier initiated in the Joint Forest Management (JFM) programme. The management of forest resources by the PRIs is another significant step to empower the local self-government at the grassroot level to preserve and protect the forest resources for the interest of the tribal people. However, in the administrative perspective, no effective coordination was found between PRIs and forestry institutions over controlling forest resources. This problem was further complicated due to the overlapping of functions on management of forest resources in the same legal jurisdiction. The linkage of PRIs and JFM committees is further complicated in the Fifth Scheduled Areas under the Constitution. The Fifth Scheduled Areas are those, which are primarily dominated by tribal people (Upadhayay, 2003: 3631) except the states of Assam, Meghalaya, Tripura and Mizoram, which come under the Sixth Scheduled Area, where autonomous district councils administer to protect the interests of the tribal people. As per the Constitution of India, the governor is empowered to administer in the Fifth Scheduled Areas; he can also make, repeal or amend any Act of parliament or of the state legislature or any existing law, if he thinks them to be detrimental to the interests of the tribals. The governor may make regulations for good government in the Fifth Scheduled Areas; he can prohibit or restrict the transfer of land of the tribal people and regulate the carrying on of business of money-lending in this area (Sharma, 2000: 221).

In post-independent India, it was found that the interests of the tribal people had not been addressed. When the state governments started enacting Panchayat laws, they continued with the past practice of not taking into account the needs and interests of the Scheduled Areas. Keeping in mind the interest of the tribal people, this was challenged in the high courts of Andhra Pradesh, Bihar, Orissa and Maharashtra. The courts held the extension of State Panchayat Acts to the Scheduled Areas as *ultra vires* of the Constitution and declared that Part IX of the Constitution which deals with the Panchayat can be extended to Scheduled Areas only through an Act of parliament. This created an unprecedented situation in the Scheduled Areas of the country as the formal institutions created under the new provisions of the Constitution were declared illegal and the traditional tribal institutions were unrecognized by law. At this juncture, political parties, tribal Members of Parliament and people's organizations took up the issue and demanded justice for the Scheduled Areas. Consequently, a need was felt by the Government of India to extend the provisions of Part IX of the Constitution to the Scheduled Areas.

The Government of India in June 1994 appointed a committee headed by Dileep Singh Bhuria to look into the customary rights over forest resources and cultural identities of the tribal people in the same decentralized democratic structure. The committee submitted its reports with the recommendations of village governance, participatory democracy, community control over resources and suitable administrative framework for the Scheduled Areas. The committee felt that while shaping the new Panchayati Raj structure in tribal areas, it is desirable to blend the traditional with the modern by treating traditional institutions as the foundations on which a modern superstructure should be built. It also recommended that the Gram Sabha should be given complete command and control over natural resources (Mukul, 1997: 928-9). Based on the recommendations of the committee, on 24 December 1996, the PESA Act, 1996 was enacted (Bakshi, 2001: 186). This Act has extended the Central Act (73rd Constitution Amendment Act, 1992) to Scheduled Areas mentioned under clause (1) of Article 244 of the Constitution. All states which had Scheduled Areas within their geographical boundaries were also mandated to amend their existing Panchayati Raj Acts, incorporating the provisions of PESA within a year, i.e. by 24 December 1997.

OWNERSHIP OF MINOR FOREST PRODUCE (MFP)

The Extension Act, 1996, has been voted with wide-ranging powers and functions at the grassroot level. The Act provides constitutional power to the Gram Sabha of every village, to safeguard and preserve the traditional rights of the people. The Gram Sabha shall be endowed with the ownership of MFP and both Gram Sabha and Panchayat, at the appropriate levels, shall be consulted for granting licenses or mining lease of MFP. It also suggests the need of prior recommendation of Gram Sabha and Panchayat for acquisition of land in the Scheduled Areas for development projects or for resettlement of project-affected people of the tribal communities (Singh, 1997: 8-9). In Orissa, following the provisions of the Central Act, 1996, and the State Confirmatory Acts on Panchayti Raj of 1997, the state government declared its MFP policy in March 2000. It has empowered that Gram Panchayats to own, control and manage MFP in their own areas. However, the revenue earned from MFP are still managed under the strict control of the state government.

SCHEDULED TRIBES BILL, 2005

The Scheduled Tribes (Recognition of Forest Rights) Bill, 2005 is proposed to address the needs and aspirations of the forest dwellers.

As far as the tribals are concerned, this Bill recognized that 'historical injustices' done to them by the government, both in the colonial and post-colonial period and that the forest policies of these government have denied them the right to use and manage forest and have over-exploited the forest for commercial gains (Munshi, 2005: 4406). The main provision of the Bill is to legally entitle forest land of 2.5 hectares to those tribals who have occupied the land before 25 October 1980. But the tribals who have occupied forest land after the above-mentioned date will simply be evicted from there. However, it is the responsibility of the government to take necessary steps to address these people as well. Long-term economic interest can and does become a strong motivation of protection for resources.

FOREST POLICIES AND STATE CONTROL: OVERVIEW

British Period

State control over forest was started by the European pattern of resource use. To control over the forest, the British government for the first time, introduced the Forest Policy of India in 1855, under which they restricted the rights of the forest dwellers over forest resources (Chaudhuri, 1997: 234). The very objective of the British Government of India was to treat forest as state property and restrict the rights of forest dwellers (Human and Pattanaik, 2000: 25). The first forest policy in the country was formulated in 1894. This policy made two major communications: first the claims of cultivation was stronger than the claims of forest presentation; second, the public benefit was the sole object of forest administration (Lal, 1989: 20). It clearly stated that the government could impose restrictions on the rights of the forest dwellers because the state was the sole administering authority over the forest. Due to this restriction, the tribals and rural landless could be easily deprived of their source of livelihood because they were the only groups without any bargaining power.

The Indian Forest Act, 1927, was a new codified forest legislation on people's rights over forest land and produce. As per this Act, the government, instead of conserving the forest for the interest of people, allowed export of the valuable forest resources for remunerative purpose, and destroyed a large part of natural forests of the country in order to serve the interest of the Empire (Fuchs, 1992: 375-6). The Government of India Act, 1935 brought forests in the provincial legislative list. In fact, the British forest policies were mainly aimed at commercial exploitation of forests resources at the cost of the tribals in the name of national interest. Under the 1935 legislative policy, the tribals again became the victims of commercial exploitation of forests (Chaudhuri, 1997: 235). Through various measures the British restricted the rights of the tribals and extended administrative control over forests, which resulted in its increasing commercial exploitation.

Independent India

In the post-Independence period, the first forest policy was formulated in 1952, with the emphasis on national interest rather than the natural forest resources. The policy clearly pointed out that local interest and priorities should be subservient to national interest. However, in the name of national interest, the Government of India used the forest resources to meet the requirements of defence, communications and vital wood-based industries. Indeed, it enhanced the income of the government but it also resulted in larger-scale depletion by forest resources (Kannan, 1983: 76-7). In most parts of the country large sections of ecologically sensitive areas were destroyed to make way for power projects, mining, irrigation, industrial ventures and infrastructure like roads and railways. Through the contract lumbering system, huge areas of forest were clear-felled to raise revenue for the state (Human and Pattanaik, 2000: 26).

The right of the tribal people over forest produce in independent India was ensured in the draft of the Indian Forest Bill, 1980. It clearly stated that the provisions of the bill recognized the state's right over forest lands and forest produce and ignored the rights of large sections of communities, especially those who were connected with forest produce. It also denied the real worth of forest as a source of livelihood for millions of poor tribals. The historic 1988 Forest Policy highlighted the symbiotic relationship between the tribal people and forests. This policy emphasized on safeguarding the interest of forest dwellers (http://envfor.nic.in/nfap, MoEF). The Government of India identified that one of the major causes for degradation of forest is illegal cutting and removal of wood by contractors. In order to put an end to this practice, contractors, were replaced by institutions such as tribals cooperatives, labour cooperatives and government corporations. However, the authority over the forest remained in the hands of the government and illegal destruction of forest continued.

In the 1990s, the policy planners began to develop new strategies to reduce the conflict between the state and tribal people. An attempt was made to facilitate the emergence of collaborative forest management systems that responded to both national needs and local resource requirements. In this strategy, it came to widely recognize that the active involvement of tribal people living in and around forest was crucial for the ultimate success of forest protection, regeneration and management activities. In this perspective, the National Forest Policy, 1988 outlined the scope for people's participation in forest management in one of its basic objectives. The policy emphasized on creating a massive people's movement for achieving these objectives and to minimize pressure on existing forests. The broader parameters of people's participation were determined in a June 1990 circular of the Government of India. The circular outlined the *modus operandi* for involvement of forest dwellers and the civil societies in jointly regenerating the degraded forests in the country. The initiative of the government for the participation of people in forest management was widely welcomed in the country. With this national resolution, 22 states approved the guidelines of JFM, but none of the Union Territory did so (http://envfor.nic.in/nfap, MoEF).

The primary objective of JFM is to ensure sustainable use of the nation's forest to meet local needs equitably while achieving India's broader environmental goals. Most state forest departments have been authorized to establish formal dialogues with communities and devolve some management responsibilities to them which are central to their survival. Despite the policy of participatory management of forest, many conflicts have existed between people's expectations and needs and state guidelines for forest management and product sharing. At the official level, the forest department is reluctant to grant greater rights to forest protection groups because they have been controlling the forests for more than a century (Poffenberger and Singh 1996: 62-3). The government's control over forest contradicts the community management system of forest at the village level. In this regard, the community management groups have responded differently in different regions. Some contend that the forest department's recognition of independent community forest management activities may be a tool to co-opt and bring them under government control. In some areas villagers are extremely wary of the forest department's involvement and have banned them from entering their areas. In other regions, village communities are anxious that the forest department staff register their groups and demarcate their protected forests.

STATE POLICY: ORISSA

The forests of Orissa first time came under the notice of the authorities in 1862, although the Orissa Forest Division was created only in 1883 Orissa was then a part of the lower provinces of Bengal. The policy of the then government was to bring more and more forest areas under Reserved Forest and exercise control over it. In the post-Independence period, the forests in Orissa are managed under the mainframe forest law, i.e. the Orissa Forest Act, 1972. Prior to that, the forests in the southern part of Orissa were being managed under the Madras Forest Act, 1882 and forests in the rest of Orissa under the Indian Forest Act, 1927. Various acts and rules have been formulated in the state to facilitate management of forests and forests produce, such as (i) the Orissa Forest Act, 1972, (ii), the Orissa Kendu Leaves (Control of Trade) Act, 1961, (iii) the Forest Conservation Act, 1980, (iv) the Orissa Forest Produce (Control of Trade) Act, 1981, (v) the Schedule of Rate of Forest Produce in Orissa Rules, 1977 and (v) the Orissa Timber and Other Forest Produce Transit Rules, 1980.

In the 1960s, the Government of Orissa started the Orissa Forest Corporation to harvest and manage bamboo, which was being supplied to the paper mills at very subsidized rates. It continued until 1990 even after the nationalization of bamboo in 1988. The state government had appointed the Orissa Forest Development Corporation Ltd. (OFDC) as the sole agency for extraction and trade in bamboo at over the state. The paper mills were virtually harvesting bamboo from the forest under the guidance of the corporation. After the National Forest Policy 1988 these companies were engaged as raw material procurers. Presently the OFDC is directly managing bamboo and the paper mills are no more interested in bamboo as they have shifted to hardwoods. Similarly, Kendu leaves were brought under strict state control in 1973; prior to that it was managed under monopoly leases by a few traders. The Sal seed, which was not given any importance during the 1950s and 1960s, was nationalized in 1983. During the 1970s the Forest Corporation and Tribal

Development Cooperative Corporation (TDCC) was set up by the state government. However, the rest of the MFP was not being managed properly until 1990.

In 2000 the state government formulated the policy of NTFP. The NTFP trade in Orissa was monopolized mostly by private business houses which had been granted long-term lease to procure specific forest produce from specific forest divisions. Such monopoly trade arrangement created problems of low payment to tribals, erratic and arbitrary procurement, and revenue loss to the state. Therefore, in order to streamline the system of collection and disposal of NTFP, which is a major source of livelihood of the tribals, especially women, the state government came out with a new policy guideline on 31 March 2000. The guideline gives ownership rights to the Gram Panchayats over forest resources (Singh, 2005: 74-6).

CASE STUDY

Profile of the Districts

Koraput is one of the southern district of Orissa. The district was formed under the province of Orissa on 1 April 1936, when Orissa became a separate province [Bhatt (ed.), 1988: 679-80]. Prior to separation, it was under the control of Madras Presidency. In 1950, the president issued an order, derived from the constitutional provision of Scheduled Areas, by which the entire Koraput district was declared a Scheduled Area (Senapati and Sahu, 1966: 273-4). Koraput district is spread over 8,807 sq. km. (*District Statistics Handbook*, 2001: 1, 16), most of it covered by hills, primarily the Eastern Ghats. The highest peak of the district, and the whole of Orissa, is Deomali (5,486 ft.) (Bhatt, 1988: 681). The total forest cover of Koraput is 1,879.53 sq. km. (Table 8.1). As per the 2001 census report, Koraput is a tribal dominated district, where the tribals constitute 49.62 per cent of the entire district's population (Table 8.2). The literacy rate of the entire district is 36.20 per cent, while the literacy rate of tribal peoples is 18.68 per cent (Table 8.3).

Methodology

Koraput was selected for an intensive study primarily because it falls under the Fifth Schedule Area and the provisions of the PESA Act are equally applicable in the district. Secondly, Koraput is

TABLE 8.1: CLASSIFICATION OF FOREST AREA BY LEGAL STATUS IN KORAPUT DISTRICT

Classification of Forest	Area in sq. km.
Reserved Forest	478.86
Demarcated Protected Forest	984.58
Undemarcated Forests	0.00
Unclassified Forest	0.68
Other Forests	415.41
Total	1879.53

Source: District Statistical Handbook, Koraput, 2001, p. 32.

TABLE 8.2: POPULATION SIZE OF THE DISTRICT**

Category	Persons*	Scheduled Tribes (%)	Scheduled Castes (%)
Total	1,177,954	49.62	13.04
Male	5,89,438	49.14	12.99
Female	5,88,516	50.10	13.08

Sources: * 'Orissa Rural-Urban Distribution of Population', Census of India, 2001, p. 164.
** Important Statistics State *vs.* District, *Census of India*, 2001.

TABLE 8.3: LITERACY RATE OF THE DISTRICT**

Category	Persons* (%)	Scheduled Tribes (%)	Scheduled Castes (%)
Total	36.20	18.68	35.43
Male	47.58	29.25	48.52
Female	24.81	8.38	22.45

Sources: * 'Orissa Rural-Urban Distribution of Population', *Census of India*, 2001, p. 184.
** Scheduled Castes & Scheduled Tribes Development Department, Government of Orissa, 2001.

predominated by the tribal people and traditionally forest is a major source of livelihood for them. Lastly, large-scale destruction of forest resources, displacement and marginalization has been happening in the district in the name of industrialization.

The field study was located in the Lamtaput block and Damonjodi (falls under Koraput and Pottangi blocks) in the Koraput district of Orissa. Lamtaput is a tribal dominated block, they constitute 46.27 per cent (Census 2001) of the total population of the block. The socio-economic and cultural life of these tribal people and their livelihood is closely linked with the forest resources. As per the 2001 census report, 78 per cent of the people are below the poverty line (*District Statistics Handbook*, 2001: 88). In this block the proportion of the household living below the poverty line is the highest among the tribes. It is not possible to say that agriculture is the primary source of livelihood because the cultivable lands of the block are primarily hilly land. The irrigation facilities in the Lamtaput block are severely limited, the tribal people do not get sufficient irrigation facilities for farming. Moreover, they are skeptical about the use of modern technology and fertilizers. These factors explain the low agricultural productivity in this block.

Damonjodi was selected for this study due to the large-scale destruction of forest and displacement of the poor and marginalized tribal people from their source of livelihood by industrialization, i.e. the setting up of National Aluminium Company (NALCO). High-grade bauxite was discovered at the Panchapatmali hills of Koraput. The total length of the mining area in the hill is about 21 km. and the breadth ranges between 1 and 2.5 km. NALCO was established at Damonjodi in 1981 (Muthayya et al., 1984: 1-2). For establishing the factory, the company acquired 3,444 ha. of land. The establishment of the factory resulted in the displacement of 610 families from 15 villages. In addition to the 15 villages, four more villages were partially affected—they lost their cultivable land but their home remained intact (Muthayya et al., 1984: 2). As per the provisions of the rehabilitation and resettlement programme of the company, these displaced families were identified and provided houses in a rehabilitation colony in Amlabadi and Khalpadi villages, both of which are 2 km. away from the factory. Among the displaced families, the majority were tribal. Prior to displacement, the forest used to be the tribal homestead land and their primary socio-cultural life was revolved around the forest.

Destruction of Forest and Tribals Life

Much of the tribals food and other daily needs are met by the forest. As a result of the illegal destruction, commercialization of forest resources and industrialization the tribal people have been marginalized and further pushed into poverty. Illegal destruction and commercialization by the wood contractors and mafias has destroyed the forest resources in Lamtaput block. Table 8.4 shows the impact

TABLE 8.4: IMPACT OF FOREST DESTRUCTION ON TRIBAL PEOPLE (LAMTAPUT)

Villages (*#)	Source of Livelihood Lost	Losts of Employment	Deteriorated Health Condition
Hingaiput	12	10	09
Bankeiput	13	10	11
Dasuput	15	11	09
Kadamguda	12	09	07
Devgondna	13	11	08
Bhimariput	15	13	10
Tusuba	14	12	11
Ghumalput	13	11	08
Total	107 (89. 16 %)	87 (72.5 %)	73 (60.83 %)

Notes: * The total number of respondents in each village was 15.
As some respondents had given multiple answers to a single question the addition of the total number of responses is not the same as the number of respondents interviewed, i.e. 15.

of the destruction of forest. The tribal people have lost their source of livelihood, employment and their health too has been adversely affected. The tribals used to collect fruits and roots, seasonal vegetables and leaves for their household consumption. They also engaged in collecting MFP and selling it in the market to meet their household expenditure. In most cases it has been found that the women lost the source employment because traditionally they were the primary gatherers of MFP. Since the dietary pattern of tribal people was a combination of fruits, roots and leaves, they stayed healthy and also protected themselves from various diseases. However, due to destruction of forest resources neither are they getting sufficient nutritious food nor are they able to meet the high cost of modern heath care facilities.

In Damonjodi, the problems faced by the displaced people at the resettlement colony are not only due to the destruction of natural environment but also because of the change in their economic and social life. They regard the new place as a desert. Table 8.5 shows the problems faced by the tribal people in the resettlement colony, including:

(i) *Food Insecurity:* This is one of the major problems for the displaced tribal people. Prior to their displacement, every tribal family preserved food grains for the whole year. Following

TABLE 8.5: PROBLEMS FACED AT THE RESETTLEMENT COLONY: DAMONJODI

Villages (*#)	Food Insecurity	Unemploy-ment	Social Disin-tegration	Indeb-tedness	Health Problem
Sindhipar	12	12	13	13	12
Gaudaguda	14	10	14	11	09
Sukriguda	13	09	12	10	14
Damonjodi	11	13	14	13	11
Jhodiguda	12	08	13	12	13
Patiasil	15	13	15	09	10
Kantaguda	12	10	12	07	12
Gadipapli	13	09	11	12	13
Total	102 (85 %)	84 (70 %)	104 (86.66 %)	87 (72.5 %)	94 (78.33 %)

Notes: * The total number of respondent in each village was 15.
As some respondents gave multiple answers to a single question, so the addition of the total number of responses is not same as the number of respondents interviewed, i.e. 15.

displacement, they have lost their common property resources and agricultural lands, which has resulted in chronic food insecurity among the tribal people. Presently they have to buy the food items from the market out of the money earned from jobs or wage labour. As the family size is big and for everything to depends on the market, the people are struggling to run the house on one person's income.

(ii) *Unemployment:* Traditional occupations like collecting MFP, agriculture, cattle rearing, and poultry have been lost due to industrialization. The resettlement colony provides no opportunities to carry out traditional activities, viz., cattle rearing, poultry, kitchen gardening, and so on. On the other hand, at the time of displacement none of the tribals were educated or skilled enough to get employment. It has often been found that the tribal families are migrating to the neighbouring states in search of employment and living in inhuman conditions without social security. Also unemployment has led to psychological problems among many young tribal people.

(iii) *Social Disintegration:* The social organization of the tribal people disintegrated following industrialization and displacement. The kinship groups have scattered and there is no community solidarity and cultural identity. It has been hard for the tribals to rebuild their old social organization in the resettlement colony. Presently, the displaced people are busy in making money with little time to think about the community. They maintain social relation with those who are in similar income group as them. Even in sociocultural ceremonies, the higher income families are not willing to participate with the lower income families. Thus, socio-cultural and community solidarity of tribal society has disappeared following industrialization.

(iv) *Indebtedness:* Due to displacement, the tribal people have to borrow to meet their household expenses. They borrow money from the moneylenders, who take advantage of the poor condition of the tribal people and charge high interest.

(v) *Health Problems:* Prior to displacement, the tribal people depended on the forests medicinal plants for their health care. However, post-displacement they have to turn to modern medicine, which adds to the marginalization of their economic condition. One way or the other, the tribals are the worst sufferers of the displacement process.

Traditional Institutions and Forest

The traditional institution of tribal society, the *Gaon Kutum* is the apex body of the village. The head of the traditional institution is known as the *Jani/Disari*. The villagers vest the authority to head of the institution of *Gaon Kutum* and to control and command all the affairs of the village on the *Jani/Disari*. If any person violates norms or goes against the society, the institution would take action as per its customary laws. In the perspective of preserving the forest resources, the *Gaon Kutum* has been managing the forests to meet the requirements of the tribal people. Later the tribal people initiated the Community Forest Management (CFM) system to protect the forests adjoining their village. In the Lamtaput block out of the eight survey villages, three (Devgondna, Bhimariput and Hingeiput) have the formal CFM system. In the rest five villages the *Gaon Kutum* looks after the preservation of the forest. The CFM systems are participatory bodies because they are constituted within a homogeneous group or a single village.

Though the traditional institutions play a significant role in controlling the forest resources, Tables 8.6 and 8.7 clearly show that

TABLE 8.6: DECLINING ROLE OF THE TRADITIONAL INSTITUTIONS: LAMTAPUT

Villages (*#)	Control by the Forest Officials	Restriction to Use the Forest Resources	Commercialization of Forest Resources
Hingeiput	12	14	15
Bankeiput	15	13	13
Dasuput	10	15	13
Kadamguda	15	14	14
Devgondna	13	09	12
Bhimariput	10	09	15
Tusuba	14	12	13
Ghumalput	15	10	14
Total	104 (86.66 %)	96 (80 %)	109 (90.83 %)

Notes: * The total number of respondenr in each village was 15.
As some respondents gave multiple answers to a single question the addition of the total number of responses is not the same as the number of respondents interviewed, i.e. 15.

TABLE 8.7: REASON FOR THE INABILITY OF THE TRADITIONAL INSTITUTIONS: DAMONJODI

Villages (*#)	Lack of Social Integrity	Busy in Search of Livelihood	Lack of Support from Industrial Authority/ Government Agencies
Sindhipar	09	13	12
Gaudaguda	11	10	08
Sukriguda	08	12	11
Damonjodi	10	09	10
Jhodiguda	12	11	09
Patiasil	11	08	12
Kantaguda	08	12	13
Gadipapli	09	10	13
Total	78 (65 %)	85 (70.83 %)	88 (73.33 %)

Notes: * The total number of respondent in each village was 15.
As some respondents gave multiple answers to a single question the addition of the total number of responses is not same as the number of respondents interviewed, i.e. 15.

the present scenario in the study areas suggest that the traditional institutions are losing control over the forest resources because of their inability to protect the interests of the tribal people. In Lamtaput block large-scale commercialization, control by forest officials and restrictions on tribal people to collect the MFP are some of the major causes for the disablement of the traditional institution. The most worrisome part is that the mafias and wood traders smuggle timber and various forest products in the night. Though the villagers often lodge complaints with the police or forest officials, no action has been taken so far against the defaulters because of corruption at the local level. Over the years it has been found that despite the control of forest officials over the resources, illegal destruction has not been reduced. Thus control over forest by the forest officials has gone against the interest of the traditional rights of the tribal people.

In Damonjodi, the traditional institutions have become weak and no more functional in the resettlement colony, as it was prior to their displacement. Table 8.8 shows that after the displacement, the social integrity of the tribal society has disappeared. This disintegration has further weakened the traditional institutions and made them non-functional. In the context of management of forest resources, the traditional institutions could not regain their position to preserve and protect the resources to meet the requirements of the tribal society. Having lost their source of livelihood, the displaced tribal people are busy in search of sustainable livelihood. Since Damonjodi is an industrial area, it is not possible for the traditional institutions

TABLE 8.8: ROLE OF GRAM PANCHAYAT IN MANAGEMENT OF FOREST: LAMTAPUT

Village (*#)	Illiteracy	Lack of Awareness Campaign	Bureaucratic Apathy	Role of Influential Persons
Hingaiput	12	09	10	08
Bankeiput	13	11	13	11
Dasuput	15	13	09	09
Kadamguda	14	11	10	10
Devgondna	09	12	10	14
Bhimariput	15	14	12	08
Tusuba	13	10	12	06
Ghumalput	15	12	11	15
Total	106 (88.33 %)	92 (76.66 %)	87 (72.5 %)	81 (67.5%)

Notes: * The total number of respondent in each village was 15.
As some respondents gave multiple answers to a single question, the addition of the total number of responses is not same as the number of respondents interviewed, i.e. 15, but it is more than that.

to manage the forest without the effective support of the government agencies and the industrial authorities, even if the institutions take some serious steps to restore the forests. Thus, to survive the traditional institutions and to grow forest in the displacement areas, the social integration of the tribals needs to be strengthened. This will happen only if the authorities ensure sustainable livelihood to the displaced tribals.

PESA AND FOREST

As per the provisions of the Scheduled Area Act, Koraput district falls under the Scheduled Areas (Annual Report, 2003-4: 127). The PESA Act, 1996 and the state Act of 1997, equally apply to the Koraput district. The PESA Act is a significant step to devolve power to the local self-government to preserve, protect and manage the forest resources, in the context of the traditional rights of the forest dwelling communities. The Act also empowers the Gram Sabha to preserve and protect the traditional rights and ownership of MFP at the village level. However, over the years it has been found that the Panchayats, because of adhering to a particular functioning, could not grow as units of self-governance, as per the provisions of the PESA Act. Instead of functioning as an enabling and empowering institution to protect the rights and interest of the tribal people, it tried to project itself as an administrative and controlling authority, which resulted in creating a gap between the Panchayat members and the people at large. Further, the bureaucratic system instead of operating as a facilitator exercised authoritative control over the Panchayats. Today, the Panchayats are mere implementing units. The dream of self-reliance, self-governance and self-managed Panchayats seems to have faded from the people's minds. In the perspective of management of MFP, there have been various shortcomings.

(i) Devolution of Power

The provision of PESA specifically endows Gram Sabhas the ownership over the MFP, to manage and preserve them in the Scheduled Areas in the larger interest of the forest dwelling community. However, in practices, no such power has been given to the Gram Sabha by the Government of Orissa. The government, has not followed the provisions of the 1996 Act in its true spirit. As per the provisions of the Orissa Gram Panchayat Act, every village has a Palli Sabha, which consists of all persons registered by virtue of the Representation of the People Act, 1950. The Palli Sabha is empowered to recommend to the Gram Panchayat on various development works and programmes at the village level (S.S. Singh, 1997: 356). This clearly shows that the Gram Sabha does not have any power to play a vital role in the management of forest resources at the village level.

Further, there is contradiction between the Orissa Forest Policy and the PESA Act. Section 77 of the Orissa Forest Act, 1972 invests the Divisional Forest Officers with the power to enter upon any land to survey, demarcate and prepare a map of the same; power to hold an inquiry into forest offences and in the course of such inquiry to receive and record evidence. The criminal procedure authority is also under the jurisdiction of forest officials (*Orissa Forest Manual*, 2005: 660). Taking the advantage of this Act, the local forest officials are misusing their power and controlling the forest, which is affecting the traditional rights of the tribal people over the forest. It also completely contradicts with the PESA Act, where even though the Gram Sabhas as are empowered to manage the forest, they have no authority to take legal action against the offenders. To put it differently, the Gram Sabhas have only civil power not judicial power.

(ii) Role of Gram Panchayats

The tribal people are completely ignorant about their powers over the management of forest resource as per the provisions of the Panchayati Raj Act (Table 8.8). They have little knowledge that the Panchayat is an institution which can implement various welfare scheme at the village level, that the elected members of the Panchayat, i.e. the president, members and the secretary (official staff) should hold a village meeting to select beneficiaries for various anti-poverty programmes. The issue of management of forest resource and protection of tribal rights has not been discussed ever in the Panchayat meetings. Since the activities and functions of the Gram Panchayat are carried out under the direction of the influential persons of non-tribal communities, the rights of tribals has not been addressed ever. It is a fact that even the elected members of the Panchayat do not know about the provisions under the PESA and the role of Gram Panchayat in the management of forest resources.

In Damonjodi, the resettlement colony falls under the jurisdiction of Matalput Panchayat. On paper the provisions of PESA Act have been equally applied to the resettlement colony but not in practice. Table 8.9 shows that since the resettlement colony is situated within the periphery of an industrial area, the Panchayat officials argue that it is the responsibility of the industrial authority to think about the interest and rights of the tribal people. The perception of the elected members is that the industrial authority has been providing benefits to the tribal people. It is also a fact that bureaucratic apathy is also rampant in Damonjodi. The bureaucrats do not pay attention to the rights of the tribal people under the provision of the PESA Act. Though PESA came into force to protect the interests of the tribal people, it has failed to fulfil its promises in Damonjodi. It is industrialization which has caused the destruction of forest resources, but as per the provisions of PESA, the concerned Panchayat officials and bureaucrats should protect the interests of the tribal people through necessary steps to conserve the forests.

TABLE 8.9: ROLE OF GRAM PANCHAYAT IN MANAGEMENT OF FOREST: DAMONJODI

Villages (*#)	Resettlement Colony in the Periphery of Industry	Prejudice by the Elected Members	Bureaucratic Apathy
Sindhipar	10	12	09
Gaudaguda	08	10	11
Sukriguda	11	13	10
Damonjodi	09	11	08
Jhodiguda	07	09	13
Patiasil	09	11	06
Kantaguda	11	08	09
Gadipapli	12	10	10
Total	77 (64.16 %)	84 (70 %)	76 (63.33 %)

Notes: * The total number of respondent in each village was 15.

\# As some respondents gave multiple answers to a single question, the addition of the total number of responses is not the same as the number of respondents interviewed, i.e. 15, but it is more than that.

CONCLUSION

From the field assessment, it was observed that forest is the main source of livelihood for the tribal people even through the government is spending huge amounts to eradicate poverty in the tribal society. Even today the tribal people largely follow their traditional economic system. However, due to commercialization, industrialization and illegal destruction of forests, the tribal people have been losing their source of livelihood. A number of policies have been made to protect their interests but have failed to address the need and problems of the tribal people. Democratic decentralization is one of the significant steps of the government to empower the local people to participate in the decision-making process, but still large sections of tribal people are not aware of the provisions of the grassroot democratic institutions.

The PESA Act, 1996 came into force to protect the interests of the tribal people. The Act empowers the Gram Panchayat to preserve and protect the forest resource at the village level. It also bestows ownership authority to the Gram Sabha to own and manage the forest-based resources at the village level. However, it has been found that the state government is reluctant to implement the provisions in their true spirit. In the case of ownership of MFP, no significance changes can be seen. The MFP policy of 2000 clearly mentions that the Gram Panchayat has ownership rights over MFP. However, the ownership over MFP still lies undefined and it is the forest department that enjoys ultimate authority over the resources. On the other hand, the Gram Panchayat can only exercise control over those forest produce that the Forest Department decides as MFP. The important issue is that even after handing over responsibility to the Gram Panchayats, the government has not really taken any significant step to create a facilitating environment for the Gram Panchayats to own, control and manage the MFP. Most Panchayats do not even have the desired information with them on the devolution of power and authority. No efforts have been made to capacitate the Gram Panchayats and Palli Sabhas to own and control the resources. On the other hand, the forest department is no more showing any interest in the management and control of resources for the interest of the tribal people. Even if the ownership rights have been vested with the Gram Panchayat, the judicial power lies with the forest department. Lastly, it has been seen in the study areas that under the PESA Act the real sufferers are the primary users of the resources. In both Lamtaput and Damonjodi, the act has failed to gain in terms of protecting and preserving the rights and interests of the tribal people.

REFERENCES

Annual Report 2003-2004, Ministry of Tribal Affairs, Government of India.

Bakshi, P.M. (2001), *The Constitution of India*, New Delhi: Universal Law Publishing Co.

Bhatt, S.C. (ed.) (1988), *The Encyclopaedic District Gazetteers of India*, New Delhi: Gyan Publishing House.

Chaudhuri, Buddhadeb (1997), 'Forest and Tribals', in Georg Pfeffer and Deepak Kumar Behra (eds.), *Contemporary Society, Tribal Studies*, vol. I, New Delhi: Concept Publishing Company.

Deeney, John and Walter Fernandes (1992), 'Tribals: Their Dependence on Forests, Their Traditions and Management Systems', in Walter Fernandes (ed.), *National Development and Tribal Deprivation*, New Delhi: Indian Social Institute.

District Statistics Handbook Koraput (2001), Directorate of Economic and Statistics, Bhubaneswar, Orissa.

Fuchs, Stephen (1992), 'Indian Tribals and the Forest', in Buddhadeb Chaudhuri (ed.), *Economic and Agrarian Issues*, New Delhi: Inter-India Publication.

Human, Joe and Manoj Pattanaik (2000), *Community Forest Management*, New Delhi: Oxfam.

Kannan, K.P. (1983), 'Forestry Legislation in India: Its Evolution in the Light of the Forest Bill-1980', in Walter Fernandes and Sharad Kulkarni (eds.), *Towards a New Forest Policy*, New Delhi: Indian Social Institute.

Lal, J.B. (1989), *India's Forest: Myth and Reality*, Dehra Dun: Natraj Publishers.

National Forest Policy 1988, Ministry of Environment & Forests, http://envfor.nic.in

Mukul (1997), 'Tribal Areas: Transition to Self-Governance', *Economic and Political Weekly*, vol. XXXV, no. 17, pp. 928-9.

Munshi, I. (2005), 'Scheduled Tribes Bill, 2005', *Economic and Political Weekly*, vol. XL, no. 41, p. 4406.

Muthayya, B.C. et al. (1984), *Rehabilitation of Displaced Villagers: A Study in NALCO Complex Damonjodi, Koraput District, Orissa*, Hyderabad: National Institute of Rural Development.

Orissa Forest Manual 2005, Cuttack: Orissa Law Review.

Poffenberger, Mark and Chatrapati Singh (1996), 'Community and the State: Re-establishing the Balance in India's Forest Policy', in Mark Poffenberger and Betsy McGean (eds.), *Village Voices, Forest Choices: Joint Forest Management in India*, New Delhi: Oxford University Press.

Sarkar, Amitabha and Samira Dasgupta (2000), *Ethno-Ecology of Indian Tribes*, Jaipur: Rawat Publications.

Senapati, Nilamani and N.N. Sahu (1966), *Orissa District Gazetters, Koraput*, Cuttack: Orissa Government Press.

Sharma, B.D. (2000), *The Fifth Schedule*, vol. I, New Delhi: Sahyog Pustak Kuteer Trust.

Singh, S.K. (ed.) (2005), *Self-Governance for Tribals: Management of Minor Forest Produce and Common Property Resources,* vol. III, Hydrabad: National Institute of Rural Development.

Singh, S.K. (1997), 'Panchayat for Scheduled Areas', *Mainstream*, vol. XXXV, no. 43, pp. 8-9.

Singh S.S. et al. (1997), *Legislative Status of Panchayti Raj in India*, New Delhi: Indian Institute of Public Administration.

Upadhayay, S. (2003), 'JFM in India: Some Legal Concerns', *Economic and Political Weekly*, vol. XXXVIII, no. 35, p. 3631.

Vidyarthi, L.P. and B.K. Rai (1985), *The Tribals Culture of India*, New Delhi: Concept Publishing Company.

CHAPTER 9

Development or Destitution: Rethinking Tribal-State Relationship in Orissa

JAGANNATH AMBAGUDIA

INTRODUCTION

The 1990s has witnessed a proliferation of scholarship around the topic of tribes and the state. Tribes and their relations to the state have been the mutual interest of anthropologists, historians and political scientists in modern scholarship. In recent years, they have discovered fruitful opportunities for intellectual exchange and even collaboration in their effort to understand continuity and change in different societies. Historians and political scientists have turned to the concepts and tools of anthropology to examine certain questions that are directly or indirectly related to understand the diversified democratic nature of the Indian society. In the first decade of the twenty-first century, different factors are shaping and re-shaping the tribal-state relations. The future of these relations is unclear, but the interaction among these trends and relative influence of each will do a great deal to determine not only the shape of those relations but the future of the Indian nation.

This paper looks at the cohesion, conflicts and contradictions within the Orissan state with reference to vulnerable tribal communities. By looking at the tribal situation in Orissa, the paper tries to find out how tribes define themselves in terms of their relationship with the state and what would be the impact of such a relationship in shaping and re-shaping tribal structure. Within this backdrop, it examines the interrelationship of tribes and the state at different times and parts of the state. It examines the continuous interaction of tribes and state, changes in the interaction over the spans of time, the similarities and differences those changes produced across the state. It proceeded to argue that the role of the Orissan state is coercive or predatory in nature that leads to the destitution of tribal communities of Orissa.

TRIBAL SITUATION IN ORISSA

Orissa has many tribal communities and occupies a unique position in the tribal map of India. According to 2001 census, Orissa has 8,145,081 tribal persons, out of which 4,066,783 are male and 4,078,298 are female, contributing 22.19 per cent to the state population of 36,706,920. To put it in another way, one out of every four person is a tribal in Orissa. It is nearly 9.64 per cent of the tribal population of the country, third in terms of tribal concentration, only next to Madhya Pradesh (14.48 per cent) and Maharashtra (10.15 per cent). They are drawn from 62 communities, the largest number in the country. They belong to different ethnic, linguistic and religious groups. They maintain socio-economic and cultural characteristics. Each one of the tribal communities has its own language different from the others. The Parliament in its winter session passed the Scheduled Castes and Scheduled Tribes Orders (Amendment) Act, 2002 (No. 10 of 2003) on 7 January, 2003 with some modifications and prepared the list of 62 communities.

The tribal communities living in the state range from small communities like Chenchu, Banda, Juanga, Didayi to a larger groups like, Munda, Santhals, Kandha, Oraon, Saura and Bhuiyan. Among the 62 tribal communities of Orissa, Government of India identifies only 13 tribes as Primitive Tribal Groups (PTG). They are namely, Birhor, Bonda, Didayi, Dongria Kondh, Juang, Kharia, Kutia Kondh, Langia Saora, Lodha, Mankirdia, Paudi Bhuiyan, Saura and Chutia Bhunja. They live in the area of Sambalpur, Koraput, Malkangiri, Keonjhar, Sundargarh and Mayurbhanj. Each of these group is small in number, have attended various levels of social and economic development and generally, they live in remote habitat with poor administrative and infrastructure back up. They have been characterized by a low level of literacy, declining or stagnant population, a pre-agricultural level of technology and are economically backward. However, these communities have similarities of their dependence on the nature for livelihood and in adherence to nature spirit complexes. For better administration and effective implementation of developmental programmes for the benefit of STs, almost 44.21 per cent of the total land area of the state has been constitutionally declared as Scheduled Areas by taking into account the concentration of tribals in different parts of the state.

The tribes of Orissa have been classified ethno-linguistically into three groups: (i) Austro-Asiatic or Munda group; (ii) Dravidian group; and (iii) Indo-Aryan group (Das and Pradhan, 2002: 41). Some others like, N.K. Behura classified the tribes of Orissa, according to their economic practices, into following six categories: (i) hunting gatherer nomads living in hilly and forest areas; (ii) hunting gatherer shifting cultivators; (iii) simple artisans; (iv) shifting cultivators; (v) settled agriculturists; and (vi) the industrial and urban unskilled and semi-skilled workers (Behura, 2002: 63; Mahapatra, 2000: 170). The core of the tribal population is concentrated in three belts: the south-west belt comprises the district of Koraput; the north-west belt consists of Mayurbhanj and Sundargarh in the north of Orissa. The tribes of Orissa have their distinct ethnic identity, which is overtly marked in their language, culture, art and craft, beliefs and value judgement and lifestyle. Nearly 25 tribes speak their own language or have distinct languages. Some of the tribal languages are Santhali, Ho, Mundari, Kol, Kharia, Sadri, Kuvi, Koya, etc. They use these languages to communicate among themselves. Ironically, most of these tribal languages have no script. In recent times, however, Santhals have been able to develop a script known as 'Olchiki' and Saoras a script called as 'Sorang Sompe'.

DISTRIBUTION OF STs IN DISTRICTS

The STs are distributed in almost all districts including those in the coastal belts. The analysis of census data shows that the tribes such as, Juang, Gadaba, Paraja, Banda, Koya, etc., live in a compact area; while the Saura, Kandha, Gond and Bhuiyan have a wide distribution in different districts. The particular block or district is not confined with a particular tribe. There are more than one community living in every village. The distribution of ST population among districts is greatly uneven. As Table 9.1 indicates, the STs are much larger proportion to the total district population compared to the state average of 22.19 per cent in districts like, Malkangiri (57.42 per cent), Mayurbhanj (56.59 per cent), Rayagada (55.75 per cent), Nabarangpur (55.02 per cent), Kandhamal (51.96 per cent), Sundargarh (50.19 per cent), Gajapati (50.78 per cent), Koraput

(49.61 per cent), Kendujhar (44.27 per cent), Nuapada (34.71 per cent), Sambalpur (34.49 per cent), Debagarh (33.60 per cent), Jharsuguda (31.34 per cent) and Kalahandi (28.64 per cent) and the rest are below the state average. Just below the 50 per cent of districts have the higher proportion of tribal people than the state average. According to 2001 census, the proportion of tribal population to

TABLE 9.1: DISTRIBUTION OF STs IN DISTRICTS

District	Total	ST	ST Population % to the state	ST Population % to the district
Angul	1,140,003	132,994	1.63	11.66
Bolangir	1,337,194	275,822	3.38	20.62
Balasore	2,024,508	228,454	2.80	11.28
Bargarh	1,346,336	60,691	3.20	19.36
Bhadrak	1,333,749	25,141	0.30	1.88
Baudh	373,372	46,557	0.57	12.46
Cuttack	2,341,094	83,591	1.02	3.57
Debagarh	274,108	92,103	1.13	33.60
Dhenkanal	1,066,878	136,501	1.67	12.79
Gajapati	518,836	263,476	3.23	50.78
Ganjam	3,160,635	90,919	1.11	2.87
Jagatsinghapur	1,057,629	8,640	0.10	0.81
Jajpur	1,624,341	125,989	1.54	7.75
Jharsuguda	509,716	159,757	1.96	31.34
Kalahandi	1,335,494	382,573	4.69	28.64
Kandhamal	648,201	336,809	4.13	51.96
Kendrapara	1,302,005	6,822	0.08	0.52
Kendujhar	1,569,990	695,141	8.53	44.27
Khordha	1,877,395	97,186	1.19	5.17
Koraput	1,180,637	585,830	7.19	49.61
Malkangiri	504,198	289,538	3.55	57.42
Mayurbhanj	2,223,456	1,258,459	15.45	56.59
Nuapada	530,690	184,221	2.26	34.71
Nabarangapur	1,025,776	564,480	6.93	55.02
Nayagarh	864,516	50,836	0.62	5.88
Puri	1,502,682	4,482	0.05	0.29
Rayagada	831,109	463,418	5.68	55.75
Sambalpur	935,613	322,770	3.96	34.49
Sonapur	541,835	52,978	0.65	9.77
Sundargarh	1,830,673	918,903	11.28	50.19

Source: Government of India, *Census of India, 2001*, Final Population, Series 1.

the total population of the district is highest in the district of Malkangiri (57.42 per cent). This district was also the first among districts in 1991 with 58.54 per cent.

The proportion of STs is lowest in districts of Puri (0.29 per cent), Kendrapada (0.52) and Jagatsinghpur (0.81). If we compare the tribal population of Malkangiri district between 1991 and 2001, we notice that it has gone down by 1.12 per cent. Puri district was also the last among districts in 1991 with 0.27 per cent. Similarly, if comparison will be made between 1991 and 2001, there has been a marginal increase of 0.02 per cent. Reckoning against the total population of the state, more than one-third of the tribal population lives in Mayurbhanj, Sundargarh and Kendujhar.

SOCIAL ORGANIZATION

Tribes in India are not a homogeneous category. They differ widely among themselves in respect of regions they live in, language they speak, physical feature they display, geographical terrain they inhabit, modes in which they make their living, levels of development at which they are placed and size of community they represent. The tribal structure does not subscribe to the pattern of social stratification according to the *varna* or *jati* as found in Hindu society. As V.P. Varma says:

> The Adivasis is not organised on the basis of the endogamous structure of the caste that is prevalent in the Hindu society. The tribal social system, on the contrary, is structure on the basis of inner differentiation among the tribes themselves. It is true, however, that with the infiltration of Hindu priest, traders and other citizens into tribal society; some kind of Hinduization is taking place. But the tribal population, not being organised on the caste lines, will have differentiation in getting Hinduized. It is also observed that their process of Hinduization is being counteracted by the intensification of the Christian proselytization. (Varma, 1972: 383-4)

Some tribes of Orissa, for instance, like the Kandha and the Saora have developed internal social differentiation along the line of occupational specialization such as, potters, weavers and basket makers. Some other tribes like the Bhuiyan, the Bathudi, the Gond and the Binjal of northern and western Orissa have been very much Hinduized and their status is equal to that of the clean Hindu castes. Thus, in tribal society, two broad dimensions of stratification can be seen: firstly, it is to be seen in the background of caste *versus* tribe and tribe *versus* tribe; and secondly, in the relevance of intra-tribe setting.

Among the tribes of Orissa, the family is of patriarchal type and the rule of residence is patrilocal. The oldest male member of the family, unless he is very old and is leading a retired life or is handicapped or infirm, is the ***mukhia***, the head of the family. He plays a dominant role in all family matters. The ***mukhia***, however, consults usually grown-up male members of the family in social and economic matters. The eldest son occupies an important position in the family. Division of labour in the family is based on age and sex. Women take the responsibility of all the household work, plus go to the field with their husbands to help them in various agricultural activities and collection of firewood. The anthropological study shows that men exclusively do the ploughing (Singh, 1995: 106). But female members are now also practising this and the Koya tribe of Malkangiri district can be demonstrated in this context.

The STs dispersing all over the country differ from one another in racial traits, language, social organization, cultural pattern, etc. Marriage, as an institution, has a different connotation to people on the basis of their ethnic and cultural identities. The customary and legal procedures, provisions, ceremonial practices, etc., vary from one country to another and also within the country on the basis of people's ethnic and cultural affinities. Social organization of any culture reflects the core and the intensity of social bond existing in that culture. So, the need of marriage is for a dependable social mechanism for the care of children and also the transmission of culture from one generation to the other.

Most of the tribes in Orissa (for instance, the Kuvi Kandha and the Bhumia) practice cross-cousin marriage. Predominant form of marriage among the tribal people is monogamy but polygamy is also practised. They believe that having more than one wife is the indication of the higher status (Singh, 1995: 107). It has been perceived that, if more wives are there, they will produce more children so that workload is distributed. In this context, the notion that a small family means better economic status does not apply. For them, marriage by negotiation is always considered as socially approved and most prestigious, however, they also follow some other ways of acquiring mates such as, marriage by capture, marriage by exchange and marriage by service. To make the marriage ceremony more enjoyable, they introduce liquor. Country wines called *Mahula* and *Salapa* are in use among them. There must be dance and feast with plenty of liquor for everyone to get some pleasure out of the marriage event (Elwin, 1954: 532). The drinking of wine is so much a part of their social and religious life that the Government of Orissa while introducing prohibition had excluded the districts with a large Adivasi population out of its purview (Dash, 1997: 80).

In Orissa, certain tribes practice the paying of bride price and the bridegroom acquires his bride only after making payment towards it. This categorically differentiates what is happening in the contemporary Indian scenario. The Bhumias call this system as *jala* and *modar* as the Dongria Kandhas name it. The logic behind the bride price, according to tribals of Orissa, is that the parents have taken the responsibility of her growing up. So, it is also her responsibility towards the parents. The groom sometimes comes to serve as a suitor-servant in his would be father in-law's house till the time he is able to pay the entire amount of the finalized bride price. Once it is paid, he can take back his bride. But the story of bride price does not take full shape at this juncture. It goes much beyond that. To maintain some form of balance, they also practice another kind of bride price termed as *sagarta* by the Bhumia tribe of Malkangiri. This system clearly shows that if married woman/widow gets remarried then her previous husband's family demand bride price more than they had actually paid to the girls family. It may take the form of negotiation, but he is bound to pay either in cash or kind.

ECONOMIC ORGANIZATION

K.S. Singh (1992) analyses that the economy of tribes is a projection of tribal society, a response to the economic system in which it is placed. Its functions of production and distributions are governed by the bond of kinship within or between families, clans and kindred. Production is based on the exploitation of resources locally and easily available with a crude technology largely for consumption. Family is the unit of production, with little specialization and division of labour based on sex and age. The tribal civilization is predominantly rural in character and its political economy is very primitive.

The tribes of Orissa belong to different socio-cultural situation and show a considerable variation in their basic economy. Because of their adherence to habits that are either located in the hills and forests, hills-plains fringe regions or the plains and subsequent ecological adaptation to the immediate physical as well as social environment, they have been found with different primary occupation or technoeconomic levels like food gathering and hunting, shifting cultivation, settled agriculture, industrial urban labour, etc.

On the other hand, there are backward shifting cultivating groups like the Kutia Kandha, the Bonda, the Hill Juang, the Paudi Bhuiya, etc., and there are assimilated groups who are undistinguishable from the general rural population of the country. The most interesting aspect of tribal economy is that they rarely follow one occupation exclusively. For instance, in Orissa, the tribals like Kharia and Birhor follow the occupations of hunting, collecting and gathering types. Birhor, although, are identified as the hunting and gathering community, their main occupation is making ropes out of the siali. Similarly, Saora and Gadaba both adhere to shifting and settled agriculture (Das and Pradhan, 2002: 42-3). As far as Santhals are concerned, they were formally engaged in collection of forest produce, hunting, fishing and cultivation on hill slopes. At present, they are engaged in cultivation with the capacity of sharecroppers, agriculture labourer and small farmers (Kar, 1999: 244). Above all, agriculture is the main source of their income substantiated by shifting cultivation.

The tribal economy of Orissa is primarily a subsistence oriented and based upon a combination of agriculture, forestry and wage labour. Nearly 90 per cent of tribals depend on agriculture. Although agriculture is the main source of their income, agricultural productivity of tribals is quite low in Orissa due to traditional farming practices, low use of yield stimulating inputs like, high yielding variety (HYV) seeds, chemical fertilizer, inadequate irrigation facilities that are available and low investment in agriculture. So, the financial position of tribals does not present a good picture. The development gaps between tribals and non-tribals vary across states and so do the resource requirements to bridge the gap. The inter-state variations in the level of deprivation of tribals *vis-à-vis* the rest of the population may also exist in each area of social concern. It is impossible to assess quantitatively the relative deprivation of tribals *vis-à-vis* the rest of the population for each state. Corresponding to their income, the per capita monthly income of tribals is Rs. 124.16 as against Rs. 131.17 in case of non-tribals in Orissa (Hooja, 2004: 30).

The state government of Orissa has failed to provide quality life to the tribal community. This is because of financial crisis, low level of economic growth, per capita income, etc. Although agriculture continues to be the mainstay of the state's economy with a contribution of about 28.13 per cent of NSDP during 2001-2, it suffers from many hazards. Droughts and floods are not only the permanent feature of Orissa's economy, the production pattern is also defective in Orissa. Orissa also suffers from serious financial burden and it raises a loan over the years. In Orissa, for instance, the per capita loan burden during the year 1999-2000 was Rs. 5,014.07 and was raised to Rs. 8,473.62 in 2003-4. In other words, the Government of Orissa failed to provide quality life to the people, including tribals, due to its financial constraints (Misra, 2003: 87-97; Dash, 2004: 433-56).

POLITICAL ORGANIZATION

Political organization of tribals can be seen as a curious blend of democracy and monarchy (Padhy and Tripathy, 1994: 54). The head of every community or village or an area or a class exercises the supreme power over his subjects and he is the source and interpreter of all laws. Socially, tribals in most cases are well organized into many groups. In this context, Verrier Elwin says: 'There is a regular village hierarchy. Every village has its own chief who is its spokesperson and general organiser. In some tribes, he has great authority; in other words he is a mere figure head' (Elwin, 1954: 2/10). The Savar headman is known as *Gomango*; the Kondhs call him *Samanto*, or *Majhi*; the Parojas call him *Janni* or *Muduli*; the Koyas call him as *Pedda*, *Goantia* or *Naik* and the head of the Bhumias is known as *Naik*. As political life, behaviour and role of an individual are influenced by the socio-economic conditions of the family/community, his office is a hereditary one. In the case of Dongria Kondhs, after his death his son becomes the head. If he is not blessed with a son, his younger brother and failing that any other competent consanguine relative becomes his successor. The careful analysis of political organization of the Bhumias of Malkangiri district in Orissa seems quite different. Considering the Bhumias, after the death of the head, his younger brother becomes his successor or failing that his son becomes the head. The democratic nature of the tribal political organization can be demonstrated by the fact that the tribal leader governs the community only because the majority or the whole of the nation backs him. It has been observed that tribal leadership cannot be changed if not backed by heredity. If anybody does, he is not going to be recognized as the leader of the respective community.

In Orissa, the political organization of tribals has been empowered to enjoy legislative, executive and judicial powers. It stands for the safeguard of judicial rights and the enforcement of the judicial obligation on people. Law and order is maintained by a few village elders in consultation with the adult male members. They categorically announce that violation of any law is punishable. Generally, tribes do not have any judicial institutions in Orissa, but they have their panchayat system and village council of which the elders of the village are members. They try to settle all types of controversies within the village. The party found guilty will be fined with cash or kind. Ironically, they spend the cash fine on drinking as well as entertainment. This village council is also the ultimate arbiter of ensuring peace and justice, solving disputes and regulating social life by the enforcement of customary laws. If the village council fails to resolve the difference then they will move to the panchayat. If again it fails, the sarpanch forwards the case to the police station, which is very rarely used by tribal people in Orissa. The tribals keep it as the last option of resolving differences. So, we can observe that tribal communities of Orissa try to resolve all types of controversies irrespective of their nature at their disposal by hook or by crook and show their apathy in modern political institutions.

TRIBAL AND NON-TRIBAL RELATIONSHIP

There is a wide variety of literature which exists to demonstrate that the British policy tried to separate tribes from non-tribes. When British entered tribal areas, there were encounters and uprisings. Hence, the administration of such regions was separated from civil administration. In 1874, the Scheduled Districts Act was passed with the aim to keep the tribal areas separated from the general administration. This came to be known as 'non-regulation system'. This endorsed the British government to reveal that tribals were native and indigenous groups, who were different and isolated from the mainstream. But the nationalists, under the leadership of Gandhi, opposed the segregation of tribals from rest of India. They held that tribals were a part of Hindu society and at the very least, they were backward Hindus.

When we address the question of tribal and non-tribal relationship, it is clear that the relationship is based on cross-cultural assimilation and conflict. Taking note of active process of cultural assimilation, large number of land granted to Brahmins to the upland hilly forest areas of Orissa, which led to the process of Brahminization. This process facilitated the acculturation of tribals. Some tribal elements were incorporated with the Hindu society and there was an upward mobility, described by M.N. Srinivas as 'Sanskritization' (Sarkar, 2003: 3-4), which were assimilated in the Brahminical caste hierarchy. But Xaxa prefers to use the term 'Hinduization' in the place of Sanskritization (Xaxa, 1999: 1520-2). This is because climbing up the caste ladder is not the overriding concern among tribes. Such interaction of tribal and Brahminical culture led to the cross-cultural assimilation in Orissa as manifested in the worship of Shakti in the form of mother Goddess and the cult of Jagannath. Another example can be substantiated. The people of Malkangiri district in Orissa celebrate *Badayatra*, which takes place in every alternative year, irrespective of their caste, class, colour, sex, etc. This shows their cooperation as well as cultural assimilation. Thus, the tribals have played a major role in shaping the history and culture of Orissa.

On the contrary, the Hindu caste hierarchy demonstrates the latter. According to historian Niharranjan Ray, 'In Indian historical tradition there were two sets of *janas*, one who are still recognized by anthropologists and sociologist as tribes . . . and another set who are at a higher level of socio-economic and political organisation and of aesthetic and religious culture' (Ray, 1972: 123). This dynamic of social stratification between tribals and non-tribals continued from the formation of princely state, which led to a sort of king-subject relationship between the non-tribal king and tribal subjects (Joshi, 1997: 460). In the context of preferential treatment, the tribal and non-tribal relationship has turned into conflict in Orissa. For instance, Mathili block of Malkangiri district in Orissa witnessed a bloody struggle between the Kandha tribe and non-tribals in 1999-2000. The conflict arose on the ownership pattern of land, where the non-tribal (upper caste) people felt the sense of relative deprivation. In the recent years, it has been observed that the struggle for survival among tribals of Malkangiri district is being initiated by some civil society organizations. The main motto of this struggle is to restore the land rights of tribals, which are transferred to non-tribals illegally. To put it differently, this pattern of ownership of land has more aggravated in the recent years. Notwithstanding these cultural assimilation and conflict, what is seen as the most pronounced mark of differentiation as compared to non-tribes is that they are more self-contained than the non-tribal social groups (Xaxa, 2001: 203) and they fall outside civilization (Beteille, 1986: 316). The tribals of Orissa have also contradictory relations with another constitutionally recognized group for preferential treatment such as SCs. It reveals the state's perhaps worst ever incident of caste violence, months of bloody caste war between Dalits and tribals in Phulbani (Kandhamal district) of Orissa during February-June 1994 (Ambagudia, 2006: 289-90). This conflict was also aggravated due to the words of upper caste people of Phulbani, where they told the tribals that 'Dalits loot the illiterate tribals and disrupt the moral order of the village' (ibid.).

STATE AND TRIBAL RELATIONSHIP

There is an open debate about the tribal-state relationship that is alarming. It is essential to know something about the historic foundation upon which the relationship between the tribes and the state is based. In a broader or narrow sense, it is not an easy task to draw a clear-cut relationship between the state/nation and tribals. To be specific, it is a truly complex process and controversial to assess the relationship between the state and tribals in Orissa, as they have different attitudes towards each other. The existing literature claims considerable diversity, substantiated by their relative field studies, in their approaches, methods and inferences. This part starts with one of the significant aspects of Oriya identity or nationalism, i.e. language.

Let us examine the view of Georg Pfeffer. His thesis follows: 'The Scheduled Tribes (ST) in Orissa are inimical and antithetical to Oriya identity/nationalism' (Pfeffer, 1998: 20-4). As language is a maker of identity, Orissa gained the status of separate state due to its exclusive identity as a province of the Oriya-speaking people on 1 April 1936. According to Georg Pfeffer, STs are not glamorous, fashionable, feasible and reliable for strengthening Oriya identity. He goes on to the extent of ratiocinating that STs know Oriya language and they do have the talent to communicate with others in Oriya but they are reluctant to disclose Oriya as their mother tongue.

For instance, it has been observed that, whether it may be Bhumia or Koya tribe, first of all, they prepare to respond in their respective tribal dialect as the mother tongue and then come to Oriya. To put it differently, tribal dialects are primary and Oriya language is secondary for them. This may be due to the kind of discrimination, the tribal population faced from the Oriyas. In contrast, tribals, in fact, experience gender equality in their own cultural context. This argument can be more strengthened if we look at the Constituent Assembly debates. In the Constituent Assembly, tribal representatives demanded to develop according to their own genius and culture because there was no gender discrimination among tribals and this trend of tribals is yet to become irrelevant (Ambagudia, 2005: 105).

The question of 'tribals as an inimical to Oriya identity or Oriya nationalism' has, however, been increasingly found to be of little significance. In this context, Biswamoy Pati's study can be quoted as an instance. Citing an example of coastal Orissa (comprising Cuttack, Puri and Balasore) and that the language spoken in this tract is the real Oriya and this area is the centre of Oriya culture, he argues that some of the remotest tribes of the province, i.e. the Bandas of Koraput district, speak a language which sounds like the seminal variant of Oriya spoken in the coastal region today (Pati, 1993: 2). Some scholars argue that the tribal deity Jagannath is the prime symbol of Oriya identity (Kanungo, 2003: 3294; Pathy, 188: 43-4). It is more significant that prior to the colonial period, Oriyas did not have a strong consciousness of their identity (Mohapatra, 1996: 203-21). The virtual 'common sense' emerged with the emergence of Jagannath as a key player in the political arena of the province. The most important feature, however, is the unique position of Jagannath of Puri in the religio-cultural and political traditions of Orissa. Though Jagannath is identified as Orissa's 'god/cult', he has a strong adivasi connection (D'Souza, 2006: 87-102; Nayak, 2001: 25-48). However, throughout these centuries, Jagannath remained as a potent rallying symbol, reinforcing the collective regional and ethnic identity of the territorially fragmented Orissa.

During the freedom movement, tribals of Orissa took part in large numbers. By the 1940s, tribal involvement in the freedom movement had become widespread, even though there was less manifestation of unrest than in 1930-2. Several regions of tribal middle India, which had not been affected by the Civil Disobedience Movement, felt the impact of the Quit India Movement. A typical example was Laxman Nayak, a Bhumia from Koraput (now Malkangiri) district of Orissa, who had given up hunting and become a vegetarian under the influence of Gandhian ideology, offered Satyagraha in 1939-40. He organized resistance to payment of taxes and led a march of the Bondo highlanders on 31 August 1942. They picked up liquor shops and there was a scuffle in the course of which a forest guard was killed. Laxman Nayak was implicated in this case and his history came to an end when he was hanged on 29 March 1943, even though he was universally believed to be innocent (Das, 1967-8: 22-8; Pathy, 1988: 23). Before Laxman Nayak was hanged, he uttered his last words, 'If the sun and the moon are true, then India will achieve freedom. Swaraj will definitely come. I cannot see it. Its my only grief' (Panigrahi, 2006: 30). Even it is most unfortunate that the people involved in the entire process of Laxman Nayak's arrest and death penalty were able to get all government facilities, employment and promotion during the post-Independence period.

Orissa witnessed a series of tribal revolts since the beginning of the nineteenth century. The Koyas of Malkangiri in erstwhile Madras Presidency rose against the administration in 1879 and 1880. The Kondh of Phulbani rose in revolt under the leadership of Chakra Bissoyi in 1850. Being oppressed by the mutta heads, the Saura rose twice in 1890 and 1940. Bhuyians and Juanngs of Keonjhar were equally vociferous against the native chiefs. All these events claim that tribals resisted the alien rulers, who overlooked their traditions and felt needs. It is worth acknowledging that tribal women of Orissa were also not out of the scene during the national movement. For instance, Bangara Devi, a Koya princess, who ascended the throne of Malkangiri in 1835, launched an attack on British troops in 1860. Similarly, Khare Parvati, a Banda tribal woman, carried out a guerrilla war against the British during the early twentieth century. In short, the most dominant characteristic of the tribal resistance movement was that it was essentially a movement against the foreign rulers. So, tribals of Orissa had great attachment with the state and that continues to exist even today.

In order to attain national integration and maintain national Independence, it is thought that the primordial ethnic and religious identities must be replaced by the loyalty to the 'national mainstream' or at least made them compatible with the 'national interest'. Paradoxically, the formation of the nation state led to the denial of diversity of cultures and value system of people and their language and religion severely impaired and stigmatized. The assimilationist policy of nation-building devastated tribal cultures, languages and their collectivities. It would be dangerous for the Indian state to ignore social bases of ethnicity and treat their upsurges merely as a law and order problem. Meanwhile, the key to survival of tribal people with dignity rests in their struggle for recognition of their inalienable traditional rights over local resources and right to self-determination in the legitimate cultural, social, linguistic and political spheres.

The tribals of Orissa, however, maintain *we-feeling* or their 'distinct identity' within the broader framework of 'unity in diversity'. The simultaneous presence of similarities and differences in social organization of tribes lies at the heart of the question of identity. According to Myron Weiner, 'policy feedbacks' (Weiner, 1989: 30), i.e. government policies in the form of entitlement and reservations induce groups to organize for political action, have had their impact on the intensification of the self-identity of tribals in Orissa. Differences or boundaries of caste/tribe or the other inside/outside levels (such as class, religion, language, etc.) are essentially maintained because they represent their separate and distinct identities.

Society without boundaries cannot sustain. Boundaries are where one encounters others; they imply the recognition of other's autonomy and their specificity as well as the realization of one's own identity. Boundaries are often a matter of cultural proximity: natives and aliens are constructions anchored to preferred categories. The tribal people too create boundaries/identities, socio-cultural in content, so that they can find roots and identities to emancipate themselves from the rudderless and chaotic urban milieu. Virginius Xaxa's study reveals that the articulation of identity is most pronounced among tribes where an educated middle class has emerged (Xaxa, 2005b: 1368-9). With the emergence of middle class, the issue of culture, tradition, livelihood, even control over land and resources as well as demand for a share in the benefit of projects of modernity has become an integral part of identity articulation among tribes. However, the consciousness evident in such articulation is not the consciousness of tribe as a category but consciousness of being a people different from the others and especially the dominant regional community. The articulation of tribal identity also related primarily to the state and resources or the benefits that it may make available. To put it differently, the articulation of tribal identity emerges more in the context of tribal people's relation with the state, facilities of reservations and other forms of affirmative action and that is not anti-nationalism or against the Oriya identity. In short, the exclusion of other and the exclusiveness of the own are almost absolute in the tribal society of

Orissa but that is not compatible with the anti-nationalism or against Oriya identity.

WELFARE STATE: ORISSA

As in many other countries, in India debates central to tribal rights and protection have a longer history than these recent transnational concerns. Colonial and post-colonial history resulted in a series of positive discrimination policies and special administrative and territorial concessions for India's constitutionally recognized ST populations (Shah, 2007). At the end of the long drawn debates in the constituent Assembly, Dr. Ambedkar lucidly pointed out that 'although theoretically, it is good to have the principle that there shall be equality of opportunities, there must at the same time, be a provision made for the entry of certain communities which have so far been outside the administration' (Ambagudia, 2007a: 152). This principle works out as one of the most significant steps to adopt welfare state in India.

The principle of social justice in a welfare state demands for its fulfilment not only equality before the law and equality of opportunity for all individuals, castes and classes; it requires, especially in the Indian society, positive measures by the state for promoting education, health, employment opportunity, and economic condition in generally, of the comparatively backward or weaker sections of the society. Consequently, Article 46 of the Indian Constitution under the Directive Principles of State Policy laid: 'The state shall promote with special care the educational and economic interests of the weaker sections of the people, and in practice, of the Scheduled Castes and Scheduled Tribes, and shall protect them from social injustice and all forms of exploitation'. So, the Indian state has adopted both the constitutional provisions or constitutional framework and statutory provisions or legal framework to address the various issues of weaker sections of the Indian society.

Guided by this humanitarian understanding, Orissa state has adopted preferential policies and programmes in the spheres of education, politics and public service. The state has adopted different humanitarian policies and programmes for the educational development of STs since Independence with the express purpose of not only to bring socio-economic transformation but also to reduce the gap between tribals and non-tribals. The logic of providing preferences in education for tribals in Orissa is based on the fact that the preference in public service and politics is meaningless tribes have education. How can tribes without education get recruited to public service even within the reserved quotas? How can tribal legislators discharge their functions unless they have education and understanding? Therefore, the Orissan state has adopted humanitarian approach towards the STs.

Along with preferences in education for STs, the Government of Orissa has undertaken a number of important measures to improve the educational level of STs through steps like provisions of scholarships, boarding facilities, free distribution of nationalized textbooks (NBTs), school uniforms and imparting special coaching for appearing in various competitive examinations (Planning Commission, 2002: 450). Orissa has introduced midday meals in all primary schools to check the drop out rate among the tribal students. The collective impact of these sustained and uninterrupted efforts on the educational status of tribal society of Orissa is positive in nature. When we compared across different census reports, it is clear that the literacy status of tribal communities of Orissa has increased from 7.36 per cent in 1961 to 37.37 per cent in 2001.

Orissa has also provided reservation for STs in politics in proportion to their population. The quantitative presence of STs at different levels of power in Orissa is due to the political base provided by the policy of preferential treatment. The policy aimed at integration of the deprived in the political system in order to secure accommodation of their rising aspirations. In Orissa, as a consequence of preferential policy in politics, five out of 21 and 34 out of 147 seats are reserved for STs in Lok Sabha and Legislative Assembly respectively. After the enactment of the 73rd Constitutional Amendment Act in 1992, this kind of facility is also extended to all tiers of local governance. Though the recent data on the representation of the tribals in the local governance of Orissa is not available, by the year 1997, they have represented 22,854 (24.72 per cent) candidates in three tiers of Panchayati Raj Institutions in Orissa (Ambagudia, 2007b: 36; SCSTRTI, 2001). As these seats are reserved for tribals, which kept the non-tribals away from contesting from these constituencies, seats have periodically filled up. At least some of them have been able to occupy the political space that would otherwise be lacking (Ambagudia, 2006: 285-94).

Similarly, Orissa also provides preferences in public services to tribals. Orissa is the first state in the country to make a law called

'The Orissa Reservation of Vacancies in Posts and Services (for Scheduled Caste and Scheduled Tribe) Act, 1975' (Planning Commission, 2002: 448; DESPCD, 2004: 20/9-20/10; Srichandan, 1993: 131). The rules and regulations framed under this Act came into force with effect from 1 July 1976 to tighten up measures for securing increased representation of Scheduled Castes and STs in services through preference. The state government has also issued separate instructions to the organizations (public sector undertakings, corporations, autonomous bodies and universities, etc.) receiving grants-in-aid from the government to conduct their recruitment to fill up the vacancies according to the principles laid down in the Reservation Act. This unambiguously indicates the greater concern on the part of the state government for the adequate representation of the STs to the public services.

Over the years, sizeable numbers of candidates from the tribal communities are appointed to the central and state government on the basis of preferential policy in services (Article 335). There are several special provisions permitted by the Government of Orissa, in consonance with the central government, designed to enhance the ability of preferred groups to compete successfully for government posts. To give impetus to the fulfilment of quotas, several relaxations have been provided in terms of age, fee, educational qualifications/standards, experience, etc. So, preferential policy helps the tribal society of Orissa to enter the competition, they would not otherwise be eligible. In few cases, it works as a project of capacity building through coaching. By examining the available data, as on 1 April 1986 their representation was 0.88, 1.56, 5.62 and 12.02 per cent in groups A, B, C and D (NCSCST, 1987). The data sheet prepared by Scheduled Castes and Scheduled Tribes Research and Training Institute, Bhubaneswar, Orissa shows that the ST represented only 1.95 and 2.91 per cent in Indian Administrative Service (IAS) and Indian Police Service (IPS) respectively on 1 August 2000. So, when we look at the overall impact of preferential treatment policy in Orissa at three levels such as, education, politics and government services, the vulnerable tribal communities of Orissa have successfully been able to represent in education and politics but a very large number of reserved seats in services have gone unfulfilled. Indifference or apathy on the part of the appointing authorities, insufficient advertisement of vacancies, sheers expense of application forms, etc., contribute to the low tribal representation in services in Orissa.

Besides these preferences in three spheres, Government of Orissa has also adopted numerous outreaching policies and programmes and welfare measures for the necessary development of the tribals in all spheres. All these measures are of two types: (a) overall planning at the micro-level, and (b) specific tribal development schemes for the welfare of the tribal communities at the micro-level.

Large scale industrialization, agricultural development, communication, education and their welfare measures at the national level belong to the first category, while specific projects for the welfare of tribal communities belong to the second category. The various developmental initiatives taken for all round development of the tribals include adoption of tribal sub-plan, integrated tribal development agencies, cooperative and LAMPS societies, small farmers development projects, modified area development approach, dispersed tribal development programme, Orissa tribal empowerment and livelihood programme, micro-projects for the development of primitive tribal groups, etc. Besides, International Fund for Agricultural Development assisted Orissa tribal development project for all round development of Kashipur block of Rayagada district, anti-poverty programmes that have a bearing upon the economic development of STs and scheduled areas of the state have been taken up. Through all these welfare measures, government tries to eradicate all forms of exploitation from tribal societies to ensure better income through just price for tribal products and to facilitate adoption of modern ways of life and avail new economic opportunities. All these anti-exploitative, protective, social, economic, cultural and welfare measures have proved the welfare nature of the Orissan state. In other words, tribal and state relations are by no means always of ones of conflict. Nevertheless, tribes and tribal leaders, independently of whatever role they might play in the institutions of government, cherish and forcefully protect their interests. Furthermore, newness of the modern state, rampant corruption, and a stalled democratic reform process also create the conducive environment to enjoy their citizenship rights.

COERCIVE STATE: THE CRISIS?

The welfare state is the affirmative politics of redistribution. While the state may be acknowledged as a player in these relations, what is missing in the redistribution/recognition framework is appreciation of the state as 'a crucial source of oppression' (Feldman, 2002: 41).

The state follows controversial moves in the name of protection of tribal rights and globally they have induced renewed and heated debates amongst historians and anthropologists. With the initiation of economic reforms in India, it is widely believed that the Indian state is reneging on its welfare promises, and thereby compromising its fundamental defining ideals. In this backdrop, the Orissan state may be more appropriately characterized as an interventionist rather than welfare state. Even the Orissan state failed to fulfil the basic objectives of the welfare state. Interventionism can subsume a welfarist orientation but being a vastly more encompassing concept, suggests the legitimacy of the state intervention for a variety of tasks, not all of which need be justified in terms of welfare objectives. The primary purpose of interventionism and indeed its inspiring and guiding force was developmentalism. This was not a state that self-consciously and deliberately took on the responsibility of providing for its citizens, in clearly defining areas which bore some relationship to the idea of needs, especially basic needs.

The exploitative role of the old political system has remained unchanged to this day. Those in the government, continuing to practice the same old style of politics, tend to become corrupt with the result that people are demoralized by submitting to them and are ineffective in opposing them. Coercion, accepted as the defining feature of the state, has a dual character. It guarantees the reproduction of domination and order and suppresses changes to state authority. Continuous use of force to suppress dissent, resolve social conflicts and maintain order may lead to the erosion of legitimacy and undermine the capacity of the state to rule. According to Amartya Sen, the democratic state can generally handle the problems like famine, hunger, starvation, etc., more effectively because of popular pressure (Misra, 2003: 90). The stability of a democratic state depends on the way it responds to social conflicts arising in society and the way it uses force to settle them. The state's activity in the maintenance of order in society can best be understood as coercive-legitimation process.

This kind of state-society synergy reflects the uneasy relationship or crisis between the tribes and the state in Orissa. There is an open debate about the tribal-state relationship that is alarming. It argues that the state will not hesitate to manipulate tribes in order to achieve greater political power. In Orissa, the state is establishing trade-off relationship with the tribals by legitimizing its activities. Some scholars argue that in the name of development and extending reservations to tribals, the state is legitimizing its systematic control over their land and resources (Xaxa, 2005a: 119-35; Behura and Panigrahi, 2002: 54; Mohanty, 1997: 10). The rights and status of tribal people are subordinated through their presumptive incorporation to the state. In the name of development, the state of Orissa is controlling huge amount of tribal land. The study of Mohanty (1997) shows that there are 18 large schemes in Koraput district occupying 50,000 acres of land (or 7.42 per cent of the total areas) depriving 10 per cent of the tribals of their livelihood. These developmental projects involve the displacement of some people who are called upon to sacrifice for the greater interest of the nation. On the other hand, it appears that the pains of development have to be borne out quite unequally by the poor tribal communities of Orissa. The statistical figure of the Planning Commission (2002) indicates that more than 40 per cent of the displaced families in developmental projects in Orissa are the tribals. D.K. Behura shows that the installation of steel plant in Rourkela of Orissa resulted the displacement of 32 tribal villages. In other words, the vulnerable tribal communities of Orissa are forced to bear the massive burden of development, they are sacrificed at the alter of development that robs them out of their homes, traditional survival mechanisms, of the lands, forests and the eco-system of which they had been custodians for centuries.

Whether under colonial state or the welfare state after Independence, the dominant role of the state based on 'Eminent Domain' has struck at the root of the customary rights of the tribal people. This doctrine empowers the state to take property for the public use even without the owner's consent. The concept provided the legal justification for an entirely expedient political process that had progressively deprived the tribal of his land in colonial era. British rule and subsequent sub-proposition of laws dictated by the needs of colonialism led to the tribals being deprived of the customary rights of the tribal communities in respect of land and other resources. Paradoxically, the foundation of the nation states in the past hundred years has led to a corresponding marginalization and pauperization of tribal communities. In Orissa, despite the continuation of the positive responsibility of the tribal people towards the state since the colonial period, it did not give respect to the material context of survival strategy of the tribals. The land reforms and other laws are based on the formal system whose framework is in contradiction with the society and economy that the tribals are accustomed to. That becomes the basis of their alienation from land and other natural resources. This is quite contradictory to the UN declaration on Racism and Racial Discrimination of 1978 where it states that '. . . the right of indigenous people to maintain their traditional structure of economy and culture and stressed that their land and natural resources should not be taken away from them' (quoted in Pathy, 1989: 20). Their relations with the land remain intact.

Land is perhaps the most important resource of all: humans rely on it for their very existence and it forms the basis for most human activity and development. Land continues to be the pivotal property in terms of both income and employment around which socio-economic privileges and deprivations revolve. Land is not only a source of livelihood for tribals but it is also connected with their sense of history and is a symbol of social prestige for them (Elwin, 1963: 50). Land has not merely an economic significance as a survival resource, it has also a social (the basis of person's sense of belonging to a specific cultural community), cultural (the link to tradition, ethos and ways of life) and political significance (the material basis for the power of the elder to manage the community). To put it differently, land is the basis of polity, economy and culture of the tribal people. The tribals become bonded or semi-bonded labourers in their own land. In Orissa, there have also been many cases where the land is in the name of the tribals but non-tribals who had given money to tribals as loan cultivate it. This sorry state of affairs enabled some of the civil society organizations to fight back for the rights of the tribals on land in Malkangiri district during 1999-2000. The progressive erosion of the tribal ways of life, the break up of their land system, land alienation and imposition of the values and dominance of outsiders in collaboration with government has ensured the tribals to be impoverished. The colonial rulers as well as their successors in so-called independent India made laws with the intention of safeguarding the interests of the tribals. Despite the enactment of several important legislations by the Government of Orissa to render social and economic justice to the tribals, the ground reality in Orissa, however, remains disturbing.

A state's coercive power is represented best by the deployment and behaviour of its police and paramilitary forces. In a democracy, police are the visible symbol of state authority expected to safeguard the interest of the society and protect basic individual rights. It is the instrument of coercion but also the essence of governance, which is to maintain internal order. The police are perceived as corrupt, prone to high-handed behaviour and readily available as an instrument of political abuse of power. But the Orissan police have rarely had a positive image among the vulnerable tribal communities. This is due to the discriminatory role of the police in Orissa. When people across the world were exchanging New Year greetings in 2006, the tribal people of Kalinga Nagar in Orissa's Jajpur district witnessed perhaps the bloodiest day of their lives. On 2 January, the police gunned down 12 of them (including a 13-year-old schoolboy and three women) who opposed the construction of a boundary wall for the proposed steel plant of Tata Steel. To put it differently, the vulnerable tribal communities of Orissa were not opposing the developmental works of the state but they were fighting for their rights on land and natural resources. The state, the highest political organ that usually involves itself directly in matters of large projects, finds its authority eroded. It's decisions no longer go unchallenged. The means with which the state sets out to develop, distribute and value resources appear to be contested.

The police has also an indifferent attitude towards the tribals even when the conflicts arise between tribals and non-tribals in Orissa. On June 24, 2001, two tribals were murdered by the Bengali settlers (land grabbers) in Jambodora village in the presence of the police. By giving communal colour to the clash between the tribals and Bengali settlers in Nabarangpur district, on 30 October 2001, the armed police of the state entered Rengabhati village in the Raigarh police station of Nabarangpur district and opened fired at a gathering of 400 tribals. Two of them were instantly killed and most of them were injured. This conflict has nothing to do with ethnicity or language or caste. The main source of conflict in the area is primarily relating to control over the precious resources of forest and land and this conflict took place between an organized group of tribal defenders of forest and the people who are destroying forest under one pretext or another.

The discriminatory role of the state towards the tribals is also visible in Orissa. When the central government decided to settle the Bengali refugees in Dandakaranya areas of Orissa, the complete responsibility of the Bengali refugees was taken by the state government through the Dandakaranya (DNK) project. Consequently, the settlers were given seven acres of land per family. After 1965, the land given to settlers got reduced to five acres in non-irrigated areas and three acres in irrigated areas. By 1962, 91,652 acres of land had been given officially to settlers in Malkangiri and Nabarangpur subdivisions of undivided district of Koraput, Orissa. But how did the state arrange such a huge amount of land for the refugees. The government decided to clear good number of forests to meet the requirements. It is estimated that an area of 432.20 sq. km. of forest was cleared for the rehabilitation of around 10,000 Bengali refugee families in Malkangiri and Nabarangpur areas under the centrally sponsored DNK project. At the beginning of the project, the tribal families were also promised land but the idea was later scraped. The project itself showed partial treatment for the non-tribals. For instance, the tribes used to depend more on millet than on rice or wheat, but there had been hardly any research on the maximization of production of millets and no market facilities were created for its sale. In contrast, research was done on the crops of the settlers and market facilities were provided for sale of their maize crop. This brings back the predatory role of the state. The tribal communities of Orissa have their own problems and the modern state does not look at them. So, the Indian state has been more sensitive to the demands of communities defined by religion and caste and has arguably been less receptive to claims made by tribal communities, and considerably more invasive and predatory in its relationship towards the tribals (Jayal, 1998: 231; Barik, 2006: 97). Thus, the tribes perceive it as a conscious undermining of their interest by the state.

In a number of respects, state-tribal relations exacerbate the range of conflict situation. Firstly, the tribes continue to feel marginalized and excluded from decision-making process. Tribal leaders are not happy with the state's failure to deliver basic infrastructure and provide for social services such as education and health. And, secondly, the state continues to have a negative view of tribals as a bunch of people who are often regarded as being 'backward', incapable of making informed decisions or effective use of resources and aid they are given and in need of guidance or control by the state. In the initial phase of Constituent Assembly debates, this reason had formed the platform on which to argue against the creation of Autonomous District Council in the tribal areas of Assam (Ambagudia, 2005: 105).

So, in the Indian context, the state is facing the greatest challenge from those very people who are being increasingly politicized by the expansion of democracy but are dissatisfied by with the pace of socio-economic change. The lopsided development together with lack of emphasis on institutionalizing democratic norms has rendered the Indian state weak and vulnerable to a variety of social changes. Organic linkages between people's aspirations and the translation of those aspirations into performance have weakened the state democratic institutions.

CONCLUSION

This paper started by noting how vulnerable tribal communities of Orissa have positive responsibility towards the state, especially during the colonial period, and the welfare policies of the state, which are bound by the constitutional provisions. It proceeded to point out the coercive/predatory role of the state that leads to the destitution and marginalization of the tribal communities of Orissa. It is inferred from the preceding analysis that there has been a systematic exploitative relationship between the state and the tribals. The vulnerable tribal communities of Orissa are protesting for the meaningful rights over their resources. In the name of development and extending reservations, the state is legitimizing its domination over the customary rights of the tribals on land and other resources in Orissa.

Looking at the relationship between the tribals and the state, an important question needs to be asked: how do tribals of Orissa view their predicament? In popular notion, the relationship between the state and the tribals is treated as cooperative in which policies of the state are viewed as if it were conducted for the welfare of the tribals. The state and tribal relationship is perceived by the tribals not through the prism of the policies and programmes of generally well meaning government at the centre and in the state but through the behaviour and action patterns of numberless minions spread over the sprawling tribal areas in the state like patwari, the forest guard, the police force, etc. The latter personify the state to the tribals. But their actions are parasitic and sometimes illegal. Consequently, for tribals, the state stands for exploitation. In the present context, the future of the tribal-state relationship is not clear or there is a growing crisis in the relationship between the tribes and the state in Orissa, especially in the 1990s. This is because in the era of liberalization, privatization and globalization (LPG), should tribals oppose or support the state, however, remains a subject of further deliberations and discussions. This is due to the fact that during the period of LPG, the state is the only institution that can protect the tribals. On the other hand, the

Orissan state has every administrative apparatus to respond in an authoritarian manner to deal with emerging social challenges. But there is absolutely no reason to believe that the Orissan state will be able to manage deep social crisis through 'authoritarian' interventions. A weak state in its inability to manage serious crisis can lead to social anarchy or even disintegration of the state.

REFERENCES

Ambagudia, Jagannath, (2005) 'Policies of Protective Discrimination: Locating Scheduled Tribes in the Constituent Assembly Debates', *Punjab Journal of Politics*, vol. XXIX, no. 2: 99-114.

———. (2006), 'Standing at the Edge: Representation and Electoral Reservation for Scheduled Tribes in Orissa', *The Indian Journal of Political Science*, vol. LXVII, no. 2: 285-94.

———. (2007a), 'Scheduled Tribes, Protective Discrimination and Social Justice: Exploring Constituent Assembly Debates', in B.T. Lawani (ed.), *Social Justice and Empowerment*, New Delhi: Om Publications.

———. (2007b), 'Empowering the Powerless: 73rd Amendment and Emerging Leadership among the Scheduled Tribes in Orissa', in B.T. Lawani (ed.), *Social Justice and Empowerment*, New Delhi: Om Publications.

Barik, R.K. (2006), 'Faulty Planning in a Tribal Region: The Dandakarany Development Authority', in Govinda Chandra Rath (ed.), *Tribal Development in India: The Contemporary Debate*, New Delhi: Sage.

Behura, N.K. and N. Panigrahi (2002), 'Marginalisation of the Vulnerable Tribal Communities in the State of Orissa through the Process of Sponsored Development', *Journal of Anthropological Survey of India*, vol. 51, no. 2: 41-72.

Beteille, Andre (1986), 'The Concept of Tribe with Special Reference to India', *Journal of European Sociology*, vol. 27, no. 2: 297-318.

D'Souza, Leela (2006), 'The Jagannath Cult in Orissa: Its Tribal Origin', *The Eastern Anthropologist*, vol. 59, no. 1: 87-102.

Das, Jagannath and Suresh Chandra Pradhan (2002), 'Tribes of Orissa and their Population', in R.N. Pati and Jaganath Das (eds.), *Tribal and Indigenous People of India: Problems and Prospects*, New Delhi: A.P.H. Publishing Corporation.

Das, Nityanand (1967-8), 'Martyr Lakshman Naik: A Hero of the Freedom Movement', *Adibasi*, vol. IX, no. 1: 22-8.

Dash, Satya Prakash (2004), 'State Administration: Development, Finance and Crime', *The Indian Journal of Political Science*, vol. LXV, no. 3: 435-56.

Dash, Shreeram Chandra (1997), *States of our Union: Orissa*, New Delhi: Publications Division, Ministry of Information and Broadcasting, Government of India.

Directorate of Economics and Statistics, Planning and Coordination Department (DESPCD) (2004), *Economic Survey (2003-2004)*, Bhubaneswar: Government of Orissa.

Dwivedi, Ranjit (2006), *Conflict and Collective Action: The Sardar Sarovar Project in India*, New Delhi: Routledge.

Elwin, Verrier (1954), *Tribal Myths of Orissa*, London: Oxford University Press.

——— (1963), *New Deal for Tribal India*, New Delhi: Ministry of Home Affairs, Government of India.

Feldman, Leonard C. (2002), 'Redistribution, Recognition and the State: The Irreducibly Dimension of Injustice', *Political Theory*, vol. 30, no. 3: 410-40.

Fürer-Haimendorf, Christoph Von (1982), *Tribes of India: The Struggle for Survival*, Berkeley, Los Angeles, Oxford: University of California Press.

Government of India (2001), *Census of India, Final Population Series-I*, New Delhi.

Hooja, Meenakshi (2004), *Issues and Strategies for Tribal Development*, Jaipur: Rawat Publications.

Iveson, Duncan, Paul Patton and Will Sanders (eds.) (2000), *Political Theory and the Rights of Indigeneous Peoples*, Cambridge: Cambridge University Press.

Jayal, Niraja Gopal (1999), *Democracy and the State: Welfare, Secularism and Development in Contemporary India*, New Delhi: Oxford University Press.

Joshi, Vidyut (1997), 'Genesis of Tribal Problem', in Ghanashyam Shah (ed.), *Social Transformation in India*, vol. II, Jaipur: Rawat Publications.

Kanungo, Pralay (2003), 'Hindutva's Entry into a "Hindu Province": Early Years of RSS in Orissa', *Economic and Political Weekly*, vol. XXXVIII, no. 31.

Kar, P.K. (1999), 'Social Transformation and the Tribes of Orissa', in V.K. Pant and B.S. Bisht (eds.), *Backward Communities: Identity, Development and Transformation*, New Delhi: Gyan Publishing House.

Kaviraj, Sudipta (1984), 'On the Crisis of Political Institutions in India', *Contribution to Indian Sociology*, vol. 18, no. 2: 223-4.

Mahapatra, Khageswar (2000), 'The Ethno-Linguistic Identity of the Tribes of Orissa', in Kishore C. Padhy (ed.), *The Challenges of Tribal Development: Essays in Honour of Dr. N. Patnaik*, New Delhi: Swarup & Sons.

Mishra, Nita and Arundhati Roy Choudhary (1993), 'Voices of the Indigenous Peoples', *Seminar*, no. 412: 48-53.

Misra, Baidyanath (2003), 'Problems and Prospects of Revival of Orissa's Economy', *IASSI Quarterly*, vol. 22, no. 1: 87-97.

Mohanty, Bibhuti Bhusan (1997), 'State and Tribal Relationship in Orissa', *Indian Anthropologist*, vol. 27, no. 1.

Mohapatra, Bishnu N. (1996), 'Ways of Belonging: The Kanchi Kaveri Legend and the Construction of the Oriya Identity', *Studies in History*, vol. 12, no. 2: 203-21.

Mohapatra, Bishnu N. and Dwipayan Bhattacharyya (1996), 'Tribal-Dalit Conflict: Electoral Politics in Phulbani (Orissa)', *Economic and Political Weekly*, vol. XXXI, nos. 2&3: 160-4.

National Commission for Scheduled Castes and Scheduled Tribes (1986-1987) *The 28th Report of the National Commission for Scheduled Castes and Scheduled Tribes (1986-1987)*, New Delhi: Government of India.

Nayak, Prasanna K. (2001), 'Jagannath and the Adivasis: Reconsidering the Cult and Its Traditions', in Herman Kulke and Burkhard Schnepel (eds.), *Jagannath Revisited: Studying Society, Religion and the State in Orissa*, New Delhi: Manohar.

Nayak, Ramanath (2002), 'A Forgotten Hero: Saheed Laxman Nayak', *Times of Bahujan*, July-August: 14-16.

Padhy, K.S. and P.P. Tripathy (1994), *Voting Behaviour of the Tribals in India*, New Delhi: Kanishka.

Panigrahi, N.P. (2006), 'Laxman Naik: The Leader of the Leaders', *Orissa Review*, August: 28-30.

Pathy, Jaganath (1988), *Under Development and Destitution: Essays in Orissan Society*, New Delhi: Inter-India Publishers.

———. (1989), 'Indian State and the Tribal Question', in J.P. Singh and N.N. Vyas (eds.), *Tribal Development: Past Efforts and New Challenges*, Udaipur: Himanshu Publications.

———. (1999), 'Tribe, Region and Nation in the context of the Indian State', *Sociological Bulletin*, vol. 48, nos. 1&2: 97-111.

Pati, Biswamoy (1993), *Resisting Domination: Peasants, Tribals and the National Movements in Orissa, 1920-1950*, New Delhi: Manohar.

Pfeffer, Georg (1998), 'The Own and the Other: Construction of Oriya Identity in Orissa', *The Fourth World*, no. 8, October: 20-4.

Planning Commission (2002), *Orissa Development Report*, New Delhi: Government of India.

Rao, B. Shiva (1967), *The Framing of India's Constitution: Selected Documents*, vol. II, New Delhi: Indian Institute of Public Administration.

Rath, S.N. (1977), *The Development of the Welfare State in Orissa, 1950-1960*, New Delhi: S. Chand.

Ray, Niharranjan (1972), 'Introductory Address', in K.S. Singh (ed.), *Tribal Situation in India*, Shimla: Indian Institute of Advanced Study.

Sarkar, Jayanta (2003), 'Transition, Change and Transformation: Impacting the Tribals in India', in Jayanta Sarkar and Jyotirmoy Chakrabarty (eds.),

Transition, Change and Transformation, Kolkata: Anthropological Survey of India.
Satapathy, Sachidananda (ed.) *Orissa Vision 2020: Towards Building a New and Modern Orissa*, New Delhi: New Age Publications.
Scheduled Castes and Scheduled Tribes Research and Training Institute (SCSTRTI) (2001), *Tribes in Orissa: A Data Sheet*, Bhubaneswar: Government of Orissa.
Shah, Alpa (2007), 'Keeping the State Away: Democracy, Politics and the State in India's Jharkhand', *Journal of Royal Anthropological Institute*, vol. 13, issue 1: 127-45.
——— (2007), 'The Dark Side of Indigeneity?: Indigenous People, Rights and Development in India', *History Compass*, vol. 5, issue 6: 1806-32.
Singh, K.S. (1992), *People of India: An Introduction*, Calcutta: Anthropological Survey of India.
Singh, K. Suresh (ed.) (2002), *The Tribal Situation in India*, Shimla: Indian Institute of Advanced Study (revised edition).
Singh, Nishi (1995), 'Family and Marriage among Khonds of Koraput, Orissa: A Comparative Study', *Man in India*, vol. 75, no. 1: 105-10.
Srichandan, G.K. (1993), *Tribal Development and Welfare Legislation in Orissa*, Delhi: Pratibha Prakashan.
Varma, Vishwanath Prasad (1972), 'Political System of Tribal Bihar', *The Indian Journal of Political Science*, vol. XXXIII, no. 4: 381-400.
Weiner, Myron (1989), *The Indian Paradox: Essays in Indian Politics*, New Delhi: Sage.
Xaxa, Virginius (1999), 'Transformation of Tribes in India: Terms of Discourse', *Economic and Political Weekly*, vol. XXXIV, no. 24: 1520-2.
——— (2001), 'Empowerment of the Tribes', in Debal K. SinghaRoy (ed.), *Social Development and the Empowerment of the Marginalised Groups: Perspectives and Strategies*, New Delhi: Sage.
——— (2005a), 'Electoral Reservation for Scheduled Tribes: The Legitimization of Domination', in Stephanie Tawa Lama-Rewal (ed.), *Electoral Reservation, Political Representation and Social Change in India*, New Delhi: Manohar.
——— (2005b), 'Politics of Language, Religion and Identity: Tribes in India', *Economic and Political Weekly*, vol. XL, no. 13: 1368-9.

CHAPTER 10

Engendering Disability in the Developmental Agenda in India: A Policy Perspective

RENU ADDLAKHA

This paper explores the situation of persons with disabilities in India with special reference to the plight of women with disabilities. Tracing the development of the disability movement, the first part of the paper shows how the issue has moved from a marginal state-sponsored welfare programme to a social development issue highlighting the role of local and global factors in the process. The Persons with Disabilities (Equal Opportunities, Protection of Rights and Full Participation) Act, 1995 (henceforth referred to as the PWD Act) has transformed the political and public discourses on disability. The terms of the debate have moved from segregation and exclusion to integration and inclusion, from charity and tokenism to human rights and entitlements. Globalization has given a fillip to this new identity politics based on a hitherto unacknowledged axis of oppression, namely disability. Although a rights-based approach has entered the disability rights movement in India, the specific concerns of women with disabilities have not yet found a place, neither in the government policies and programmes nor in the private or the voluntary sectors. The paper discusses the implications of the absence of a gendered perspective in the disability movement. It not only explores the lacunae in the laws, programmes and policies for persons with disabilities from a gender-sensitive perspective, but also makes recommendations for gender mainstreaming in the areas of legal reform, policy planning and implementation.

IDENTITY POLITICS AND PUBLIC POLICY

Persons with disabilities are the most neglected and disempowered sections of the population. Due to their marginalized status, they are denied the fundamental civil, political, social and economic rights that are the prerogative of all citizens in a democracy. Two events, which triggered public outrage and a nation-wide debate, clearly highlight the extent of the utter dehumanization of persons with disabilities in our society. One was the forced sterilization of women in a home for the mentally retarded in Pune district in 1994. The primary reason given for the hysterectomies was maintenance of menstrual hygiene. The other was the burning to death of 28 inmates in a private mental asylum in Tamil Nadu in 2001. The inmates of the Erwadi Dargah were chained to their beds and could not escape the flames that engulfed their thatched huts. Their cries for help were ignored by the asylum owners, mistaking them for the usual outbursts of the mentally ill. The Supreme Court of India took *suo motu* cognizance of this horrific incident and called for a nation-wide review of treatment facilities for the mentally ill both in the public and private sectors.

According to conservative estimates derived from the 2001 Indian census, 1.8 per cent to 2.1 per cent of our population of 1.2 billion suffers from some form of disability which in absolute numbers is approximately 18.49 to 21.92 million persons. Using a wider definition of disability which includes conditions like diabetes and cardiovascular disease, the World Health Organisation (WHO) estimates that 6 per cent to 10 per cent of the population suffers from identifiable physical or mental disability. That comes to over 70 million persons in India. Such phenomena as war, ethnic conflict, HIV/AIDS, industrial injuries and road accidents are increasing the number of persons with disabilities. Ironically, enhanced life expectancy has increased manifold the incidence of old age-related, chronic disease-induced disabilities worldwide as well.

But what is a disability and what does it mean to have a disability in the first place? Disabilities may be congenital, or from birth. For instance most mental retardation is congenital. Malnutrition and micronutrient deficiencies may result in disabling conditions in children in the form of stunted physical and mental growth. When disabilities are acquired later in life due to accidents, injuries or advancing age, they may be characterized by episodic upsurge of symptoms and/or progressive degeneration. Many mental illnesses like schizophrenia, multiple sclerosis and Alzheimer's disease fall in this category. A disability may be static such as the loss of a limb due to an amputation. Then there are also hidden and visible disabilities. Diabetes and epilepsy are hidden disabilities while leprosy and blindness are visible conditions. A disability generally has two components, i.e. the medical limitation and social prejudice, which often gets translated into discriminatory behaviour towards the person with disability. In legal documents and policy statements disability is defined in terms of what qualifies for public assistance.

Major social movements such as the black civil rights movement in the United States, the women's movement and the counter-culture revolution led by university students in France during the 1960s brought identity politics into the political and academic landscape. Following the minority group paradigm, the organization of disabled persons themselves into a vibrant social movement was an outcome of this larger process of assertion of group identity and the goal of empowerment. Through self-advocacy, the concept of disability was redefined not as personal tragedy necessitating therapy but as collective oppression necessitating political action (Oliver, 1996). In this perspective the focus shifts from the inability of persons with disabilities to adapt to the so-called 'normal' environment to the failure of the social and structural environment to adapt to the needs and aspirations of persons with disabilities. As advocates for equal rights, the disability organizations lobbied with national governments for a barrier-free environment, inclusive education, affirmative action in employment, in addition to the whole range of civil, political, social and economic rights to which all citizens are entitled in a democracy.

The Universal Declaration of Human Rights enunciated by the United Nations (UN) in 1948 introduced a rights-based approach to disability. Every person has certain natural or inalienable human rights by virtue of being a person. These rights cannot be violated under any circumstance. They constitute what in essence it means to be human. Article 25 of this UN Declaration explicitly states that each person has the right to security in the event of unemployment, sickness, disability, widowhood, old age or other lack of livelihood in the circumstances beyond his control. Persons with disabilities are entitled to all the rights upheld by the Human Rights Charter as also other rights instruments such as the International Covenant on Civil and Political Rights (1976a) and the International Covenant on Economic, Social and Cultural Rights (1976b).

The international climate was made more disabled-friendly by subsequent UN declarations specifically for the welfare of persons with disabilities. In 1971 the General Assembly adopted the Declaration on the Rights of Mentally Retarded Persons which stipulated that the mentally retarded are not only entitled to basic human rights like everyone else but they also have special rights corresponding to their special needs in medical, education and social fields. In 1975 the Declaration on the Rights of Disabled Persons was adopted, which proclaimed their equal civil and political rights. The year 1981 was declared as International Year of Disabled Persons. A World Plan of Action Concerning Disabled Persons was adopted by the General Assembly in 1982 for the implementation of which 1983-92 was proclaimed the United Nations Decade of Disabled Persons. In 1993 the General Assembly adopted the Standard Rules on the Equalisation of Opportunities for Persons with Disabilities. More recently in 2006 the UN adopted a comprehensive Convention on Rights of Persons with Disabilities (CRPD) (the CRPD and its optional Protocol was adopted on 13 December 2006 and was opened for signature on 30 March 2007), which has been signed till date by over 128 countries including India.

The impact of the international human rights movement and anti-poverty initiatives have transplanted the issue of disability from that of social welfare to one of social development. Development essentially means inclusion. If the needs and aspirations of a whole population group are not taken account of, then social development in the true sense of the word has not taken place. Disability is both a cause and consequence of poverty. They reinforce each other leading to increased vulnerability and exclusion. Poverty exacerbates the opportunities of persons and disability further marginalizes them, making it impossible for them to have access to basic conditions of life like health, education, transportation and employment. For women with disabilities there is the added burden of gender bias and discrimination, which further exacerbates their life conditions.

Instead of giving rights to citizens with disabilities and empowering them, a culture of charity and welfare has been systematically promoted in India since the colonial period. Medical rehabilitation, including distribution of assistive aids and appliances, special schools, vocational training in low-end occupations and sheltered employment, have been the pillars of state policy on disability. Furthermore, electoral politics of caste and gender have pushed persons with disabilities to the margins of the political landscape making them a weak political constituency. They have, in fact, been systematically disenfranchised by the political system. Things began to change marginally after 1981 (International Year of Disabled Persons) when the issue of disability was opened up at the national level. The changing international climate focusing on human rights and empowerment of marginal groups impelled the government to make some policy changes such as token reservations in educational institutions and employment. But real progress in the form of concrete legislation to deliver the promise of equality of opportunity and social justice only came in 1995 with the passage of the Persons with Disabilities (Equal Opportunities, Protection of Rights and Full Participation) Act. In addition to the active role of the United Nations, one of the positive outcomes of economic liberalization and globalization has been the introduction of a view of disability as a human rights and development issue rather than simply a matter of charity and welfare.

A QUESTION OF GENDER

The 2001 census estimated that there are over 9 million women with disabilities in India constituting less than 1 per cent of the population. Some researches estimate that there are over 35 million women with disabilities in the country (Bacquer and Sharma, 1997). Others put the figure at 20 million; 98 per cent of them are illiterate; less than 1 per cent can avail health care and rehabilitation services (Action Aid, 2003). It needs to be remembered that estimates of the total number of persons with disabilities in a country vary depending on the definition of disability used, degree of impairment, survey methodology including use of scientific instruments for identification and measurement. But these statistics are only the tip of the iceberg when it comes to gauging the level of neglect, isolation, stigma and deprivation that characterize their lives. The majority of women with disabilities suffer the triple discrimination of being female, being disabled and being poor. Indeed, not only are they a socially invisible category but their plight is worse than both men with disabilities and other non-disabled women.

While being a man and having a disability are culturally very incongruous, being female and having a disability also implies a certain level of continuity as both are to varying degrees associated in our society with notions of weakness, passivity and dependence. But the likeness is only superficial because a woman with a disability is also considered incapable of fulfilling the normative feminine roles of homemaker, wife and mother (Fine and Asch, 1988). Then, she also does not fit the stereotype of the normal woman in terms of physical appearance. Since women embody family honour in many cultures including India, girls with disabilities are kept hidden at home by families and denied basic rights to mobility, education and employment. They are less likely to be given in marriage than male counterparts. Doubts around the capacity of women with disabilities to be sexual partners, homemakers and mothers abound. They are not considered capable of performing household chores efficiently, having meaningful sexual relationships or producing and rearing healthy children. Under these circumstances, they may be married off to older already married men or men in poor health. In short, women with disabilities do not have the same options of marriage and motherhood as non-disabled women. Being nurturing and caring are core characteristics of normative constructions of femininity, but women with disabilities are themselves in need of care. This inversion reduces them to the status of being lesser than women.

Being powerless, isolated and anonymous, women with disabilities are extremely vulnerable to abuse and violence. In addition, the need for assistance in activities of daily living like dressing, eating and other bodily activities renders them more vulnerable to abuse both at home and in institutions. She will be less able to defend herself in a risky situation because she may not be able to run or scream for help. Then, persons with developmental disabilities may be too trusting of others and hence may be easier to trick, bribe or coerce. They may not understand differences between sexual and non-sexual tactile behaviour. Persons with speech and hearing difficulties may have limited communication skills to report abuse. Furthermore, since persons with disabilities are often taught to be obedient, passive and control their behaviour, this will render them easy victims.

Women with disabilities face violations of their rights at every level. They are considered a financial burden and social liability by their families; they are denied opportunities of movement outside the home and access to education; they are viewed as asexual, helpless and dependent; their vulnerability to physical, sexual and emotional abuse is enormous; their aspirations for marriage and parenthood are often denied; they grow up ensconced within the walls of their homes or special institutions, isolated and neglected with no hope of a normal life. A poignant picture of their plight is depicted in the Bollywood movie *Black* (Bhansali, 2005) in which high socio-economic status and family compassion are only partially successful in alleviating the life of the female protagonist who has multiple disabilities.

Although a rights-based approach has entered the disability rights movement, the specific concerns of women with disabilities have not yet found a place, neither in the government policies and programmes nor in the voluntary sector. Ironically or expectedly, the disability rights movement all over the world, including India, is male-dominated. It may even be blatantly sexist. Even within the women's movement, women with disabilities rarely figured as a distinct group in international covenants until the Beijing Declaration in 1995. In its platform for action, this document specifies women with disabilities as a particularly vulnerable group with little access to information on their fundamental rights. This is a serious lacuna, which needs to be rectified.

While presenting an overview of various policies and programmes for persons with disabilities in this paper, an attempt will be made to highlight how the invisibility of gender prevents these efforts from reaching a vast target group, namely women with disabilities. Legislation is a key tool for social empowerment but existing legislation on disability is silent when it comes to the concerns of women with disabilities. Gender mainstreaming is only possible when there is sound knowledge of ground realities. What are the salient issues in the lives of women with disabilities in rural and urban India? What are their experiences of the health and education systems? What are their marital and maternal experiences? What are the problems faced by women with disabilities in old age? These are all grey areas which require systematic research that can directly feedback into programme development and implementation.

SOCIO-DEMOGRAPHIC PROFILE OF PERSONS WITH DISABILITIES IN INDIA

Disability has featured as a variable in both the Census and in the periodic surveys carried out by the National Sample Survey Organisation (NSSO). In 1981 which was also the International Year of Disabled Persons, disability was incorporated into the census. Due to the use of extreme criteria for defining impairment (totally blind, totally deaf and totally cripple), the 1981 census came up with a meagre 1.1 million figure of persons with disabilities in the country. It took no account of the mentally disabled or the leprosy-affected persons. Using a less restrictive definition of disability the NSSO came up with a figure of 12 million persons with disabilities in the same period constituting 1.8 per cent of the total population. Disability was dropped in the 1991 census. But the 47th Round of NSSO in 1991 came up with a figure of 16 million persons with disability (including those suffering from mental retardation) constituting 1.9 per cent of the population.

Disability was incorporated in the 2001 census literally at the last moment through a public interest litigation filed by the Disability Rights Group in the Delhi High Court. Using a more comprehensive definition of both physical and mental disability, a total of 18.49 to 21.92 million persons were found to be suffering from some form of disability constituting 1.8 to 2.1 per cent of the population. Indeed, it appears that the percentage of persons with disabilities in the population has remained more or less constant ranging from 1.8 to 2.1 per cent. However, there has been an increase in absolute numbers over the years in proportion to the rate of population growth in the country.

For the purpose of this paper I have chosen to draw largely upon the NSSO data on disability collected in 2002 for a number of reasons. Firstly this is the most recent national-level survey providing an in-depth profile of the disabled population in the country. Secondly, limited comparisons can be made, since three surveys on disability have been carried out by NSSO during 1981, 1991 and 2002. While there has been relative uniformity in concepts, definitions and operational procedures for locomotor, hearing and speech and visual disabilities in the three rounds, mental disability (comprising both mental retardation and mental illness) was introduced in the 2002 survey. It may be noted that the population estimates in NSSO data are lower than Census population or its projection; but the figures are expected to be closer to the true situation. To illustrate this point, Table 10.1 gives an overview of the overall prevalence of different categories of disabilities from recent census and NSSO surveys.

Although the time-lag between the census and NSSO surveys is only a year, there are marked differences in the data. There appears

TABLE 10.1: NUMBER OF PERSONS WITH DISABILITIES (IN LAKHS)

Disability	NSSO 2002	Census 2001
Locomotor	106.34 (51.19%)	61.05 (27.86%)
Visual	28.26 (13.60%)	106.35 (48.54%)
Hearing	30.62 (14.74%)	12.62 (5.78%)
Speech	21.55 (10.37%)	16.41 (7.49%)
Mental	20.96 (10.09%)	22.64 (10.33%)
Total	207.73	219.07

Source: From relevant tables of Census 2001 and NSSO 2002.

to have been an overall decline in the total number of persons with disabilities by 11.34 lakh. Secondly there are differences between relative prevalence of different types of disabilities. The census data placed visual disability at highest prevalence followed by locomotor, mental, hearing and speech. This order got changed in the NSSO data set with locomotor taking the top bracket followed by hearing, visual, speech and mental (see Table 10.1).

Main Findings of National Sample Survey Organisation Survey 2002

The survey was carried out between July and December 2002 covering a total of 48,557 rural households spread over 4,637 villages and 24,731 urban households spread over 3,354 urban blocks. A total of 49,300 rural and 26,679 urban-based persons with disabilities were interviewed. As in the census medically-based simple operational definitions of different types of physical and mental disabilities were used taking into account the non-medical status of field investigators.

Like the 2001 census, NSSO data put the total number of persons with disabilities in India at around 1.8 per cent of the total population; 8.4 per cent of rural households and 6.1 per cent of urban households had at least one member with a disability. A high 92 per cent of households in both sectors had one disabled member, 7 per cent had two and 1 per cent had more than 3 such members. The average size of such households was 5.7, which is higher than the national average. One may speculate that the presence of a child with either congenital or adventitious disability is a factor in the decision to increase family size for a number of reasons including gender. Since the birth of a disabled child is considered both an economic liability and a social misfortune, especially if it is a girl child, the need for compensation through more offspring would be felt. Other children, particularly sons, would not only be expected to provide long-term security for parents but would also take on the role of caregivers for the disabled sibling, who would be conceived of as a life-long economic and social burden for the household.

Other major findings show that 84 per cent of persons with mental retardation and 82 per cent of persons with speech impairment have a congenital disability. Majority of hearing, visual and locomotor disabilities are acquired and mainly associated with old age (above

60 years). It may be noted that more persons with adventitious disabilities were to be found in rural areas probably due to lesser availability of and accessibility to quality health care services. About 37 per cent of total persons with disabilities were working before the onset of disability. Of these 41 per cent were males and 37 per cent females.

According to the NSSO data, 10.64 per cent of persons with disabilities had multiple disabilities (co-existence of more than one disability). Of this 13 per cent could not manage self-care activities of daily living like eating, sitting, standing dressing and personal hygiene even with the help of mechanical aids. Of these 12 per cent were males and 15 per cent females. Reasons for higher number of males engaging in self-care than females could be related to differential gender-based expectations and lifestyle options. Girls, in general, are more home-bound: and when female status and disability combine, it may mean literal incarceration at home abjuring the need for developing self-care skills. Boys with disabilities would, on the other hand, be encouraged to be mobile and hence concerted efforts might be made to inculcate self-care skills. Then, basic biological factors related to female anatomy like managing incontinence and menstrual hygiene might render girls more dependent on others for help in the household. Consequently, functional capacities of women with multiple disabilities are lower than those of men with disabilities, which is largely attributable to social factors.

The prevalence of disability is uniformly higher in rural areas and among males. Several factors may be interacting to produce this situation. Firstly, there is greater concentration of population in rural areas implying a corresponding higher number of both non-disabled and disabled persons. While there may be some underlying biological reasons for higher prevalence of different disabilities among males, lower prevalence of disabilities in women may actually be an outcome of lower survival rates of female infants due to sex selective abortions and systematic neglect of the female child (see Table 10.2).

Prevalence of all types of disabilities, except blindness, is uniformly higher among males. In the case of blindness there is an over-representation of women both in urban and rural areas. One reason for this could be that eye care is not considered a priority for women who are mostly engaged in domestic work that does not require a high level of visual acuity. While speech impairment is again higher in males, more in-depth analysis reveals that muteness or total absence

TABLE 10.2: PREVALENCE OF DISABILITY BY SEX AND SECTOR PER 100,000 POPULATION

	Rural (%)	Urban (%)
Persons	1.85	1.50
Males	2.12	1.67
Females	1.51	1.31

Source: NSSO 2002.

of speech is much higher in females than males. Like hearing and visual impairment, mental illness was also more often reported as a problem of old age. This raises the need to address the special needs of elderly women with disabilities, many of whom may be widows. The combination of physical/mental disability and widowhood raises the spectre of a very precarious existence (see Table 10.3).

As Table 10.4 shows the male-female differences in marital status are quite significant. A significantly large number of adults with disability (47 per cent) were found not to be married. Sharp differences were also observed in the distribution of marital status over various categories of disabilities. Highest number of never married persons was found among the mentally retarded followed by hearing disabled. One can speculate that factors like mental stability, independence and communication are determinative in the social assessment of persons with disabilities to enter wedlock. A higher proportion of urban-based

TABLE 10.3: PREVALENCE OF DIFFERENT TYPES OF DISABILITIES BY SEX AND SECTOR PER 100,000 POPULATION

Type of Disability	Prevalence per 100,000 Population (Rural)	Prevalence per 100,000 Population (Urban)	Prevalence among Males (Rural)	Prevalence among Females (Rural)	Prevalence among Males (Urban)	Prevalence among Females (Urban)
Locomotor	1,046	901	1,274	804	1,058	750
Blindness	296	194	191	230	116	166
Hearing	310	236	379	301	234	238
Speech	210	187	242	176	221	151
Mental Retardation	110	100	113	69	118	81
Mental Illness	92	89	128	91	105	71

Source: NSSO 2002.

TABLE 10.4: MARITAL STATUS BY SEX/1000 DISABLED PERSONS

Sex	Never Married Rural	Never Married Urban	Currently Married Rural	Currently Married Urban
Male	471	484	448	450
Female	489	415	460	284

Source: NSSO 2002.

females were unmarried in comparison to their rural counterparts pointing to possibly higher levels of stigmatization and discrimination of women in cities. Not surprisingly, 30 to 31 per cent of females with disabilities were found to be widowed, divorced or separated. The corresponding figure for males was only 7 to 8 per cent. Annulment of marriage on account of disability is a major factor in the lives of women with disabilities. Very often, this happens because the natal family chooses to conceal the disability, especially if it is an invisible one like mental illness, at the time of marriage. At other times the married woman with a disability may be expelled from the marital home for other reasons, ranging from her inability to satisfactorily perform household chores to bearing a child with a disability (see Table 10.4).

Of the disabled, 45 per cent were literate but only 9 per cent of these 45 had studied up to secondary level and beyond. Of these 7 per cent were in rural areas and 18 per cent in urban areas. Kerala and Delhi have the highest number of literate persons with disabilities in both urban and rural sectors.

On an average out of every 1,000 persons with a disability, 15 would have completed some vocational training in rural areas and 35 in urban areas. This is not a surprising finding given the higher concentration and greater accessibility of educational institutions and vocational training centres in urban areas.

There is an overrepresentation of boys with disabilities in education, both in special and mainstream schools. Due to differential gender-based role expectations, education is not considered a priority for girls with disabilities. Drop-out rates for girls with disabilities are higher than for boys with disabilities. Parents become more protective and restrictive especially after the daughter with a disability reaches puberty. Travelling to school is a double problem: transport difficulties and the danger of sexual abuse and violation also loom large.

Furthermore, there is the reasoning that there is no point investing in the education of a girl with a disability as it is presumed that she will never be able to earn. She is perceived be a life-long burden on the natal family because marriage is also not a realistic option. So, it is economically unsound to invest in her education or vocational training. Distribution of school-going children in terms of different types of disabilities shows the highest enrolment rate for those having locomotor disability and lowest enrolment rate for the mentally retarded.

There are around 1,200 special schools in India (with an enrolment of about 55,000 students), which are almost exclusively concentrated in cities reducing their accessibility to the majority of children with disabilities in rural areas. The upshot of this situation is that it necessitates some integration of children with disabilities in the mainstream educational system, especially in rural areas. However, integration into mainstream schools without the necessary infrastructure and trained manpower to address the special needs of such children results in high school dropout rates, especially of girl children with disabilities (see Table 10.5).

Overall 26 per cent of all persons with disabilities in the productive age group of 18-44 years were employed. The rural-urban gap is not too large, since 22 per cent of rural and 24 per cent of urban persons with disabilities were employed respectively. Not surprisingly, the employment rate was higher for males (37-8 per cent) in comparison to females (9 to 11 per cent) with disabilities. Among different disabilities the lowest rate of employment was among the mentally retarded (6 per cent) and the highest among the hearing impaired (34 per cent).

Family composition of the households in which there was a member with a disability was examined (Table 10.6).

Not surprisingly the family remains the mainstay of care for persons with disabilities.

TABLE 10.5: SCHOOL ENROLMENT IN MAINSTREAM AND SPECIAL SCHOOLS OF CHILDREN WITH DISABILITIES (5-18 YEARS)

Type of School	Rural (%)	Urban (%)
Mainstream	47.8	44.4
Special	1.0	11.0

Source: NSSO 2002.

TABLE 10.6: LIVING ARRANGEMENT OF DISABLED IN INDIA

Living Arrangement	% of Disabled
Living alone	3
Living only with spouse	5
Living with family with/without spouse	92

Source: NSSO 2002.

It will be noted that the census and NSSO use a narrow medical definition of disability wherein it is defined in terms of functional limitations imposed on an individual due to the presence of some congenital or adventitious sensory, physical or mental anomaly. There are many chronic conditions like asthma, cardiovascular disease, diabetes and even HIV/AIDS which have disabling consequences on a person's life which have been excluded from this restricted definition. Similarly, learning disabilities like dyslexia also do not find a separate mention. Although for purposes of national-level surveys one can understand the need for applying restrictive criteria, it needs to be borne in mind that disability is a heterogeneous multi-dimensional concept extending beyond very basic sensory, physical and mental dysfunctions.

As against a medical definition of disability that is grounded in individual suffering and personal misfortune, the international disability rights movement and disability researchers subscribe to a more socially-based definition of disability in which the focus of attention shifts from an individual suffering from a range of limitations or incapacities to the inability of the social system to provide the necessary conditions which may enable persons with disabilities equality of opportunity and full participation in all spheres of social, economic, political and cultural life. This perspective derives from the human rights discourse and ideas of empowerment that have developed within the framework of national democratic institutions, the United Nations and a globalized NGO movement. Every human being including a person with a disability is entitled to a dignified, productive life of self-reliance and personal fulfilment. According to the social model of disability, impairment is not the problem, society oppresses through ableism (prejudicial attitudes and discriminatory practices towards persons with disabilities). Consequently, persons with disabilities are a minority group like other marginalized racial, caste or ethnic groups. The social model of disability is a proactive approach, which focuses on changing social conditions and mindsets that obstruct the full development and integration of persons with disabilities.

While the census and NSSO surveys have tried to estimate the magnitude of the population with disabilities in India on the basis of medically-based definitions of physical and mental disability, the legislative enactments and policy statements have tried to look at disability more from the social model perspective. To this end various constitutional provisions espousing the cause of social justice and affirmative action have been deployed to justify special measures for the welfare of persons with disabilities. Indeed, there is no denying that the existence of a disability at the individual level does require additional resources to cater to the specific needs of activities of daily living, education, training and employment for a person with a disability to lead an economically productive, socially meaningful and personally fulfilling life. Without these additional imputs, his/her capacity for equal participation and economic productivity will be curtailed. For this to happen there is a need to remove the material, social and attitudinal barriers that inhibit access. The rationale for inclusion is mainstreaming of marginalized groups so that they are able to become full citizens with the same social, economic, cultural, civil and political rights that others enjoy.

LEGISLATIVE REGIME FOR EMPOWERMENT OF PERSONS WITH DISABILITIES

There is a broad provision in the Preamble of the Indian Constitution (1950) on the part of the state to guarantee equality of opportunity and a life of dignity to all its citizens including persons with disabilities. Although there are no explicit references to persons with disabilities as such in the Constitution, they may, however, be derived from provisions dealing with welfare of other identified vulnerable groups. Article 14 guarantees equality before the law: Article 15(3) enjoins the state to make provisions for welfare of women and children. Article 39(A) of the Directive Principles of State Policy directs the state to ensure that no citizen is denied justice on the basis of economic and other disabilities. Similarly, Article 41 enjoins the state (within the limits of economic policy and development) to make effective provisions for securing the right to work, to education and to public assistance in cases of unemployment, old age, sickness and disablement and in other cases of undeserved want. Then, Article 46 of the Directive

Principles of State Policy enjoins the state to promote with special care the social and economic interests of the weaker sections without mentioning persons with disabilities in so many words.

If a chronological analysis of the Indian state's policies on disability is undertaken, the period can be broadly divided into two phases. The first phase would extend from Independence in 1947 to 1995 when the Parliament enacted the Persons with Disabilities (Equal Opportunities, Full Participation and Protection of Rights) Act. In this period some administrative measures to alleviate the plight of persons with disabilities were undertaken which gained momentum after 1981, the International Year of Disabled Persons. But the major fillip came with the passage of the PWD Act. This is a landmark legislation, which has catapulted disability as a central human rights issue. Today, it is the lynchpin of all state policies on disability in the country. It is the main tool of redressal for individual violation of human rights. It frames the partnership between the government agencies and the NGOs working in the disability sector. It is increasingly being used to encourage the private and corporate sectors to enhance employment opportunities for persons with disabilities. Several shortcomings notwithstanding, one can safely aver that it is the most elaborate measure for empowerment of persons with disabilities in the country. The main objectives of the PWD Act are to lay down modalities for comprehensive development of programmes and services and equalization of opportunities for persons with disabilities by making special provisions for their integration into the social mainstream. The other objectives are:

1. To spell out the responsibilities of the state towards prevention of disabilities, protection of rights, provision of medical care, education, training, employment and rehabilitation of persons with disabilities.
2. To create barrier-free environment.
3. To remove any discrimination against persons with disabilities in sharing of development benefits *vis-à-vis* non-disabled persons.
4. To counteract any abuse or exploitation of persons with disabilities.

It will be noted that the implementation of the Act requires a multi-sectoral collaborative approach of the central and state governments, their respective ministries and other local authorities. In prevention and early detection of disabilities, the pivotal role has to be played by the Ministry of Health and Family Welfare and the

Department of Women and Child Development. For inclusive education and ensuring a barrier-free environment in schools, the responsibility lies with the Ministry of Human Resources Development. For increasing physical accessibility and modifications in the built environment, it is the Ministries of Surface Transport, Railways, Civil Aviation and Urban Affairs that have to work together. In the area of employment, the Ministry of Labour has the central role.

Although this act was a veritable milestone in the government's approach to the issue of disability, it is open to criticism on a number of counts:

1. The Act is criticized for being a mere tokenism. For instance, the Chief Disability Commissioner was only appointed in 1998, a full three years after its ratification.
2. Bureaucratic structure of boards and committees creates distance between providers and beneficiaries, i.e. persons with disabilities.
3. There is no systematic machinery to ensure enforcement, including a penalty for those failing to implement its provisions.
4. The Act is not gender-sensitive.
5. Not enough effort has been made to create awareness about the Act, especially among beneficiaries.
6. The government is itself not following the provision of 3 per cent reservation in its own agencies and departments.

Such limitations notwithstanding, the PWD Act is a powerful tool of empowerment for the disabled in the country.

In addition to the PWD Act, there are three other legislations that directly concern physical and mental disability. These are:

The Mental Health Act, 1987

Keeping pace with scientific developments in psychiatry and the international human rights movement, the Government of India replaced the obsolete Indian Lunacy Act of 1912 with the Mental Health Act in 1987. This Act has a whole section dealing with the protection of human rights of mentally ill persons. It also differentiates between the mentally ill and the mentally retarded and eschews the use of stigmatizing terms such as 'lunatic', 'insane', 'idiot' and 'unsound mind'. A mentally ill person is simply defined as one who is in need of treatment by reason of any mental disorder other than mental retardation. The Act calls for regular visits by visitors to duly licensed psychiatric hospitals and also contains provisions for setting up of mental health authorities.

It needs to be remembered that unlike those with physical disabilities, there have historically been many legal disqualifications for both the mentally retarded and mentally ill based on a presumption of mental incapacity and incompetence. For instance, under the Indian Contract Act (1972), a person of unsound mind is ineligible to enter into a contract and under the Indian Succession Act (1925) s/he does not have testamentary capacity to dispose of property. A person of unsound mind cannot engage in litigation nor can s/he be charged in a court of law. Under the Hindu Marriage Act (1955), insanity will automatically render a marriage null and void. Unlike in the case of persons with physical disabilities, employment in government service, voting and election to public office are other deprivations which affect persons with mental disabilities

The Rehabilitation Council of India Act, 1992

One of the major lacunae in the disability sector has been the lack of trained manpower. The Rehabilitation Council of India (RCI) was constituted in 1986 as an apex body to standardize and monitor training in the disability sector in the country. In 1992 it was converted into a statutory body under the Rehabilitation Council of India Act. Prior to this, existing programmes in the fields of rehabilitation and special education were ad-hoc and uncoordinated in nature with no standardized syllabi. There was a need not only to standardize manpower training and service delivery, but also to regulate organization and institutions. One way of maintaining both standards of professional practice and quality of services is through the creation of a central register of certified rehabilitation professionals and organizations. In establishing uniform standards in the field of rehabilitation, the RCI Act covers a range of professionals such as psychologists, speech therapists, social workers, physiotherapists, occupational therapists and other specialists working in the field of disability.

The National Trust for the Welfare of Persons with Autism, Cerebral Palsy, Mental Retardation and Multiple Disabilities Act, 1999

This is a special legislation operationalizing the constitution of a national-level trust to look into the welfare of the most vulnerable among persons with disabilities. Its aim is to work for affirmative action for categories of persons whose disability may render them incapable of self-care in daily life and independent living. The purpose of this legislation is to empower specific groups of persons with disabilities to live in the community. Essentially protectionist and promotive in nature, the trust is created to safeguard the interests and protect the rights of a highly vulnerable population. The national trust supports programmes which promote independence and guardianship where necessary, and addresses the life concerns of those people who do not have family support and protects interests of such persons after the death of their parents and care-givers. It also supports organizations rendering support in the event of crises in the family of such persons.

The trust comprises a board of public servants, parents associations, NGO representatives and persons with disabilities. It received from the government a one-time contribution of Rs. 100 crore for the corpus fund. It receives contributions in the form of donations, bequests, benefactions and transfers from private individuals and organizations. In rendering assistance preference is given to women with disabilities, persons with severe disabilities and the disabled elderly.

DISABILITY AND STATE DISCOURSE: FROM WELFARE TO HUMAN RIGHTS

It needs to be remembered that even prior to the enactment of the above legislation, a number of multi-sectoral programmes were in operation for persons with disabilities. However, they were framed within a welfare orientation rather than a rights-based regime. During the first three five-year plans (1955-69), support to the disability sector took the form of grants-in-aid to NGOs and the establishment of national training institutes. A number of policy measures for improving the status of persons with disabilities in the country were undertaken by the government during the 1960s and 1970s, ranging from reservation in educational institutions and in employment to junior levels of government service to expanding the network of national institutes and vocational training centres. Support was also provided to the voluntary sector with emphasis being on service delivery. Persons with disabilities were configured as a vulnerable group in need of protection and care rather than as equal citizens with rights.

Table 10.7 presents an overview of concessions available to persons with disabilities under various schemes even before the passage of the PWD Act.

TABLE 10.7: CONCESSIONS FOR PERSONS WITH DISABILITIES IN INDIA BEFORE 1995

Concession	Details
Reservation in Government Jobs	3 per cent reservation in government jobs at C and D levels for the blind, hearing and speech impaired and locomotor disabled.
Railway Travel	75 per cent rebate in fares for four categories of disabled (blind, hearing and speech impaired, locomotor and leprosy-affected) and 50 per cent for the escort in all classes.
Free Postage	Free postage of literature for the visually impaired within the country and abroad.
Telephone Concessions	50 per cent concession on telephone rental to blind persons: quota allotment of public telephone booths to disabled persons.
Custom Duties	Exemption of custom duties on import of various equipment and aids by individuals with disabilities and by registered institutions in the disability sector.
Conveyance Allowance	Conveyance allowance to blind and orthopedically impaired central government employees at the rate of 5 per cent of basic pay.
Children's Educational Allowance	Tuition fee reimbursement for education of children with disabilities of government employees not exceeding Rs. 100 per month.
Income Tax Rebate	Deduction for medical treatment and rehabilitation of a dependant with disabilities up to Rs. 41,000. Tax rebate of Rs. 40,000 on personal income for a person with disability.
Allotment of Agencies by Oil Companies	7.5 per cent reservation for persons with disabilities, widows of government employees deceased in course of duty and government employees disabled in harness (other than defence personnel).
Age Relaxation	Relaxation in age by 10 years for recruitment to C and D cadres in public sector.
Loans	Public sector banks offer loans at low interest rates for self-employment projects.
Waiver of Application Fees	No application fees for candidates with disabilities applying for government jobs.

Source: Collated by author.

With the declaration of 1981 as International Year of Disabled Persons followed by the International Decade of Disabled Persons (1981-91), disability moved from a peripheral concern to an important issue in state discourse. Firstly, it was incorporated into the 1981 census. Efforts were made at generating public awareness about the special needs of persons with disabilities. The reservation policy in education and employment was pursued more vigorously. The Bahrul Islam Committee was appointed in 1988 by Prime Minister Rajiv Gandhi to go into the whole issue of formulating a comprehensive legislation on disability. Identification of suitable jobs for persons with disabilities at senior cadres was undertaken. As a signatory to the Asia Pacific Proclamation on Disability, India was obliged to proactively work for ensuring the human rights of persons with disabilities through appropriate legislative instruments and administrative measures.

The Division of Disabilities in the Ministry of Social Justice and Empowerment is responsible for programmes on disability in the country. For effective implementation of various schemes, it co-ordinates with other ministries like Railways, Civil Aviation, Surface Transport, Housing, Posts and Telegraphs, Human Resource Development, among others. For instance, conservative estimates put the number of employable persons with disabilities in the country at 7 million but the rate of employment has been a mere 4,000 per annum. With the objective of empowerment of persons with disabilities and the implementation of the policy of affirmative action for employment, the Ministry of Labour has set up 55 special cells in general employment exchanges and 22 special employment exchanges. Over 70,000 persons with disabilities are registered with special employment exchanges in the country. This scheme is implemented through the labour department at the state level.

The main activities of the Division of Disabilities in the Ministry of Social Justice and Empowerment are described below:

Prevention of Disabilities

A large proportion of disabilities can be prevented. Research indicates that the socio-economic cost of prevention of disabilities are lower than the cost of rehabilitation. Environmental sanitation and hygienic living conditions can immensely reduce incidence of disabilities. For example, worm infections can cause anaemia resulting in high mortality, morbidity and disability among neonates. Defecating in the open can lead to the growth of wild polio virus. Similarly, polluted water causes rota virus infection which results in diarrhoea. Diarrhoea, in turn, is known to cause growth retardation. Unsanitary conditions enable spread of trachoma, which can lead to blindness. Even leprosy can be caused by unsanitary living conditions resulting in the development of deformities.

Then, malnutrition and deficiency of essential micronutrients can also lead to the onset of disabilities, particularly in women and children. For instance, iron can cause anaemia especially among pregnant women resulting in greater proneness of infants to disease and disability. Vitamin A deficiency is a major cause of blindness among children. Studies indicate that iodine deficiency impairs brain development significantly. Various micronutrient deficiencies account for a large percentage of low birth weight in babies which is associated with poor physical and mental development of surviving infants. Malnutrition during infancy and early childhood is believed to have adverse effects on both physical growth and intellectual performance in later life.

Prevention is promoted through various national health programmes like Programmes on Blindness Prevention, Leprosy Elimination, Pulse Polio Immunization and various reproductive and child health programmes.

Maintenance and Creation of Institutional Infrastructure

In addition to the Rehabilitation Council of India and the National Trust for Welfare of Persons with Autism, Cerebral Palsy, Mental Retardation and Multiple Disabilities, there are other national, regional, and district-level institutes on disability. Six national institutes were established during the 1970s and 1980s for purposes of training, manpower development and research for different types of disabilities. These institutes are, namely:

- National Institute for the Visually Handicapped, Dehra Dun (Uttarakhand);
- National Institute for the Orthopaedically Handicapped, Kolkata (West Bengal);
- Ali Yavar Jung National Institute for the Hearing Handicapped, Mumbai (Maharashtra);
- National Institute for Mentally Handicapped, Secunderabad (Andhra Pradesh);

- National Institute for Rehabilitation, Training and Research, Cuttack (Orissa);
- Institute for the Physically Handicapped, New Delhi.

These institutes offer a comprehensive package of welfare, pedagogic and research services addressing the multi-dimensional needs of persons with physical and mental disabilities. They run degree and certificate courses in physiotherapy, occupational therapy, prosthetic and orthotic engineering, special education, audiology and speech rehabilitation, and so on. They also offer consultancy services to state governments and NGOs.

In addition, a network of regional, composite regional and district rehabilitation training centres have been set up across the country. The aim of these centres is to provide comprehensive rehabilitation services to persons with disabilities in rural areas right at their doorstep, including availing of facilities and concession offered by the state governments such as pensions, aids and appliances and other medical services, vocational training and job placement. As resource centres, they aim at creating an integrated environment for persons with disabilities through information dissemination, networking and skill development to ensure a system of community-based rehabilitation exists in the most inaccessible and deprived regions of the country.

Other Schemes to Promote Welfare of Persons with Disabilities

The Disability Division in the Ministry of Social Justice and Empowerment is running a number of other schemes to mainstream disability and promote the welfare of persons with disabilities in the country. These are:

- Assistance to Disabled Persons for Purchase/Fitting of Aids and Appliances;
- Scheme to Promote Voluntary Action for Persons with Disabilities;
- Scheme of National Awards for the Welfare of Persons with Disabilities;
- Scheme of National Scholarships for Persons with Disabilities.

In addition, there are schemes and concessions of different state governments to promote welfare of persons with disabilities, which may take the form of disability pensions, scholarships, free transport, uniforms and books for schoolchildren.

NON-GOVERNMENTAL ORGANIZATIONS IN THE DISABILITY SECTOR

There are more than 2,000 NGOs working in the disability sector in India. They are mainly engaged in service delivery in connection with specific disabilities operating at district, state and national levels. For instance, National Association for the Blind, All India Federation of the Deaf and Spastics Society of Northern India (now known as Action for Abilities, Development and Inclusion (AADI) operate at national and regional levels. On the other hand, Jan Madhyam, Family of Disabled and Samadhan are Delhi-based NGOs working on disability. NGOs working in any sector often work in isolation. There is also intense competition for limited funds. There is a general mistrust of NGOs regarding the nature of work being done and utilization of funds. Those working in remote areas are unaware of new developments in the field. The converse is also true, as new, innovative and successful practices developed are not disseminated to the other practitioners in the field. Advocacy efforts of a single NGO are less effective and the changes sought may not be implemented. The NGO-government interface is often underwritten by mistrust.

The long-standing isolation among NGOs, divided on grounds of the type of disability, was partially dented when it came to lobbying for the passage of the PWD Act. In 1994 a cross-disability forum under the aegis of the Disability Rights Group was formed, which has come to serve as a common platform for advocacy with the government. The first convenor of the Disability Rights Group Javed Abidi is a leading disability activist in Delhi, who even contested for the New Delhi parliamentary seat as an independent candidate during the 2004 general elections. He is the founder of the National Centre for Promotion of Employment of Disabled Persons (NCPEDP), which is engaged in promoting higher education and employment for persons with disabilities, especially through networking with the private sector.

Subsequently, there has been limited networking and coalition-building among major NGOs in the disability sector, since power to lobby increases with increase in number of actors. Besides the passage of the PWD Act has also played a role in bringing different groups together. Since 1999 a National Disability Network has been functioning and a number of cross-disability national-level conventions have been held. For instance, in March 2004, a National Political

Convention of Persons with Disabilities was held in Delhi just before the general elections. The aim of the convention was to ensure that voting booths were disabled-friendly, so that persons with disabilities could exercise their franchise as equal citizens and participate in the democratic process.

One of the negative outcomes of globalization is that privatization has reduced the state's participation in the social sector in the areas of employment and education. Consequently, some concessions, reservations and other facilities for persons with disabilities offered by the public sector are diminishing. Retrenchment, voluntary retirement schemes and automation have impacted employees with disabilities, most of whom are at the lower-end job levels. In the context of structural adjustment policies of the governments, NGOs can play a major role in undertaking activities for persons with disabilities. Central and state governments should take advantage of the grassroot presence of NGOs and support them to implement various schemes. On the other hand, NGOs in the disability sector need to ensure that a large number of their employees come from the population with disabilities. They have to lead by example.

While priority should be given to NGOs working for persons with disability, the isolation of these NGOs should be broken by encouraging networking and coalition-building with other NGOs in the development sector, because disability is after all a developmental issue. By the same token, NGOs working in other areas should also be encouraged to have a component on disability in their work. This kind of inclusive funding and programming will go a long way in making visible persons with disabilities as a minority group and empowering them to fight for their rights.

AN AGENDA FOR RESEARCH AND ACTION FOR WOMEN WITH DISABILITIES

Key terms in disability discourse are dignity and respect, inclusion, participation, equalization of opportunities and empowerment. The paper has shown that many of the programmes and laws are mere tokens or symbolic gestures as far as women with disabilities are concerned. There is an urgent need to ensure rights to security, health, education, employment and parenthood for women with disabilities. Gender mainstreaming in programme development, research and advocacy is the need of the hour. Very often the three go together. This gender mainstreaming must be within a multi-sectoral and rights-based approach.

The legal framework on disability makes no provisions for women with disabilities. The PWD Act is gender neutral. It does not address the specific concerns of women with disabilities in the areas of health, education and employment. Although the National Trust Act does mention that preference will be given to helping vulnerable groups among the disabled such as the disabled elderly and women with disabilities, it is not being used by parents of daughters. A gender-based analysis of existing legislation on disability would go a long way in highlighting both the obstacles faced by women with disabilities and their possible remedies.

Anecdotal reportage by doctors reveals that they see most girls with disabilities only as children when parents come for treatment for the disability. Rarely are they seen in obstretic and gynaecological settings as adults. Reproductive health of women with disabilities is another grey area. From the socio-demographic analysis we have seen that the stereotype that women with disabilities will not marry and bear children is only partially true. What are the experiences of such women in the medical system? Is it in fact accessible to them? What kind of morbidities are they more prone to? What are their special needs during pregnancy, delivery and lactation? Till date, these are issues which do not even find mention in the reproductive and child health (RCH) programmes. Both disability and reproductive health are about access to information, services and finally rights. In India they are both enveloped in stigma and taboo, blocking individuals' access to resources. Incorporating disability into the RCH programmes is a critical avenue for empowerment.

Women with disabilities are particularly vulnerable to violence and abuse. They may not have accurate knowledge about their bodies, abuse prevention and self-protection. Being often viewed as asexual, lacking intelligence and non-credible victims, they can easily be taken advantage of. There are sporadic media reports on assault of women with disabilities in the family, on the street and in institutions, but there is again no systematic data on this phenomenon. Violation of their reproductive rights in the form of forced sterilization, contraception and abortion, especially in institutions, are not uncommon. Self-defence should be made a part of the special education system for adolescent girls. Violence against women is a central concern of the women's movement and this issue should feature both as an agenda for research and advocacy.

Women with disabilities are quite often excluded from gender equity programmes. They should be included not only as beneficiaries but also as fieldworkers and project facilitators, survey designers and field investigators in projects with disability components. This will enhance their visibility in highly positive roles and challenge negative attitudes that reduce them to objects of pity and helplessness.

Various levels of state administration and the NGO sector dealing with the welfare of women need to be oriented on the problems of women with disabilities. This would ensure that the diversity of women's experiences are part of the agenda of the women's movement and the structures within the state that focus on women and child development. There is a need for more sensitization workshops, especially with women's groups and government departments like Women's Commission, Department of Women and Child Development. Furthermore, there should also be a separate wing for women with disabilities in the office of the Chief Commissioner of Persons with Disabilities. Women with disabilities should also be represented on the central and state co-ordination and executive committees mandated by the PWD Act.

Besides personnel dealing with women's welfare, health care staff should also be trained to respond to needs of women and girls with disabilities. Similarly, police and judiciary should also be trained to handle cases involving women with disabilities in a sensitive manner.

Negative media representations of women with disabilities further reinforce their negative public perceptions as women with defects. There is an urgent need to develop and propagate more realistic and positive images of women with disabilities as capable and productive persons in the mass media, especially radio and television. Inclusive programming and highlighting the achievements of women with disabilities will go a long way in changing entrenched mindsets and creating positive role models for girls with disabilities. Such role models provide a subject with a face and success story worthy of emulation.

There is a need to develop support services for families with a member with disability. As principal caregivers, mothers are particularly vulnerable to emotional stress. The situation is exacerbated for mothers of daughters, who also suffer the taint of disability as those who did not only produce sons but instead gave birth to a bigger burden for their families in the form of a daughter with a disability.

There is immense scope for gender mainstreaming within pedagogy. Whether it is courses in special education, rehabilitation or women's studies, the concerns of women with disabilities should feature as a special module, if not as a separate course. Rehabilitation Council of India can go a long way in promoting this process, since it is the nodal agency responsible for standardizing teaching and curricula in the disability sector in the country. So, a two-pronged approach in training is the need of the hour, namely, gender mainstreaming in curricula on disability and rehabilitation and disability mainstreaming in curricula on gender and women's empowerment.

Allocation of funds to NGOs in the disability sector is also an area amenable to gender mainstreaming. Projects focussing on the welfare of women with disabilities should be promoted or a gender component built into any project that receives support. NGOs started by women with disabilities should be provided extra support.

Technology is also a path to empowerment. Government policies in the disability sector encourage development of innovative, adaptive technologies. For instance, the Scheme on Science and Technology Projects in Mission Mode in the Ministry of Social Justice and Empowerment provides 100 per cent research funding for such work. There is a need not only to make such assistive technologies women-friendly but also to involve women with disabilities in their development.

In conclusion, it may be emphasized that there is an urgent need to increase the ambit of inclusiveness by ensuring that women with disabilities are part of the programmes of government, NGOs and women's groups. Opposition to such a focus could emanate from two main sources, namely that the concerns of women with disabilities are subsumed within programmes for gender equity in general, which is not true. And secondly, the Constitution and the PWD Act itself offer an escape route when it is averred that the provisions are subject to the limits of the state's economic policy and development plans. Furthermore, research on disability not only in terms of gender but also in terms of the cross-cutting of gender with ethnicity, religion, caste and class and even sexual orientation needs to be carried out. Positive attitudinal change can be brought about by strengthening alliances between women with disabilities and non-disabled women and men with disabilities as partners. Eventually, for women with disabilities in India, visibility and participation in social life is the path to empowerment.

CONCLUSION

This paper attempts to present an overview of disability discourse in India with a special focus on the concerns of women with disabilities. In addition to a brief socio-demographic analysis, the paper discusses the legislative provisions and policy measures instituted by the state to ameliorate the life conditions of persons with disabilities. However, due to the absence of a gender-sensitive perspective, a large segment of the disabled population, namely, women with disabilities are more or less excluded from the purview of such programmes. Lastly, the paper offers an agenda for action and research to engender existing laws and programmes. It is hoped that the paper carries forward the nascent debate on disability, gender and development in the Indian context.

Conservative estimates show that 18.49 to 21.92 million persons suffer from some form of disability in India (*Census of India*, 2001). Over 9 million of them are women. Some researchers estimate that there are over 35 million women with disabilities in India. A shocking 98 per cent of them are illiterate: less than 1 per cent can avail health care and rehabilitation services. But these statistics are only the tip of the iceberg when it comes to gauging the level of neglect, isolation stigma and deprivation that characterize their lives. The majority of women with disabilities suffer the triple discrimination of being female, having a disability and being poor. Indeed, not only are they a socially invisible category but their plight is worse than that of both men with disabilities and other non-disabled women. The paper shows that gender discrepancies show up at every level in the socio-demographic analysis on disability in India.

Today there is a general recognition of the need to enhance educational and employment opportunities for persons with disabilities in order to promote economic self-reliance and independent living. In tracing the development of such a perspective, the paper identifies a number of seminal influences such as the international human rights movement and anti-poverty initiatives which have transplanted the issue of disability from one of charity and social welfare to one of social development. The United Nations has played a pivotal role in prioritizing disability at international and national levels. In addition, the new developmental discourses moving beyond modernization and industrialization theories have also focused attention on disability as a human rights issue. However, as the paper points out, a sound gender perspective on disability is still absent at the level of policy planning and implementation.

Instead of giving rights to citizens with disabilities and empowering them, a culture of charity and welfare has been systematically promoted in India since the colonial period. Medical rehabilitation, special schools, vocational training in low-end occupations and sheltered employment have been the pillars of state policy. Things began to change marginally after 1981 (United Nations International Year of Disabled Persons) when the issue of disability was opened up at the national level. The changing international climate focusing on human rights and empowerment of marginal groups impelled the government to make some policy changes such as token reservations in educational institutions and employment. But real progress in the form of concrete legislation to deliver the promise of equality of opportunity and social justice only came in 1995 with the passage of the Persons with Disabilities (Equal Opportunities and full Participation) Act. Other legislations soon followed. One of the positive outcomes of economic liberalization and globalization has been the introduction of a view of disability as a human rights and development issue rather than simply a matter of charity and welfare. The paper discusses the disability legislation regime in India highlighting the need for engendering the same.

A number of government programmes are in operation for the welfare of persons with disabilities. They range from disease control to prevent the onset of disabilities in children to provision of aids and appliances and reservation in education and employment. However, there are a number of obstacles to the optimum utilization of such schemes. Very often, persons with disabilities and their families are not aware of such schemes. Then, there are too many bureaucratic procedures in availing the benefits such as provision of medical certificates. Last, but not the least, the callous attitude and behaviour of government functionaries makes many persons with disabilities reluctant to undertake the effort to avail of the benefits. In this situation, women with disabilities find it almost impossible to avail of these schemes.

Consequently, there is an urgent need to incorporate the concerns of women with disabilities at different levels in policy planning, programme design and implementation and research. In the neo-liberal political and economic context, developmental activity is strategically dependent upon state-NGO collaboration. Women's groups occupy a significant swathe of the developmental sector. Therefore, joint initiatives on gender and disability through networking and alliance-building between these different agencies in the areas of health, education, legal reform, pedagogy, technology development among others could go a long way in mainstreaming the needs of women with disabilities. This paper proposes an agenda for action and research as a first step in this direction.

REFERENCES

Action Aid (2003), *Just People: Nothing Special, Nothing Unusual*, Bangalore: Books for Change.

Bacquer, A. and A. Sharma (1997), *Disability: Challenges vs Responses*, New Delhi: Concerned Action Now.

Fine, M. and A. Asch (eds.) (1988), *Women with Disabilities: Essays in Psychology, Culture and Politics*, Philadelphia: Temple University Press.

Government of India (1981), *Census of India*, New Delhi: Director General of Census.

——— (1987), Mental Health Act, New Delhi. Ministry of Justice and Company Affairs, http://nhrc.nic.in/Publications/Disability/annexure3.html

——— (1991), *Census of India*, New Delhi: Director General of Census.

——— (1992), Rehabilitation Council of India Act, New Delhi. Ministry of Justice and Company Affairs, http://rehabcouncil.nic.in/council/acts_amend.htm

——— (1995), The Persons with Disabilities (Equal Opportunities, Protection of Rights and Full Participation) Act, 1995, New Delhi: Ministry of Law Justice and Company Affairs, http://socialjustice.nic.in/disabled/act.htm

——— (1999), The National Trust for the Welfare of Persons with Autism Cerebral Palsy, Mental Retardation and Multiple Disabilities Act, New Delhi: Ministry of Justice and Company Affairs, http://rehabcouncil.nic.in/pdf/nationaltrust1999.pdf

——— (2001), *Census of India*, New Delhi: Director General of Census.

National Sample Survey Organisation (1981), *Disabled Persons in India* (36th Round), New Delhi: NSSO, Govt. of India.

——— (1991), *Disabled Persons in India* (47th Round), New Delhi: NSSO, Government of India.

——— (2002), *Disabled Persons in India* (58th Round) Report No. 485, New Delhi: NSSO, Government of India.

Oliver, M. (1996), *Understanding Disability: From Theory to Practice*, London: Macmillan.

United Nations (1948), Universal Declaration of Human Rights, General Assembly Resolution 217A (III), http://www.un.org/Overview/rights.html

——— (1971), Declaration on the Rights of Mentally Retarded Persons, General Assembly Resolution 2856 (XXVI), http://www.unhchr.ch/html/menu3/b/m_mental.htm

——— (1975), Declaration on the Rights of Disabled Persons, General Assembly Resolution 3447 (XXX), http://www.unhchr.ch/html/menu3/b/72.htm

——— (1976a), International Covenant on Civil and Political Rights. Adopted and opened for signature, ratification and accession by General Assembly Resolution 2200A (XXI), http://www.unhchr.ch/html/menu3/b/a_cescr.htm

——— (1976b), International Covenant on Economic Social and Cultural Rights. Adopted and opened for signature, ratification and accession by General Assembly Resolution 2200A (XXI), http://www.unhchr.ch/html/menu3/b/a_cescr.htm

——— (1993), Standard Rules on the Equalization of Opportunities for Persons with Disabilities, General Assembly 48/96 annex 1, http://www.un.org/esa/socdev/enable/dissre00.htm

——— (1995), 'Fourth World Conference on Women: Action for Equality, Development and Peace', Beijing, China, http://www.un.org/womenwatch/daw/beijing/platform/

——— (2006), The Convention on the Rights of Persons with Disabilities and its Optional Protocol was adopted on 13 December 2006 at the United Nations Headquarters in New York, and was opened for signature on 30 March 2007, http://www.google.co.in/search?hl=en&q=Convention+on+rights+of+persons+with+disabilities&meta=

CHAPTER 11

Rescue and Rehabilitation of Sex Workers: A Case Study of Delhi

O.P. MISHRA

PERSPECTIVE

Rescue and rehabilitation of sex workers are logically interlinked with each other. The basic purpose of rescue is rehabilitation of the sex workers. While rescue is essentially a job of law enforcing agencies, rehabilitation lies with state and other non-governmental organizations (NGO). Before an attempt is made to discuss the rescue and rehabilitation dimension of sex workers, it is important to understand the status of sex workers, also known as prostitutes (in more popular language) in a historical perspective.

Theoretically speaking, the issue of rescue and rehabilitation of sex workers is a very recent phenomenon. The very nature of the problem and its deep rooting in the social system have always discouraged any systematic displacement/rescue of prostitutes from society. However, due to the growing menace of the problem from the social point of view and concern by various NGOs and women rights activists, over a period of time, the issue of rescue and rehabilitation has assumed significance. It would not be out of place to mention that mass rescue operation of trapped victims from G.B. Road (Garstin Bastion Road) has not been very common in the history ever since brothel houses existed. The network of traffickers and *kotha* (brothel) owners has always resisted any rescue operation of neglected and juvenile children from the brothel houses. In 1990, the rescue of 112 juvenile and neglected children from the brothel houses led to strong protests by the *kotha* Madams and traffickers at the local police station. They even did not allow the medical examination of the victims to be conducted. The present rescue operation also faced stiff resistance from the traffickers' network and *kotha* owners.

This article is essentially based on rescue operations carried out in G.B. Road brothel houses a few years back and the subsequent interviews of rescued victims in observation homes. Views expressed in the article are personal and have nothing do with the official position I occupy.

The article has been divided into the following parts:

(i) The first part deals with the issue of prostitution in general in India and how it has been changing over a period of time. It also presents some relevant statistics in this regard.
(ii) The second part understands the problem in Delhi with special reference to G.B. Road brothel houses. It also highlights the inner social structure which emerged following interaction with the rescued victims.
(iii) The third section deals with significant dimensions of the problem which emerged from the interaction.
(iv) The fourth section highlights the importance of law enforcing agencies in the process of rescue.
(v) The fifth section highlights the importance of rehabilitation and explains how a meaningful strategy can prevent entry of innocent victims in this whole trade.
(vi) Case studies: profile of a few victims.
(vii) The article concludes with a set of recommendations.

A BACKDROP

Prostitution has existed in India since time immemorial, sometimes as a deviant social behaviour and as an accepted norms at other times. To paraphrase Simone de Beauvoir,[1] prostitution has followed humanity from antiquity to the present day. So have many other phenomenon which have not created such emotional and even vitriolic response. Dr. Crooke wrote in an article on Indian prostitution in Hastings' *Encyclopedia of Religion and Ethics* that prostitutes are tolerated in contemporary India to an extent which can hardly be paralleled in any other part of the world.[2]

A close look at Indian history shows that the institution has existed under various rulers in some form or the other. Crook[3] points to passages in the *Rigveda* which demonstrate its existence in the Vedic age. During the Mauryan empire founded by Chandragupta (325-298 BC), courtesans and prostitutes occupied a privileged position at the royal court and cooperated with one of the most important departments of the imperial administration. In the famous *Arthashastra* of Kautilya, chapter XI[4] states that prostitutes shall do the duty of bathroom servants, shampooers, bedroom attendants, washerwomen and garland makers. As a matter of fact during the Mauryan empire prostitutes were even employed as member of secret services as spies. The Greek writer Stabo records that professional prostitutes cooperated with the royal spies and worked as a recognized medium of intelligence.[5]

In a similar fashion one also finds the existence of this institution in the regime of various other rulers. Abdul Razzak, who visited Vijayanagara as a Persian envoy in AD 1443 during the reign of Deva Raya II writes: 'Opposite the mint is the office of the prefect of the City, to which it is said 12,000 policemen are attached, and their pay which equals each day 12,000 fanams is derived from the proceeds of the brothels.'[6]

Prostitution also existed under Muslim rulers. One significant distinction during Muslim rule was that it was not treated by every ruler as a legitimate source of revenue for the government. For example, during Akbar's reign, according to the *Ain-i-Akbari*, prostitutes were so many that they defied enumeration. They had a separate quarter of the city assigned to them also known as 'Shaitanpura' ('Devilsville', translated by Crook). A *darogah* (overseer) and a clerk were appointed for it, who registered the names of all those who visited prostitutes or who wanted any of them to their houses.[7]

In nutshell it can be said that from a very early period in history prostitutes occupied a recognized position in the society. While during certain regimes they were part of mainstream society, in others they occupied separate hamlets. They were offered honorary positions and remained an important source of revenue, although the later rulers kept them away from being part of state revenue, prostitutes remained part of society in some form or other.

While talking about prostitution in India, we cannot negate the religious dimension attached to it. The presence of Devadasis in south India explains the existence of this institution in temples since the very beginning. Sociologically speaking one also finds the prevalence of this institution in various castes/tribes as a socially acceptable profession. The Bhedias of Rajasthan, Kolhaites of Bombay, Bedars of Mysore are important from this point of view. For example, the

Bhedias of Rajasthan reserve nearly all their girls for prostitution and the men of the tribe keep concubines from other castes. In some places, if a man marries a girl who has been reserved for prostitution, he is fined by the caste council.[8]

The gradual evolution of society and social change led to changes in various institutions. Similarly over a period of time prostitution changed in form and content. The methodology and procurement of women into this profession led to enactment of rules and criminal laws across the globe to regulate the trade. The institution has survived and acquired modern form with industrialization, urbanization and globalization. It has emerged today as a flourishing industry working on the basic economic principles of demand and supply. Trafficking of young women and children for purposes of prostitution, brothel labour and enslavement has assumed draconian dimensions today. It is very difficult to collect data on prostitution because of the clandestine nature of its operation. Hughes has rightly said, 'the trade is secretive, the women are silenced, the traffickers are dangerous and not many agencies are counting'.[9]

Despite constraints in the official compilation of data, attempts have been made to understand the magnitude of the problem. In the year 1990 a survey was conducted by the Central Social Welfare Board (CSWB) in six metropolitan cities. As per the survey, the population of women and children who are victims of commercial sexual exploitation was between 70 thousand and 1 lakh, out of which 30 per cent of them were below the age of 18 years and 40 per cent were inducted into the trade when they were less than 8 years.[10] According to another statistics of collated by Indian Association for Rrescued Fallen Women in the year 1992, there were 8 million brothel workers in India and another 7.5 million call girls.[11]

The figures of sex workers have been analysed on the basis of various criminal cases registered under different sections of law covering different dimensions of the trade. These data are available with the National Crime Records Bureau. An analysis of figures from 2002 to 2006 shows that procuring of minor girls has been increasing every year. It rose from 124 in 2002 to 231 in 2006. Similarly selling of girls for prostitution has also shown an increasing trend, from 5 in 2002 to 123 in 2006. The statewise breakup of figures under different categories my be seen in Table 11.1. While Table 11.2 shows increasing trend of minor girls being trafficked for various purposes between 2002-6. Table 11.3 reflects share of cases under human traffciking in over all Indian Penal Code (IPC) cases from 2002-6.

TABLE 11.1: CASES REGISTERED UNDER HUMAN TRAFFICKING DURING 2006

State/ UT	Buying of Girls for Prostitution	Selling of Girls for Prostitution	Procuration of Minor Girls	Importation of Girls	Immoral Trafficking Prevention Act 1956	Child Marriage Restraint Act 1929	Total
Andhra Pradesh	5	6	35	0	657	17	720
Arunachal Pradesh	0	0	0	0	0	0	0
Assam	0	1	0	0	29	1	31
Bihar	0	0	4	42	13	2	61
Chhattisgarh	0	0	0	1	13	5	19
Goa	0	0	1	0	26	0	27
Gujarat	0	0	9	0	78	12	99
Haryana	0	0	0	0	85	7	92
Himachal Pradesh	0	0	2	0	0	1	3
Jammu & Kashmir	0	0	0	0	5	0	5
Jharkhand	0	0	26	5	11	0	42
Karnataka	0	0	2	0	786	6	794
Kerala	0	0	35	0	189	1	225
Madhya Pradesh	0	0	6	0	12	4	22
Maharashtra	23	1	15	1	378	15	433
Manipur	0	0	0	0	0	0	0
Meghalaya	0	0	3	0	1	2	6
Mizoram	0	0	0	0	0	0	0
Nagaland	0	0	0	0	9	0	9
Orissa	0	0	0	12	44	3	59
Punjab	0	1	0	2	67	9	79
Rajasthan	2	0	1	3	143	1	150
Sikkim	0	0	0	0	0	0	0
Tamil Nadu	0	0	1	0	1,732	6	1,739
Tripura	0	0	0	0	0	1	1
Uttar Pradesh	0	0	0	0	70	0	70
Uttaranchal	0	0	13	0	3	0	16
West Bengal	4	114	77	1	66	6	268
Total (States)	34	123	230	67	4,417	99	4,970
A&N Islands	0	0	0	0	0	0	0
Chandigarh	0	0	0	0	3	0	3
D&N Haveli	0	0	0	0	0	0	0
Daman & Diu	0	0	0	0	1	0	1
Delhi	1	0	1	0	112	0	114

Lakshadweep	0	0	0	0	0	0	0
Pondicherry	0	0	0	0	8	0	8
Total (UTs)	1	0	1	0	124	0	126
Total (All-India)	35	123	231	67	4,541	99	5,096

TABLE 11.2: CRIME HEAD-WISE INCIDENCE OF VARIOUS CRIMES UNDER HUMAN TRAFFICKING DURING 2004-6 AND PERCENTAGE VARIATION IN 2006 OVER 2005

Crime Head	Year					Percentage Variation in 2006 over 2005
	2002	2003	2004	2005	2006	
Procuration of Minor Girls (Sec. 366A)	124	171	205	145	231	59.3
Importation of Girls (Sec. 366B IPC)	76	46	89	149	67	-55.0
Selling of Girls for Prostitution (Sec. 372)	5	36	19	50	123	146.0
Buying of Girls for Prostitution (Sec. 373)	9	24	21	28	35	25.0
Immoral Trafficking (Prevention) Act, 1956	6,598	5,510	5,748	5,908	4,541	–23.1
Child Marriage Restraint Act, 1929	113	63	93	122	99	–18.9
Total	6,925	5,850	6,175	6,402	5,096	–20.4

TABLE 11.3: PROPORTION OF CRIMES UNDER HUMAN TRAFFICKING TOWARDS TOTAL IPC CRIMES

Year	Total IPC Crimes	Cases under Human Trafficking	Percentage of total IPC Crimes
2002	17,80,330	6,925	0.39
2003	17,16,120	5,850	0.34
2004	18,32,015	6,175	0.34
2005	18,22,602	6,402	0.35
2006	18,78,293	5,096	0.27

LOCATION: FROM TRADITION TO MODERNITY

Prostitution has existed in Delhi as elsewhere since ancient times. During the nineteenth century, Delhi had licensed prostitutes who were required to go through a medical check-up every week at a hospital situated behind the Jama Masjid where the municipal dispensary is situated now.[12] During the pre-Partition days Delhi had brothels restricted to the walled city; the professionals hardly came out of city walls. In the evenings the entire Chawri Bazar area used to reverberate with the sound of dance and music. This part of Delhi was known as Delhi of *jaam*, *saqi* and *paimana*. There was nothing 'immoral' about these dancing girls. This scenario particularly refers to an era when prostitution was regarded as a decent profession.[13] Many of the prostitutes during this time catered to the needs of noblemen. The sons of the latter were sent to the prostitutes for learning the art of polite behaviour and social etiquette.[14] A professor of Persian narrated his first visit to a dancing girl in 1947. In order to test the knowledge of the dancing girl he requested her to sing a composition of Hafiz or Sadi, the greatest Persian poets. The dancing girl replied, 'Sir, can I present a Persian composition of mine'. The professor was surprised to hear this.

G.B. Road came into existence in 1932 as an alternate site for those dancing and singing girls who held their *mujras* in Chawri Bazar.[15] The same G.B. Road is now known as Shraddhanand Marg. It is surrounded by Lahori Gate on one side and Chawri Bazar on the other side. This is also known as the biggest market of iron, hardware and machine tools in Asia. On both sides of the road, are multistoreyed buildings ranging from two floors to four floors. The ground floor of all the buildings is occupied by shopkeepers who are either on rent or have bought the premises. The upper floors both on right and left hand sides are occupied by prostitutes.

There are nearly 100 premises. Each premise had 2-3 floors. The upper portion of the *kothas* are so closely connected to each other that one can easily move from one portion to the other without using the stairs. The sex workers have utilized this upper portion for escape and concealment during police rescue operations. While the leading and prosperous *kothas* have been bought by the rich brothel owners, many of them are still operating on rented premises whose owners cannot be identified easily. Ever since the *kothas* shifted to G.B. Road the composition and social profile of the sex workers has changed with the passage of time.

Several dancers who claimed themselves to be *Tawaifs* (prostitutes) practising respectable arts have also realized the change in the profile. They complain that man of fine taste who could appreciate *mujras* have practically disappeared. Their patrons of today are common place and vulgar.[16] The number of typical dancing and singing *kothas* have gone down with the changing times. The same place where once upon a time no 'immoral' activities happened is today the cauldron of immoral and traffic today. The physical location of the red light area in Delhi differs from other red light areas situated in metropolitan cities like Kolkata and Mumbai. Since it is situated in a busy marketplace and close to the railway station, it attracts a floating population of businessmen and commuters as customers on a daily basis.

Social Structure Within

The social system of a *kotha* understood in the following diagram:

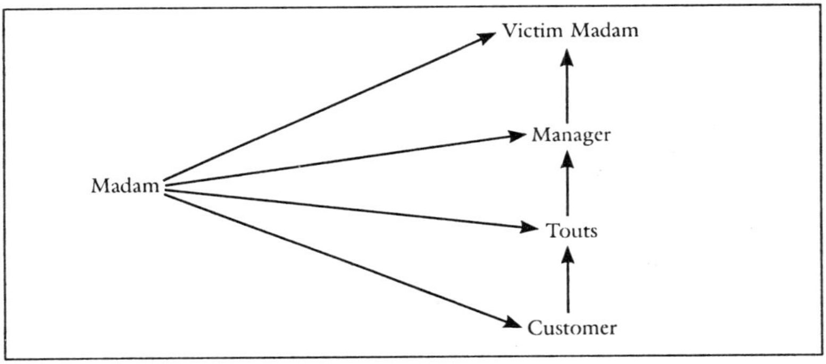

The 'Madam' is the owner of the brothel for all practical purposes. She may be the real owner of the property or may have rented it. She is responsible for coordinating the procurement of minor and new girls for the brothel house through the traffickers and through her own network. She assigns the day-to-day management of the premises to a full-time paid manager. She can be physically present or may stay away from the premises.

The manager can be a male or a female. His/her basic job is to ensure smooth running of the premises. He/she is also responsible for procuring logistical services for the inmates on a regular basis. The first contact point of the customer at a brothel is the manager.

In order to compete with the other *kothas*, the owners appoint touts whose job is to procure customers and at times even girls for the *kothas*. These touts loiter outside premises and motivate customers to visit the *kothas*. They are being paid commission for every customer they get. Various *kothas* have dedicated touts whose network extends among the *panwalas* (betelnut sellers), tea sellers, rickshaw-pullers and auto drivers, who act as agents and help the *kothas* by providing various utility services.

There are three categories of victims.

Bonded victims: These victims are procured for the *kotha* by various traffickers. They are sold directly to the owners for a price. They remain in the brothel house as private property and slaves of the owners. They get space to live inside the *kotha* and all their expenses are taken care of by the brothel keeper. They cannot enjoy any free status till their bought amount is realized. But the catch is that the everyday expenses are added to the sale amount. So in effect the victim can never repay the debt and is at the mercy of the Madams. This is the first and initial stage through which every victim has to pass. This is the stage at which most of the trafficked minors are kept. The period of stay in this stage depends on the age at which the girls enter the *kotha*, but in no case is it less than 4-5 years.

Nayikas: These sex workers procure victims directly and the procured girls are their victims. The Nayikas do not enjoy the same status as that of the *kotha* owner. However, they exploit their victims in the same manner as the bonded girls are exploited by the brothel owners.

Commission-based workers: This is the stage in which a victim gets physical space to operate her business, while she bears her own expenses. A victim moves to this stage when she is slightly older and is unable to attract too many customers.

Managers: A customer visiting a *kotha* first contacts the manager whose counter is situated at times in the corner or in the middle of the house. The customer discloses his demand and gets a slip for a particular girl and a cabin. The rates for minor victims are higher than for the older ones. It would not be out of place to mention that *kothas* having minor girls attract more customers than the ones which do not have minors. Normally charges are calculated on an hourly basis, though charges for the night are different. Half of the amount by the customer is credited to the victim's account in a rough accounts register. The rest of the paid amount goes to the owner for all the expenses incurred on the victim including structural facilities inside the *kotha*. In exchange for residence and protection provided by the brothel, the prostitute shares a large portion of her earnings with the pimp or the owner.[17]

The victims (sex workers) keep the customer slips in safe custody as the proof of their earnings, which over a period of time accumulates to a handsome amount. The register clearly mentions the expenses incurred against individual sex workers. It also has entries of money paid to various people including the police. The sex workers cannot dare to claim this money as a matter of right. Instances have also come to light where the victims maintain bank accounts and an individual who visits all the *kothas* and deposits their money in the banks in exchange for a small commission.

The brothel house has a full-fledged kitchen which is managed by professional cooks who also act as part-time pimps and touts and procure customers for the brothel house in general or for a particular sex worker.

There is a stark difference in the standard of living of common sex workers and the *kotha* owners. While the brothel house owner has a well-furnished room equipped within all modern living facilities, the sex worker is deprived of even basic amenities like a proper bed for sleeping. Several of the victims spend their nights on the floor after the end of business hour. The conditions of living are unhealthy and unhygienic, which exposes them to various health problems. Several of them suffer from malnutrition and other chronic diseases. At times 10-12 sex workers share one room. Every *kotha* takes need of its customers' requirements inside the *kotha* itself. Thus the services of eating stalls and musicians are common at the *kothas*.

Middlemen: Although an earlier customer familiar with the location directly reaches the *kotha*, pimps, touts and middleman loitering around the shops on the ground floor surround any prospective customer. These middlemen operate in three shifts (morning, afternoon and night) which also is the business hour for the *kotha*.

The profile of the middlemen varies with the shifts. The morning and the afternoon (before 7 p.m.) shift have more sophisticated touts, since this is the *time* when businessmen who visit, the area for work, may visit brothels. Touts have been found using mobile phones during these two shifts. However, business is in full swing after 7 p.m. when the market is closed.

The touts get a commission from the sex workers for every customer they get. The touts include tea sellers, rickshaw-pullers and TSR (auto rickshaw) drivers. Most of these touts have also been found involved in petty crime and extortions from the customers. Thus, the distinction between a petty criminal and a tout at times is very thin. This is why small-time criminals and drug addicts find it very convenient to indulge in extortions. Most of these cases go unreported due to the floating nature of the complainants.

MODALITIES OF TRAFFICKING

After talking to various rescued victims it emerged that they have been pushed into brothels through a very systematic and organized network of traffickers and *kotha* owners. For the sake of better understanding, the procurement of a victim can be summarized in the following stages.

Locating source area: A trafficker first locates a source area from where a victim can be easily trafficked.

Locating vulnerable families: After selecting the source area the trafficker then locates the most vulnerable families and abandoned and neglected children.

Establishing rapport: Once the target is selected, a rapport is established and the process of brainwashing and promise of better economic opportunities is extended to the victim.

The actual trafficking: If the trafficker has established meaningful rapport and convinced the victim she readily agrees to the request put forward. Minor reluctance is taken care of through clandestine methods, which might even include administering of intoxicants.

On reaching the destination: In order to avoid easy suspicion and initial revolt by the trapped victim, traffickers keep them in a transit accommodation which could be in a residential area or even a hotel. Depending upon the category and profile of the trapped victim, she could stay at the transit place even for a month. In between the intervening period she could be engaged in some domestic jobs also. In the meantime, negotiations are on with the *kotha* owners and traffickers at the destination through their contacts.

Delivery to the kotha: Finally, the girl is handed over to the *kotha* owner at a place other than the *kotha* and subsequently brought to the *kotha*. The delivery places may include busy markets and community parks. The victim is always kept in dark about the place. Traffickers introduce the *kotha* Madams as their relatives.

Initial socialization, brainwashing and exposure to the trade: As soon as a victim reaches the *kotha* a meeting is organized in a separate room where she is counselled and brainwashed by the managers and other sex workers who have gone through the same process. If a victim easily adjusts to the situation things become easy. All victims are told in the beginning that they have been sold to the *kotha* and that they can leave the place only if the buying amount is repaid. The initially trapped victims are concealed and at times kept locked in cubicles, cabins, secret pipes and false ceilings to avoid easy detection during police searches.

It is at this stage that the victim gets a new name. She is asked to change her parentage age and real address and acquires an anonymous identity in an anonymous place. This stage is the most traumatic and painful period of the victim's life through which every trafficked girl goes through. The initial initiation of the new entrants to the trade starts with mild persuasions, changing gradually to threats, intimidation, severe beating, gang rape, denial of food, confining to dark cubicles without food and water—all with a view to making the girls surrender to the brothel owner's wishes. Some of the victims had to even undergo physical torture beyond imagination.

Surrender to the situation: The statistics of rescued victims revealed that 90 per cent of the victims are from outside Delhi. A trapped victim is so terrorized that it is very difficult for her to run away from the *kotha*, due to continuous surveillance of traffickers, agents and pimps working for the brothel. The mafia aborted several attempts by brave victims on several occasions. So finally a victim reconciles to her fate and situation reluctantly and grudgingly.

The trafficker networking is a vicious cycle that can be seen in the flow chart depicted in Figure 11.1.

Source Areas

The analysis of figures of rescued girls reveals that the major source areas are Andhra Pradesh, West Bengal, Karnataka, Nepal, Rajasthan and Maharashtra. The worst affected districts in Andhra Pradesh are Kurnool, Chittur, Cudappah and Anantpur. Ironically out of the rescued girls there was only one girl from Delhi.

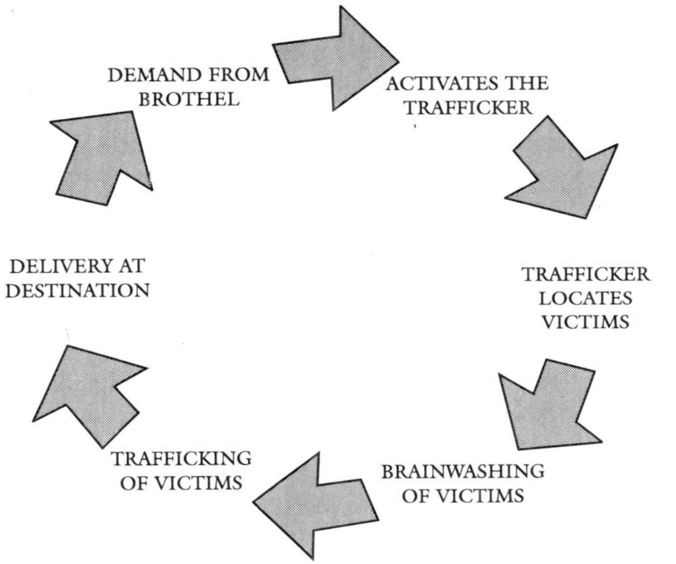

FIGURE 11.1: DEMAND AND SUPPLY CYCLE OF PROCUREMENT OF VICTIMS AT BROTHEL HOUSES

There is a very close relationship between the source area and the *kotha* from where the victims were rescued. The maximum number of girls belonging to a particular state were rescued from that *kotha* which was owned and managed by the *kotha* owner hailing from the same state. For example, maximum girls of Nepal were rescued from a *kotha* owned by Bhakti Ram Pandey who also hails from Nepal. Strategically it is easy for traffickers and their network to locate and operate among a set of people who are closely knit with each other in their own native area. After all, a Telugu-speaking trafficker will be in a better position to convince and establish rapport with a potential Telugu target rather than a non-Teulgu-speaking person. An economic profile of the source area reveals that the affected districts are drought prone and suffering from acute poverty.

TRAFFICKER: THE INVISIBLE AND ANONYMOUS MONSTER

An investigation into the various criminal cases registered has revealed that victims have been pushed into the trade by traffickers who came into contact with the victims at the early stage and vanished later. In some cases the traffickers are known and their identity is established but in most cases they are invisible characters. In several cases they have disappeared after the initial deal and payment of their commission. During the examination of various victims and investigation of criminal cases, it has emerged that traffickers use different *modus operandi* while operating in their source areas. State-wise *modus operandi* of major source areas can be summarized as under. Major source areas of victims rescued from G.B. Road can be seen in Figure 11.2.

Bangladesh and Nepal: Organized gangs and groups were found trafficking girls. Young boys and women are members of these groups. They target girls working in small factories, offering them better job opportunities in India. They have a very organized network for transit stay in Delhi, Loni and even in some hotels in Paharganj area near the railway station. As soon as girls arrive in town the *kotha* owners and Madams are contacted on phone and the final delivery point is finalized. Some Nepali citizens too run *kothas.* Bhakti Ram Pandey is the kingpin who has amassed so much wealth that he owns several properties in Delhi apart from a prosperous *kotha* on G.B. Road. He has been recently convicted for seven years in a case. The traffickers in these localities have adopted procurement of girls with a promise of better and lucrative jobs in Gulf and other Asian countries.

Andhra Pradesh: Apart from a few organized gangs who procure and deliver victims at *kothas*, this state has a very peculiar *modus operandi* as far as entry of girls into prostitution at G.B. Road is concerned. The sex workers who are already into flesh trade in G.B. Road visit their parental homes after 2-3 years and present themselves with new clothes and a lavish style of living to impress their peer group. Girls from the same age group are very impressed with their style of living. A request comes from the girls and parents for arranging better jobs in Delhi for improving their financial status. In this process every old girl brings one-two girls with her after vacation, who are either minor or of tender age. Entry of such girls is very smooth and straight without much hastle.

Karnataka and Maharastra: In these states, *modus operandi* is similar to that in Andhra Pradesh. Apart from this, a gang of traffickers with one or two women and a male moves around bus stands, railway

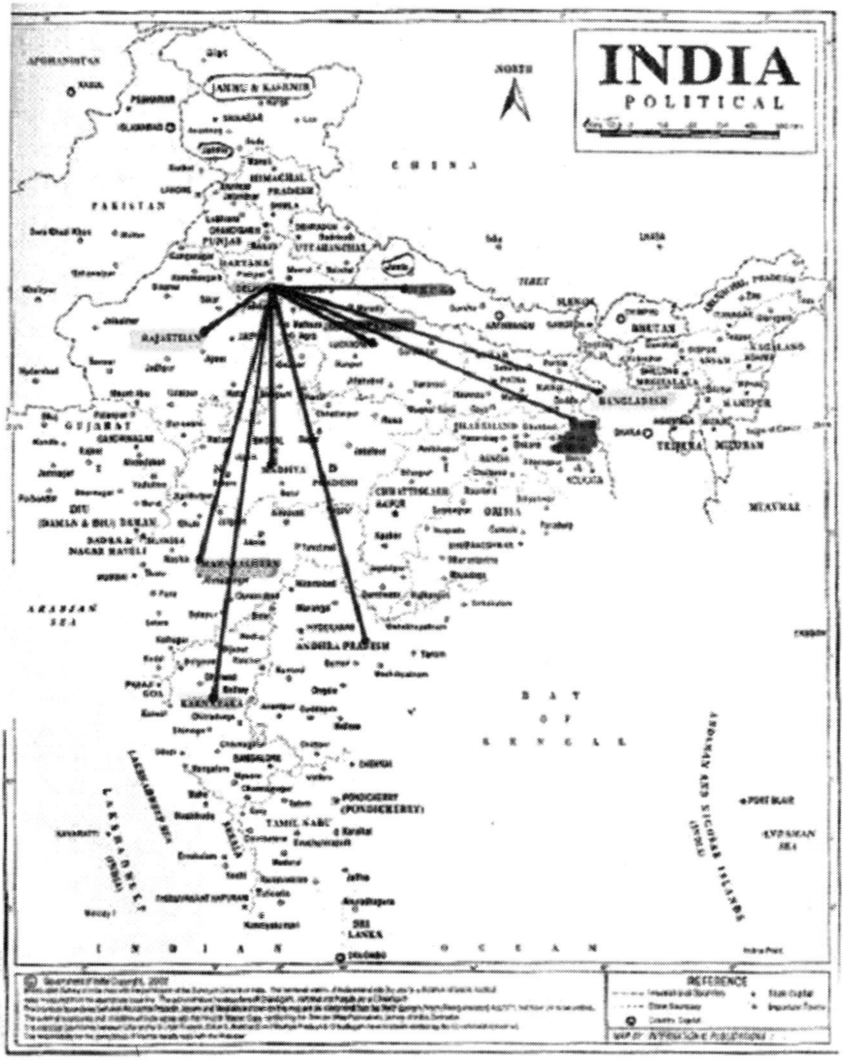

Source: opmdel@gmail.com

FIGURE 11.2: SOURCE AREAS OF VICTIMS

stations and industrial units to allure younger girls with better opportunities in Delhi and sell them at G.B. Road *kothas*. Several victims from Maharashtra were from the earthquake-hit area of Latur.

West Bengal: In West Bengal too two middle-aged women and one man move around industrial units, bus stands and railway stations to identify girls. The gang follows the targeted girls for a week and strikes friendship with them. They also simultaneously make local enquiries. These girls are promised better jobs in factories or as domestic helps. Many of these traffickers have even drugged victims, who finally finds themselves at *kothas*. These traffickers mostly stay in hotels in Delhi till the deal is finalized and the girl is handed over. Traffickers are very shrewd in staying in hotels. They at times do not make entries in the register and even stay in the servant's quarters of the hotels.

A visit to most of these places during the process of rehabilitation revealed that the affected source areas in these states had very acute poverty and the per capita income and standard of living of the affected families 'was much below the average of the state'. Economic inequality and poverty act as a very strong push factor for migration of these victims.

LAW-ENFORCING AGENCIES

The role of law enforcing agencies in rescue can be conceptualized at two levels:

1. Proactive
2. Reactive

Proactive Stage: The proactive role essentially refers to the prevention aspect wherein the law enforcing agencies play a vital role in preventing the entry of minors and other helpless victims into the sex industry using their own network of surveillance. The information regarding trapped victims also comes through area policing and intelligence network. On several occasions information is also given by members of the public and meaningful social activists/NGOs.

Reactive Stage: There are three important stages in a rescue:

1. *Initial Stage:* This sets into motion the whole process of agencies involved in the rescue operation. This stage actually locates the

target of rescue. Credible information regarding trafficked persons is received at this stage through reliable sources.

2. *Planning Stage:* This stage evaluates the practical feasibility and operational viability of the credible information received in the initial stage. The important things to be kept in mind at this stage are as under:

   (i) Mandatory legal requirements.
   (ii) Rescue by designated officer (Special Police Officers only).
   (iii) Presence of NGO/independent member of public in the rescue team.
   (iv) Presence of female police officer.
   (v) Recce of the area, topography.
   (vi) Assessment of manpower and other logistics for the rescue.

Final Stage: The outcome of this stage depends on how much ground work and meticulous planning has been done in the earlier two stages. While executing the rescue operation the following things shall be kept in mind:

(i) Simultaneous rescues at all the suspected places.
(ii) Segregation of trafficked minors and others in confinement.
(iii) Segregating customers, traffickers from sex workers.
(iv) Shifting them and transportation to safe place for further necessary action.
(v) Rounding up of *kotha* owners and managers.

Post-rescue Formalities

Immediately after the rescue operations the following important steps are taken for initiation of proper legal action:

(i) Medical examination of rescued girls to establish their age to clearly know their status as minor/major as per law.
(ii) Initial rescue of minors under relevant section of Juvenile Justice Act/other sections of IPC.
(iii) Initial recording of statement reflecting circumstances under which forced to indulge in prostitution.
(iv) Registration of criminal cases under relevant sections of law as per the statements given.

(v) Shifting of the rescued girls to observation homes run by the Social Welfare Department as per the direction of the Juvenile Justice Board.
(vi) Further recording of statement for initiating criminal cases against responsible persons.
(vii) Counselling of rescued victims at remand homes by trained psychologists and meaningful NGOs.

Investigation

Investigation of criminal cases registered on the basis of statements given by rescued girl is very important. For the investigation of all such criminal cases, the following points are important:

(i) Proper investigation of the case from various angles.
(ii) Collection of evidence.
(iii) Recording relevant statements with reference to important ingredients of offence committed.
(iv) Submission of final report to facilitate trial.
(v) Assigned to designated court for trial.
(vi) Identification of traffickers and effective legal action against them.

Legal Back-up

- Juvenile Justice Act
- Immoral Traffic Prevention Act
- Indian Penal Code

While conducting rescue operations and interrogation of victims at subsequent stages reflected some concerns, both on the part of law enforcement agencies as well as the victims.

ROLE OF LAW ENFORCING AGENCIES AND CRIMINAL PROSECUTION

A close look at police action against sex workers reveals that the tilt of legal prosecution has been more towards the victim. The police has been accused of having an ambivalent and tolerant attitude towards sex workers. The law enforcing agency has been accused of promoting flesh trade in connivance with traffickers and *kotha* owners. While commenting on the role of police, Joarder has pointed out that it is common practice for the police to forewarn brothel keepers about raids so that they can leave the building. Many of the sex workers are advised to put vermilion on the parting of their hair and pose as wives of local people.[18] In the event of a police raid, no brothel keeper is found and the women can safely argue that they are operating independently and no crime is being committed.

Sharing the confessions of one of the police officers, Joarder further says that the police even suggest some procedures to the *kotha* owners so that they can escape the law. The principle is to 'live and let live', because if the brothel business runs smoothly the policemen get *haftas* (weekly bribe).[19]

Since the new ITP Act is more stringent more money is demanded to avoid legal prosecution. This payment of money has also been termed as protection money. The comments made by Joarder relate to the Sonagachi red light area in Kolkata. However, things are not different elsewhere. While reflecting on the role of local police in G.B. Road it has been said that the police involved in staged processes called 'Registering the victims'. After a minor is brought to the *kotha*, the owner calls the local beat and division staff and requests them to make entry of a newly purchased minor girl and pay Rs. 10,000 to the police. A trumped up case is registered against the minor alleging that she was soliciting in a public place. After arrest she is shown as 21 years, transforming her into a major overnight. The next morning she is produced before a magistrate and released as being a major. She returns to the *kotha* to escape further harassment by the local police.[20] Sherwani adds that the police's demand for bribe from *kothas* varies with the number of minor girls they have. A *kotha* having 10 minors has to pay Rs. 50,000 while those with 20 to 50 have to pay Rs. 1 lakh to Rs. 3 lakh respectively.

This aspect of the role of police in the context of sex workers does not vary in other countries of the world. While looking into possible illegal activities and associated police misconduct, the chairperson of Queensland Commissions of Enquiry, Tony Fitzgerald confirmed the involvement of drug distributors in Brisbane parlours, of links between parlour operators and officers of Queensland police department licensing branch, which was common knowledge among senior officers. There were also reports of payments in money and sexual favours.[21]

Since the attitude of the local police towards the sex workers has been that of 'live and let live', the enforcement of legal provisions and acts to deal with this issue has been different. Perusal of records at the national level compiled by the NCRB as well as own records of the Delhi police in the police station in whose jurisdiction the red light area falls, reveal that despite a special act to deal with the menace of traffickers the law is strict on the victims than on the traffickers and *kotha* owners—the real tormentors who have procured and pushed the helpless victims into flesh trade.

A very important factor for non-effective action against Madams and traffickers has been the reluctance of victims in coming forward against them. This is evident from the fact that out of more than 300 rescued victims, only 70 of them volunteered to give a statement before the police. Due to selective enforcement of provisions of a special act the industry has always prospered at the cost of the helpless and vulnerable victims pushed into trade every year by unscrupulous traffickers and brothel owners. However, the enforcement aspect of the local police has changed. With mass rescues, traffickers and *kotha* owners have been effectively brought under the legal net after a very long time. For the first time a rescued victim was given an opportunity to nail her tormentor and exploiter, to fix legally someone who has played with her innocence and dignity of being a human being. She has got an opportunity to prosecute and punish all those who thought women to be objects of pleasure and enjoyment in the same land where women are being worshipped. Easier said than done.

The change in the attitude of the police as well as the attitude of the rescued victims has not been smooth sailing. It took time for the rescued victims to accept this new role of the local police and their pleas and counselling for statements against *kotha* owners and traffickers. The victims were skeptical about this new face of the local police, which was a bit different from the role, which they had been playing during their visit to the *kotha* to collect *hafta*. The rescued victims considered the plea for statements against *kotha* owners and traffickers initially as another ploy against themselves. Due to constant counselling by an NGO associated with the police in rescue operations, committed and sensitized police officers, officers of the Social Welfare Board victims finally came forward and gave statements which became the basis for registration of several cases against the *kotha* owners and traffickers. It took days for a victim to mentally prepare herself against the *kotha* owner who once provided her all help. Seventy such cases were registered against the traffickers and *kotha* owners not only under relevant sections of the ITP Act but also under stringent sections of the IPC. Some of the applied IPC sections included kidnapping, confinement, rape and criminal intimidation. Then began the arrest of *kotha* owners and traffickers.

All the leading *kotha* owners were sent to jail and are facing trial today. As per the orders of Delhi High Court three special courts were assigned the job of speedy trial on a day-to-day basis. Securing conviction in criminal cases is very difficult. The continuous monitoring due to speedy trial and bold statements of the victims made this Herculean task seem easy and convictions up to 7 years have been announced in several cases. On the request of the prosecution, for the first time in the country, sealing orders were obtained in the convicted cases and several *kothas* have been sealed.

Some significant features of the rescue operations in Delhi can be summarized as under:

- Mass level rescue started in the year 2001.
- More than 350 minor girls rescued.
- More than 75 criminal cases registered.
- Paradigm shift from treating victim as an offender to one as a complainant.
- Application of stringent IPC sections along with ITP sections as per the victim's disclosure in her statement (Sections 323, 342, 363, 366A, 366B, 368, 372, 373, 376, 506 of the IPC are some sections under which traffickers can be booked).
- Speedy trial of these cases in specially designated courts as per the High Court's order.
- Proper follow-up of trial proceedings by investigating officers.
- Convictions awarded with exemplary punishment in several cases.
- A well-coordinated rehabilitation and reintegration scheme with the involvement of meaningful NGOs. Several marriages of victims were organized through the intervention of the court.
- Sealing of *kotha* on conviction initiated for the first time in the country. Many premises were sealed by the order of the trial court.
- Constitution of separate medical boards for conducting medical examination of rescued victims.
- Meeting with rescued victims only through intervention of Court. (Cases of fake guardians and parents came to notice.)
- Excellent coordination between law enforcing agencies, NGOs and other partners.

- Funds allotted to police to take care of post-rescue expenses of the victims till they are sent to observation homes.

REHABILITATION

So far we have been talking about rescue and post-rescue formalities, which is exclusively the domain of law enforcement agencies. To be precise one can say that the rescue operations are being carried out primarily by law enforcement agencies with the assistance of public/ NGOs. But rescue is not the end of the whole problem. As a matter of fact the real problem of the victim starts once they have been removed from the confines of the *kothas* or the brothel houses. In concrete terms rescue is also economic displacement of the victim. It is in a way eviction of the victim from a safe environment or home to which she has been used to for several years. Against this backdrop it is actually the responsibility of the civil society, NGOs and the government. The future of the rescued victims largely depends on the effective rehabilitation schemes adopted for them. A meaningful rehabilitation scheme will actually ensure that the victim starts living a new life with economic independence without any stigma or reference to her past.

While planning the rehabilitation of a trafficked victim, the following points are important:

1. Psychological counselling of the victim.
2. Victim should not be reminded of her past.
3. The focus should be on making the victim economically independent.
4. Integration with the family only with the consent of the victim after the family has been taken into confidence and a proper ground work has been done in this regard.
5. The rehabilitation package should be participatory in nature. While planning the rehabilitation of a victim, the feelings and concerns of the victims should be given top priority. What each girl intends to do should be the guiding principle for her rehabilitation rather than what has been already designed without taking victim into confidence.
6. The focus of rehabilitation should be holistic in nature rather than unidimensional. A scheme intending to provide rehabilitation support base to a victim should be self-sufficient in terms of infrastructure, logistical and financial support base.

During the course of rescue and rehabilitation scheme I had an opportunity to interact with some of the victims belonging to Andhra Pradesh who were rehabilitated with active participation and involvement of an NGO called 'Prajwala'. Many of the victims were managing ice-cream kiosks and other vending stores independently run by them. Similar efforts were made by NGOs of other states also.

TALE OF TRAP AND TERROR: SOME CASE STUDIES

Rekha (name changed) comes from a very poor family. She got married at an early age and gave birth to a child. Her husband died soon after, but social customs and traditions did not permit her to remarry. She came back to her parent's house but once again the social customs did not permit her to stay with her parents for a long time. One day Rekha fought with her parents over a small issue and left the house in anger with her newborn baby. At the railway station she met an aged lady who sympathized with her and showered love and affection on the baby and the mother. The woman prodded Rekha about her background, and learning that she had no one to look after her, promised get her a job in Delhi.

Rekha landed up in Delhi, from a remote village in UP. She was kept in a transit home in Delhi and promised a job for which she would have to abandon her child. She agrees to the job. The child is sold to an issueless couple in UP.

Rekha is taken to a brothel house on G.B. Road and she reluctantly becomes part of the system. After five years the police rescue her. Her child is recovered, along with the trafficker and as per the court orders and her own wish the child is handed over on *superdari* to the same couple who brought him up. Rekha recently expressed her desire to meet the child, who comes to Delhi with her social parents. The child does not recognize the mother. The aged couple fear that the child will be snatched from them. They are even willing to accept the mother in their family. Rekha is yet to decide whether to go with the family or forget her child. The state is trying to rehabilitate Rekha according to her own wishes.

* * *

Since birth Reena (name changed) has only seen poverty. Her father supports the six-member family with a lot of difficulties. A person in her village promises her a job in Delhi and approaches Reena's parents.

After brainwashing Reena's parents he brings her to Delhi. In Delhi Reena comes into contact with her own aunt in a transit stay. She is arranged a maidservant's job which she quits because of maltreatment and sexual harassment. She finally lands up on a G.B. Road *kotha* through her own aunt. She initially revolts her initiation into the trade but succumbs to the torture.

Rescued by police Reena returns to her village without making any statement to the police. Despite counselling by the NGO and the police she does not give any statement while at the Nari Niketan. After a year, she approaches a representative of the same NGO that repatriated her and volunteers to record her statement. On that basis Reena's aunt and uncle are apprehended from a hotel along with minor who was being promised to be sent to a Gulf country. Reena now tries to convince rescued victims to come forward and speak against their tormentors and get them punished. The loss and damage to Reena's self-esteem and dignity cannot be compensated in any manner but she has the satisfaction that those responsible for her misery are behind bars.

* * *

Simmi (name changed) was promised a job in Delhi like others through an anonymous trafficker. Instead of a job she lands up in a brothel house. At a very early age she is subjected to the most inhuman treatment and perpetual sexual assault. After rescue, she came forward to give a statement against her oppressors who were subsequently arrested. Simmi stood by her earlier statement at the trial stage too. Realizing the fatality of her deposition at the trial stage the defence lawyers get her cross-deferred three times. She is undeterred. In the meantime she is approached by the *kotha* owners and is offered Rs. 50,000 for changing her statement. She turns down the offer. The little girl has only one mission—the demons responsible for her plight must be punished.

There are many more Rekhas, Reenas and Simmis whose tales of agony, torture, ill-treatment and oppression question the very ethos of civic life in the new millennium.

CONCLUSION

Rescue and rehabilitation are two sides of the same coin. The purpose of former is to facilitate the latter. The interview of various victims revealed that except communities where there is a family tradition (like among the Bhedias) the victims end up in brothels through the evil design of brothel owners and traffickers. Many of the victims are not even aware of the place. This also demystifies the age-old myth that sex workers are in this profession of their own choice. This notion presents a lopsided and myopic picture of the profile of a sex worker. Every sex worker has a different story regarding her entry in the trade. Prostitution cannot be a voluntary choice. It is always a compelled choice through either violence or destitution. Theoretically speaking it defies all stereotypes and any generalization will suffer from epistemological fallacy.

It is precisely because of these reasons that it is better to use the term 'victim' for a sex worker then to call her a prostitute. At some point of time she has been a victim and continues to occupy the same status. We have seen that this paradigm shift in treating the sex worker as a victim and a complainant by law enforcing agency has affected the nexus of various players in the whole trade.

The interaction with various victims helped in drawing some important recommendations regarding rescue and rehabilitation. These recommendations are more proactive in nature and can be summarized as under:

Guidelines for Making Rescue/Rehabilitation Meaningful and Effective

- Proper counselling of rescued girls by dedicated social activists/ NGOs.
- Creating an amicable atmosphere for dialogue.
- Concrete rehabilitation and reintegration programme.
- Preparing the victims to come forward and make statement against *kotha* owners and traffickers who responsible for their plight.
- Acceptability at OHG/Observation Homes. Integration with other inmates at home to avoid isolation.
- Detailed examination of victims, assessment of various socio-economic reasons for entering into the trade, classification of causative factors, formulation of adequate preventive, protective, proactive strategies to stop further/future flow of vulnerable sections into the trade.
- Speedy trial and exemplary punishment by special courts.
- Provision of separate homes other than police stations for examination and putting up of rescued girls.

- Sensitization of and attitudinal change in policemen handling rescued girls. Orientation and training of police officers may be organized.
- Creation of separate institutional arrangements for handling various aspects of investigation, for example, formation of a medical board for initial examination of victims.
- Adequate institutional support from various agencies involved in the criminal justice system to officers associated in the rescue, investigation and prosecution of traffickers, to help them in their discharge of duties against malafide designs and allegations levelled by traffickers, sex workers and other interested persons in the organized racket.
- Disclosure regarding place, time and so on, to be kept secret and in the knowledge of only responsible persons.
- Financial support to law enforcing agencies to meet the expenses of rescue operations.
- Complainants in the criminal cases to be escorted separately by police for production in the court at the trial stage.
- Comprehensive plan for education of vulnerable sections of society who sell their girls for such trade knowingly, and have a family tradition (like the Bhedia community in Rajasthan who have a tradition of sending young girls for prostitution).
- Better co-ordination and mutual trust amongst various agencies involved in rescue operations.
- Legal provision for prosecution of customers. Effective preventive action against pimps, agents and brothel keepers as per prevailing laws of the land.
- Effective preventive action against pimps, agents and brothel keepers as per prevailing laws of the land.
- Missing reports, particularly of minors, lodged at the police station to be taken seriously by law enforcement agencies.
- Creation of a national data bank of traffickers along with their photographs and finger prints and continuous updating and sharing of information by affected states and source areas.
- Effective surveillance at border check points, railway stations and airport, particularly regarding movement of minors in groups.
- Only designated police officers as per ITPA to conduct rescue operations.
- All complaints related to brothel houses to be looked into by Special Police Officers only.

- Effective legal action against traffickers in source areas.
- Medical examination and bone X-ray of rescued victims by a board of doctors.
- Effective psychological counselling of rescued victims for preparing them to make statements for criminal prosecution.
- In-camera trial to be ensured.
- Meaningful rehabilitation and reintegration package.
- Constant counselling and reassurance of meaningful rehabilitation of rescued victims at remand homes.
- Women arrested under Sections 7 and 8 of ITPA should be offered necessary assistance as victims and not treated as offenders.
- Website of missing children to be developed.
- The term 'Trafficking Police Officer' should be replaced by 'Anti-Trafficking Police Officer'.

The prime concern of any stakeholder involved in the rescue and rehabilitation of prostitution should be to remove victims from the sex industry and provide them with shelter and rehabilitation. Counselling, health care, economic empowerment are required rather than advocating the continuance of these helpless victims in the sex industry.

The network of traffickers, brothel owners and other partners in this industry is very strong and organized. The anti-trafficking network still stands divided in terms of ideology, theory and praxis despite the participation of a large number of governmental and non-governmental bodies. The need is for a more focused, holistic and well-coordinated action plan taking the best from everyone involved in it.

NOTES

1. Simone De Beauvoir, *Second Sex* (1972).
2. *Crime in India*, p. 71.
3. Ibid.
4. Ibid., p. 72
5. Ibid., p. 74.
6. Ibid., p. 76.
7. Ibid., p. 77
8. Ibid., p. 85.
9. 'Action Research on Human Trafficking', NHRC, 2004, p. 21.
10. Ibid., p. 16 (NHRC).

11. 'Action Research on Trafficking', NHRC, p. 16.
12. *Gazetteer of Delhi*, p. 174.
13. Bopegamage, p. 178.
14. Ibid., p. 178.
15. Ibid., p. 175.
16. The *Illustrated Weekly of India*, 26 November 1972.
17. *Encyclopadia of Britannica*, p. 737.
18. Jorder, 1985, p. 106.
19. Ibid.
20. Azim Sherwani, 1998.
21. *Sex Industry and Public Policy*, p. 168.

REFERENCES

BOOKS

Beauvoir, Simone De (1972), *Second Sex*, Penguin: Middlesex.

Foucault, M. (1981), *The History of Sexuality: An Introduction*, Middlesex: Penguin.

Bopegmage, A. (1957), *Study in Urban Sociology*, Bombay: University of Bombay.

Joarder, B. (1984), *Prostitution in Historical & Modern Perspectives*, New Delhi: Inter India Publication.

Sherwani, Azim (1998), *The Girl Child in Crisis*, Delhi: Institute of Social Science.

Delhi Administration (1976), *Gazetteer of Delhi*, Delhi: Publications Division, Government of India.

Edwards, S.M., 1924, *Crime in India*, Delhi: Oxford University Press.

REPORT AND JOURNALS

IJJ (2002), *From Darkness to Light*, Institute of Juvenile Justice, New Delhi: Prayas.

MHRD (2001), Protecting Children from Trafficking and Sexual Abused, Initiatives in India', New Delhi: Department of Women and Child Development, Ministry of Human Resource and Development.

NCRB (2000), *Crime in India*, New Delhi: NCRB, 2000.

NHRC and ISS (2004), 'Action Research on Trafficking in Women & Children in India', National Human Rights Commission and Institute of Social Sciences.

Illustrated Weekly of India, 26 November 1972.

The Statesman, 12 April 1970.

III. CIVIL SOCIETY, LOCAL AND CORPORATE INITIATIVES

CHAPTER 12

Social Development and the Empowerment of Marginalized Women: A Study of SHGs

DAMAYANTI MUKHOPADHYAY
S.A.H. MOINUDDIN

INTRODUCTION

Over the last sixty years, India's development goals have changed from time to time. The aim of 'growth with stability' just after the Independence was changed in the mid-1960s to 'growth with social justice' (SinghaRoy, 2001). Through the expression of 'social justice', the government wanted to convey the message of caring for the marginalized. However, understanding that setting the goal alone could not bring the desired level of positive change for the marginalized people, the Government of India has also made consistent efforts and allocated considerable amount of resources for bringing sustained social development. Social development is a process that results in the transformation of social structures in a manner which improves the capacity of the society to fulfil its aspirations and desires. It is a process of increasing the assets and capabilities of individuals to improve their well-being. Society develops by consciousness and social consciousness develops by its organization. It is realized that as long as the marginalized people do not become conscious of their own rights, speak for themselves, become socially and economically self-reliant, it would not be possible to free them from the shackles of age-old deprivation and subordination.

Women, in general, despite being half the population of the world, are considered as marginalized in every society all over the world. They occupy an asymmetric social position and fare worse than their male counterparts in every aspects of socio-economic development (Narasimhan, 1999). The rural women are especially handicapped for various reasons, which include their gender identity as women, as rural populace and as poor and backward. However, while they have subordinate positions in the society, various studies show that upliftment of women helps directly to uplift their families and improve the socio-economic conditions.

Considering their crucial role, women's development has featured in the priority list of every country's development agenda. However, the issue of development of women should be understood in the right perspective. Being half of the populace it is expected that half of the benefits of development should go to women. Women, equally with men, are expected to be the beneficiaries as well as partners of development. Therefore, the process of making the benefits of development available to women is not, in itself, women's development but merely a natural expectation of development in general.

Gender development and women empowerment are among the ten key commitments made at the World Summit for Social Development 1995, Copenhagen. In India, it was in the Fifth Five Year Plan (1974-8) that for the first time women's development was clearly articulated for overall development of the country. In the Ninth Plan (1997-2002) the focus shifted from 'development' to 'empowerment' and the government suggested the adoption of the National Policy for the Empowerment of Women 2001 (Sinha, 2006). As a result, empowerment of women, especially their economic empowerment, has consistently gained increasing importance in the development of the country. Economic empowerment is considered as the most essential and primary component for the empowerment of women on one hand and to remove poverty on the other.

From the beginning of the 1980s, the term empowerment has become fashionable in the development field. It is felt necessary to share power with the powerless people to carry out the social development agenda. Empowerment, in short, indicates informed decision making power in social, economic, political and all other spheres of life. And 'women's empowerment', in its broadest sense implies development of women in every sphere of their life. It is a process of social transformation where women gain control over their own body, financial and other resources and hence influence decisions that affect their life (Parvin, 2005).

However, despite the government's efforts to eradicate rural poverty and to improve women's position in the society through various programmes, poverty levels have reduced a little bit, but with the growing population the absolute number of rural poor has more or less remained static over the years. The most recent effort in this direction is the Swarnjayanti Gram Swarozgar Yojana (SGSY) which was launched in April 1999 and is continuing till date. The programme covers all aspects of self-employment including organization of poor through Self-Help Groups (SHG), training, credit, technology, infrastructure and marketing. The objective of SGSY is to bring the assisted poor families above the poverty line by ensuring appreciable increase in incomes over a period of time (SGSY Guideline, GOI). More specifically it aims to bring about the economic and social betterment of marginalized rural women to improve the welfare of their families and their status both within the family and in the community.

The concept of SHG was first introduced by Nobel Laureate Prof. Mohammad Yunus, an economist, in 1995 and has been popularized through the activities of the Grameen Bank of Bangladesh. Later on, nearly 53 developing countries, including India, have adopted the SHG movement to deal with the serious problem of poverty and to empower the poorest section of the population through micro-credit (Suguna and Rani, 2007).

The present study has been carried out in Paschim Medinipur district, which is one of the pioneering districts of West Bengal with nearly 20,000 SHGs under the SGSY programme. Nevertheless, of the 20,000 SHGs in Paschim Medinipur, until March 2007 only about 2.5 per cent, i.e. 500 groups had been recognized as credit-linked groups. Project loans are sanctioned to make the groups economically self-reliant through one or more pre-decided micro-economic activities chosen by the group members themselves. This study also motivates one to look deeper into factors that affect the actual functioning of SHGs. It encourages judging the level of empowerment of the members of the groups.

OBJECTIVES

The study primarily focuses on the institutional and financial functioning of groups as well as the level of empowerment of group members. The specific objectives of the present study are to examine the:

- institutional functioning of SHGs
- financial functioning of SHGs
- level of empowerment of the group members.

METHODOLOGY

The present study has been carried out in 100 credit-linked groups from six blocks, namely, Garbeta I, Garbeta II, Garbeta III, Kharagpur I, Kharagpur II and Midnapur Sadar of Paschim Medinipur district. Names of the SHGs have been provided by the District Rural Development (DRD) Cell of Paschim Medinipur. Separate selection of groups is not in the purview of the present study. Data has been collected both from the leaders as well as the general members of each SHG. Altogether 500 members have been interviewed from 100 SHGs. Moreover, it is felt that in the functioning of the SHGs, banks also play a crucial role. Keeping that in mind, information has also been collected from the respective bank managers who are dealing with the groups for all financial and other matters related to project loans.

Data has been collected both from primary and secondary sources. For primary data collection, structured questionnaire, focus group discussion, observation and interview methods have been applied. Secondary data has been collected from the DRD Cell, concerned Gram Panchayat, records of the SHGs, bank records and the published reports, journals and so on.

Collected data is analysed by using simple statistical methods.

IDENTITY OF SHGs

Altogether 100 groups have been studied from six blocks of Paschim Medinipur, namely, Kharagpur I, Kharagpur II, Midnapur Sadar, Garbeta I, Garbeta II, and Garbeta III. All these groups have passed the second gradation and found eligible for receiving credit through sanction of project loan. Eligibility for getting project loan depends on multiple factors including SHGs functioning as well as the role played by the local authority responsible of nurturing the groups. Banks also play an important role in it. However, among all the factors performance of the groups is the most crucial and important aspect. Therefore, the number of credit-linked groups varies to a large extent across the blocks. Table 12.1 reveals the block-wise distribution of the groups.

Institutional Functioning of Groups

SHGs are associations, as defined by McIver and Page (1950), where people from one or more hamlets or villages, especially from BPL

TABLE 12.1: BLOCK-WISE DISTRIBUTION OF GROUPS

Name of the Block	Number of Groups
Kharagpur I	10 (10%)
Kharagpur II	16 (16%)
Midnapur Sadar	6 (6%)
Garbeta I	12 (12%)
Garbeta II	27 (27%)
Garbeta III	29 (29%)
Total	100 (100%)

families, come together for particular purposes, form groups and deposit fixed amounts of money. They then become eligible to get credit from the government to initiate economic activities with a long-term goal of sustainable livelihood which will ultimately uplift those people and their families above poverty line and empower them economically as well as socially. Hence, the functioning of SHGs would have to be judged based on the extent to which these groups are able to meet the above purposes. For assessing the functioning of groups, meetings convened by the groups, their savings status, inter-loaning capacity, leadership capability as well as change in leadership, social consciousness and capacity building aspects have been evaluated.

Meeting

Meeting is one of the most important activities considered as a pre-requisite for the smooth functioning of any group. It is not only important for carrying out organizational activities, but also creates a platform for interaction among the group members.

The present study looks into the frequency of the meetings convened, average attendance of the group members in the meetings and their participation in discussions. It is found that 48 (48 per cent) groups organize three meetings in a month, whereas 22 (22 per cent) groups organize four meetings, 18 (18 per cent) groups meet two times in a month and no meetings are convened by 12 groups.

Data also reveals the trend of attendance in meetings among the members and their nature of participation. In 43 groups, more than 90 per cent members are present in the meeting. In 40 per cent groups their presence is 70-90 per cent and in 5 cases it is found that members' presence in the meeting is less than 70 per cent. Moreover, it has also been seen that in 12 per cent cases no regular meetings are being held.

Similarly, in case of members' participation it is seen that other than 12 groups where no meeting is held, in 94 per cent of the 84 groups most of the members participate in the discussion. It is found that in 2 groups (2.3 per cent) only a few members and in another 2 groups (2.3 per cent) only the leaders participate in the discussions.

Group Savings

The study shows that 40 per cent groups have savings between Rs. 20,000 and 50,000, 34 per cent groups are in the range of Rs. 5,000 to less than Rs. 20,000. On the other hand, 7 groups have less than Rs. 5,000 savings and 19 groups have savings of more than Rs. 50,000. It is also revealed that among these seven groups which have less than Rs. 5,000 savings, six groups are in Garbeta III Block and one group is in Garbeta II Block. Moreover, except one (10 per cent) group all the nine groups (90 per cent) in Kharagpur I Block have savings of more than Rs. 20,000. In addition, while most of the studied groups (29 per cent) are in Garbeta III Block, there is no group in that block which has savings of more than Rs. 50,000. Among the 19 groups which have savings of Rs. 50,000, 2 groups each are in Kharagpur I, Kharagpur II and Midnapur Sadar, seven groups are in Garbeta I and 6 groups are in Garbeta II Blocks.

Utilization of Savings

The study intends to know whether groups are utilizing the savings amount through inter-loaning and for other purposes. Inter-loaning not only ensures utilization of the amount and profit out of loan repayment, but it also shows the enterprising ability of the group members. The data reveals that 32 per cent groups do not utilize the amount for inter-loaning or other purposes and 5 per cent groups make use of more than 90 per cent of the total savings amount. Among these five groups, three groups are in Garbeta I Block and one each in Kharagpur I and Garbeta II Blocks. Other 63 groups (63 per cent) have used up to 90 per cent of their savings. Among these 63 groups 28 groups have used up to 30 per cent of their savings, whereas 35 groups utilize 31 to 90 per cent of their savings.

Leadership

In this study, the leadership aspect is measured through leaders' presence in meetings, change in leadership and their ability to maintain the registers as well as state of the registers at the time of the survey. While it is found that only in four groups leaders are either not regular or does not come to the meeting at all, meeting registers of all other groups show that leaders are very regular for meetings. However, remarkable information has come out regarding the change in leadership.

According to the SGSY programme, leaders may be changed every year to maintain democracy in the group. Nevertheless the data shows that in 90 per cent of groups no change in leadership has taken place, even though there are groups which are more than six years old. It is felt that many a times the present leaders are the only capable members in the group in respect to their educational level and organizational ability.

Bookkeeping

Regarding bookkeeping primarily status of five registers are studied. These registers are the meeting register, loan register, saving register, pass book and cash book. It is seen that in most of the groups saving registers, pass books and cash books are maintained regularly. However, meeting registers and loan registers in some cases are not up to date.

However, if three books out of five are up to date it is assumed that the status is up to date. It is found that in 72 per cent case books are up to date while 28 groups (28 per cent) do not maintain their registers properly. No group is found where no registers are maintained.

Similarly, in case of leaders' capacity to maintain the books and registers the study reveals that in 62 per cent case books are maintained by outsiders. These outsiders include any members' children, husbands or any other close relatives, local youth, panchayat personnel, and so on. In 10 per cent cases registers are maintained by group members other than leaders. On the other hand, in case of

28 groups, leaders themselves maintain the registers. This data also corroborates the earlier assumption that leaders are the most capable among all the members. Therefore, wherever leaders are unable to maintain books, they have to depend on outsiders. Out of 100 groups only in 10 groups books are maintained by group members other than leaders.

Social Consciousness

It is expected that the SHG groups under SGSY programme would also perform or take part in some social activities. Study intends to know that whether the groups have taken part in any type of social activities. Moreover, it also tries to find out what kind of activities, if at all, have been performed by the groups. The study categorizes primarily four types of social activities, namely awareness creation, environmental protection, voluntary action for creation of resources and voluntary action as well as donation for resource creation.

The study reveals that 66 groups (66 per cent) have taken part in varied kinds of social activities, including awareness creation on Pulse Polio, sanitation, bad effects of alcoholism or counselling of school drop-outs, tree plantation or cleaning of pond, construction of meeting place or village road, and so on.

Capacity Building

Training is an important part of capacity building of the SHG group members. For effective functioning of the groups, trainings have been imparted on leadership and bookkeeping. It is found that among 100 groups while 74 groups have received training either on leadership or bookkeeping or both, other 26 groups have received no training. Detailed inspection shows that among the 74 groups which have received trainings, 2 persons each from 30 groups have received training, whereas 4 members each from 23 groups, 1 member each from 13 groups, 3 members each from 7 groups and 10 members each from 2 groups have received trainings. Therefore altogether 206 persons from 100 groups have received trainings on leadership and bookkeeping.

Institutional aspects show that except for change in leadership or maintaining registers most of the groups have attained a level of maturity in their activities. While it cannot be denied that there is much scope for improvement, considering the importance of the programme and in view of the difficulties in involving rural women, the progress is commendable.

Financial Status of the Groups

Financial status of the groups ultimately indicates the outcome of their functioning as well as the sustainability of the groups. To assess the financial status as well as the capacity of the groups, the study has focused on certain aspects of cash credit, project loan, training on skill development and marketing.

Cash Credit

Assistance under the SGSY to individual Swarozgaris or SHGs is given in the form of subsidy by the government and credit by the banks. Credit is the critical component of the SGSY, subsidy being a minor and enabling element. The SGSY also seeks to promote multiple credits rather than a one-time credit injection. The credit requirements of the Swarozgaris need to be carefully assessed. The Swarozgaris are allowed and, in fact, encouraged to increase credit intake, over the years (SGSY Guideline, GOI). It is assumed that it will impart credit discipline and financial management skills to the members so that they become creditworthy.

Keeping these in mind the present study intends to see the number of transactions made by the SHGs, their repayment status as well as pattern of repayment.

In case of number of transactions, data shows that the maximum number of groups has performed transactions for four times. While it indicates a positive trend, these groups are only 35 per cent in number.

In the present study, repayment status has been judged based on the groups' ability to repay loan or at least show regular trend in repayment. The study shows that 38 per cent groups have paid back the total amount with interest. However, while it indicates part credit discipline, the purpose of cash credit is not entirely served. According to the SGSY guideline, the credit requirements of the SHGs need to be carefully assessed. They are allowed and, in fact, encouraged to increase credit intake over the years. The rest 62 groups (62 per cent), however, could not repay the amount and also could not show positive trend in transaction.

Project Loan

Every SHG which has passed through second gradation and prepared a project according to the stipulated criteria is entitled to get a project loan. The size of the loan under the scheme would depend on the nature of the project. The study examines aspects of loan receipt, loan repayment, utilization as well as skill development training. It is found that at least in 18 cases (18 per cent groups) though the project loan has been sanctioned the SHGs have not received the loan amount as yet.

Detailed study of repayment status of project loan illustrates that the 82 groups which have received project loans vary in regard to repayment. While 26 groups (32 per cent) have started repayment of loan, 49 groups (59 per cent) have not yet started. Moreover, in 7 groups (9 per cent) there are confusions regarding loan repayment. Among these who have not started the repayment have just received the loan. However, the rest 34 groups (41 per cent), in spite of receiving the project loan, are yet to start repayment.

Skill Development

The SGSY seeks to lay emphasis on skill development through well-designed training courses. Those who have been sanctioned loans are to be assessed and given necessary training. The design, duration of training and the training curriculum are tailored to meet the needs of the identified key activities.

The present study indicates that before the sanctioning of the project loan, only 31 groups (31 per cent) got any kind of skill development training. Whereas, after approval of project loan it has risen to 67 per cent. However, it is important to note that apart from traditional skill-based project it is crucially important to impart skill development training to enable the members to utilize the project loan judiciously and to meet the project objectives.

Resources and Infrastructure

Resource development and infrastructure building are two important aspects which indicate the capability of SHG groups, availability and utilization of fund and many more. In this study, resources denote the products developed by the SHGs or equipments and other things used for development of products, for example, livestock, sewing machine or husking machine, etc., as well as milk, cow dung cake, goat, chicken, tailored clothes, vegetables, milk, and so on. On the other hand, infrastructure represents the permanent structure built to use for production purposes, like training sheds or cowsheds.

Data reveals that, resources have been developed by 50 per cent groups, whereas rest 50 per cent groups could not yet develop any resources. On the other hand, in case of infrastructure, 62 groups do not have any common infrastructure, and 38 per cent have built so.

Marketing

The SGSY provides support for promotion of marketing of the goods produced by the SHGs, by organizing exhibitions/*melas* at district/state/national/international levels for exhibition and sale of goods produced by the SHGs, provision of market intelligence, development of markets and consultancy services, as well as institutional arrangements for marketing of the goods including exports. In the present study the availability of markets has been explored in reference to local and outside markets. The study investigates whether the groups have explored the facility to sell their product locally or outside the locality or both.

The study shows that 63 per cent groups have reported that local markets are available for their products. All these groups have not yet started to produce from their project but have explored that local markets are available for their product. On the other hand, in 28 per cent cases it is reported that no local market is available.

Moreover, among 18 groups which have not received loan yet, 9 groups have reported that they have not started to explore the local market. Similarly, 20 groups have reported that they know or have already explored the outside market, while in 80 per cent cases the SHG members are not aware of the outside market.

Data reveals that groups are yet to achieve financial discipline. Moreover, in this aspect the linked banks and the DRD personnel have important roles to play. Considering the lack of education among women and their social position they need to be trained with utmost care.

Empowerment of Group Members

The process of women's development has been already discussed as a process to overcome the gender inequalities in particular, and to achieve development goal of the country in general. This needs an understanding of the issue of women's empowerment—the process to achieve social equality and promote development.

Empowerment is a multifaceted concept and not always easily comprehensible. However, it is assumed that empowerment is not a one-time agenda; rather it is a lifelong process. In a nutshell it implies the decision-making ability of a person. It is assumed that economic independence is a necessary and essential step for women's empowerment. It is expected to enable them to take decisions regarding household expenditure or in other financial matters. At the same time, it will also help them achieve an improved social position. They will have improved access to information and resource. In the present study, the empowerment is judged on the basis of their awareness, ownership of property, ability to take decisions in household expenditure, sense of freedom, issue of vulnerability, mindset about women's role, confidence and self-reliance. The study also wanted to know whether these factors could bring change in their social condition, division of labour in household activities or leisure time activities.

Changes in Income

To assess the direct impact of the SGSY programme, the present study examines the change in status of income level of the group members. It shows that while 98 per cent has been reported, increase of income at family level it is nearly 88 per cent at the personal level. Enhancement in personal income is directly related to the SGSY programme. In case of family income, the direct linkage could not be ascertained. However, close probing has revealed that in a few cases the loan amount has been given by the women to their husband or other family members to pursue their activities.

Ownership of Property

Ownership of property is considered one of the most important indicators of women's economic status which is believed to be a necessary condition, if not a sufficient condition, in the process of development. The data shows that while 35 per cent (175) members have at least some amount of money in their name, in case of ownership of house it is 9.6 per cent and for landed property it is only 7.4 per cent. Detailed enquiry suggests that even if some of the women have purchased land from their own income, in accordance to their socialization those are in the name of their husbands.

Ability to Decide on Household Spending

It is usually believed that women's earning bring economic freedom for them in any society. However, in reality it is also found that one does not bring the other naturally. The study intends to see whether women's personal earning could change their spending ability and how much the change is felt. The present study shows that 83 per cent SHG members feel that their ability has been enhanced, whereas 17 per cent members feel there is no such change. Moreover, while more than 21 per cent reported that they are economically independent, i.e. they can take decisions on their own, 70 per cent feel their independence is partial. However, 9 per cent members feel that they do not have any freedom to spend according to their wish.

Issue of Vulnerability

Women in our society not only have asymmetric position but are also exposed to different levels of vulnerabilities. This vulnerability acts as the cause and effect for lack of empowerment among women. This study has made an effort to understand their perception regarding future security of themselves and their families. The study reveals that only 17 per cent members have taken life insurance policies as a mark of future security, while the rest 83 per cent have not thought about it.

Changes in Social Condition

Social status of the members has been judged at the family level as well as in the neighbourhood. In both the cases most of the members have confided that due to their engagement in the SGSY programme their social status has been elevated. While 442 members (88 per cent) feel that their status in the family has elevated, 58 (12 per cent) members feel it is the same as before. Similarly, out of 500 members,

456 persons (91 per cent) feel that status has also been elevated in the neighbourhood, while 44 persons (9 per cent) feel it is unchanged.

Division of Labour and Cooperation Received at Home

The study intends to see whether women's elevated status in the family could bring change in the working pattern in the family—whether they receive support from the members of their family. It is assumed that if the family members are content with the activities performed by the SHG members they will also extend support and cooperation in household chores. In this regard it is found that 87 per cent members (435) told that they receive cooperation from their family members. However, the rest 13 per cent do not get that kind of cooperation.

In case of division of labour, 194 (39 per cent) members reported that both male and female members of their households carry out daily household activities. However, in case of 36 per cent (178) members it is only the female members' responsibility and in 25 per cent (128) members' family the household activities are entirely members' own responsibility.

Leisure Time Activities of the Members

The study reveals that 239 members (48 per cent) spend their leisure time watching TV, listening to the radio or chatting with friends; 196 members (39 per cent) read newspaper or do some productive work for additional income. Only 65 members (13 per cent) have shared that during their leisure time they also help children in studies.

The above discussion reveals that a silent change is taking place in the village society. Women, being the members of the SHG group, have started to earn and take decisions in household matters. Moreover, they have begun to believe that it has elevated their social position. Close probing also revealed that it is not only the individual membership; rather the sense of being a part of the group has helped to create a feeling of assurance and self-esteem among the members.

EFFECT OF EMPOWERMENT

The outcome of empowerment is reviewed on the basis of the level of social consciousness among the members, their perception regarding primary role of women and sense of confidence and self-reliance. Social consciousness is judged on the basis of members' awareness about the different government programmes, laws and legislature for the benefit of the women, such as age at marriage, etc., and various kinds of oppressions faced by the women.

Data reveals that while 296 (59 per cent) members are aware of various programmes launched by the government for the development of women, rest 41 per cent could not mention even one programme. Those members who can share at least one programme have been considered as aware. However, it should be mentioned here that in most of the cases it is found that members can only mention about the SGSY programme.

It is found that 439 (88 per cent) members could point out a few laws related to age at marriage or dowry. Similarly 88 per cent members (440) have shared that they are aware about the various kinds of oppression and discrimination faced by women in society.

Women members were asked about their perception regarding the primary role of women. While 234 (47 per cent) members feel that a woman's role is to assist the family by earning money, 106 (21 per cent) members feel that earning is mainly for being economically independent. However, 159 (32 per cent) members say women's primary role is to become a good wife and mother.

Finally, it is seen that 437 (87 per cent) members feel self-confident whereas 63 (13 per cent) members lack confidence in themselves. On the other hand, 370 (74 per cent) members find themselves self-reliant and 130 (26 per cent) members do not feel so about themselves.

It is well understood that no direct correlation can be established between this awareness and new-found empowerment through the SGSY programme. Their experiences in life have taught them the hard reality. However, life is a process in which varied experiences create an enabling environment to learn, get informed and take decisions, which ultimately empower people.

CONCLUSION

In the present study an effort has been made to find out the level of empowerment of the women members of SHG groups formed under the SGSY programme. The study tries to learn whether women in spite of their marginalized position in rural society, are successful in their new endeavour to mobilize the SHGs institutionally and financially and how their new role as members of the group could empower them socially and economically. Data have been collected from 500 members of 100 SHGs.

The study reveals that overall there is a positive change in the lives of the group members. Most members have reported that after membership their economic independence has increased and social status has enhanced.

More specifically it is seen that out of the 100 groups, 88 are meeting on a regular basis at least once a month. All the SHGs have savings account in bank. As all the studied groups are considerably mature in terms of their age, it is expected that their savings should reflect that. However, the amounts of savings vary across the groups. Moreover, nearly 40 per cent groups have developed a kind of credit discipline in cash credit transactions, which indicates certain maturity in financial transactions. However, in terms of utilization of savings amount and in the aspect of leadership, these groups did not impress. As many as 32 groups (32 per cent) have kept the money untouched and thus losing the opportunity of earning more from that resource. With respect to change in leadership it is found that in 90 per cent groups (90 groups) there is no change in leadership since the formation of the groups. It reveals that second line of leadership has not been developed, which is not in favour of sustainability of the groups. Most of the groups could not be elevated from individual effort to organizational effort.

However, membership in SHGs has brought remarkable and significant changes in the life as a whole for most of the women. Income has increased for most of the women and for the first time in their life many of them are able to save some money in their name. Their ability to earn has also provided them with a kind of economic freedom. They are now able to, at least partially, decide on household spending.

In most cases their social status has also been elevated in the family as well as in the neighbourhood. They have been able to get support from the family members.

Finally this paper reveals that the SGSY programme has brought overall positive changes in the lives of the marginalized women. These changes are to be noticed in their level of awareness, feeling of empowerment as well as in their economic freedom. In a way it has brought a social revolution among the rural women. They have learnt to dream and make that dream a reality. Economic independence is opening a broad horizon in front of them. A continuous facilitation, persuasion and capacity building from the side of the authority and self-reliance and determination from the SHGs' side will take this social movement to its desired goal.

After Independence, the government agenda of creating social justice conveys the message of caring for the marginalized. To bring the desired level of positive change for the marginalized people, the Government of India has put consistent efforts and allocated considerable amount of resources for bringing sustained social development. It is realized that as long as the marginalized people do not become conscious of their own rights, speak for themselves, become socially and economically self-reliant, it would not be possible to free them from the shackles of age-old deprivation and subordination. From the beginning of the 1980s the term empowerment has become fashionable in the development field. It is felt necessary to share power with the powerless people to carry out the social development agenda.

Empowerment, in short, indicates informed decision-making power in social, economic, political and all other aspects of life. And 'women's empowerment', in its broadest sense implies development of women's life in every sphere. It is a process of social transformation where women gain control over their own body, financial and other resources and hence influence decisions which affect their life (Parvin, 2005). Considering the various problems faced by the rural women as well as their immense power to uplift their families and improve the socio-economic conditions, economic empowerment is considered as the most essential and primary component for their empowerment on one the hand and to remove poverty on the other.

The SGSY is the most recent effort in this direction, which was launched in April 1999. The programme covers all aspects of self-employment including organization of poor through SHGs, training, credit, technology, infrastructure and marketing. The objective of SGSY is to bring the assisted poor families above the poverty line by ensuring appreciable increase in incomes over a period of time. More specifically it aims to bring about the economic and social betterment of marginalized rural women and to improve the welfare of their families and their own status both within the family and in the community.

The present study has been carried out in 100 SHGs from six blocks of Paschim Medinipur district. The six blocks are Garbeta I, Garbeta II, Garbeta III, Kharagpur I, Kharagpur II and Midnapur Sadar of Paschim Medinipur district. To understand their nature of functioning it is felt prudent to study those groups which have already passed through the stages of initial enthusiasms as well as problems. Therefore, the study focuses only on the SHGs which have become eligible for receiving credit as project loan. These groups are loosely known as credit-linked groups. Data has been collected both from the leaders as well as the general members of each SHG.

The study primarily focuses on the institutional and financial functioning of groups as well as the level of empowerment of the women members of the groups. This paper reveals that the SGSY programme has brought overall positive changes in the lives of the marginalized members. These changes are to be noticed in their level of awareness, feeling of empowerment as well as in their financial ability. In a way it has brought a social revolution especially among the rural women. They have learnt to dream and make that dream a reality. Economic independence is opening a broad horizon in front of them. Continuous facilitation, persuasion and capacity building from the side of the authority as well as self-reliance and determination from the SHGs' side will take this social movement to its desired goal.

REFERENCES

Government of India (1999), *Swarnjayanti Gram Swarojgar Yojona Guideline*, New Delhi: Government of India.

McIver, R.M. and C.H. Page (1950), *Society: An Introductory Analysis*, New Delhi: Macmillan.

Narasimhan, Sakuntala (1999), *Empowering Women: An Alternative Strategy from Rural India*, New Delhi: Sage.

Parvin, M. Razia, (2005), *Empowerment of Women, Strategies and Systems for Gender Justice*, New Delhi: Dominant Publishers and Distributors.

SinghaRoy, D.K. (2001), 'Critical Issues in Grassroots Mobilisations and Collective Action', in D.K. SinghaRoy (ed.), *Social Development and Empowerment of the Marginalized Groups: Perspectives and Strategies*, New Delhi: Sage.

Sinha, Patrali (2006), 'Impact of Globalisation on the Rights of Women in Third World with Special Reference to India', *Socialist Perspective*, vol. 34, nos. 3-4: 149-68.

Suguna, B. and G. Sandhya Rani (2007), 'Women's Empowerment and Self Help Groups', in Kamal K. Misra and Janet Huber Lowry (eds.), *Recent Studies on Indian Women*, Jaipur: Rawat Publication.

World Bank (2005), New Frontiers of Social Policy, Development in a Globalising World, Tanzania, December 2005 http://go.worldbank.org/

CHAPTER 13

Social Mobilization of the Marginals: A Case Study of Tribal Development Project

SILIMA NANDA

This paper analyses the *Wadi* (orchard) project as an instrument of sustainable tribal development in the Dangs district of Gujarat. The *Wadi* programme is an integrated livelihood programme. It includes income generating activity through horticulture, soil and water conservation, improved farming and forestry, health and women's development and micro-finance, implemented by Dharampur Udhdhan Vahini Agency (DHRUVA) covering 3,483 families, on 3,400 acres and across 88 villages. DHRUVA-BAIF (Development Research Foundation—an organization running many developmental schemes in south Gujarat) started working in the Dangs district in the year 2001-2. This programme constitutes the foundation on which the organization has built its wide ranging development interventions. It is implemented with a grant from the Indo-German Bank, Kreditanstalt Fiir Wiederauf Bau (KFW—a German government owned development bank) through the Government of India and National Bank for Agricultural and Rural Development (NABARD) and Rashtriya Sam Vikas Yojna (RSVY) scheme of the Government of India. NABARD is the nodal agency on behalf of the Government of India and the project executive agency is a sister agency (voluntary organization) of BAIF, DHRUVA. The *Wadi*-based comprehensive tribal development project is being implemented in three blocks of south Gujarat, i.e. Dharampur, Kaprada and Vansada since 1995. The term *Wadi* is a local term for a fruit orchard. In the programme, at the beneficiary level, which is mostly the tribes, one acre of plot is selected to plant fruit trees, namely mango and cashew. Recommended distances are followed and a variety is planted, keeping in requirement the demand for market and processing. Inter-cropping of vegetables is also practised, which gives an additional and frequent income. Along the boundary, forest plantation is normally done, with the dual purpose of both fencing as well as an investment. Such an arrangement helps in generating periodic income flow for the families. But over the years, the families have also been diversifying into other enterprises. One of the most common ones is mango nursery, which most of the households are growing in their homestead land. The other major activity promoted in the area is dairy, with the help of credit from the mobilized savings of the Self-Help Groups (SHG).

Prior to appreciating the performance and impact of the project, the demographic information about Dangs district is of relevance. Located on the south-eastern part of Gujarat, and bordering Maharashtra, Dangs is the smallest district of Gujarat, covering a geographical area of 1,764 sq. km., with a population of 2,25,802, of which the tribals constitute 93.80 per cent (*Indian States at a Glance* 2006-7: 88). The predominant tribal groups are the Kotwalia, Kolga, Kathodi (all primitive tribes), Warli, Dangi Bhils and Kunbi (Konkana) tribes. All these groups form the present-day population of Dangis, a heterogeneous mixture of several tribes.

Warli are a primitive tribe living in the forested region. They live in Umargaon, Dharampur, Vanda Talukas in Valsad and Dang districts in areas near the Maharashtra border. Warli are a sub-tribe of Bhils and the language that Kunbi and Warli speak is Gujarati. Living in the hilly and remote forest areas they retain their primitive lifestyle. These tribes migrate in search of work, collect forest produce like gum, honey, *doli*, *mahua*, *amla* and *timrou* leaves to sell in the market. The Warli are considered to be the children of nature and to them the forest is more important than agriculture. Farming and cattle herding form their main occupation. About 26 per cent of the Dangs tribal population belong to the Bhil tribal group. A good proportion of Nayaka, Naikada, Patalis, Rathwa and Koli are the other tribes. The aborigines settled in the Dangs are Bhils, Kuntie, Kukanes and Warlis. Bhils derive their names from the Dravidian word called 'Bilu', which means 'bow'. Bhils thus are seen with bows and arrows. They live in isolation, practice hunting, fishing, shifting cultivation and are not very progressive in farming. Kunbi, Konkana and Konkani are the tribes that migrated from Konkan in south India and settled down in the Dangs. Kunbis are progressive agriculturists and are often orthodox Hindus. They occupy important posts within the tribal groups and are more cultured than the Bhils.

The district has a good forest cover, including the Poorna Wildlife Sanctuary. Since the formation of Gujarat state, Dangs has been given considerable attention, but due to its hilly terrain not much industrial development could take place. At present, it is one of the slow developing *talukas* which has been identified by the state government for intensive attention.

THE DANGS PROFILE OF THE PRIMITIVE TRIBAL GROUPS

Demographic Profile

Community-wise population in Dangs

Community	No.
Kotwaliya	1,141
Kolgha	28
Kathodi	972
Total	2,141

Sex-wise population

Sex	No.
Male	1,108
Female	1,033
Total population	2,141

According to a ranking of 447 districts based on the index of backwardness prepared by the Planning Commission, Dangs is the poorest district. The index of backwardness incorporates the percentage of Scheduled Caste (SC) and Scheduled Tribe (ST) population, agricultural wages and output per farm worker.

Some of the socio-economic indicators which explain the poverty of the district are:

1. Lowest per capita income at Rs. 10,664.
2. Workers dependent on the agricultural sector are highest (85.90 per cent) and those dependent on non-agricultural sector are lowest (14.10 per cent).
3. Amount of deposits stand at Rs. 8,829 lakh, which is the lowest in the state.
4. Penetration of services such as LPG (1,795 households) and electricity (42.60 per cent) are lowest, indicating lack of affordability.

5. Poor health services, especially for women as 89.34 per cent have used their homes for the delivery of babies and 27.25 per cent of women have not received ante-natal check-ups following their pregnancy in 2003-4 (*Indian States at a Glance 2006-07*: 90-115). Out of the 19 districts of Gujarat, the Dangs ranks 18th on infant mortality rate at 87 per 1,000 births.

Occupational Pattern

The Dangs predominantly has a subsistence-based economy, where the people are dependent on the natural resources. Poverty levels and inability of people to take risks due to high degree of vulnerability are the reasons for subsistence agriculture. Apart from agriculture, animal husbandry, collection and sale of non-timber forest produce, labour in forest and migration are the options available to tribals (Figure 13.1).

In the beginning, DHRUVA got the required grant from KFW for initiating the programme. After initial success and stabilization of the programme, DHRUVA attracted funds from multiple sources: from the state government through the District Rural Development Agency (DRDA), DPAP as well as NABARD. The Government of Gujarat helped in the establishment of Wadi through the tribal Sub-plan in Vansada, Dharampur Kaprada as well as in Dang districts.

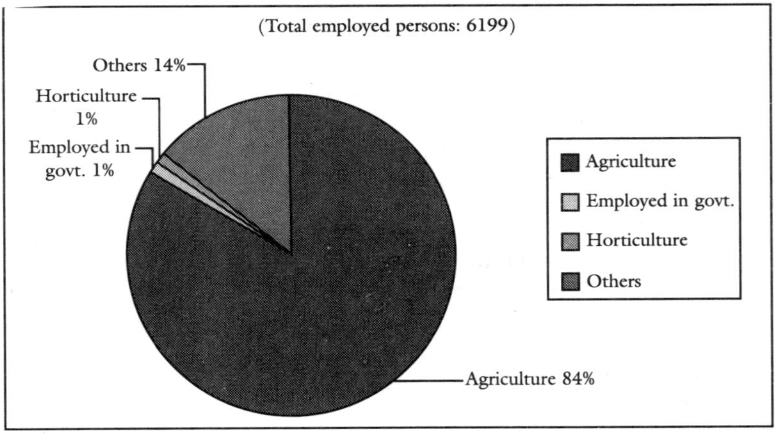

FIGURE 13.1: DISTRIBUTION OF TRIBALS IN DIFFERENT OCCUPATIONS IN DANGS

SWOT ANALYSIS OF THE DANGS DISTRICT

Strengths	Weaknesses
People • Special skill in herbal treatments • Mesmerizing Dangi group dances • Skills in carpentry and bamboo crafts	• Mostly illiterate villagers living in reserved forests • Cut-off from the mainstream • No marketable skills other than traditional ones • About 50 per cent of the population have to migrate for livelihood for 6-7 months • No self-help groups in 50 per cent of the villages, leading to poor orientation for saving
Forest • 90 per cent forest cover out of total area of 1,764 sq km • Dense forest in 1,008 sq km • Rich in teak, sissoo, khair, bamboo, medicinal/aromatic plants • 550 species of plants • Vast area under bamboo plants and land suitable for growing bamboo	• Rights of tribals on forest land not adequately enforced • Rights on collection of MFP is questionable • Poor quality of bamboo (in terms of distance between nodes) • Cutting of teak and other trees relentlessly without rejuvenating
Rainfall • Heavy rainfall	• Despite heavy rainfall, Dangs doesn't have adequate drinking water • No rainwater inflow to Dangs from neighbouring areas due to its elevated level • Rainfall and floods cause land erosion
Social and physical infrastructure • Remoteness could be an advantage in promoting eco-tourism	• Poor rural connectivity due to eroded roads • Lack of all-weather roads • No banking/credit facilities in villages • Poor housing • Only 27 villages have facilities for higher education beyond primary, and only one college at Awha • Poor public transport

Agriculture	
• Organic cultivation practices followed without use of chemical fertilizers or pesticides • Local weekly *haats* for trading/ marketing surplus food grains/ pulses	• Soil erosion decreases soil fertility as there is no forest land cover to protect soil erosion, leading to poor yields • Lack of adequate water recharge facilities • Poor irrigation facilities • Land use only for 3-4 months, and slope land cultivation of selected few crops • Landholding size is small and scattered • Poor soil conditions • Low agricultural productivity
Institutional System	
• Growth of SHGs and their positive impact on savings, migration, education and women's activities	• Poor community development infrastructure
Animal Husbandry	
• Dairy activity is growing in selected pockets • Poultry growing as a household business • 59 milk cooperatives	• Limited support of infrastructure

Opportunities	*Threats*
• Huge reservoir of medicinal plants and herbs a natural asset of the forest • District headquarter has an Ayurvedic hospital to explore the possibility of utilizing the traditional medicinal system. This would be an opportunity for integrating the two knowledge systems and in that way making health care more accessible • With regard to farm-based income generation, horticulture has a strong potential • Animal husbandry also a good option for generating regular and sufficient income for families • Scope to promote economic activities such as eco/adventure tourism,	• No ready access to MFP due to inadequate recognition of rights of tribals (minor forest produce) • Fear of exploitation by traders dealing in medicinal plants and herbs • Irrigation facilities for horticulture are a major concern • Without proper planning to tackle the issue of biomass and water availability, taking up animal husbandry will be a liability rather than an asset • Without availability of efficient veterinary service, it will not be feasible to go for large-scale animal husbandry practices • Development threat to eco-system

processing of medicinal plants, bio fuel/clean energy production	• Losing cultural identity • Fear of involvement of the local tribals in the process and hence benefits of value addition not accruing to them

Note: SWOT analysis prepared by Asian Centre for Entrepreneurial Initiative, May 2007.

DHRUVA also tapped the financial resources from the Department of Agriculture and Cooperation, Ministry of Agriculture, Government of India, for promotion of integrated horticulture, especially homestead vegetable and floriculture. In the year 2003-4, the cost of establishing 1,500 Wadi had been sanctioned through the Rashtriya Gram Vikas Yojna. The promotion of SHGs helped in mobilizing savings as well as extending credit for various income generating activities. A total of 436 SHGs have been formed in 135 villages with their cumulative savings and credit around Rs.19.4 lakh and 18.5 lakh, respectively. As mentioned earlier, DHRUVA has also promoted a community-based credit programme, known as Sahabhagi Vikas Yojna, for need-based credit for farm and non-farm activities, including working capital loan for cooperatives.

The Wadi programme implemented by DHRUVA BAIF is committed towards sustainable development of tribals in Dangs district. The health intervention forms an integral component in improving the quality of lives of tribals. There is special emphasis in the Wadi programme on the involvement of women in the family-based development programme. The other interventions include micro-finance to provide credit to invest in activities and enterprises facilitating further development. One of the reasons for the success of the programme is the well-defined strategy of forward and backward linkages in the project. This is facilitated with the establishment of producers' cooperatives, which helped in both aggregation of produce as well as distribution of inputs, thereby creating economies of scale in both the functions. The strategy of local value addition through people's institution helped in higher retention and thereby better income for the producers. This was done through the establishment of processing centres in a cluster of villages for both mango and cashew. For marketing the produce, the creation of the brand 'Vrindavan' is another significant step which helped in tapping the local retail market for mango pickles and pulp. These institutions are engaged in mango and cashew processing, marketing of farm produce, purchase of inputs in bulk and distributing the same in a decentralized manner. The Wadi farmers have contributed Rs. 14.2 lakh as share capital. The Vasundhara Cooperative is the oldest cooperative, providing marketing support to all newly formed cooperatives. In the financial year 2003-4, about 192 tonnes of cashew and 560 tonnes of mango were processed. The sales turnover of Vasundhara Cooperative in 2000-1 was Rs. 72.61 lakh and it increased to Rs. 204.21 lakh in 2003-4, registering a growth of around 200 per cent. Thus, the Wadi programme is a holistic, participatory and dynamic programme for the economic development and socio-cultural enhancement of tribals in the Dangs district.

Wadi has promoted over 350 SHGs in Dangs who have saved more than Rs. 32 lakh. Amongst them, 300 SHGs are linked with banks for availing credit for income generating activities. These groups are involved in capacity building, village sanitation, vermic composting, *papad* making, garments, forest nursery raising, roof tile making, and so on. The women are trained in the manufacturing of new born baby units. Two NGOs have also started ethnic restaurants *Nabne* which serve traditional food to tourists. DHRUVA is working as a mother NGO for Reproductive and Child Health (RCH) programme being implemented in Dangs, with assistance from the state Ministry of Health and Family Welfare. Reducing maternal mortality and child mortality are major challenges in the district and to address these grave problems, DHRUVA has promoted local SHGs for awareness and total sanitation among the tribals. The success of the project is apparent from the scale it has achieved in two decades and the number of the beneficiaries it has supported. This has been made possible through an array of phased interventions in the area. Concomitant with the flow of economic projects, the programme built human resource institutions which provide the much required support services around these activities. In the process, the project developed the capacity of the people in institution management as well as in the activities the beneficiaries pursued.

The watershed development programme in the district is implemented by DHRUVA with support from the central and state governments and is has spread over 3,000 hectares. This programme benefits more than 3,200 families in 18 villages. The net cropping areas have increased to 50 per cent and the increase in crop yields has motivated the tribals to bring degraded lands under cultivation. The Table 13.1 gives a clear picture of the area distribution in Dangs

TABLE 13.1: EXTENT OF AGRICULTURE IN DANGS DISTRICT

Year	Gross cropped area (ha)	Net sown area (ha)	Production (tonnes)	Net Irrigated area (ha)	Area under food crops (ha)	Area under Horticultural crops (ha)	Area under fruit crops (ha)
2001-2	69,484	48,300	1,02,187	4,650	68,970	117	397
2002-3	69,252	48,000	90,060	6,150	68,623	231	398
2003-4	70,964	50,620	1,07,470	7,350	69,953	520	491
2004-5	70,964	50,620	1,07,470	7,350	69,953	520	491
2005-6	73,521	51,510	1,40,117	7,500	73,521	N.A.	N.A.

and its steady rise in terms of irrigation and horticultural development.

The NGO is taking every opportunity to develop and train community organizations to manage existing programmes as well as create new ones as the need arises. The *Ayojan Samitis* and 17 *Gram Vikas Mandals* are being trained as key agencies of the watershed development as well as Wadi programmes in Dang. The people's organizations are increasingly responsible for the design, implementation and monitoring of all activities in the village.

DHRUVA undertook a pilot exercise of processing cashew nuts with a view to developing the technology for a processing unit. The first cashew nut processing unit was started in Dangs at Jamalpade village. Four thousand kilograms of raw nuts were processed during 2005 at Jamalpade unit with encouraging results. The unit now is capable of generating employment for 20 persons per day and over the next seven years the project's yield is expected to increase to 40 tonnes, requiring the setting up of two such processing units.

The analysis of the progress of the project discussed in terms of the financial parameters as well as physical indicators may be briefly summarized.

Wadi-related impact:

- Most of the beneficiaries (75 per cent) regarded the NGO itself as the source of information on the Wadi project. Role of information media was just 5 per cent.
- The quality of land for Wadi was poor in the sense that 81 per cent wadi had 'unirrigated land.

- Hardly 5 per cent beneficiaries could expand the Wadi after joining it.
- Almost 99 per cent beneficiaries said they had received financial input/support in Wadi development.
- 77 per cent producers had undergone one or other type of capacity building training programme.
- 66 per cent said they had utilized the training in the practice but almost one-third beneficiaries expressed their inability to use the training.
- Training is reflected in the fast adoption of soil and water conservation practices. It is quite remarkable that in our sample 96 per cent farmers had taken up soil conservation measures. Bund construction is followed by 86 per cent beneficiaries. Similarly, rearly 70 per cent respondents followed water harvesting techniques including *nala* plugging, well repairs and development of *jalkunds* (farm ponds).
- The systematic 'Wadi' development with best use of scientific approach and actions show almost 85 per cent survival rate of Wadi plants, 93 per cent in case of cashew and 86 per cent in case of mango, having much less variation by clusters.
- The marketed surplus recorded by beneficiaries was 87.55 per cent in case of mango and 95.15 per cent in case of cashew nuts.
- Employment and income benefits during the process of Wadi development was also found remarkable, as on an average 42 days' of work Rs. 1,543 wage was made available to Wadi farmers to work on their own farms.

Quality of Life

Almost eight variables were used to judge the impact on quality of life and the findings are encouraging. We may highlight the main findings as follows:

- There is no starvation; substantial food availability with better quality have ensured 'food security'.
- Consumption basket of the beneficiaries has improved with greater quantum of quality items of non-food consumption indicating definite change in the standard of life.
- Assessment of better quality living sources and equipment did not find much rise. In fact, except for radio (36 per cent), wall

clock (31 per cent) and cycle (28 per cent) the beneficiaries had little other 'urban life' equipments.

- Seventy-one per cent of the beneficiaries had only *kuccha* houses and hardly 2.46 per cent and 7 per cent had separate toilets and bathrooms. However, 70 per cent had separate kitchen and separate drinking water facility, 76 per cent houses had separate cattle shed while 60 per cent reported to have electricity.
- It is a matter of great satisfaction that quality drinking water was available to 92 per cent respondents; 50 per cent received chlorinated water though 42 per cent had to walk for water for over 1 to 3 km.
- Family planning-related impact was quite positive, as 93 per cent had started to receive some health service and guidance through these project and health guides. While 94 per cent had been vaccinated, 83 per cent delivery was done at home by trained *Dayans*—village maids trained by DHRUVA health guides. Almost 95 per cent reported to have only casual sickness, skin disease was reported by 2 per cent but 10 per cent reported anaemia. A high 93 per cent sample households asserted positive medical assistance by DHRUVA and the project. As much as 70 per cent have followed family planning.
- Gender issues were examined and it was interesting to find that:

  (a) 78 per cent women expressed that they have a voice in the economic affairs of the family.
  (b) 90 per cent women accepted that their in-laws take care of their children while they go for work.
  (c) 80 per cent women showed interest in assisting their children in their education, which is a positive sign of acceptance of education.
  (d) The remarkable change in women's life was that as much as 90-8 per cent denied any discrimination in food consumption both in terms of quality and quantity.
  (e) Due to Wadi, income generating activities for women had increased and 'women-beating' was almost non-existent. Non-consumption of alcohol and relatively better life had also played their role in elimination of this vice.

The Wadi as a sustainable development model has proved its basic worth by achieving the objectives of sustainable livelihood along with sustainable environmental development. The Wadi model has proved that a committed, and professionally managed NGO could be successful to uplift the poor, depressed and dependent tribals through mutual cooperation, collective effort and confidence building activities. However, the replication of the Wadi model is more an opportunity than a challenge due to the path already carved by BAIF following many experiments and failures in last three decades. Wadi-based *Adivasi* development has been doing well and there is still scope for better performance and shaping a better model of tribal development.

As of now, every village has a motor bike and between every two villages one vehicle is sighted. Such vehicles carry emergency cases to hospitals, whenever ambulances are not available. The forest department has been asked to take up more than thirty places for joint forest management by involving the local *Bhagats*, so that the herb tubers and roots along with horticulture, dairy, bamboo and other timber-related trees could be grown. This would fetch the people more income and make the district a busy supplier of medicinal herbs and commercial bamboo. It would also indirectly address the problem of illegal cultivation leading to clashes between tribals and the forest department over ownership issues. Skill upgradation programmes have been undertaken by Wadi for providing skill training to the tribals so that the unemployed tribal men and women can work in the service industry for alternative sources of income. Propagation of tribal millets, marketing of *Nagalis* (local names for millet), making products of bamboo and expediting the process of 'Maliki' tree payment through the forest department are other measures to help the tribal farmers generate income.

The eastern pocket of Dangs is water deficient and thus sees heavy migration. Emphasis has been made through schemes like land levelling, soil conservation and check dams by joint efforts of forest and panchayat so that there's agricultural stabilization and with that medium and large farmers can employ or deploy the landless category which would provide them with sustainable employment and thus they would not go for migration. The new scheme of the Government of India under the national rural employment programme which is being implemented through the village panchayat is also being used to take care of asset creation for irrigation and other water purposes so that it can provide temporary relief by giving employment to tribals and also serve as a permanent source of employment by supporting sustainable agriculture, in the long run.

On the nutritional and health side, the number of children who are malnourished is no doubt significantly high but this problem has been taken care of through increased emphasis and extension of the *anganwadi* network and also through the fortification of wheat through the *ghantis* located in the district. What is appalling is the huge number of vacancies in the district, including for specialist doctors and senior officers in the health sector who are to discharge the mandate with sincerity and seriousness. The posts of district primary education officers, poultry officers as well as civil surgeons cannot be left unmanned looking at the needs and expectations from the tribal Dangis. Though roads are good and connectivity is excellent, students still drop outs due to absence of proper transportation. Old worn out buses need replacement, there is also need for introducing bus routes in areas already connected with new roads. The schools are poorly attended by children as sending them is a risky proposition due to unworthy and unreliable transport vehicles which may get stalled in the midst of forests.

For further social mobilization of the tribals, 'retailing' units need to be introduced. Unemployed persons can be given short courses in marketing and salesmanship and instill in them standards of accountability and customer-care skills. Mainstream activities in the rural sector can also be slowly undertaken by the trained tribals. The companies should encourage such people to start their own enterprises, which may range from cooking to plumbing, from electrical repairing to automobiles.

In addition to the Wadi programme recent initiatives have been launched by the Government of Gujarat. In order to bring the quality of life indicators of the tribals at par with the of rest of the state, in a time-bound manner, the chief minister of Gujarat has launched the Chief Minister's Ten Point Programme (*Vanbandhu Kalyan Yojana*) for the development of tribal areas. This programme aims at improving the civil and social infrastructure in these areas. It also aims at doubling of the income of the tribal areas, involving all stakeholders including the private sector, and developing the urban habitations in such a way that they become growth engines for wealth creation in these areas. Mainstreaming of specially disadvantaged groups like primitive tribals, women-headed households, migrant families and people suffering from disabilities are also major goals of this programme. The programme's strategies include harnessing of private initiative, technology, infrastructure development and training to enable the tribal communities lead a better life. The programme has the following ten components:

1. Quality and sustainable employment for 5 lakh tribal families.
2. Emphasis on quality education and higher education.
3. Accelerated economic development of tribal areas
4. Health for all
5. Housing for all
6. Safe drinking water to all
7. Irrigation
8. All weather roads
9. Universal availability of electricity
10. Urban development

The strategy for the Ten Point Programme is outcome-oriented, with time-bound interventions and people's participation. The programme will be implemented in the mission-mode through strengthened Integrated Tribal Development Project (ITDP) machinery with a quarterly review of progress by the chief minister. Experts and professionals, including the private sector, will be closely involved in the programme for capacity building, project development and implementation, service delivery and other aspects. The impact of the programme will be assessed through independent, third-party monitoring at the household level. Water and Power Consultancy Services of India has already been engaged for monitoring civil works in Dahod and Panchmahal, while other agencies are being identified for the remaining districts. The framework and formats for Management Information Systems and concurrent monitoring are being developed by Gujarat Institute of Development Research.

Due to the magnitude of the Ten Point Programme and its implementation in the mission-mode, it was found necessary to create an autonomous society that allowed flexibility and innovation. Accordingly, the Development Support Agency of Gujarat (DSAG) has been set up by the state government as an autonomous body under the Societies Registration Act, 1860 and Bombay Public Trust Act, 1950 with the Chief Secretary, Government of Gujarat, as the chairman. The society will receive its funding from the state government and will have the freedom to involve skilled professionals to carry out certain key tasks. It is the apex institution for co-ordination, evaluation, supervision and monitoring the work of corporations, boards and other bodies set up by the state government and are given the responsibility of assisting tribal communities for their economic development. DSAG also has an advocacy role by extending help and assistance for furthering government policies and programmes for the development of tribal communities and areas.

The Government of Gujarat, through a resolution (GR No. VKY-102007-244(1)/P, dated 10 April 2007), has laid down broad guidelines for the involvement of the private sector in implementing large-scale projects under the chief minister's Ten Point Programme. The programme will implement projects with private sector participation in three areas—farm-based activities; dairy-based animal husbandry activities; and service sector. Private sector units have been invited for developing and implementing projects that can provide assurance that a minimum committed number of poor families will cross the poverty line and will receive an assured minimum income annually. The project period will be of around five years, and each project would cover about 3,000-5,000 BPL tribal families. A few high-technology-based small projects may also be launched on a pilot basis if there is scope for scaling them up later.

The nature and extent of government support will vary from project to project. However, in general, the average cost of assistance will not exceed Rs. 30,000 per BPL tribal family. Government support to the projects will be extended through the Tribal Development Department, which will leverage its Tribal Area Sub Plan (TASP) stream funds as well as funds of other departments. The government will also help in the development of project-specific infrastructure like construction and strengthening of roads, power and water supply, broadband connectivity facilities, etc. Since the programme is outcome-oriented, the state government will monitor project progress through every individual participating BPL family.

The incidence of seasonal and distress migration is high in the tribal pockets of Gujarat, with studies indicating that nearly 30 per cent of the tribal population migrating out temporarily every year in search of work. Most of these migrants take up jobs as unskilled labour at very low wages. Areas surrounding large urban cities such as Ahmedabad, Vadodara and Surat are the popular destinations due to the booming construction sector. However, present trends point to shrinking demand for unskilled workers. Unless the skill base of these migrant workers is improved, their avenues for earning livelihood will only continue to get narrower. With steady advancement in the technical specifications and skill requirements in the construction industry, there is a need to involve competent organizations to establish skill training centres in tribal areas. In addition to the construction sector, the other potential areas that need skill improvements are the transport sector, hospitality industry, agro services, parameds, patient care, stone carving, and garment industry.

The Tribal Development Department seeks to invite experienced private sector organizations who have considerable expertise in their fields to establish training centres in tribal areas. Interested organizations can suggest their own outcome-based models for imparting training to about 1,000 tribal youths every year. At the end of the training period, the participants should be in a position to double their wage income due to the high-quality support they have received.

The Eklavya School Project for classes 6-12 was launched across in the Gujarat in 1999-2000, and currently, ten schools have been sanctioned in the state. The project is part of the national initiative to provide quality education to tribal students and is based on the public school model. The thrust of the project is to promote excellence in students by providing them with modern educational and extra-curricular infrastructure along with professionally trained teachers. The state government has promoted an autonomous society under the Tribal Development Department to implement the project. Since establishing and running a large number of high quality schools requires professional management and expertise, the Eklavya School Society in Gujarat will offer the management of these schools to external, competent organizations. These organizations can adopt the schools on a medium term basis for about five years, with clearly defined financial terms and performance norms. Each school will have about 420 students, primarily from tribal communities. Since the focus of the project is to provide quality education to tribal children, the society will monitor the performance of the students and the other agreed performance parameters only. It will not interfere with the actual management of the schools. Inducting of teaching staff and other academic decisions will be the responsibility of the managing organization.

The other likely activities that can be taken up as a roadmap for economic regeneration and social mobilization of the tribals are suggested below:

- Given the ample rainfall, mini hydel plants could be encouraged although they would be operable only during the monsoons.

This activity has to be implemented as a commercial activity through the formation of a company owned by the local tribals and other stakeholders. Once the feasibility of energy production is established, the extent of surplus power could be estimated and measures could be put in place to generate revenue.

- While sufficient water is available, there is a need to find innovative and cost-effective techniques of water harvesting and conservation. This could be accomplished through village-level committees as a social activity benefiting the locals.
- With the limited or no use of chemical fertilizers and pesticides, organic farming can be taken up in a commercial manner as a seasonal activity. Co-owned organic farming on a large scale by tribals and agri business firms could be encouraged for the following crops:

    - ➢ Ragi millet
    - ➢ Ambadi edible oil
    - ➢ Mushroom
    - ➢ Strawberry
    - ➢ Cashew nut growing and processing
    - ➢ Medicinal/herbal plants growing and processing units
    - ➢ Bio Fuels Park

- The uncultivated land area of about 4,000 hectares and wasteland of about 1,500 hectares could be put to productive use through the plantation of oil-seed bearing trees such as *jetropha*. Madhya Pradesh has initiated such a project to enhance the income of the locals and reduce migration.
- Given the availability of medicinal and aromatic plants now largely sold through middlemen without value addition, there is scope to organize this activity in a way that is more beneficial to the tribals. It is suggested that the tribals be equipped with skills to 'harvest' the produce scientifically and process the same at least to the stage of an intermediate product. This shall be an attractive proposition to the processors since they would save on the transport cost.
- Although bamboo is available in plenty, it has short inter-nodal distance, deterring value addition for applications other than paper making. To facilitate value addition, the following steps are required:

- With the current skill levels, setting up of *agarbati* units with the help of leading brands like ITC and Cycle brand and retail chains.
- Through the interventions of the Bamboo Mission and research centres, explore the possibilities of replacing the current varieties of bamboo with more suitable ones that have long inter-nodal distance and better industrial applications.
- Once feasibility is established, generate awareness among the locals and the forest department about the advantage of replacing the current bamboo varieties.
- Facilitate formation of SHGs for collection and conversion of bamboo into value-added products such as eco-friendly furniture.

• The tribes are known for their mesmerizing group dances and other forms of tribal art. Their way of life is also different from mainstream society. This resource could be applied to promote cultural tourism. The remoteness of the district, lack of ready accessibility, hilly terrain, heavy rains and other conditions could be positioned as advantages for promoting eco-tourism and adventure tourism. The tourist centre at Saputara has already found place on the tourism map. The other areas that could be focused on are Sabari, Waghai and Ahwa.

• Agro processing units can be set up in the north and east to create employment for at least 100 persons in allied activities. The following steps need to be taken to facilitate value addition in a market-driven manner:

- Establishing the feasibility of value addition and processing activities such as small scale oil extraction units, formulated protein foods such as a combination of nagali and soyabean, etc.
- Linking the above with clean energy production to fulfil the energy needs of such projects.
- Encouraging farmers to come together to set up co-owned processing facilities in the interest of synergy.
- Establishing marketing facilities through linkages with agro-processing companies.
- Farms with larger landholding size (beyond 10 hectares) who form 15 per cent of the landowners in Dangs could be roped in.

- While there is a large amount of timber coming from the Dangs, as of now, there is no value addition taking place. The following measures could be taken to promote clusters:
    - ➢ Identify timber collection points.
    - ➢ Identify farmers following *malki* practice and those locals with carpentry skills and bring them together in co-ownership mode.
    - ➢ Identify processing opportunities such as solar seasoning plant, wooden components for textile sector, furniture, etc.
    - ➢ Generate awareness on processing possibilities among the pre-identified group.
    - ➢ Facilitate the setting up of processing units with joint stakes by skilled workers, farmers following *malki* practice and marketing agencies.
    - ➢ Organize skill training wherever necessary.
    - ➢ Establish linkages with institutions such as National Institute of Design (NID), Ahmedabad for design inputs wherever necessary.
    - ➢ Establish marketing facilities through linkages with traders.
- Current trends indicate that animal husbandry activities are on the rise in certain parts of Dangs. There is a well-developed route to reach the chilling plant at Waghai. The following steps can be taken to promote the activity:
    - ➢ Identify milk collection points and marketable surplus.
    - ➢ Identify farmers already engaged in cattle rearing and bring them together in a co-ownership mode.
    - ➢ Identify processing opportunities through mini-dairies, taking due care to formulate a product mix that has a relatively longer shelf life given that the market segment is outside the district.
    - ➢ Generate awareness on processing possibilities among the pre-identified group.
    - ➢ Facilitate setting up of processing units jointly owned by farmers and marketing agencies.
    - ➢ Establishing marketing facilities through linkages with traders.
- Most villages in the district do not have small business units. As per the sustainability norms for Special Business Units (SBU)

with a standard profit-operating margin of 12-15 per cent, business turnover of Rs. 30,000 a month will provide sustainable income for at least one family in each village. Given the limited population, one SBU can cover a cluster of villages. The ten SBUs that have been identified include saloon; retail shops for fruits, fodder and cosmetics; medical shop; storage; entertainment facilities/cultural centres; restaurants and eateries; repairs and maintenance of electric appliances and hand pumps; telephone booths; tailors and bakery units. These SBUs can be established through the micro-enterprise development mode.

- Local artisans are by and large engaged in producing bamboo products, carpets and wooden toys. However, these are not suitable for urban markets and cannot be taken up as entrepreneurial activities. The following steps can thus be taken to transform handicraft activities into entrepreneurial ones:
    - ➢ Identify the most promising artisan centre in the district and set up a common facility centre on a pilot basis.
    - ➢ Follow a group entrepreneurship mode and integrate it with a co-owned company having artisans as stakeholders.
    - ➢ Facilitate marketing tie-up through private and state-owned handicraft dealers.
    - ➢ Facilitate provision of design inputs through tie-ups with design institutions.

In the days to come, social mobilization of the tribals will be complete and successful and they too will also start competing in the global markets. However, educational opportunities need to be intensified and such courses are to be popularized that will help the tribals in self-employment, through the opening of ITIS, polytechnics and other vocational institutions.

REFERENCES

BAIF Development Research Foundation, *Progress Reports of Comprehensive Tribal Development*, 2007.

BAIF Journal, vol. 24, no. 2, April 2001. http://cinicell.org/research_documents/11.%20 BAIF-DHRUVA%20casestudy.pdf

Bhosale, B.V (ed.) (2004), *Mobilisation of Backward Communities in India*, New Delhi: Deep and Deep.

D.D.O. (Dangs), *Dangs Development Report*, 2007.

GITCO (2003), *Development of Dang Report*, Ministry of Finance, Government of India.

Hegde, N.G. (2003), *Wadi Users in Hope Untribal Communities Edition, BAIF Journal.* http://cinicell.org.research_documents.

Mahajan, S.G. (1990), *Tribal Rehabilitation through Development of Wadi, BAIF Journal.* http://cinicell.org.research_documents.

Prasad, Jitendra (2005), *Tribal Movements in India*, New Delhi: Kilaso Books.

CHAPTER 14

Cooperative Movement and Social Development of the Marginalized: A Case of Lift Irrigation

SARJERAO SALUNKHE

INTRODUCTION

In predominantly agricultural societies such as India's issues relating to the expansion of irrigation, ownership and distribution of water resources have emerged as crucial. Though water is a common property resource, in reality, water rights in the area of irrigation are linked to ownership of land. The skewed distribution of land necessarily denies access to water resources to the marginal/lower sections of the farming community. Under such circumstances, institutional mechanisms whereby farmers come together and jointly strive to bring water to their farms and manage the distribution of water on their own becomes not only desirable but also necessary. The formation of farmers' cooperative lift irrigation schemes could be a viable solution for providing access to irrigation to the farmers.

In the absence of development of canal irrigation in the hilly parts of western Maharashtra, the cooperative efforts enabling an access to irrigation have been normally articulated through farmers' lift irrigation cooperatives. The available statistical data reveal that in the year 1998, there were 4,433 lift irrigation cooperatives in Maharashtra state. Out of these, more than half (i.e. 2,881) were in Pune Division which includes Pune (1,392), Satara (467), Sangli (234), Solapur (253) and Kolhapur (535) districts (Government of Maharashtra, 2000: 70-3). Thus, the formation of farmers' lift irrigation cooperatives is an important segment of the cooperative movement in western Maharashtra.

There are very few empirical studies focusing on the social aspects of water cooperatives and their impact. Some scholars have emphasized the role of farmers' participation in land and water management (Deshpande, 1998: 247-56). Bokil's case study (1996: 42-7), of a 'Vishwambhar' lift irrigation cooperative established in Karanjgaon Budruk village located in Sangamner taluka of Pune district has demonstrated the success of collective management of water resources. The author's own case study of 'Dhantek' lift irrigation cooperative located in village Mangle (in Shirala taluka of Sangli district in Maharashtra) has found that the water resources made available by this cooperative are being fairly distributed among the poor and well-to-do sections of the farming community, according to their needs, based on their rights in land (Salunkhe, 1998: 253). In addition to the earlier case study, the author took up another study to examine the impact of lift irrigation cooperatives in the broader context of 'sustainable development'. The notion of sustainable development incorporates an integrated view of ecological, economic and social dimensions of developmental sustainability. In the context of the present paper, a brief elaboration of the conceptualization of social development is in order.

CONCEPTUALIZATION OF SOCIAL DEVELOPMENT

While it cannot be denied that the idea of 'social development' was implicit in the general notion of 'development', it has gained prominence after a critique of the 'economic growth' model of development. The early development debate focused attention on the consequences of the 'economic growth' model of development. An examination of early development experiences of many countries, which adopted the 'economic growth' model of development, revealed that through there was the economic growth it was accompanied by the widened gulf between the countries in the north and the south. It also promoted economic disparities between the rich and the poor sections within societies. As Srivastava points out, 'the problem that most of the countries face today is not that of lack of economic development but that of a problem of distorted development' (1998: 70-1). He further observes that 'during past decades investments in development efforts have produced limited results to avert the increasing socio-economic inequity and inequality, both within and amongst nations' (ibid.: 71).

It was realized that 'development' conceived simply as 'economic growth' was an inadequate notion, and that economic growth does not necessarily lead to the development of all sections of society, specifically the economically marginalized and socially underprivileged. As a result of the critique of the economic growth model of development, there occurred a shift in development thinking and it eventually led to the inclusion of some additional criteria of development such as distributive justice or equity, and improvement in the overall quality of life of the masses (Dhanagare, 1996: 7-9), which signified the importance of social dimensions of development.

The 'ultimate purpose of development', according to a UN document (1975), 'is to bring about a more equitable distribution of income and wealth for promoting social justice; alleviating poverty; maximizing productive employment; and expanding and improving facilities for education, health, nutrition, housing and social welfare for the deprived and disadvantaged individuals, groups and communities' (quoted from Srivastava, 1998: 73).

The Social Development Summit at Copenhagen in 1995 contributed to crystallize the world-view on social development. The summit emphasized that the economic policies and social programmes require placing the human person at the centre of all thinking and all decisions; and promotion of social development as being fundamental to the life and future of any society. It recommended the integration of economic and social components of development (ibid.: 74-5).

As Srivastava notes, like 'development', the term 'social development' too has several connotations and continues to be used in a broad sense to refer to improvements in human and/or social well-being. The term is understood to mean 'economic growth with social justice, eradication of poverty and minimization of economic inequalities, emphasis on human resource development, and development of social services which are inclusive of welfare services but also extended to cover health, education, housing, rehabilitation etc.' (Srivastava, 1998: 75-6).

When it comes to centrally important aspects of social development such as minimization or removal of social inequality, elimination of exploitation and oppression, the empirical study of 'social development' becomes a difficult task. This is because it is not so easy to operationalize the concept of social development and understand the ongoing developmental processes, practices and their consequences.

Partha N. Mukherjee's elaboration of the conceptualization of 'social development' provides some valuable insights for operationalization of this concept for conducting empirical investigations. According to him, in the context of the Third World,

> The two basic values that should define development—are *equality* and *freedom*. These diffuse value-laden terms are subject to varied interpretations, hence there is need to specify them in concrete structural terms . . . these values can be better comprehended by their *structural counter-concepts*, viz., *Discrimination, Exploitation* and *Oppression* (DEO) which require operationalization . . . it can be argued with conviction that, a progressive diminution in DEO would indicate a commensurate increase in equality and freedom, and hence in societal development. (Mukherji, 1989: 37-8)

Mukherji further writes that,

> Each of these counter-concepts refers to sets of asymmetrical relationships between groups, such that one or more exercise dominance over the other groups. *Discrimination* essentially conveys the content of a *social* relationship which is asymmetrical and legitimated by societal norms. It operates at the level of groups identified by ascriptive criteria such as kinship, caste, religion, race, language, sex and so on—identifications into which individuals are born. If groups identified by ascriptive criteria are not in an asymmetrical relationship with each other, there is no discrimination between them. *Exploitation* is best applied to the content of economic exchanges emanating from within a normatively defined system of exchange and market. The extent of freedom from exploitation would refer to the degree of access to the available economic resources by existing groups and individuals and also to their capacity to resist or withstand unequal exchange. Exploitation is further reflected in asymmetrical relationships between those who are the owners of the means of production at one end, and those whose labour is utilized for production, at the other. Equality in this context will naturally concern itself with the reduction in this asymmetry, the distributive aspects of goods produced, the management of surpluses, a shift from large scale private ownership of the means and forces of production towards collective ownership, and so on. *Oppression* is clearly a political concept, which defines the relationship between the dominant and the dominated. It is the means by which the dominant group is able to impose its conditions on those who are weak or unwilling or are deviants. More simply, oppression is overt behavioural manifestation of power, which is conceptualized as force. (ibid.)

Mukherji further states that, 'any process of development will attempt to reduce the asymmetries' (ibid.).

In the light of the above framework, social development may be conceived as a process of social transformation guided by the ideals of equality and freedom and characterized by non-discriminatory, non-exploitative and non-oppressive practices, which result in the reduction of asymmetries in social, economic and political relationships.

There are three points which need to be stressed while empirically examining the role of lift irrigation cooperatives in promoting social development. The points are:

1. First, we have to examine whether cooperative lift irrigation schemes are contributing to changing the traditional asymmetrical relationships between groups based on ascriptive criteria such as caste or religion. If the relationships that they are encouraging are not asymmetrical, it can be inferred that this would lead to gradual reduction in discrimination and they are promoting social development.
2. Secondly, we have to examine whether the lift irrigation cooperatives are promoting non-exploitative relationships or relationships based on equality among their members. Equality in the context of lift irrigation cooperatives would refer to the distributive aspects of goods produced, i.e. equality in distribution of water resources made available and a shift from private ownership of water resources towards collective ownership of these resources. The extent of freedom from exploitation would refer to the degree of access to the available water resources for existing groups and individuals. If the members of lift irrigation cooperatives do not feel that there is discrimination in water distribution and if they get water in sufficient quantity when it is required, it may well be inferred that, these cooperatives are establishing non-exploitative practices and hence they are promoting social development.
3. Thirdly, we have to examine whether there is oppression of one group by the other group in the cooperatives. Oppression essentially being the political concept, empirically we have to examine the composition of power structure of lift irrigation cooperatives. If we find that the farmers belonging to the lower strata of the village peasantry and socially underprivileged sections are able to occupy seats of power within the cooperative power structures, we can say that the cooperatives are promoting social development. We will come to these three points later after looking at the empirical data.

THE STUDY AND METHODOLOGY

The study was undertaken to examine the impact of Lift Irrigation Cooperative Schemes (henceforth LICS) in Warana River basin (western Maharashtra) on the ecosystem of Warana region. The data were collected by using two techniques: mailed questionnaire and interview schedule. The questionnaire was posted to 84 lift irrigation cooperatives located in Warana River basin, which covers parts of Sangli and Kolhapur districts in Maharashtra. We received filled in questionnaires from 57 lift irrigation cooperatives. The secretaries of the lift irrigation cooperatives were the respondents. The postal correspondence relating to the data collection through mailed questionnaire was made between February and April 2002.

Then, using the list of 57 LICSs as the sampling frame (which gave positive response to the mailed questionnaire), 14 lift irrigation cooperatives were purposively selected for collecting the relevant data directly from the beneficiary farmers of these cooperatives. These LICSs represented all the 7 talukas which form part of the Warana region. Four LICSs were drawn from Hatkanangale taluka, three from Walva taluka, two each from Shirala and Panhala taluka, and one each from Miraj, Shahuwadi and Shirol taluka. Eight LICSs belonged to Kolhapur district while the remaining six went to Sangli district.

Out of the 2,992 total members of the 14 LICSs, 493 members (16.47 per cent) were selected, while out of the 496 non-member beneficiaries, 60 (12.09 per cent non-members) were selected for the present study. The 'member' beneficiaries of lift irrigation co-operatives were selected by adopting a systematic sampling procedure and 'non-member' beneficiaries were selected by resorting to the accidental sampling procedure. The total number of beneficiaries of 14 selected lift irrigation cooperatives (2,992 members + 496 non-members) was 3,488. The aggregate sample of both member and non-member beneficiaries of 14 selected LICSs was 635 (18.20 per cent beneficiaries). The data collection work, with the help of an interview schedule, was carried out from April to December 2002, by the project staff including the Principal Investigator, Project Fellow and the field-workers appointed for data collection work. This paper shares some of the findings of the study and focuses on the role of lift irrigation cooperatives in promoting the development of marginal sections of the village peasantry.

DATA AND DISCUSSION

Now, let us examine the data in order to understand whether the lift irrigation cooperatives are contributing towards promoting social development of the marginalized sections of the rural communities. For the purpose of the present study, the marginalized sections include: (i) lower strata of the village peasantry (marginal and small farmers), (ii) socially underprivileged sections such as OBCs, SCs, NTs (former Nomadic Tribes), and (iii) farmers belonging to religious minorities. The social dimension of development is examined here in the context of getting answers to questions such as: (a) Are lift irrigation co-operatives in the Warana region benefiting the lower strata of the village peasantry? (b) Are they eliciting participation of socially underprivileged sections of the village community in the process of development? (c) Are members of socially underprivileged sections of the village community able to occupy positions of power in the management (i.e. body of board of directors) of lift irrigation co-operatives? And, (d) are the members satisfied with the functioning of lift irrigation cooperatives? The data are presented and analysed and discussed below.

Social development is linked to economic development. Due to the water resources made available by the LICSs, beneficiary farmers' income from agriculture has increased. The data on this aspect were collected from both the secretary respondents and beneficiary farmers themselves. Overall, the range of increase in the income of farmers judged and reported by an overwhelming majority (48 or 84.2 per cent) of the secretary respondents is between 50 to 100 per cent. Similarly, after beneficiary farmers started getting water for their farms they have started cultivating cash crops (mainly sugar cane) and consequently all of them have reported increase in their income. As the data collected from farmer beneficiaries revealed, in case of an overwhelming majority (482 or 75 per cent), there is increase in income which is twice the income that they were getting before the establishment of lift irrigation cooperatives. It should be noted here that this is a very general assessment of the rise in agricultural income without taking into account the trend of rising expenditure on agricultural inputs. However, the general trend of increased agricultural income is indicative of the fact that the lift irrigation cooperatives in the region are contributing to the economic betterment of the beneficiaries.

LICSs and Lower Strata of the Village Peasantry

The study of landholding pattern will provide insights into the category of farmers which are benefiting from the lift irrigation co-operatives. Therefore, let us look at the data relating to the distribution of beneficiaries according to the landholding pattern in terms of (a) total land owned by them, (b) their total land under irrigation, and (c) total land in the command areas of lift irrigation cooperatives.

Beneficiary Farmers: Family Landholding Pattern

The data relating to the total land owned by the respondents' families are classified and presented in the Table 14.1.

The data presented in Table 14.1 clearly reveals that in terms of total family landholding, the majority (359 or 56.5 per cent) of the beneficiary farmers of the lift irrigation cooperatives belong to the category of marginal farmers, followed by those belonging to the category of small farmers (182 or 28.7 per cent). The proportion of middle and big farmers is comparatively less (9.9 and 4.9 per cent, respectively). Thus, taken together, majority of the beneficiaries of the lift irrigation cooperatives in the Warana region constitute marginal and small farmers.

Beneficiary Farmers: Family Land under Irrigation

The analysis of social background may be more realistic if we consider the family land under irrigation. In the present study, the data relating to the family land under irrigation were also collected.[1] For classification of the respondents under the present study, farmers having irrigated land up to 1 acre are considered as marginal farmers; those having

TABLE 14.1: DISTRIBUTION OF THE RESPONDENTS ACCORDING TO THE TOTAL LAND OWNED BY THE THEIR FAMILIES

Total Land Owned	Category of Farmers	Frequency	Per cent
Up to 2.5 acres (up to 1 ha.)	Marginal farmers	359	56.5
2.5+ acres to 5 acres (1.1 to 2 ha.)	Small farmers	182	28.7
5+ to 10 acres (2.1 to 4 ha.)	Medium farmers	63	9.9
10 and above acres (above 4 ha.)	Big farmers	31	4.9
	Total	635	100.0

irrigated land between 1.1 and 2.5 acres are treated as small farmers; those having irrigated land of more than 2.5 but up to 7.5 acres are considered as medium farmers; and those having irrigated land above 7.5 acres are considered as big farmers. The data are presented in Table 14.2.

The data presented in Table 14.2 reveals that among the beneficiaries of lift irrigation cooperatives, small farmers constitute the single largest category (235 or 37.0 per cent) followed by the category of marginal farmers (29.6 per cent). The rest are divided between medium (26.9 per cent) and big farmers (6.5 per cent). Taken together, majority (66.6 per cent) of the farmers constitute marginal and small farmers, the lower section of the village peasantry.

Beneficiary Farmers: Landholding Pattern in the Command Areas of Lift Irrigation Cooperatives

The data regarding the land that is owned by the beneficiaries in the command areas of respective lift irrigation cooperative schemes are presented in Table 14.3.

TABLE 14.2: DISTRIBUTION OF RESPONDENTS ACCORDING TO THE FAMILY LAND UNDER IRRIGATION

Family Land Under Irrigation	Category of Farmers	Frequency	Per cent
Less than 1 acre	Marginal farmers	188	29.6
1 Acre to 2.5 acres	Small farmers	235	37.0
2.5+ to 7.5 acres	Medium farmers	171	26.9
7.5 and above acres	Big farmers	41	6.5
	Total	635	100.0

TABLE 14.3: RESPONDENTS' DISTRIBUTION ACCORDING TO THE LANDHOLDING CATEGORIES IN THE COMMAND AREAS

Land Size Categories	Category of Farmers	Frequency	Per cent
Less than 1 acre	Marginal farmers	281	44.3
1+ acre to 2.5 acres	Small farmers	226	35.6
2.5+ to 7.5 acres	Medium farmers	113	17.8
7.5 and above acres	Big farmers	15	2.4
Total		635	100.0

Looking at the land-holding categories, the data presented in Table 14.3 clearly shows that marginal farmers constitute the single largest category (44.3 per cent) among the respondents, followed by small farmers (35.6 per cent). The proportion of medium and big farmers among the beneficiaries is relatively less (17.8 and 2.4 per cent, respectively). Thus, the benefits generated by the lift irrigation co-operatives in terms of availability and access to the water resources are being shared by all the sections of village peasantry having land in the command areas of respective irrigation cooperatives. It needs to be underscored that among the beneficiaries, the proportion of lower sections of the peasantry is much higher as compared to medium and big farmers.

An important finding that emerges from the study of landholding pattern of the farmer beneficiaries of lift irrigation cooperatives [in terms of: (a) total land owned by them, (b) their total family land under irrigation, and (c) their total land in the command areas of their lift irrigation cooperatives] is that the bulk of the beneficiaries consist of marginal and small farmers. These farmers constitute the lower strata of the village peasantry. Therefore, it is safe to conclude that the lift irrigation cooperatives have enabled the lower strata of village peasantry to have an access to water resources. The LICSs have paved the opportunities for their agricultural development, and therefore, they are promoting social development.

LICSs and Socially Underprivileged Sections of the Village Community

Among the variables relating to the social background of individuals in rural society, the study of caste/community background occupies central importance in sociological analysis. This is so because the institution of caste is pervasive, powerful and a distinctive feature of the Indian social structure. More often than not, an individual's social status and opportunities and access to developmental inputs are structurally conditioned by the prevailing caste hierarchy. Social development implies participation of socially underprivileged sections of the village community in the process of development. In order to understand to which social categories are benefiting from LICSs a study of the social background of beneficiaries in terms of their caste/community is important. In the Indian society, the castes and communities classified as OBCs, SCs, STs, NTs and minorities are generally considered the socially underprivileged sections of society.[2]

Therefore, let us see whether the lift irrigation cooperatives in the Warana region are eliciting participation of socially underprivileged sections of the village community in the process of rural development. This can be seen by examining the caste/community-wise distribution of the beneficiaries and the proportion of beneficiaries belonging to OBCs, SCs, STs, NTs and minority communities among them.[3] The caste/community-wise distribution of the beneficiaries is presented in Table 14.4.

The data presented in Table 14.4 reveals that the respondents belong to 26 different castes/communities. An overwhelming majority (432 or 68.0 per cent) of the beneficiaries belong to the Maratha caste. It is not surprising because the Marathas constitute the numerically preponderant, landowning and cultivating caste in this region. Among other castes having relatively more representation, are Brahmins and Mahars (4.7 per cent each) followed by Dhangars (20 or 3.1 per cent) and Lingayats (16 or 2.5 per cent). Among the beneficiaries, Muslim and Jain minority communities constitute another significant category (29 or 4.6 per cent and 24 or 3.8 per cent, respectively). The rest of the respondents belonging to different castes have less than 2 per cent representation in the sample.

TABLE 14.4: DISTRIBUTION OF THE RESPONDENTS ACCORDING TO THEIR CASTE/COMMUNITY BACKGROUND

Sr. No.	Caste/ Community	Frequency	Per cent	Sr. No.	Caste/ Community	Frequency	Per cent
1	Maratha	432	68.0	14	Shimpi	3	.5
2	Brahmin	30	4.7	15	Koli	2	.3
3	Mahar	30	4.7	16	Gosavi	2	.3
4	Muslim	29	4.6	17	Gondhali	2	.3
5	Jain	24	3.8	18	Teli	2	.3
6	Dhangar	20	3.1	19	Hanbar	1	.2
7	Lingayat	16	2.5	20	Gurav	1	.2
8	Chambhar	11	1.7	21	Ramoshi	1	.2
9	Mali	6	.9	22	Sutar	1	.2
10	Mang	5	.8	23	Koshti	1	.2
11	Nhavi	5	.8	24	Gavandi	1	.2
12	Kumbhar	4	.6	25	Sonar	1	.2
13	Parit	3	.5	26	Sali	1	.2
			Total			635	100.0

It is important to note that along with the numerically dominant cultivating Maratha caste, farmers belonging to almost all castes and minority communities having land in the command areas of lift irrigation cooperatives have become beneficiaries of the cooperatives. This indicates that the LICSs do not discriminate on the basis of caste or religion while recruiting members. The beneficiaries get water based on their rights in land. Table 14.5 presents the classification of respondents in terms of caste categories to which they belong.

The data presented in Table 14.5 reveals that among the beneficiaries, those belonging to the upper/savarna caste category are numerically predominant (75.3 per cent). However, it is also significant to note that farmers having land in the command areas of lift irrigation co-operatives and belonging to minority communities (8.5 per cent), SCs (7.2 per cent), OBCs (4.9 per cent), and NTs (4.1 per cent) have become beneficiaries. Thus, lift irrigation cooperatives in the region have enabled the members of underprivileged sections of rural communities to have an access to water resources. To the extent they are contributing to the development of socially underprivileged sections of the rural community, the lift irrigation cooperatives can be seen as promoting social development in the rural areas where they are operating.

Representation of Underprivileged Sections in the Management of Lift Irrigation Cooperatives

The power to manage water distribution and lift irrigation cooperatives rests with the elected (in some cases selected by consensus) body of board of directors of the cooperatives. Let us now see the extent to which the lift irrigation cooperatives in the Warana region are giving

TABLE 14.5: DISTRIBUTION OF BENEFICIARY FARMERS ACCORDING TO THEIR CASTE/COMMUNITY CATEGORY

Caste/Community Category	Frequency	Per cent
Upper/Savarna Castes	478	75.3
OBCs	31	4.9
SC	46	7.2
NTs	26	4.1
Minorities	54	8.5
Total	635	100.0

opportunity to socially underprivileged/weaker sections of the village community to participate in the management functions. This can be seen by looking at the proportion of their representation in the board of directors of irrigation cooperatives on positions such as directors, vice-chairman or chairman.[4]

The data on this aspect were collected through the questionnaire. The data relating to the 14 sampled LICSs included in the study are presented in Table 14.6. The data reveals that the 14 lift irrigation cooperative schemes had 14 positions of chairman, 14 positions of vice-chairman and 117 positions of members of board of directors, thus making a total of 145 positions of power.

If we look at the caste-wise distribution of these positions, it can be seen that out of the 14 positions of chairman, 11 (78.6 per cent) positions were occupied by persons belonging to the upper caste category, 2 (14.3 per cent) by the members belonging to minority communities, and 1 (7.1 per cent) by the SC community. Among the persons occupying the position of vice-chairman, there were 10 (71.4 per cent) belonging to the upper caste category, 2 (14.3 per cent) belonging to the SC category and 2 (14.3 per cent) belonging to the minorities.

TABLE 14.6: BENEFICIARY FARMERS' CASTE/COMMUNITY CATEGORY AND THEIR POSITION IN LIC CROSS-TABULATION

Caste/Community Category	Position in LICSs			
	Chairman	Vice-Chairman	Director	Total
Upper/Savarna castes	11 (78.6%)	10 (71.4%)	79 (67.5%)	100 (69.0%)
OBCs	–	–	1 (0.9%)	1 (0.7%)
SCs	1 (7.1%)	2 (14.3%)	12 (10.3%)	15 (10.3%)
NTs	–	–	8 (6.8%)	8 (5.5%)
Minority communities	2 (14.3%)	2 (14.3%)	17 (14.5%)	21 (14.5%)
Total	14 (100.0%)	14 (100.0%)	117 (100.0%)	145 (100.0%)

Among those who were occupying the position of director, there were 79 (67.5 per cent) persons belonging to the upper caste category, 1 (0.9 per cent) belonging to the OBC category, 12 (10.3 per cent) belonging to the SC category, 8 (6.8 per cent) belonging to the NTs category and 17 (14.5 per cent) belonging to minority communities. Overall, in the power structure of lift irrigation cooperatives, there is domination of persons belonging to the upper caste category (69 per cent), followed by those belonging to minorities (14.5 per cent), SCs (10.3 per cent), NTs (5.5 per cent) and OBCs (0.7 per cent).

The power structure of lift irrigation cooperatives is influenced by both the numerical preponderance of members belonging to different castes/communities and caste-wise landholding pattern in the command areas of these lift irrigation cooperatives. The domination of upper caste category persons, particularly Marathas, is not surprising because they are the numerically dominant, cultivating and landowning caste. Yet, it needs to be pointed out that persons belonging to all other caste categories have got space in the power structure of the lift irrigation cooperatives. Thus, the lift irrigation cooperatives in the Warana region have given opportunity to the socially underprivileged sections (such as SCs, OBCs, NTs, and minorities) of the village community to occupy positions of power (31 per cent positions) and to participate in the management of the cooperatives. In this sense, they are replacing traditional primordial hierarchical relations and promoting social development, which ensures participation of representatives belonging to weaker sections of the village community. Bokil's (1996: 42-7) case study of a Vishwambhar lift irrigation cooperative located in western Maharashtra has also pointed out that a Dalit member could become the vice-president of that cooperative due to his own merit and socialization of other leaders in the cooperative movement, which teaches lessons of politics of compromise and development.

Respondents' Assessment of the Functioning of the LICSs

In order to have an insight into the functioning of the lift irrigation cooperatives, respondents' responses were elicited regarding whether they get sufficient quantity of water for their crops, whether they get timely supply of water, whether there is a feeling of discrimination among them regarding water distribution and to what extent they are satisfied with the present system of water distribution. Let us look at the major findings in this regard.

An overwhelming majority (84.7 per cent) of the respondents reported that they get sufficient quantity of water from the cooperatives. The responses also revealed that majority (79.2 per cent) of the farmer beneficiaries get timely supply of water for their crops.

An impressive majority, 518 or 81.6 per cent of the respondents do not feel that there is discrimination in water distribution. Another set of data made it clear that an overwhelming majority (88.7 per cent) of the respondents had never launched any complaints regarding unfair distribution of water, indirectly indicating that they do not find any serious discrimination or injustice in the water distribution mechanism. In all the lift irrigation cooperatives, water is distributed among the member and non-member beneficiaries using the rotation method. The analysis of responses clearly revealed that those 'fully satisfied' with the present system of distribution of water constitute the single largest category (420 or 66.1 per cent) among the beneficiaries.

Yet, not all is well with the functioning of lift irrigation cooperatives. There are financial problems, lack of maintenance of the pipelines and resultant leakage of water, irregular supply of electricity disturbing rotation of water supply, untrained and inefficient staff, occasional favouritism in water distribution, over-use of water resources by some farmers, non-supply of water to some farmer members in the command areas due to non-availability of sufficient branch pipelines and political factionalism. However, the existence of problems in lift irrigation cooperatives does not undermine the positive trends of socio-economic change that these cooperatives have set in, in the larger context of social development in rural areas.

MAJOR FINDINGS AND CONCLUDING REMARKS

Let us summarize the major findings noted above. The lift irrigation cooperatives in the western Maharashtra region: (a) have been contributing to the economic betterment of the beneficiaries, (b) have enabled lower strata of village peasantry to have an access to water resources and paved the opportunities for their agricultural development, (c) do not discriminate on the basis of caste or religion while recruiting their members, (d) have enabled the members of underprivileged sections of rural communities—such as OBCs, SCs, NTs and minorities—to have an access to developmental input in the form of water resources, and (e) could be seen as institutions ensuring distributive justice in the context of water distribution among the resource-rich and resource-poor sections of the village community.

It may be pointed out that the beneficiaries are getting water resources made available by the LICSs on the basis of their rights on land, and therefore, increase in their agricultural incomes may be in direct proportion to the size of the land owned by the different beneficiaries. Yet, the real significance of the lift irrigation cooperatives lies in making available the developmental inputs in the form of water resources to the resource-poor lower sections of the peasantry and the socially underprivileged sections of village community, which was otherwise impossible due to the lack of individual assets. On the basis of the data, analysis and findings presented above, we may conclude as follows:

Firstly, the cooperative lift irrigation schemes are contributing to changing the traditional asymmetrical relationships between groups based on ascriptive criteria such as caste or religion. The formal relationships based on the membership of LICSs that these cooperatives have established are not asymmetrical. Therefore, it can be said that there is no discrimination in the LICSs on the basis of ascriptive criteria such as caste or religion and in this sense they are promoting social development.

Secondly, the lift irrigation cooperatives are promoting non-exploitative relationships or relationships based on equality among their members. As mentioned earlier, equality in the context of lift irrigation cooperatives refers to the distributive aspects of goods produced, i.e. equality in distribution of water resources made available and a shift from private ownership of the water resources towards collective ownership. In the present context, the extent of freedom from exploitation refers to the degree of access to available water resources to the individual members of the LICSs based on their rights on land. As the data reveal, majority of the members of lift irrigation cooperatives do not feel that there is discrimination in water distribution and they get water in sufficient quantity when it is required. Therefore, it can be said that the lift irrigation cooperatives are promoting social development.

Thirdly, social development implies that there should not be oppression of one group by another. More generally, powerful groups tend to oppress less powerful ones. The management of lift irrigation cooperatives is basically a democratic power structure since it is made up of a body of elected members. We have noted that the farmers belonging to the lower strata of the village peasantry and those belonging to the socially underprivileged sections have also occupied seats of power within the cooperative power structures. As such, there is less likelihood of oppression of one group by the other in these member-controlled cooperatives.[5] Therefore, it can be said that the lift irrigation cooperatives are promoting social development.

In short, to the extent that lift irrigation cooperatives are contributing to eliciting participation of the lower strata of the village peasantry and socially underprivileged sections of the rural community in the process of development and have created space for them in the power structures of their management system, they could be seen as promoting social development in the rural areas of south-western Maharashtra where they are operating.

NOTES

1. The total land (irrigated) that the respondents' families own may not be in the command areas of the LICSs. Some part of the irrigated area may be in other areas and under well irrigation.
2. The Jain community is a religious minority; therefore, while classifying the respondents on the basis of their caste/community background Jains are included under the category of minorities. However, this community is not considered as underprivileged in this region as in the case of some other communities.
3. However, it is important to note that, only those farmers may have opportunity to become beneficiaries of these cooperatives who own land in the command areas of lift irrigation cooperatives. Hence, it is clear that the caste-wise landholding pattern in the command areas of the lift irrigation cooperatives will have decisive influence on the social composition of the beneficiaries.
4. As per the bye-laws that govern cooperatives, there is a provision of reservation of seats for different categories such as women, backward castes and economically weaker sections. The number of reserved seats depends on the total number of members on the board of directors. This institutionalized mechanism has also contributed to ensure participation of weaker sections in the power structure of cooperative bodies.
5. Dore has made a distinction between member-controlled cooperatives and techno-bureaucratic organizations disguised as cooperatives. The member-controlled cooperatives are characterized by what he calls 'institutionalization of suspicion'. This refers to the built-in checks and balances and the periodic re-election of officers. They are also governed by certain rules of accountability, in the sense that the administrators and

elected office-bearers are answerable to the general body of members. Member-controlled cooperatives are managed by leaders elected by their shareholders (Baviskar, 1980: 2-4).

REFERENCES

Baviskar, B.S. (1980), *The Politics of Development*, New Delhi: Oxford University Press, pp. 2-4.

Bokil, Milind (1996), 'Collective Management of Water Resources in Rural Development: A Sociological Study of Two Patterns of Lift Irrigation' (in Marathi), in *Samajshastra Sanshodhan Patrika,* A journal of Marathi Samajshastra Parishad, vol. 5, March 1996, pp. 42-6.

Deshpande, V.V. (1998), 'Farmers' Participation in Land and Water Management', in S.N. Pawar and R.B. Patil (eds.), *Sociology of Environment,* Jaipur: Rawat.

Dhanagare, D.N. (1996), 'Development Process and Environmental Problems' (in Marathi), *Samajshtra Sanshodhan Patrika*, vol. 5, March 1996, pp. 7-19.

Government of Maharashtra, (2000), Cooperative Movement at a Glance in Maharashtra, A 35th Issue of the Report, Commissioner for Co-operatives and Registrar of Cooperative Societies, Maharashtra State, Pune Division, Pune, pp. 70-3.

Mukherji, Partha N. (1989), 'Development Dilemmas: Towards a Conceptualisation of Social Development', in P.N. Pimpley, K.P. Singh, and A. Mahajan (eds.), *Social Development: Processes and Consequences,* Jaipur: Rawat, pp. 26-39.

Srivastava, S.P. (1998), 'Social Development Discourse: Dimensions and Directions', in S.P. Srivastava (ed.), *The Development Debate: Critical Perspectives,* Jaipur: Rawat, pp. 70-87.

Salunkhe, Sarjerao (1998), 'Water Management Through Cooperatives: A Case', in S.N. Pawar and R.B. Patil (eds.), *Sociology of Environment*, Jaipur: Rawat.

_____ (2006), 'Co-operatives and Socially Sustainable Rural Development: A Case of Lift Irrigation Cooperatives in Western Maharashtra', in *Indian Co-Operative Review*, vol. 43, no. 3, January 2006, pp. 618-38.

CHAPTER 15

Role of Corporate and Community Partnerships in Social Development

RITAMBHARA MALAVIYA

THE PHENOMENA OF MARGINALIZATION AND EMERGENCE OF CORPORATE SOCIAL RESPONSIBILITY

Historically, the developed countries of the world have prospered at the cost of the developing and the least developed countries, something vividly illustrated in the history of colonialism. The European countries exploited the resource base of their colonies for increasing their profits, and proceeded with the inhuman practice of using slaves for producing surplus. Even after gaining Independence, these post-colonial and semi-colonial countries continued to be exploited due to unjust terms of trade imposed on them. Subsequently, the World Trade Organization (WTO) became a forum where the least developed states, because of their low bargaining power and weak economic clout could not defend their interests. In the WTO member states took positions to defend the interests of their influential corporate sector, while the concerns of the marginalized communities of these countries were neither raised nor heard. The developing economies like India and Brazil energetically bargained for getting the concerns of their big corporate houses reflected, while the small-scale industries and vulnerable sections of the economy were the losers in the process.

Marginalization at the international level is manifested in various policies and actions of the developed countries. These countries consider the developing and poor countries as their dumping yard to which they can source all the hazardous activities (Table 15.1). The British company Thor Chemicals became notorious for attempting to use its South African subsidiary to 'recycle' mercury. David Fig

TABLE 15.1: HAZARDOUS WASTE EXPORT SCHEMES BY OECD COUNTRIES AND RECEIVING NON-OECD REGION, 1989-94

Exporting OECD Country		Receiving Non-OECD Region							
	Volume of Waste Generated (1000 tons)	Africa	Pacific	East Asia	South-East Asia	South Asia	Middle East	Latin America	Total
Australia	426	0	0	13	13	6	0	0	32
Austria	550	1	0	0	1	0	1	1	4
Belgium	776	1	0	0	0	0	0	1	2
Canada	5,896	0	0	28	4	5	0	0	37
Denmark	250	0	0	0	0	0	0	2	2
Finland	559	0	0	0	0	0	2	0	2
France	7,000	1	0	0	0	0	0	0	1
Germany	9,100	1	0	1	9	4	0	9	24
Italy	2,708	2	0	0	0	0	0	2	4
Japan	n.a.	0	1	1	0	0	0	2	4
Luxembourg	180	0	0	0	0	0	0	0	0
Netherlands	1,520	0	0	0	1	0	0	0	1
New Zealand	110	0	2	0	0	0	0	0	2
Norway	500	0	0	0	1	0	0	1	2
Spain	1,708	0	0	0	0	0	0	0	0
Sweden	440	0	0	0	0	0	0	0	0
Switzerland	854	2	0	0	0	0	0	2	4
UK	1,844	16	0	20	31	15	11	15	98
USA	213,620	8	8	31	24	14	0	109	194
Total	248,041	22	11	94	84	44	14	144	413

Source: Adapted by Adeola (2001) from: (1) UNDP Human Development Report, 1998, and (2) The Greenpeace, Database of Hazardous Waste Trade Export Schemes from OECD to Non-OECD Countries (1989-94).

points out, 'Poor storage of the irrecoverable mercury had resulted in deaths, comas, brain damage and other forms of mercury poisoning to on-site workers and downstream residents' (Fig, 2005: 602). The motives of the developed countries are far from innocent, as can be inferred from a comment by Lawrence Summers, who while at the World Bank said, 'Just between you and me, shouldn't the World

Bank be encouraging more migration of dirty industries to the LDCs? . . . I think the economic logic behind dumping a load of toxic waste in the lowest wage country is impeccable and we should face up to that . . .' (cited in Kovel, 2002: 76).

The developing and the least developed countries have many communities which could never be properly integrated into the development process of their economies. The ever expanding capitalist state has pushed such communities to the periphery, wherein they find themselves marginalized—economically, socially and politically. Furthermore, globalization has created a global space of exploitation and extended the reach of many gigantic monopolies into the domains of the local. These communities have been impoverished due to the irresponsible practises of the MNCs, which have ruined the lives and livelihoods of the people. The poverty and underdevelopment have been further worsened by the civil wars and accompanying famines. A number of incidents highlighted the compliance of corporations in human rights violations and denial of access to resources to the people and brought to the fore gross cases of corruption, tax evasion and violation of labour rights. Corporate irresponsibility has increasingly come to limelight in cases like the leakage of military industrial complex (MIC) in Bhopal (India) due to the criminal negligence of Union Carbide, oil spills by Exxon Valdez, and pharmaceutical companies' bid to block the import of cheap generic AIDS medicines by South Africa. It might be pointed out that Nigeria had more than 300 oil spills in the early 1990s which far exceeded such accidents in the developed countries (Frynas, 2005: 595).

Wherever the tentacles of the have MNCs extended, they have became the modern 'spaces of death' [Taussig (1984) had described exploitation of colonial people by the Europeans as the creation of 'space of death']. There are numerous examples like the plight of the people of Bougainville islands or the Ogoni people of Nigeria, and similar instances of violence and human rights violations by Africa's oil tycoons and firms like Exxon and Shell. The MNCs which expand into the developing countries do so, not for charity, but because of benefits like cheap labour, raw material and due to the lax implementation of labour and environmental standards in these countries.

The extractive nature of the activities of the MNCs converts the mineral-rich areas into zones of exploitation and plunder. While various industrialized and technologically advanced countries are engaged in a 'scramble for Africa', the people of Africa have found their lives and livelihoods at stake. A Bharat Petroleum engineer who visited an oil town in Nigeria in 1990 remarked: 'I have explored for oil in Venezuela, I have explored for oil in Kuwait, I have never seen an oil-rich town as completely impoverished as Oloibiri' (Greenpeace International, 1994: 14, cited in Eweje, 2006: 111). Wilson Akpan (2006) shows how the mining companies in Nigeria were responsible for the growth in informal settlements in proximate areas because of their insistence on having single sex hostels. It was found that single sex hostels were responsible for labour unrest, lower productivity of labour and HIV/AIDS. Yet companies considered provision of housing facilities as an unnecessary burden, something which is reflected in the statement of a company executive in Nigeria: 'We're in the business of mining, not housing' (cited in Hamann, 2004: 285).

The worldwide resentment and anger over the irresponsible behaviour of business led to an urgent need for the business to salvage its image. The chaos which resulted from the unrestricted activities of the corporates led to the building up of a strong resistance against the irresponsible practises of business. On the one hand militant movements of the people of developing countries threatened the activities of these MNCs, and on the other a worldwide movement against globalization gained strength. It is under these circumstances that Corporate Social Responsibility (CSR) emerged as a buzzword among the corporate houses which wished to manage the global opinion within the framework of the open market economy. It is paradoxical that the CSR agenda purports to help the marginalized and the vulnerable when the responsibility for their marginalization rests with these corporations.

The neo-liberal market economy which has stripped the state of all its welfare functions espouses the concept of CSR, purportedly to fill the void created by the withdrawal of the state. Yet the underlying motive is to wrest the state of all its responsibilities to distributive justice so that business is allowed to proceed unchecked and unhindered in reaping maximum profits. The agenda of bypassing the state is more than evident when corporate houses tend to replace laws and international conventions by codes of conduct and voluntary standard setting and reporting initiatives. The state is expected to keep away from regulating the corporate activities and private agencies are encouraged to take its place:

> Thus, the sphere of private law is extending to the detriment of public law not only in the choice of instruments, but also in the one of their control. The regulating power of the public authorities is being dismantled that way. This strengthens the evolution in which the neoliberal logic is imposed. Behind the social labels and codes of conduct, certification agencies are coming increasingly to the fore. (Fonteneau, 2003: 4)

David Sadler (2004) points out that the UN International Code of Conduct on Transnational Corporations which was proposed in the 1970s and 1980s had to be abandoned in favour of a CSR which favoured voluntary action because of the pressure of the corporate houses. CSR is a ploy used by corporations for precluding mandatory regulation of their activities. It is an intelligent device to bypass corporate accountability or 'compliance with state-sponsored regulations and standards' (Hamann and Acutt, 2003: 257). Voluntary codes and charters give the impression that the corporate houses are doing enough, while they continue with their irresponsible practices without fear of being coerced into mending their ways. While organizations like the Global Reporting Initiative (GRI) have recommended that companies get independent verification of reports done, Haslam points out that externally verifiable reporting in Latin America comes to only 4 per cent of the global share (Haslam, 2007: 292). Garrett Brown, an occupational health and safety professional, did extensive fieldwork in Latin America and Asia and categorically stated, 'The experience over the last decade with "operationalizing" corporate social responsibility beyond glossy annual reports indicates very little tangible progress has been made' (Brown, 2005, cited in Senser, 2007). A study of seven Asian countries found that only 2 per cent of the companies in Asia had dedicated CSR reporting, which shows the gross inadequacy of such voluntary measures (Table 15.2). CSR is a brand building tactic which builds reputation and customer loyalty while companies' commitment to it remains thin. It is used as a strategy by companies to '. . . proactively anticipate and deter draconian governmental regulations; exploit opportunities arising from increasing levels of cultural, environmental, and sexual awareness; and differentiate their products from their less socially responsible competitors' (Jones, 1996: 27-8)

TABLE 15.2: PROPORTION OF COMPANIES WITH DEDICATED CSR REPORT IN ASIA

Country	Dedicated CSR Report (%)
India	2
South Korea	8
Thailand	0
Singapore	2
Malaysia	4
The Philippines	0
Indonesia	0
Seven Country Mean	*2*

Source: Chambers et al., 2003: 12.

CSR is defined by the World Business Council for Sustainable Development as the 'continuing commitment by business to behave ethically and contribute to economic development while improving the quality of life of the workforce and their families as well as of the local community and society at large' (WBCSD 1999: 5). CSR comprises voluntary commitments by companies for promoting good governance, sound business practises, sustainable development, poverty reduction and for reducing human rights violations and corruption.

CSR: CLAIMS AND REALITIES

Corporate claims do not always correspond to reality. The commitments to CSR remain only lip service. The corporate spending on CSR also remains meagre despite the tall claims. David Sadler (2004) takes note of the fact that in 2003 the top 100 companies in the UK contributed a mere 0.8 per cent of their profits to philanthropic work, which constitutes an increase of two to three times over the spending in 2000-1. David Fig (2005) notes how the big companies and MNCs go scot-free even after committing serious crimes and violating norms of sustainability. There have been numerous such cases where the firms were absolved of all responsibility for pollution and for abusing the health of workers. Fig gives the example of Cape Plc. which took no responsibility of rehabilitation of the victims of asbestosis who got affected due to the activities of that firm. Iscor was similarly not held responsible for groundwater pollution which affected the communities around the Vanderbijlpark steel mills in South Africa. Even in case of problems which seem to get the bulk of corporate attention, the CSR efforts seem insufficient. Fig recognizes that the response of the industry to the HIV/AIDS pandemic is highly insufficient. According to a survey, there is a 'lack of wholesale and comprehensive engagement by even the largest companies on this matter, and even in the most affected areas, such as South Africa' (Bendell, 2003, cited in Jenkins 2005: 537).

Firms adopt various voluntary codes of conduct and reporting systems like the principles of the UN Global Compact, Global Reporting Initiative, AA1000 standard and Global Sullivan Principles. Yet figure notes that standards setting is no answer to problems and certification is granted to companies which continue to carry on violations of human rights and environmental standards. A good example is Eskom (based in South Africa), which enjoys the membership of the Global Compact despite being 'the country's worst polluters, undertaking massive industrial burning of low-quality coal and production of nuclear waste in its power stations' (Fig, 2005: 612). Christian Aid studied three cases of CSR adopted by Shell in Nigeria, British American Tobacco in Kenya and Brazil and Coca-Cola in Kerala, India (Christian Aid, 2004). The report points out that 'Shell's clean up of oil spills and repair of pipelines in Nigeria is scandalously inadequate and would never be tolerated in Europe or North America' (Christian Aid, 2004: 23). According to the report four community development projects financed by Shell and two by the Niger Delta Development Corporation were non-functional. Undemocratic coercive apparatus like mobile police was also being used to give protection to the activities of oil companies. It also found that tobacco cultivation done in farms contracted by the British American Tobacco was hazardous for the health of the farmers and little was being done to redress the situation by this company. Similarly in Kerala ground water depletion in an already water stressed area is associated with the activities of the Coco-Cola plant. A similar study done by Wilson Akpan (2006) in Nigeria also refers to the futility of voluntary measures. In Nigeria weak laws like the Petroleum Act merely require corporations to adopt precautionary measures against land and water pollution. In case the measures fail then it recommends prompt steps to mitigate the impact of pollution. Yet no punitive measures or sanctions are mentioned in the Act and so the oil producing corporations either get off scot-free or under the impact of strong protests determine unilaterally the amount of compensation to be paid.

Even in cases where some promises have been delivered, they are merely designed to hoodwink people to the more serious problems caused by that company: 'it is likely that the examples presented in the reports are the best practices or indeed "showcases" and that the consequences of Multinational Enterprise (MNE) behaviour are not always so beneficial in other circumstances' (Fortanier and Kolk, 2007: 18). Similarly Hamann and Acutt suggest '. . . business may be making only partial, superficial or image-related changes to give the impression that it is accommodating social interests' (Hamann and Acutt, 2003: 258). Community projects are often a means of maintaining a stable working environment and many such initiatives are left incomplete when the objective is achieved. This happened in Nigeria where Shell Petroleum Development Company provided development budget for a particular community when a pipeline was under construction and cut-off the assistance as soon as the project was completed. Oil companies were also found to publicize schemes which often did not exist or were partially functional. Frynas (2005) gives the example of Shell in Nigeria which had taken out a brochure in 1996 to advertise its rural electrification scheme in the Kolo Creek flowstation, yet on a visit to the site the author found that the scheme had not materialized: 'In Nigeria, the author witnessed many non-functioning white elephants, including unfinished buildings designed to be health clinics or schools, water projects where the water was unfit for consumption, or projects such as health clinics which lacked light, running water, basic equipment or staff' (Frynas, 2005: 587). Frynas ascribes it to the motives of the corporations which see development not as a social obligation but as a business opportunity. He cites a leaked independent audit of 2001 which had been commissioned by Shell:

> less than one-third of Shell's development projects in Nigeria were fully successful in the sense that they were functional. The audit found that Shell was still essentially trying to buy off the local people with gifts rather than trying to offer them genuine development; this followed the logic of using CSR to maintain a stable working environment and improve perceptions of Shell. (Frynas, 2005: 587)

CSR does not attempt to check irresponsible practises like tax evasion. The euphoria created by the little amount of work which corporates undertake successfully veils the fact that it is corporate profiteering, at the cost of common people's interest, which is to be blamed for poverty and inequality. Jenkins comments on how 'The current CSR agenda is as significant for what it does not include as for what it does. Corporate practices such as transfer pricing, tax avoidance or the abuse of market power are not part of the CSR mainstream . . . CSR has not explicitly dealt with the poverty impacts of business activities' (Jenkins, 2005: 528). He points out that poverty reduction or equity are not taken as criteria for assessing companies even in initiatives like the UN Global Compact. Jenkins discusses how the payment of taxes is considered less important than environmental and labour issues in the CSR policies. He discusses an OECD study which covered 246 codes of corporate conduct wherein labour standards and environmental issues were covered by 148 and 145 codes respectively and taxation by only one.

CSR in many developing countries is a mere tool for extracting concessions from governments of these countries. Frynas (2005) gives the example of Angola where Chevron Texaco used its social responsibility initiatives as a means of getting its oil stakes renewed and extended. Aid and social spending is often directed to coffers of corrupt governments and bureaucracies which strengthens their hands in carrying on the undemocratic and corrupt rule. Perhaps, it is power in the hands of people that these corporates fear the most and hence actively promote dummy governments which can play second fiddle to them.

The argument that markets can deliver social benefits is a mere smokescreen to hide the fact that corporate behaviour is universally governed by the considerations of earning maximum profits and not by the wish of conferring social benefits. Milton Friedman (1962) as a theorist of capitalism categorically states that the purpose of business is making money for stakeholders and it could be absurd to discover in it any other social responsibility. Sustainable development and profit maximization seem contradictory—business is business and ethics is ethics and never the twain shall meet. Corporate practices push more and more people to the margins as workers are laid off from factories in the name of cost effectiveness and as the poor and the vulnerable are deprived of their sources of livelihood. Rhys Jenkins (2005) explicates on how FDI in developing countries does not lead to any significant relief to the poor. Jenkins takes the help of the analysis of Alan Winters (2001, cited in Jenkins, 2005) on the impact of trade liberalization on poverty. Winters looks at three prominent channels: the enterprise channel, the distribution channel and the government revenue channel. The enterprise channel, according to Winters, helps people either by providing employment directly, or through creation of demand from the local suppliers. Yet Jenkins notes that FDI creates very little employment opportunities in proportion to the vast number of people who remain unemployed: 'UNCTAD estimated total employment by TNC affiliates in developing countries to be 19 million in 1998. This is a small proportion of the 1,200 million poor people (defined as those living on less than US $1 a day) worldwide' (Jenkins, 2005: 532) As regards the indirect impacts, often MNCs depend on imported raw material, as in the export processing zones and hence there is almost no benefit to the local suppliers.

Secondly, it is claimed that the distribution channel helps lessen poverty by making poor the consumers. Jenkins reviews the argument that fortune can be created at 'the bottom of pyramid' through the promotion of commerce and development. Jenkins does not find many evidence to support this view. He also mentions that having the poor as consumers does not successfully address the problem of poverty. He gives numerous examples—the infant formula promoted by Nestle as a substitute for breast milk was meant for the poor and yet as they were not able to buy sufficient quantities and diluted it with polluted water, it led to malnutrition and diarrhoea. The sale of incense sticks by British American Tobacco in India created difficult competition for the women who used to make them by hand at their homes. While Wal-Mart makes tall claims of its CSR initiatives, yet it is trying to enter the markets of developing countries, which could be devastating for the small-scale retail outlets.

The third channel which is regarded by Winters as instrumental in lessening poverty is the government revenue channel. This argument is based on the reasoning that revenue gains from FDI could be helpful against poverty. Jenkins shows that revenue gains from FDI are limited as governments offer tax holidays to investors and slash taxes and regulations in order to attract FDI. Thus Export Processing Zones (EPZ) and Special Economic Zones are created which benefit the corporations rather than the poor. Tax avoidance and tax evasion also minimize the benefits from FDI. Besides, sustainable development is sacrificed and human rights violated despite the tall claims of various companies.

While companies boast of their concerns for environemnt, the CSR agenda on sustainability is considered a mere 'greenwashing' by critics who argue that companies continue to pollute the environment while claiming in their reports and charters about their environmental commitments. Scholars like Kolk and Pinske (2007) point out that it was because of the opposition of various corporations in the US that it stayed out of the Kyoto process. Thus, Joel Kovel (2002) posits that it is capitalism and its principle of earning maximum profits which is actually the enemy of nature.

CSR is also a façade for covering up the violation of labour rights by the corporate houses. Companies downsize the workforce with impunity for maximizing profits, and even migrate to more profitable destinations after abrupt closures, rendering workers unemployed. Michael Blowfield comments that CSR

> . . . offers certain basic protections to workers, but at the same time indirectly shields companies from any responsibility for the consequences of disinvestment. Furthermore, because labour standards and other similar tools widely used in CSR can be promoted as a voluntary alternative to state regulation and enforcement, there is a possibility that issues ignored by CSR will not be addressed in other ways. (Blowfield, 2005: 517)

Initiatives like Global Reporting Initiative (GRI) have been criticized for limiting trade union activities. A good example is Worldwide Responsible Apparel Production (WRAP), a non-profit organization launched by American Apparel Manufacturers Association (AAMA) for implementing its concerns for 'basic standards that address labor practices, factory conditions, and environmental and customs compliance' (Bendell, 2005: 364). But Bendell finds it guilty of overlooking basic labour rights like working hours, minimum wage, maternity leave for women and their rights against harassment and even the right to freedom of association.

The real face of corporate houses is reflected in the massive MIC which fuels wars and conflicts throughout the world. The ugly face of linkages between war and corporate profiteering became very clear during the war in Iraq in 2003 when the role of corporate giants like Halliburton and Bechtel and the nexus between these corporations, politicians and war was reported. Hannah Griffiths gives the example of BAE Systems. BAE makes big claims of CSR

> but its policies have not prevented BAE from exporting Hawk ground attack aircraft to Indonesia where over 200,000 people were killed in East Timor; or from selling 60 Hawk jets to India at a time when, owing to India's dispute with Pakistan over Kashmir, the region was very unstable; or from exporting to Saudi Arabia whose governmental regime has been described

as having a 'persistent pattern of gross human rights abuses'. (Griffiths, 2005: 225)

CSR AND THE IDEA OF CORPORATE PARTNERSHIP WITH THE CIVIL SOCIETY AND COMMUNITY

Keeping in view the growing opposition from civil society, business has come up with the idea of forging partnerships to co-opt it in their agenda of maintaining the *status quo*. The interface between civil society and business thus manifests itself in two forms. One is confrontation and the other is partnership. It was the confrontation with civil society and their movements which compelled big business to put on a human face. Widespread consumer boycotts were organized against Nike which was buying goods from Indonesian sweat shops. Similarly, the decision by Shell Oil to sink the Brent Spar oil rig in the North Sea fuelled protests led by Green Peace.

Theories about Symbiotic Relationship between Corporations, Civil Society and Community

Interaction between business and civil society sometimes manifests itself in the form of multi-stakeholder partnerships which includes partnership of business organizations with various community groups, civil society and governments. The United Nations Global Compact, with more than 1,800 participating companies, has become the largest corporate citizenship initiative which tries to create partnerships between labour, civil society and corporations. Companies joining the initiative commit to ten principles in areas of human rights, labour standards and environmental sustainability.

Cooperation between business and civil society often breaks down because of the unrelenting attitude of business. A lot of literature on CSR is dedicated to considering the strategies of negotiations between the civil society organizations and business so that a compromise between different interests can be reached. While suggesting the NGOs and civil society organizations to get onto the driving seat of the CSR agenda, Hamman and Acutt (2003) point out that civil society should adopt both positive ('name and praise') and negative ('name and shame') strategies. They explicate on the concept of 'critical cooperation' between civil society and business, which depends on managing both cooperation and conflict in the same relationship. The authors believe that such relationships take shape when both business and civil society, instead of taking recourse to the language of power or rights, negotiate on the basis of interests. They also discuss the concept of 'interest-based (or principled) negotiation' as given by Fisher and Ury (Fisher and Ury, 1981, cited in Hamann and Acutt, 2003: 262). They aver that the basis for the corporate-civil society partnership lies not in 'positional bargaining' but in 'principled negotiations'. In resorting to positional bargaining partners stick to their respective positions which leads to an impasse. In comparison, principled negotiation is regarded as a better strategy. It requires that parties soften their positions and focus on interests and try to find outcomes whereby both the parties benefit. When civil society should engage in negotiating and when it should dissociate, according to Hamann and Acutt, should be determined by Best Alternative to A Negotiated Agreement (BATNA), 'a partnership, or any other form of collaboration, should only be pursued if it would provide benefits greater than would be gained by alternative strategies' (Hamann and Acutt, 2003: 263).

These ideas are based on the theories which regard the relationship between corporates, communities and civil society as symbiotic. The rationale of such partnerships is described by Jones: 'Corporations contribute finance and/or managerial expertise. NGOs give localised know-how, popular support, and publicity' (Jones, 2007: 170). Malawi is a good example of how multi-stakeholder partnerships are being formed by the corporations (Table 15.3). William Frederick (1998) tries to give allegories from nature to explain the corporate-community relationship. In his model corporations and communities are conceptualized as ecosystems whose interface produces mutual benefits. The model is lucidly explained by Deby Lee Casill and Ronald Paul Hill:

> Frederick views corporations as interconnected, energy-transforming bodies that absorb resources from their environments to produce a variety of goods and services that are placed back into the environment. One guiding principle is energy accumulation, which is combined with an energy redistribution principle so that both the wealthy and the masses may survive. In corporate terms, energy accumulation is equivalent to profit seeking; energy redistribution is equivalent to profit sharing. The management challenge is to harmonize profit-seeking and profit-sharing principles so that corporations increase their longevity. . . . (Cassill and Hill, 2007: 287)

This explanation serves to create an impression that it is natural for the processes of capitalist accumulation to result in corporate

TABLE 15.3: MULTI-STAKEHOLDER PARTNERSHIPS IN MALAWI

Type of Partnership	Name of the Campaign/Programme	Programmes
Issue-specific partnership	Satemwa and Me'decins Sans Frontieres (MSF)	Dealing with the impact of HIV/AIDS on the staff of Satemwa and their families
Collective issue-specific partnership	Together Ensuring Children's Security (TECS) between 19 companies and many civil society organizations	Tackling the problem of child labour. Scheme for 'improving localized food security, providing safe water and making access to firewood easier, thus improving the chance that children will receive an education.'
Collective, sustainability-based partnership	Growing sustainable agri-business campaign	Promoting good agricultural practices among farmers

Source: Based on Kambalame and Cleene, 2006.

social responsibility. Yet it is to be noted that the so-called 'energy redistribution' is observed more in violation and the license granted to business for earning maximum profits by economic liberalization and globalization has exacerbated inequalities in the world. It has been estimated that the total wealth of the ten richest people in the world is more than 1.5 times the total income of all the least developed countries (UNDP, 1997). Capitalist globalization which is responsible for such inequalities also propagates the idea of CSR: 'As is, the social responsibility concept and discourse places a Band-Aid over deep capitalist scars' (Jones, 1996: 8). CSR is a method of gaining legitimacy of the society by the corporations. In a similar vein, Hamann and Acutt comment, '. . . it may be argued that the CSR discourse fulfils the crucial function of legitimising the capitalist system and, more specifically, the activities of large-scale corporations' (Hamann and Acutt, 2003: 259). The real purpose of CSR is establishing the hegemony of global capitalism: 'In fact, globalised capitalism wants to impose its options, its conceptions. All societies, all people, all constituted groups must share this consensus without challenging it' (Fonteneau, 2003: 5). Capitalism adopts slogans like CSR to silence its critics by projecting that capitalism has a human face. CSR is more of a safety valve which is used to diffuse protests and discontent—'The aim is to arrive at a smooth society without conflicts, the values, criteria of which are those of the market' (Fonteneau, 2003: 6). It is touted that capitalist development lifts all boats. However, various studies and reports point out that the processes of capitalism strengthen monopolies at the cost of the interest of the common people. Thus Jones writes, 'The social responsibility discourse contributes to the ideological hegemony in which contemporary institutional arrangements are depicted as serving the general interest, whereas they in fact serve the interests of a relatively small minority' (Jones, 1996: 33).

Another theory which has gained immense popularity in CSR literature is the stakeholder theory. This theory holds that corporations are responsible for and should look after the interests of the stakeholders rather than the entire society. A corporate stakeholder is defined by Wesley Cragg as 'any individual or group likely to be affected either positively or negatively, in the short or long term, by corporate activities, policies or decisions' (Cragg, 2001: 6). The stakeholder theory, like the ecosystems theory of William Frederick, points towards a symbiotic relationship between business and community: 'From this inclusive perspective, the corporation exists at the intersection of a range of interests; it is a node in a complex web of social relationships of dependency and expectation' (Eweje, 2006: 100). The relationship between various stakeholders has been described as mutually beneficial. Jones observes that 'In the most analysed partnership schemes, between local government bodies and private firms, reciprocity is referred to as "synergy", differential benefits are claimed to accrue such as profitability for firms, additional social gains for public bodies' constituents or communities' (Jones 2007: 170). The consultation exercise is regarded as nothing less than a new paradigm: 'CSR is seen to express a new relationship between private capital and the public interest. The notion of partnerships is based on the belief in common interests and "win-win solutions"' (Hamann and Acutt, 2003: 256). Yet this rainbow vocabulary hides the reality of such partnership arrangements which are basically designed to buy-off dissenters. The Mining, Minerals, and Sustainable Development (MMSD) report warns, 'Win-win solutions are not always possible; voluntary approaches alone are insufficient where there is a compelling priority but little or no business case to justify the additional expenditures needed to meet it' (MMSD, 2002: xxiii, cited in Hamann, 2004: 279). The arrogance and size of the business partners also ensures that their interest prevails. Such a theory also serves the purpose of giving business an opportunity to shirk its broader accountability to society by selecting a few stakeholders as beneficiaries. Bakker et al. (2005) point out how the scope of CSR has been narrowed down over time—a shift from the emphasis on society to an emphasis on the stakeholder.

Criticism of the Concept of Multi-stakeholder Partnerships

Multi-stakeholder partnerships are designed to benefit business and silence the critics and dissenters. Bryn Jones shows how partnerships between NGOs and corporations are skewed in favour of business, 'businesses prefer businesslike approaches—"market solutions"—rather than political or regulatory practices and procedure' (Jones, 2007: 170-1). Hence the relationship results in the civil society often acting as mere endorsers of corporate activities. The business is often successful in taking the teeth off the criticism of civil society. Jones further observes that getting an NGO to support a particular green product is simply a market strategy for the corporate houses. He also suggests that civil society groups become financially dependent on business houses and exchange of staff and managers leads to the prevalence of 'the corporate paradigm'. The statement of an ex-official of the Nature Conservancy NGO, D. Morine, is illustrative: 'It was the wrong decision to get so close to industry. . . . These corporate executives are carnivorous. You bring them in and they just take over' (Cited in Jones, 2007: 171). Jones also notes that the NGOs endorsing products of some corporations often metamorphose into advertising or PR agencies instead of meaningful watchdogs of the process. The business hence tries to win over the critics to its own side so that it can carry on with its activities without any fear of strong opposition. For promoting the culture of corporate-community consultations and for local capacity building, corporations often create and promote social organizations. Yet this leads to corporations dictating the agenda of development in such communities and choosing groups and issues suitable to them: 'Such social engineering clearly raises the spectre of corporatism and control of so-called civil society organisations and puts in doubt their ability either to act independently or adequately represent the interests of their constituency' (Haslam, 2007: 295).

An interesting perspective is provided by Haslam who posits that the concepts like 'stakeholder' and 'partnership' are designed to pass projects promoting corporate interests as general, 'national-popular' projects. 'The key point for the purpose of this discussion is that the brand of self-regulatory global capitalism (represented by private authority) cannot be intrinsically authoritative or accepted. It needs legitimating structures or hegemonic strategies to balance it out' (Haslam, 2007: 278). Such partnerships result in the demand for change being sidelined in favour of *status quo*. Small benefits are doled out instead of the root causes of poverty and underdevelopment being addressed. This perpetuates the cycle of misery and impoverishment and attention of people is diverted in obtaining piecemeal reforms. The real motivation for business in seeking partnerships lies in taming the opposition and not in affecting any meaningful changes in their own behaviour. The motive behind such initiatives is cogently stated by Joshua Karliner of Corporate Watch: 'Global Compact Partnership and Guidelines for Cooperation do not ensure the integrity and independence of the United Nations and allow business entities with poor records to "blue-wash their image by wrapping themselves in the flag of the United Nations"' (cited in Winston, 2002: 78).

Identifying stakeholders also serves as a safety valve. The purpose is also to pacify those affected most by companies' policies before they take to extreme steps. Kytle et al. (2005) posit that CSR is a risk management strategy for companies. They argue that as a result of globalization and increased interdependence and resulting vulnerabilities, business today is facing altogether new kinds of risks. The companies try to manage conflicts with stakeholders through certain superficial consultative exercises. Yet a sincere effort at redressing the grievances of the affected comunities is not made and profit-making principles triumph over social responsibility gestures. Consultation with various stakeholders also helps the corporate houses in gaining legitimacy in the eyes of various groups. Efforts are made to diffuse resistance and build up communities supporting capitalist structures. A good example is given by Haslam who shows that the CSR agenda in Latin America is also a tactic to restore legitimacy to the idea of markets. He gives the example of how the IDB organized several Inter-American Conferences on CSR in an effort to create 'a principled belief that business can or should benefit society amidst the global epistemic community comprised of various representatives from international organisations, governmental development agencies, business houses, civil society and academia' (Haslam 2007: 291).

The corporate houses try to ignore the fact that poverty is the basic cause of the prevalence of problems like child labour, diseases and illiteracy, and hence they address the symptoms instead of the root cause. The problem of underdevelopment and poverty is a consequence of structural conditions which cannot be addressed merely by corporate-community partnerships. Newell also asserts that 'most CSR initiatives are not intended to tackle questions of poverty and social exclusion. They aim at less ambitious goals of performance enhancement and image management' (Newell, 2005: 586, cited in Sharp, 2006: 215). CSR helps in creating an atmosphere whereby small benefits are doled out to prevent people from asking for radical changes: 'The essence of accommodation as an underlying motive for CSR is hence to make small, feasible changes to how things work (including cosmetic changes), so that demands for more significant changes can be precluded' (Hamann and Acutt, 2003: 258-9).

Companies try to exclude various groups from benefits of their CSR efforts and try to limit them to as few hands as possible. They try to adopt a narrow definition of stakeholders to escape their responsibility towards people affected by their activities. Community relations department have mushroomed in many companies but it has been noted that they are selective in approach and hold consultations mostly with powerful stakeholder groups. Haslam (2007) comments on how the concept is used to exclude the weaker groups. He also comments on how those who are the most marginalized are often excluded from the definition of stakeholders. The initiatives of these companies often result in further marginalization of groups: '. . . the narrow interests of the firm and local power structures may work to exclude some potential stakeholders as legitimate participants. The firm holds most of the power in identifying relevant stakeholders and may seek to exclude those most opposed to the project in favour of more moderate "representatives"' (Haslam, 2007: 283).

It is claimed that CSR initiatives are directed towards promoting partnerships for development wherein participation of the people and self help is encouraged. Yet instead of corporate-community partnership, CSR leads to corporate patronage over communities. The process is strongly controlled by the companies who see to it that it runs according to their wishes and in their interest. Hamann also finds that at times due to their disproportionate influence 'the mining company becomes a sort of *de facto* government' (Hamann, 2004: 279). Far from empowerment of communities, CSR initiatives result in the communities becoming dependant on corporate houses for development and even for the satisfaction of their basic needs. Inherent in CSR efforts is the danger that people start looking up to the corporate houses for performing the functions of government. The corrupt governments siphon off the bulk of oil revenues which they receive from oil companies while the area remains underdeveloped and dependent on the goodwill of the companies operating in their area and their half-hearted development efforts. Frynas thus comments,

> The reason why companies such as Shell in Nigeria have been asked to build schools and hospitals is that the government has failed in its developmental role. When governance fails, local people often turn to oil companies to provide development projects, and this phenomenon can be seen in extreme form in Nigeria, where Shell has been regarded by many as a quasi-government. (Frynas, 2005: 596)

Frynas attempts an examination of the corporate claims of successful corporate-community partnerships in Nigeria. He found that the consultation exercises between oil companies and local communities are not taken seriously by the companies. The representatives of companies at the best have some meetings with the community representatives and no effort is made to go beyond this and involve the local people. The best development practises as advocated by agencies like the World Bank and Oxfam have not been practised by most of the companies. Frynas cites many cases where development projects funded by the MNCs resulted in a new set of problems. One example is Nigeria where infrastructural development led to diversion or drying up of water bodies and devastation of agricultural lands which hurt the livelihoods of people engaged in fishing and farming, thus forcing them to migrate.

David Husselbee (2000) describes 'NGOs as development partners to the corporates' by taking the example of child football stitchers in Pakistan: 'NGOs are seen as a valuable source of knowledge and experience of social and environmental issues, and as more approachable and trustworthy than government because they, like businesses themselves, are private organisations. Furthermore, their involvement may also help to neutralise campaigns against the companies concerned' (Husselbee, 2000: 377). While Husselbee finds this partnership a big success, he overlooks some of the problems which remain unresolved. The football-stitching industry in Pakistan in Sialkot tried to cut down the number of suppliers to check child labour, as it is difficult to monitor a large number of small-scale suppliers. This resulted in the loss of employment for many women homeworkers (Jenkins, 2005). Without a sound government policy of employment such efforts exacerbate the problems of poverty and underdevelopment instead of solving them.

The Case of Nigeria

The claims of successful corporate-community partnership are also studied in details by Wilson Akpan (2006). He examines the claim by Shell that it had effected a 'fundamental policy shift' by building partnerships for social development in Nigeria and its claims of having adopted 'world class standards of "community development" in the oil region' (ibid.: 223). He asserts that it was not a voluntary act, and it was only under certain conditions that Shell was forced to adopt a benign gesture, as youth unrest in the country had delivered a severe blow to its profits and oil drilling activities. Shell, taking lessons from this movement, has also started shifting its operations to off-shore locations to keep out of such troubles. He shows that CSR 'becomes a useful tool when it is used principally to create a favourable image and an atmosphere in which business can sleep peacefully with the enemy' (ibid.: 226-7). He notes that CSR reports of various oil companies operating in Nigeria often pictured incomplete and non-operational community development projects as huge achievements.

Akpan discusses how community development projects have created conflicts between various groups and have resulted in ethnic tensions in various places. Projects remain incomplete or are abandoned, thus mocking the claim of development by these companies. The author gives the example of incomplete and abandoned water projects in Oloibiri, which were projected in an NDDC newsletter as grand successes. Similarly he gives the examples of an abandoned Shell-sponsored electrification project in Oloibiri, a stinking community water borehole in Iko and an abandoned and out-of-maintenance health centre in the same community. Activities of the company had also resulted in damage of property of people. Seismic blasting activities had caused many damages to the houses of people and acid rain resulting from gas flares had corroded the iron roofs of the houses. In Ebubu too the author found an abandoned community water project. The author found that a vast stretch of land which had been rendered unusable due to a 1970 oil spill remained polluted until 2003, when he visited the site.

Oil companies intrude into and try to influence the policy making in local communities, sometimes even dictating who should be king. The companies in the name of interacting with local communities coin terms like 'stakeholder engagement' and so try to show their interest in getting the concerns of all sides reflected. Yet they try to eliminate adversaries and those protesting against their malpractises. They even interfere in their local government to the extent of removing kings who refuse to follow their dictates by blaming them for insufficient development activities. This often leads to a community getting split as the allegiance of the people gets divided among the old and new rulers. Akpan found that community governance structures like 'Community Development Committees' are also prone to manipulation by companies. In order to avoid the task of providing social amenities in all affected areas, oil producing companies adopt a policy of providing aid selectively to some regions and communities only. Thus isolated small settlements are not regarded as permanent habitations and denied benefits on these grounds. They label certain groups as migrants and squatters and try to evict them from these settlements, not recognizing their claims to any facilities, leaving them fully exposed to the hazards of their activities. Companies diplomatically use terms like 'community' and 'settlement' and specific nomenclatures like 'oil well community', 'pipeline community' and 'landlord community' for denying access to social amenities to a group while conferring them on some other group. Such policies create tensions among various groups contending for social amenities and lead to the emergence of the 'us-other' feelings and tensions among the people. There are numerous such examples, like the tensions between the Iko and Okoroette community which snowballed when Shell asserted that Iko was the only oil producing community in the region. Akpan comments on the politics of divide and rule followed by these companies so that they are spared the trouble of spending resources on all the affected communities. The consequences are disastrous:

> Ultimately, it would seem, CSR takes on a dysfunctional character when the government abandons its developmental re-sponsibilities to its citizens (as has been the case in Nigeria for many decades). Things get worse when business proportions are allowed to define how they should bring development to the people. (ibid.: 237)

Community fragmentation also takes place with the development of local development intermediaries who act as agents between a community and oil companies and government bodies. Thus various interests including leaders and elites belonging to the community clash amongst themselves for winning contracts of projects for becoming intermediaries. Cases like these reflect the attitude of companies to social development. For corporate houses, corporate-community partnership is yet another fanciful phrase in the lexicon of CSR which is used to placate the critics. Such half-hearted schemes are merely cover-ups for the human rights abuses and exploitative practises of these companies.

A MODEL OF CORPORATE HEGEMONY

The malady of the developing and least developed countries is deep rooted and cannot be addressed through superficial measures. The problem lies somewhere in the way the politics and economics of underdevelopment operate. Yet the corporate houses choose to ignore the problems inherent in the systems of accumulation and profit. All they do is adopt every possible method to subdue opposition and maintain *status quo*. The strategy of corporations is a mix of four tactics which were practised by rulers in ancient India for dealing with the enemies—*saam* (appeasement), *daan* (gift), *dand* (punishment), *bhed* (sowing dissent). Thus corporates try to diffuse resistance to their hegemony either by appeasement and gifts (e.g. corporate-community partnerships and projects bestowed upon host communities), by punitive measures (like the deployment of private forces, for example the use of mobile police in Niger Delta) or by sowing dissent (Shell's corporate-community partnership initiatives resulted in tensions between different communities in Nigeria). A model can be developed to explain this relationship between corporates and communities, a relationship which instead of being symbiotic (as pointed out by various scholars) is predatory in nature (Figure 15.1). The model tries to explain the rationale of CSR. Corporations exploit the developing and least developed countries for being resource rich and having low labour and environmental standards. Their activities result in impoverishment and further marginalization of the people. This leads to resentment among the civil society and host communities and hence leads to the adoption of the above-mentioned four strategies by the corporations. The adoption of the policies of appeasement and gift gives benefits to businesses, like enhanced reputation, increased profits as well as legitimacy from the society.

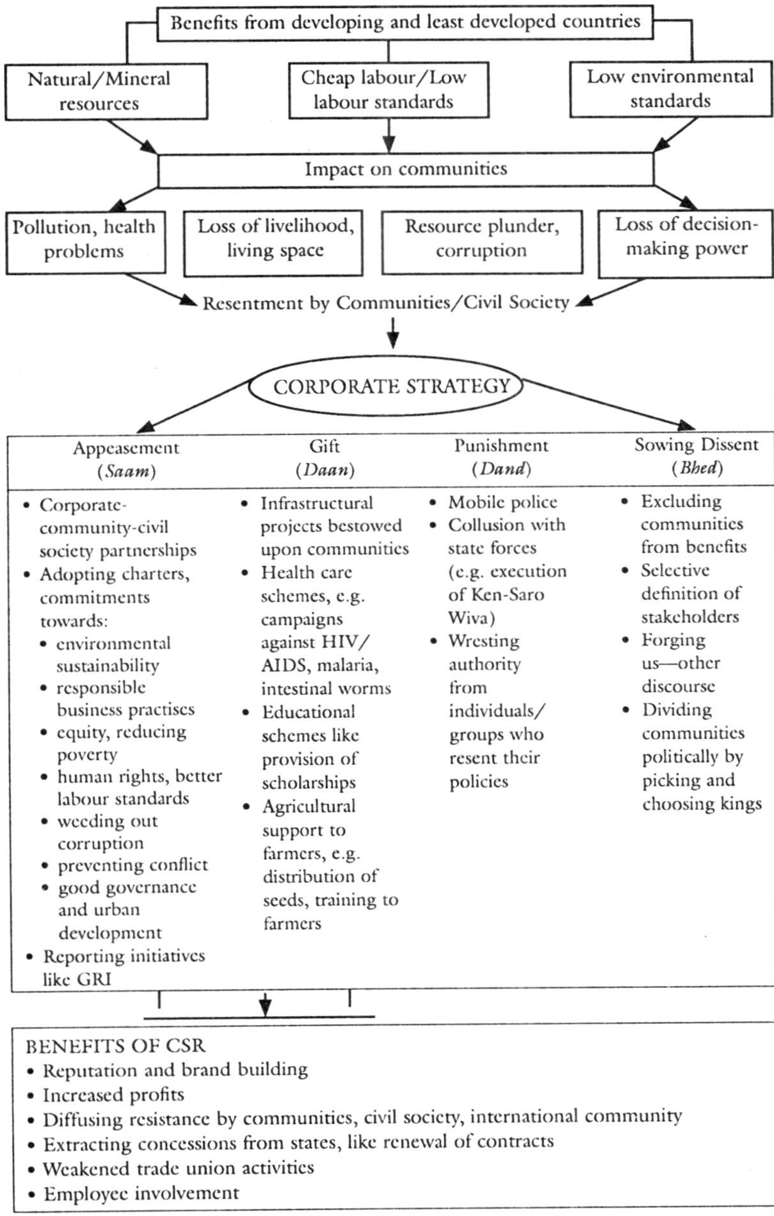

FIGURE 15.1: MODEL EXPLAINING CORPORATE HEGEMONY

CONCLUSION

Corporate-community partnership, which has become an integral principle of CSR, is thus a devise to perpetuate the hegemony of global capitalism. It seems to be fast losing its ideological hold on the people who are getting marginalized due to corporate expansion into their regions. This paper discusses how the very concept of CSR is a mask which global capitalism has put on to win over the global public opinion to its side. The corporations want to project the image that capitalism has also a human face to it. Yet the inherent motive is to gain support for the neo-liberal idea of withdrawal of state, and to show that as corporates are capable of self-regulation, there is no need for the interference of state in the process. The state should be satisfied to act as a facilitator of trade and as an institution for protecting property rights.

This paper tries to shed light on the processes through which the corporate houses gain legitimacy in the society and establish their hegemony. While the corporations continue unabated in accumulating wealth at the cost of socio-economic welfare of the common people, they also take care to diffuse resistance to their activities. CSR could be understood as a PR exercise which tries to shield business from a popular backlash by projecting the company as benevolent and socially responsible. The CSR agenda thus exacerbates the problem of under-development and marginalization by attempting to perpetuate the structural inequalities in a society. The problem of marginalization at all the three levels—international, national and local—remains unresolved—despite the adoption of the CSR paradigm by most of the big business players. This puts question marks on the neo-liberal ideology and its potential for promoting a sustainable future.

REFERENCES

Adeola, Francis O. (2001), 'Environmental Injustice and Human Rights Abuse: The States, MNCs, and Repression of Minority Groups in the World System', *Human Ecology Review*, vol. 8, no. 1: pp. 39–59.

Akpan, Wilson (2006), 'Between Responsibility and Rhetoric: Some Consequences of CSR Practice in Nigeria's Oil Province', *Development Southern Africa*, vol. 23, no. 2: 223-40.

Bakker, Frank G.A. De, Peter Groenewegen and Frank Den Hond (2005), 'A Bibliometric Analysis of 30 Years of Research and Theory on Corporate Social Responsibility and Corporate Social Performance', *Business Society*, vol. 44, no. 3: 283-317.

Bendell, J. (2003), 'Waking up to Risk: Corporate Responses to HIV/AIDS in the Workplace', *Technology, Business and Society*, paper no. 12, Geneva: UNRISD, cited in Rhys Jenkins (2005), 'Globalization, Corporate Social Responsibility and Poverty', *International Affairs*, vol. 81, no. 3: 525-40.

——— (2005), 'In Whose Name? The Accountability of Corporate Social Responsibility', *Development in Practice*, vol. 15, nos. 3 & 4: 362-74.

Blowfield, Michael, 'Corporate Social Responsibility: Reinventing the Meaning of Development?', *International Affairs*, vol. 81, no. 3: 515-24.

Brown, Garrett (2005), *Industrial Safety and Hygiene News*, Cited in Robert A. Senser (2007), 'Corporate Social Responsibility: A Fledgling Movement Faces a Crucial Test', *Dissent*, Winter, pp. 77-82.

Cassill, Deby Lee and Ronald Paul Hill (2007), 'A Naturological Approach to Corporate Governance: An Extension of the Frederick Model of Corporation-Community Relationships', *Business Society*, vol. 46, no. 3: 286-303.

Chambers, Eleanor, Wendy, Chapple, Jeremy Moon and Michael Sullivan (2003), 'CSR in Asia: A Seven Country Study of CSR Website Reporting', ICCSR Research Paper Series No. 09-2003, Nottingham: International Centre for Corporate Social Responsibility.

Christian Aid (2004), *Behind the Mask: The Real Face of Corporate Social Responsibility*. http://www.christianaid.org.uk/indepth/0401csr/csr_behindthemask. pdf

Cragg, Wesley (2001), 'Prosperity and Business Ethics—The Case for Corporate Social Responsibility in the Americas', *FOCAL Policy Papers*, Ottawa: Canadian Foundation for the Americas.

Eweje, Gabriel (2006), 'The Role of MNEs in Community Development Initiatives in Developing Countries: Corporate Social Responsibility at Work in Nigeria and South Africa', *Business & Society*, vol. 45, no. 2: 93-129.

Fig, David (2005), 'Manufacturing Amnesia: Corporate Social Responsibility in South Africa', *International Affairs*, vol. 81, no. 3: 599-617.

Fisher, R. and W. Ury (1981), *Getting to Yes: Negotiating Agreement without Giving In*, Boston: Houghton Mifflin. Cited in Ralph Hamann and Nicola Acutt (2003), 'How Should Civil Society (and the Government) Respond to "Corporate Social Responsibility"? A Critique of Business Motivations and the Potential for Partnerships', *Development Southern Africa*, vol. 20, no. 2: 255-70.

Fonteneau, Gérard (2003), 'Corporate Social Responsibility: Envisioning its Social Implications', http://users.skynet.be/gresea/csr_gf_nov03.pdf

Fortanier, Fabienne and Ans Kolk (2007), 'On the Economic Dimensions of Corporate Social Responsibility Exploring *Fortune* Global 250 Reports', *Business and Society*, vol. 20, no. 10: 1-21.

Frederick, W.C. (1998), 'Creatures, Corporations, Communities, Chaos, Complexity', *Business & Society*, vol. 37, no. 4: 358-89.

Friedman, Milton (1962), *Capitalism and Freedom*, Chicago: Chicago University Press.

Frynas, Jedrej George (2005), 'The False Developmental Promise of Corporate Social Responsibility: Evidence from Multinational Oil Companies', *International Affairs*, vol. 81, no. 3: 581-91.

Greenpeace International (1994), *Shell-Shocked: The Environmental and Social Costs of Living with Shell in Nigeria*, London: Greenpeace International. Cited in Gabriel Eweje (2006), 'The Role of MNEs in Community Development Initiatives in Developing Countries: Corporate Social Responsibility at Work in Nigeria and South Africa', *Business & Society*, vol. 45, no. 2: 93-129.

Griffiths, Hannah (2005), 'Human and Environmental Rights: The Need for Corporate Accountability', in Felix Dodds and Tim Pippard (eds.) (2005), *Human and Environmental Security: An Agenda for Change*, London: Earthscan.

Hamann, Ralph (2004), 'Corporate Social Responsibility, Partnerships, and Institutional Change: The Case of Mining Companies in South Africa', *Natural Resources Forum*, vol. 28, pp. 278-90.

Hamann, Ralph and Nicola Acutt (2003), 'How Should Civil Society (and the Government) Respond to "Corporate Social Responsibility"? A Critique of Business Motivations and the Potential for Partnerships', *Development Southern Africa*, vol. 20, no. 2: 255-70.

Haslam, Paul Alexander (2007), 'Is Corporate Social Responsibility a Constructivist Regime? Evidence from Latin America', *Global Society*, vol. 21, no. 2: 269-96.

Husselbee, David (2000), 'NGOs as Development Partners to the Corporates: Child Football Stitchers in Pakistan', *Development in Practice*, vol. 10 no. 3: 377-438.

Jenkins, Rhys (2005), 'Globalization, Corporate Social Responsibility and Poverty', *International Affairs*, vol. 81, no. 3: 525-40.

Jones, Bryn (2007), 'Citizens, Partners or Patrons? Corporate Power and Patronage Capitalism', *Journal of Civil Society*, vol. 3, no. 2: 159-77.

Jones, Marc T. (1996), 'Missing the Forest for the Trees: A Critique of the Social Responsibility Concept and Discourse', *Business Society*, vol. 35, no. 7: 7-41.

Kambalame, Daisy and Sean de Cleene (2006), 'Partnership Building as an Approach to Addressing Corporate Social Responsibility in the Agriculture Sector in Malawi', *Development Southern Africa*, vol. 23, no. 2: 281-7.

Kolk, Ans and Jonatan Pinkse (2007), 'Multinationals' Political Activities on Climate Change', *Business & Society*, vol. 46, no. 2: 201-28.

Kovel, Joel (2002), *The Enemy of Nature: The End of Capitalism or the End of the World*, Nova Scotia: Fernwood Publishing.

Kytle, Beth and John Gerard Ruggie (2005), *Corporate Social Responsibility as Risk Management: A Model for Multinationals*, Corporate Social Responsibility Initiative Working Paper No. 10, Cambridge, M.A.: John F. Kennedy School of Government, Harvard University.

MMSD (Mining, Minerals, and Sustainable Development) (2002), *Breaking New Ground: The Report of the Mining, Minerals, and Sustainable Development Project*, London: Earthscan. Cited in Ralph Hamann, (2004), 'Corporate Social Responsibility, Partnerships, and Institutional Change: The Case of Mining Companies in South Africa', *Natural Resources Forum*, vol. 28, pp. 278-90.

Nasi, J., S. Nasi, N. Phillips and S. Zyglidopoulos (1997), 'The Evolution of Corporate Social Responsiveness', *Business & Society*, vol. 36, no. 3: 296-321.

Newell, Peter (2005), 'Citizenship, Accountability and Community: The Limits of the CSR Agenda', *International Affairs*, vol. 83, no. 3. Cited in John Sharp (2006), 'Corporate Social Responsibility and Development: An Anthropological Perspective', *Development Southern Africa*, vol. 23, no. 2: 213-22.

Ramus, Catherine A. and Ivan Montiel (2005), 'When Are Corporate Environmental Policies a Form of Greenwashing?', *Business Society*, vol. 44, no. 4: 377-414.

Sadler, David (2004), 'Anti-corporate Campaigning and Corporate "Social" Responsibility: Towards Alternative Spaces of Citizenship', *Antipode*, vol. 36, no. 5: 1002–5.

Taussig, Michael (1984), 'Culture of Terror—Space of Death: Roger Casements' Putumayo Report and the Explanation of Torture', *Comparative Studies in Society and History*, Cambridge: Cambridge University Press, pp. 467-88, 492-7. In Joan Vincent (ed.) (2002), *The Anthropology of Politics: A Reader in Ethnography, Theory, and Critique*, Malden: Blackwell Publishing.

UNDP (United Nations Development Programme) (1997), *Human Development Report 1997*, New York: Oxford University Press.

WBCSD (World Business Council for Sustainable Development), *Meeting Changing Expectations: Corporate Social Responsibility*, Geneva: WBCSD.

Winston, Morton (2002), 'NGO Strategies for Promoting Corporate Social Responsibility', *Ethics and International Affairs*, vol. 16, pp. 71-87.

Winters, N., A. McCulloch and X. Cirera (2001), *Trade Liberalisation and Poverty: A Handbook* (London: CEPR). Cited in Rhys Jenkins (2005), 'Globalization, Corporate Social Responsibility and Poverty', *International Affairs*, vol. 81, no. 3: 525-40.

CHAPTER 16

Interactivity of Marginalized Indian Communities Subsisting on the Trade of Medicinal Plants with the Global Community

MOUMITA DAS

INTRODUCTION

Marginalization of a community may be defined as the exclusion of the community from meaningful participation in society. India, unfortunately, has a considerable population that falls under this category. Marginalized communities in India principally comprise tribals/adivasis/aboriginal comunities, other backward castes/Dalits, the landless, and women. Dalits and tribals constitute nearly one-fourth of the total population of India, almost all of which is marginalized. A considerable segment of this population is landless and resides in marginal lands and on the fringes of forests. These communities sustain mostly on the collection and trade of Non-Wood Forest Produce (NWFP), most of which comprise medicinal plants harvested from the wild. Marginalization has been the principal cause of extreme poverty in these communities. As a result these communities are socially and economically backward. Although efforts are being made to integrate them into the mainstream, no spectacular success has been observed so far. Integration of these communities is possible through sustainable development. Therefore, more concerted efforts are needed to understand the underlying challenges of the problem and address them accordingly. This will aid in developing effective strategies for the sustainable development of these marginalized communities and their integration into the national and global community.

Poverty eradication is the first and foremost requirement for sustainable development, as clearly identified by the United Nations Millennium Declaration, often referred to as the Millennium Declaration Goals (MDG). Strategies and plans of implementation are continuously being formulated and implemented all over the world to achieve these goals. The Johannesburg Plan of Implementation of sustainable development adopted by the World Summit on Sustainable Development dealt with, among others, the following important and strategies relevant to the issue being discussed (Plan of Implementation of WSSD, 2005):

1. *Reinforcing the goals of sustainable development*
   (a) Each country has the primary responsibility to eradicate poverty and implement sustainable development through national policies and development strategies.
   (b) Each country should promote sustainable patterns of consumption and production. They should develop production and consumption policies to improve the products and services provided, while reducing environmental and health impacts using, where appropriate, science-based approaches. They should develop awareness-raising programmes on the importance of sustainable production and consumption patterns, through education.
   (c) Each country should implement strategies to protect ecosystems and achieve integrated management of natural resources, while strengthening local capacities (capacity building).
2. *Sustainable development in a globalizing world:* The process of globalization should be fully inclusive and equitable. For globalization, policies need to be formulated with the enhanced participation and effective involvement of civil society and other relevant stakeholders.
3. *Means of implementation*: It includes providing to the stakeholders financial resources, improved trade opportunities, technologies, education and awareness, capacity building, and scientific capabilities, among others.
4. *Strengthening institutional framework at the national level*: Institutions linked to the development of communities, such as cooperatives and local governance, among others, need to be strengthened. Multi-stakeholder participation should be promoted.

Sustainable development is a complex idea that invariably requires a network of plans for its implementation. To come with a viable plan for sustainable development of a marginalized community requires the analysis of the strengths, weaknesses, opportunities and threats (SWOT) that the community faces. To address the foremost issue of poverty eradication, creation of sustainable livelihoods is a priority for these communities.

For generation of livelihoods, the preliminary requirement is capital assets/resources. The capital assets/resources are classified into five types:

1. Natural resources (e.g. environmental)
2. Social resources (e.g. networks of individuals, communities and institutions)
3. Human resources (e.g. knowledge and skills)
4. Physical resources (e.g. infrastructure, testing laboratories in this case)
5. Financial resources (e.g. credit and savings)

Livelihoods are sustainable when all the stakeholders are empowered to have enhanced access to all these resources and can maintain the livelihoods in the future while maintaining and enhancing the resources. Creation of sustainable livelihoods for the marginalized communities would entail creation of jobs that are rural-based, decentralized; jobs that require minimum capital investment, create incomes and profits, and help generate purchasing power; and jobs that create dignity and a sense of ownership in these communities.

It needs to be emphasized that the concept of sustainable livelihood is people-centric. It is very specific and meets the needs of the communities who live in close contact with their environment and derive their capital resources from it. Therefore, this approach requires the identification of the most pressing constraints faced by people as also the opportunities open to people regardless of where these may occur. It builds upon people's own definitions and understanding of constraints and opportunities and supports them to overcome the constraints and realize the opportunities.

Keeping in mind the above factors, this paper carries out a study of the existing strengths, weaknesses, opportunities and threats in the field of global trade in medicinal plants. It investigates the feasibility of a model for creating a sustainable livelihood from medicinal plants for the marginalized communities that are dependent on the collection of medicinal plants from the wild for their sustenance. Through this proposed model, the sustainable development and social integration of the marginalized communities into the mainstream and their interactivity with the global community is envisaged.

TRADE IN MEDICINAL PLANTS

The World Health Organisation (WHO) estimates that about 60-85 per cent of the world's population depends on medicinal plants for its health care needs (Traditional medicine, 2008). In recent times, there has been a steep rise in the demand for herbal medicines and other herbal products such as herbal food and nutritional supplements, cosmetics and personal care products all over the world. Some of the possible reasons for this rise may be due to the following factors as enumerated by Calixto (Calixto, 2000):

1. Preference of consumers for natural therapies.
2. Concern regarding undesirable side effects of modern medicines and the belief that herbal drugs are free from side effects, since millions of people all over the world have been using herbal medicines for thousands of years.
3. Great interest in alternative medicines.
4. Preference of populations for preventive medicine due to increasing population age.
5. The belief that herbal medicines might be of effective benefit in the treatment of certain diseases where conventional therapies and medicines have proven to be inadequate.
6. Tendency towards self-medication.
7. Improvement in quality, proof of efficacy and safety of herbal medicines.
8. High cost of synthetic medicines.

This demand has resulted in an increase in international trade in medicinal plants. Most of the pharmaceutical companies, including multinational companies, have introduced their own range of herbal products. It is estimated that the international market of medicinal plants is over US $65 billion with annual growth rates averaging from 5 to 15 per cent (Lambert, 2005). The herbal food supplement market is estimated to have an even higher growth rate of 25 per cent. A similar trend may be envisaged for the herbal cosmetics market. In 2009, a study by ASSOCHAM revealed that the Indian herbal market was worth Rs. 7,000 crore and the export of its medicines would grow at 25 per cent to Rs. 9,000 crore. The study said that by 2012, the Indian herbal industry would grow at 20 per cent per year to touch Rs. 14,000 crore (*The Economic Times*, 29 March 2008).

In India about 8,000 species of medicinal plants are used as food supplements, medicines, biocides and other phytochemicals. Around 2,500 plants are used in various Ayurvedic formulations. The international market of herbal products is estimated to be US $62 billion, which is poised to grow to US $5 trillion by the year 2050 (Aromatic and Herbal Plantations, 2009). But as compared to the US $65 billion international trade in 2001-2, India's export was only to the tune of about US $5 billion (Table 16.1) (Uniyal, 2005).

India is the third largest exporter, next to China and Hong Kong, accounting for about 13 per cent of global imports. USA is the principal market for Indian medicinal plants, accounting for about 50 per cent of exports (Exim Bank Study, 2008). According to a study by Lange, India exported medicinal plants to 95 countries and may be seen as a small trade centre for south Asia (Lange, 2007). Table 16.2 is derived from Lange's study and lists the top exporting countries in the year 2003.

At present around 90 per cent of the supply is collected from the wild, mostly by the marginalized communities living in and around the forests. The collectors sell the raw materials to village stalls, middlemen, and also to industrial city traders. The system is highly

TABLE 16.1: EXPORT OF AYURVEDIC PRODUCTS FROM THE YEAR 1999 TO 2002

Year	(US $ million)
1999-2000	3351
2000-1	4857
2001-2	5045

TABLE 16.2: SOME TOP COUNTRIES EXPORTING MEDICINAL PLANTS IN 2003

Country	Quantity [tonnes]	Value [US$]
China	150,600	266,038,500
Hong Kong	55,000	201,021,200
India	40,400	61,665,500
Mexico	37,600	14,257,500

disorganized (Lambert et. al, 1997) and the collectors get the lowest share of the market price. It is estimated that this generates about 35-40 million workdays of employment for the poor and underemployed workforce, a majority of whom are tribal women. Going by this estimate, if there is an effective management of sustainable collection, value addition and marketing of medicinal plants from the wild, the economic development of these communities can easily be envisaged.

CONSTRAINTS

While the trend shows an increase in the global demand for medicinal plants and products, India is slow in taking advantage of it. There are several factors that pose constraints to India's entry into the international market and put it in a disadvantageous position. Some of these factors are discussed below in brief (Uniyal, 2005, Singh 2006, Das, 2004):

1. *Unregulated trade:* The global trade in medicinal plants is secretive and unregulated. A substantial part of this trade is not recorded and official trade statistics either do not identify the plant individually or do not separate their medicinal use from other uses.

2. *No scientific evidence of the efficacy of traditional medicines:* Many of the traditional systems of medicine, though well documented and used safely for centuries, have no proven scientific basis of their efficacy. There is a lack of essential infrastructure at the grassroots level to carry out scientific testing. This makes the entry into the international market difficult.

3. *No uniform quality standards:* The uniformity of the collected material is often not possible owing to their different places of origin. This reflects in the inconsistent quality of the pharmacologically active secondary metabolites in the plant material, which is not desirable. Further, the processed formulations also contain contamination (mostly microbial and heavy metal) that is rejected in the international market.

4. *Lack of knowledge and information:* The people at the grassroots level do not have the necessary information about the requirements of the international market. They are also unaware of, or do not have

access to, the technologies to upgrade their produce and make them of the international quality standards. This restraints them from venturing out into international trade.

5. *Unsustainable collection and processing technologies:* The collection of medicinal plants from the wild employs unsustainable practices. Further, there is a lack of knowledge and practice of cost-effective post-harvest technologies such as storage of raw produce and standardization, processing, packaging and storage of processed materials.

6. *Lack of value addition:* The harvested materials are usually supplied in unprocessed form to the dealers. However, if the materials are processed into a more consumer useable form, the value added product would fetch a higher income as compared to the raw material. There is an urgent need of value addition at the source of collection/ production.

7. *Lack of entrepreneurship at the grassroots level:* The raw materials reach the international market through a chain of dealers with little benefits to the grassroots people involved in the collection of these plants. The promotion of medicinal plant products is also lacking. Strengthening of the financial, production, and marketing strategies is required to make the trade more organized and standardized. Then only the grassroots people can participate in the entrepreneurship endeavours of medicinal plants and claim equitable share in the profits.

INITIATIVES: NATIONAL AND GLOBAL

Efforts are being made by the Government of India (GOI) at several levels and through its various agencies, to integrate the marginalized communities into the mainstream through its developmental policies and schemes. More specifically, for the marginalized communities that are dependent on the collection of NWFP, the forest policies are being reviewed to permit sustainable forest use by these communities. Recently, the forest use rights of the tribals and other traditional forest dwellers have been strengthened through the Scheduled Tribes and Other Traditional Forest Dwellers (Recognition of Forest Rights) Act, 2007 that has become operational from 1 January 2008.

The Ministry of Environment and Forests (MoEF) has been active in developing policies for the sustainable use of forests by the communities. It has initiated the Joint Forestry Management Programme (JFM) that involves the village communities. The programme aims at conservation and satisfying the basic needs of the communities, and also aims to provide them equitable share in the benefits (Lambert, 2005). The MoEF had issued a circular that 'the beneficiaries should be given usufructs like . . . minor forest produce'. Another circular of 24 December 2004 of the MoEF recommends capacity building of the collectors and promotion of sustainable harvesting techniques. To cite an example, the JFM approach has been implemented in Andhra Pradesh in which marginalized people living on the fringes to the forests are encouraged to form societies called Vana Samarakshana Samitis (VSS) to protect and rejuvenate degraded forest areas with 100 per cent usufruct rights to the VSS. The VSS members are also encouraged to cultivate and conserve medicinal plants in the VSS areas (Joint Forest Management Extension Digest, 1999).

The Planning Commission of India in its 'Taskforce on Conservation and Sustainable Use of Medicinal Plants' had recommended that all efforts should be co-ordinated to ensure export of herbal products to earn Rs. 3,000 crore by 2005 and Rs. 10,000 crore by AD 2010 besides meeting domestic needs. The Commission had recommended the setting up of a Medicinal Plants Board for formalizing and organizing the marketing and trade of medicinal plants. The Board would include representatives of various stakeholders. The National Medicinal Plants Board (NMPB) was set up by the Government of India in 2000 to coordinate all matters relating to the sustainable use of medicinal plants including drawing up policies for conservation, cultivation, harvesting, marketing, processing, etc.; providing technical know-how for cultivation; and consultancy for management. The activities of the NMPB include survey and preparation of inventories of medicinal plants, quality planting material production, extension services including education and sensitization through training, marketing of medicinal plants, research and development, and value addition and semi-processing of products of medicinal plants. It arranges contract farming between cultivators and industrialists and also facilitates a buy-back arrangement from the farmers at reasonable prices. The Board has also formulated schemes for financial support, which is given directly to small and marginal farmers. Till the year

2006, a total of 4,254 projects worth Rs. 17.50 lakh had been sanctioned under promotional and farming schemes that cover 32 states and union territories of the country (Kala and Sajwan, 2007).

The Department of Science and Technology (DST) in collaboration with the National Botanical Research Institute (NBRI) has initiated an All India Coordinated Project on Plant Based Health System involving women. Under this, the women are trained in improved techniques related to the cultivation of medicinal plants, preparation of herbal products and their marketing. Several NGOs have also been involved in this project and they have been instrumental in implementing it in the different states of India. It has been found during the project work that the establishment of market linkages for the profitable selling of processed products is urgently required (Das, 2004).

Besides the government organizations, there are several NGOs involved in this area. For example, the Foundation for Revitalisation of Local Health Traditions (FRLHT) is a registered society that came up in 1993 (Hamilton, 2006). It seeks to revitalize the Indian systems of medicine through a range of field activities and research extension programmes. It works in collaboration and networking with state forest departments and other NGOs. Among its many activities, it has undertaken several capacity building programmes for the local communities including enterprise development, such as how to prepare herbal products and establish sales outlets. It is also working on sustainable harvesting and adaptive management of medicinal plants. There are many such NGOs that are actively working to promote awareness, documentation and conservation strategies for medicinal plants.

At the global level, there are many international organizations worldwide, such as the UK's Department for International Development (DFID), which support sustainable use of natural resources and equitable access and benefit sharing of environmental assets for poverty reduction. The DFID supports local processes that encourage sustainable development and improved capacity to manage the environment in a way that benefits poor people (DFID, 2009).

The International Centre for Integrated Mountain Development (ICIMOD) established with the collaboration of Germany, Switzerland, Nepal and UNESCO, has initiated a Medicinal and Aromatics Plant Programme in Asia (MAPPA), which promotes collaboration through national and international networks. It also promotes research on approaches to sustainable production and processing of medicinal plants. ICIMOD's strategy is based on working with its partners to identify, test, adapt and communicate opportunities for overcoming mountain vulnerabilities and transforming them into greater security and sustainability for poor and marginalized mountain peoples (MAPPA, 2009).

Continuous efforts are going on to develop techniques for the sustainable harvest of medicinal plants. In 2007, the International Conservation Union (IUCN) prepared a draft International Standard for Sustainable Wild Collection of Medicinal and Aromatic Plants (ISSC-MAP). It is designed to help those involved in the harvest, management, trade and sale of wild-collected medicinal plants to understand and comply with sustainable collection practices (ISSC-MAP, 2007).

The UN Conference on Trade and Development (UNCTAD) (UNCTAD, 2006) had started an initiative called BioTrade. BioTrade is concerned with the activities of collection, production, transformation, and commercialization of goods and services that are derived from biodiversity. This includes trade in products that are used in line with environmental, social and economic sustainability criteria. The UNCTAD established guidelines and indicators for BioTrade keeping in view the sustainability standards for wild-collected natural products (UNCTAD, 2009). These guidelines and indicators will have an impact downstream of the production process, e.g. the conservation of nature, and sustainable socio-economic empowerment of the collectors.

INTEGRATING MARGINALIZED COMMUNITIES

After examining the opportunities and constraints that are faced by the marginalized communities specifically in relation to the global trade in medicinal plants, the following three-pronged strategy is suggested which is the basis of the proposed model for the integration of the marginalized communities into the mainstream.

Community Mobilization

The first and the foremost activity to integrate the marginalized communities is mobilization of these communities. The active participation of the stakeholders, such as women, tribals and Dalits, is a must for successful mobilization of the community. A community, which is sufficiently mobilized, can set things into motion that would enhance its developmental process. Community mobilization creates the demand and supply of sustainable livelihoods. A mobilized community is aware of its position in the society, its rights and its duties. It acquires the requisite knowledge, skills and capabilities to become a self-sustaining community. It not only generates income for itself, but is also capable of supporting others. It can mobilize other marginalized communities to become developed. Community mobilization is being carried out throughout India by several NGOs with visible results. The JFM Programme of the GOI has also been able to mobilize communities to some extent (Joint Forest Management Extension Digest, 1999). More such efforts by the GOI in this direction are welcome. Institutes of higher education, such as the Indira Gandhi National Open University (IGNOU) can play a responsible role in educating and sensitizing the marginalized communities for their mobilization process through its multimedia training facilities.

Cooperatives

To ensure a sustainable livelihood based on medicinal plants, the effort would require not just the collection from the wild but a variety of standardization and value addition processes that would involve manpower. This would require a coordinated approach with mutual cooperation of the community members. Also the equitable sharing of benefits needs to be ensured. Hence, the formation of a Medicinal Plants Cooperative by these communities is very much the need of the hour. The cooperative can be modelled on the lines of the Tribal Cooperative Marketing Development Federation of India Limited (TRIFED) (TRIFED, 2009) or the highly successful Anand pattern of milk cooperatives (Brandt, 2003). The milk cooperative movement began as a network of cooperative members in two villages in Gujarat four decades ago. The milk producers were poor and were compelled to sell the perishable milk at throwaway prices to the private trader. They realized that this exploitation could be checked if they marketed the milk through their own organization, which is now popularly known as AMUL. Milk was collected from individual producers at the cooperative centre. This was then tested, pasteurized and marketed. Gradually, value addition in the form of milk products like milk powder, butter, cheese, and so on was put into operation that ensured more profits. The rural producers, with their organized efforts of application of technology and advanced management in processing and marketing have brought outstanding changes in their society. They have not only attained self-reliance and improved their standards of living, but have also built a sustainable method of cooperative development. The dairy cooperatives are organized into a network of primary, district, state and national level federations involving around six million producers. Their functions are to:

1. Create a network of policy makers, producers, professionals and technologists.
2. Make available the best technology to the producers.
3. Provide a support system to the producers.
4. Establish marketing and distribution systems reaching farthest corners of the country.
5. Ensure fair profit to the members and quality product to the consumers.

The economic development brought about by the dairy revolution has also brought about social and institutional developments. Members of the cooperative receive a dividend along with the profits and the staff gets a bonus. Out of the profits, funds are given for education, health and family welfare, animal husbandry development, tree plantation and cooperative propaganda.

A similar pattern of cooperative endeavour is required in the medicinal plants sector. The role of medicinal plant cooperative should be to:

1. Collect the produce from individual collectors.
2. Standardization and storage of raw and semi-processed materials under optimum conditions to ensure quality products to the consumers.
3. Provide financial help like agricultural credit to the members to encourage value-addition and a buyback arrangement.
4. Promote capacity building by facilitating advanced technologies and know-how to the members for producing international quality products.
5. Promote value addition products in India and abroad.
6. Implement advanced packaging, marketing and distribution strategies for the raw and semi-processed material to increase exports.

7. Ensure gainful returns for the products.
8. Guarantee equitable distribution of profits to the members of the cooperative.

Efforts should come from the communities on one hand and the financial institutions, business and industry, scientific community, government and NGOs on the other hand to bring about the successful formation and working of the cooperative.

Capacity Building

In addition to the entrepreneurship requirements (finance, marketing, promotion) that could be taken care of through the cooperatives, the individuals of the community need to be trained in several aspects to enhance their knowledge and skills in relation to their work. The language and mode of instruction would need to be adapted to the local conditions. Although some institutions are engaged in imparting some training in selected areas of capacity building, bigger education institutes such as IGNOU, with its huge infrastructure and wide reach can play a very important role in preparing the training materials keeping in mind the specific needs of the targeted communities.

The areas in which capacity building would be required are the following:

1. Sustainable harvesting practices
2. Value addition
3. Quality control standards
4. Intellectual property rights

1. *Sustainable Harvesting Practices*

Currently, the collectors of medicinal plants from the wild employ destructive harvesting methods. For example, the medicinal plants whose roots or barks are used are uprooted and the whole plant is destroyed in this process. There is, thus the loss of valuable species. This destructive trend needs to be stopped for everyone's benefit. Several studies are being carried out by various NGOs and universities on the viable methods of sustainable harvesting of medicinal plants. Guidelines and criteria have been formed by several international agencies for trade of medicinal plants (WHO, 2003, 2005) which have been harvested sustainably from the wild. Keeping in view these developments, the collectors need to be sensitized towards conservation, and educated and trained on the sustainable harvesting of plant and plant parts. For imparting the training, suitable training modules need to be developed for the collectors.

2. *Value Addition*

When the raw product is processed and sold, its value increases manifold. Efforts should be made to add value to the raw materials collected from the wild to ensure higher returns. The raw material can be processed into extracts, oils and powders. These can further be processed into creams, tablets, syrups, and other medicinal and cosmetic formulations, and nutraceuticals. The process of value addition requires skill and knowledge, which can be imparted to the interested individuals of the community.

3. *Quality Control Standards*

Ensuring and maintaining the quality of raw and processed medicinal plants is an absolute must not only for the consumers but also for the producers. The WHO and ISO have issued several guidelines on how to (i) produce quality herbal products that are contamination free (WHO, 2003), and (ii) maintain international quality control standards (WHO, 2005). Also, the Drugs and Cosmetics Act of India (Drugs and Cosmetics Act, 1940) has elaborate provisions for preparing and maintaining quality herbal products. Further, the traditional texts on Ayurveda also provide guidelines for preparing quality products. This important information needs to be passed on to these communities so that they can enforce quality control standards in their products. The people need to be empowered with this knowledge to enable them to move comfortably into the international market and ensure profitable returns.

4. *Intellectual Property Rights*

The working knowledge of intellectual property rights (IPR) is a must for people dealing with medicinal plants. This is true especially for the grassroots people. There is always the danger of losing the native medicinal plants to patents. Although plants are not patentable in India, there are instances where the same plant has been patented elsewhere in the world. The plants are however protected through the documented traditional knowledge (TKDL, 2009) and so any claim arising anywhere in the world can be opposed and rejected based on this documentation. There are several such IPR issues, which the stakeholders at the grassroots level must know. They need to be provided with this knowledge to empower them and protect their enterprises.

Based on the above discussion a model of integration and sustainable development of the marginalized communities is proposed that employs the three parameters of community mobilization, cooperatives and capacity building taken together (Figure 16.1).

CONCLUSION

Interactivity of the marginalized communities in India with the global communities is possible only when these communities are first integrated into the national mainstream. It is a fact that many marginalized communities sustain themselves on the trade of medicinal plants that they collect from the wild. The collection process is extremely unsustainable and these communities stand to gain nothing from it. On the other hand, there is a strong prospect of creating sustainable livelihoods for these marginalized communities out of the medicinal plants collected from the wild. The global market demand of products that are based on medicinal plants is rising day

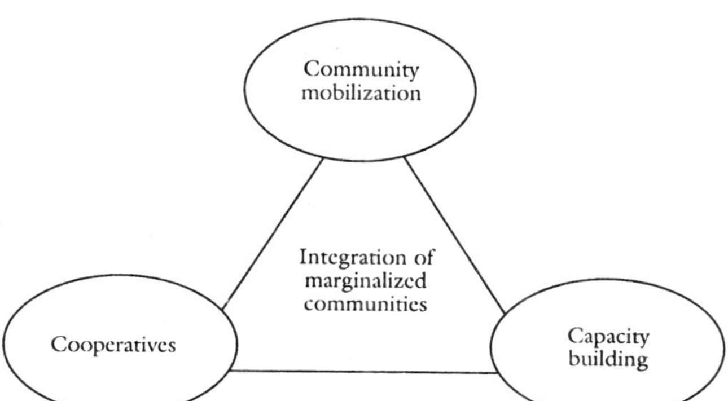

FIGURE 16.1: PROPOSED MODEL OF INTEGRATION OF MARGINALIZD COMMUNITIES SUSTAINING ON COLLECTION OF MEDICINAL PLANTS IN INDIA INTO THE MAINSTREAM

by day. The marginalized communities need to reap the benefits from this trend. They need to be mobilized sufficiently to work through cooperatives at the grassroots level towards producing international quality medicinal plant-based products. The capacity building exercise of these communities needs to be seriously carried out to empower them and enable them to enter the global market with confidence.

ACKNOWLEDGEMENT

I would like to thank Ms. Sushmita Das, Information Executive, Development Alternatives, for her help in literature survey and also her moral support while I was writing this paper.

REFERENCES

Aromatic and Herbal Planations (2009), http://business.gov.in/agriculture/aromatic_herbal_planation.php

Brandt D. (ed.) (2003), *Navigating Innovations: Indo-European Cross Cultural Experiences,* vol. II, New Delhi: India Research Press.

Calixto J.B. (2000), 'Efficacy, Safety, Quality Control, Marketing and Regulatory Guidelines for Herbal Medicines (Phytotherapeutic Agents)', *Braz J Med Biol Res,* vol. 33, no. 2: 179-89.

Das, M. (2004), 'Medicinal Plants: An Approach Towards Sustainable Development', 13th Conference of the International Association of Management of Technology (IAMOT 2004), 3-7 July 2004, held at Washington D.C.

Drugs and Cosmetics Act (1940), http://cdsco.nic.in/html/drugs&CosmeticAct.pdf; http://www.commonlii.org/in/legis/num_act/daca1940198/

DFID, http://www.dfid.gov.uk/aboutdfid/

Exim Bank Study Calls for an Inspiring National Vision for Development of Indian Medicinal Plants Sector (2008), http://www/eximbankindia.com/old/press031113.html

Hamilton, A. (2006), 'Conservation and Sustainable Use of Medicinal Plants: The Approach and Experience of FRLHT', http://www.frlht.org/

Herbal market to grow to Rs. 14,500 crore by 2012: Assocham, *The Economic Times,* 28 March 2008. http://economictimes.indiatimes.com/News/News-By-Industry/Healthcare--Biotech/Pharmaceuticals/Herbal-mkt-to-grow-to-Rs-14500-cr-by-2012-Assocham/articleshow/2910010.cms

http://business.gov.in/agriculture/aromtic_herbal_planation.php

ISSC-MAP, Medicinal Plant Specialist Group Species Survival Commission, IUCN (2007), 'International Standard for Sustainable Wild Collection of Medicinal and Aromatic Plants' (ISSC-MAP), http://www.floraweb.de/map-pro/

Joint Forest Management, http://www.manage.gov.in/managelib/extdig/Untitled-1.pdf#search=%22%22joint%20forest%20management%22%22

Kala, C.P. and B.S. Sajwan (2007), 'Revitalizing Indian Systems of Herbal Medicine by the National Medicine Plants Board Through Institutional Networking and Capacity Building', *Current Science*, vol. 93, no. 6: 797-806.

Lambert, J.D.H. (2005), 'Capitalizing on the Bioeconomic Value of Multipurpose Medicinal Plants for the Rehabilitation of Drylands of Sub-Saharan South Africa', 2005. http://lnweb18.worldbank.org/ESSD/envext.nsf/45ByDocName/CapitalizingontheBio-EconomicValueofMulti-PurposeMedicinalPlantsfortheRehabilitationofDrylandsinSub-SaharanAfrica/$FILE/CapitalizingMedPlants.pdf/

Lambert, J., J. Srivastava and N. Vietmeyer, 'Medicinal Plants: Rescuing a global heritage'. World Bank Technical Paper 355 (1997), http://www-wds/worldbank.org/external/default/WDSContentServer/WDSP/IB/2000/02/24/000009265_3971031092525/Rendered/PDF/mult_page.pdf

Lange, D. (2007), 'International Trade in Medicinal and Aromatic Plants'. http://library, wur.nl/frontis/medicinal_aromatic_plants/11_lange.pdf

MAPPA, 'Medicinal and Aromatic Plants Programme in Asia', ICIMOD, http://mappa.icimod.org/

Plan of Implementation of the World Summit on Sustainable Development (2005), http://www.un.org/esa/sustdev/documents/WSSD_POL_PD/English/WSSD_PlanImpl.pdf

Singh, H. (2006), 'Prospects and challenges for harnessing opportunities in medicinal plants sector in India', http://www.lead-journal.org/content/06196.pdf

TKDL (Traditional Knowledge Digital Library), (2009), http://www.tkdl.res.in/tkdl/langdefault/common/Home.asp?GL=Eng; http://www/tkdl.res.in/tkdl/LangDefault/Ayurveda/Ayu_Advancesearch.asp?GL=Eng

Traditional Medicine (2008), http://www.who.int/mediacentre/factsheets/fs134/en

TRIFED (2009), 'The Tribal Cooperative Marketing Development Federation of India Limited' (TRIFED), http://trifed.nic.in/profile.asp?id=pro

UNCTAD (2009), 'What is Biotrade?', http://www.unctad.org/Templates/Page.asp?intItemID= 3790&lang=1

——— (2006), 'The Biotrade Initiative and Verification', http://www.unctad.org/biotrade/BTFP/BTFP-docs/Working_docs/Bt_verification.pdf

Uniyal, R.C. (2005), 'Export Potential of Medicinal, Aromatic and Dye Plants, Medplant Network News', http://www/mappa-asia.org/uploads/tx_viewresource/medplant_PDF_oct_05.pdf

WHO (2003), 'Research Guidelines for Evaluating the Safety and Efficacy of Herbal Medicines', http://www.who.int/medicinedocs/index.fcgi?sid=rQ6TWIlB9ee80ca700000000474e0a12&a=d&d=Jh2946e.5.3.pr

——— (2005), 'Quality Control Methods for Medicinal Plant Materials', http://www.who.int/medicines/services/expertcommittees/pharmprep/QAS05_131Rev1_QCMethods_Med_PlantMaterialsUpdateSept05.pdf.

IV. ICT, EDUCATION, AND SOCIAL DEVELOPMENT

CHAPTER 17

Role of ICT in Social Development: A Critique

SUDITI NASKAR

INTRODUCTION

The usage of information and communication technology (ICT) is increasingly being seen as a major tool for development. In a huge country like India, this has deeper significance as the ICT-enabled services can be used as an alternative to the government services where the latter cannot reach directly to the citizens. However, taking ICT as a solution for various challenges in the context of development has its own set of problem. While India is increasingly appreciated globally for its magnificent growth in the IT sector, a striking majority of its people are grossly under-privileged without access to even basic modern technologies. Researches show we are a nation fraught with the worst kind of digital divide. In such a scenario, it is imperative to weigh the feasibility of using ICT as a tool for sustainable development. This paper looks into these problems, seeking to present a critique of the ongoing projects and suggesting an alternative.

METHODOLOGY

The ideas are chiefly drawn from various secondary sources, e.g. books, websites and research papers available online.

Around the world there is a movement of spreading ICT to the remotest corner of humanity. The objective is to connect with the unconnected. India as an emerging global power is also a part of this movement. The idea is that need-based application of ICT will empower rural people and make them consciously take part in the huge development process the nation is currently undergoing.

Upgrading sectors like health, education, agriculture and governance in rural India has become the focus of this development process with the initiation of various ICT-based developments that started in the late 1990s. The central and state governments, local, national, international NGOs and private agencies have come forward to give shape to various ICT projects to make the rural population a part of the developments. However, the success of such projects has been far from achieved. While India is famous for its human IT resources, it faces one of the acutest digital divide in the world. Millions of rural people have never seen a computer in their lives. A big chunk of the population is still illiterate and is evidently on the wrong side of development.

But before we get into the details of the problems, let us understand what digital divide is. In brief, this means the gap between those who can effectively make use of digital technology and those who cannot. It broadly refers to the *haves* and the *have nots* in the context of digital information (www.edutopia.org, 2007). The phrase *digital divide* was unknown until it was noted in 1996, in the United States of America (Keniston, 2002). It was that there was a gap in the United States between those who had telephones, computers and internet connections and those who did not. The phrase digital divide was invented to characterize this gap and soon the term became widely known. By 1999 the problem was so seriously felt that the former secretary-general of the UN Kofi Annan specifically mentioned digital divide as a source of growing inequality in the world, in the Human Development Report (1999). He also dedicated the UN to bridging this divide.

We usually think that digital divide is a problem that can be simply catagorized through geography and economic conditions. Many are of the opinion that the Western and the rest of the world are digitally divided. Likewise, the rich and the poor, the urban and the rural population share a digital rift. While such theories are valid to an extent, they provide a 'poor roadmap' (Warschauer, 1997) to understand the problem. To begin with, there is no such bipolar division, as we have already discussed. Various degrees of access can be seen in the developed nations. There are various places in the UK and US where people do not even understand the relevance of using a computer (McConnaughey 2008) because they cannot find information important to them. Although PC ownership has grown by 10-13 percentage points in all areas since 1994, central cities again lag behind the national average for *PC* ownership and *on-line access* (32.8 per cent, 17.3 per cent), as do rural areas (34.9 per cent, 14.8 per cent). Urban areas are slightly higher than the average (37.2 per cent, 19.9 per cent). The West's urban areas (43.9 per cent, 23.14 per cent) rank highest in PC and on-line access, while the Northeast's central cities have the lowest penetration rates (24.7 per cent, 12.6 per cent). After accounting for income, there is not a significant difference between rural, urban, and central city areas for computer penetration, although rural areas still have a significantly lower rate for on-line access. Likewise, various degrees of access and usage with regard to ICT can be seen even in the same city. So, it's basically a gradation based on different degrees of access to Information Technology and its successful usage. Oversimplification of the problem in terms of geographical location or socio-economic factors will not provide the full picture. Also, there is a risk involved in making such bipolar division. Many would see it as undue marginalization of people. For example, we often think that ICT cannot be exploited by the common villagers. Such 'stereotyping of disconnected minority could even serve to further social stratification' (ibid.) by discouraging the employers or the content writers to reaching out from those people.

We attribute too much importance to the factor of physical access. Big IT companies have usually used this as a means of expanding their market. Their way of publicizing the entire scenario in the light of physical access to computers has contributed to forming a mass misconception that the problem of digital divide revolves around the area of physical access to computers. This takes the attention away from the complex socio-economic aspects that are deeply implicated in this issue. The problem with this notion is that it tends to see computers as a larger than life solution. ICT does not exist as an external solution that can be injected from the outside to bring about certain results. Rather, it is woven in a complex manner into the social system and process. It may also imply that there is no other reliable source of gaining information and knowledge as this concept classifies the information *haves* and the *have nots* on the basis of ICT. This would minimize our scope of drawing knowledge from other resources. Our flaw in understanding the actual problem associated with this divide leads us to take initiatives that don't work and do projects that have very limited impact in serving the rural and the underprivileged people, the target clientele in question here.

However, apart from this generic problem of understanding the divide, there are some very crucial socio-economic and political issues at work. Problems at the bureaucratic level and problems related to successful implementation of the plans often create huge road blocks. Various sociocultural and political issues play a huge role in deciding upon the success or failure of a project. Most of these projects are the 'brainchild' of individuals. Hence, more than often the success of the project depends to a great extent on the enthusiasm and vision of the 'leader'. Here the leader could be an officer in the bureaucracy or a project leader in an NGO. Most of the times, the other workers do not take active interest and are not trained to carry out the project with all its vitality in the absence of the leader (Dossani and Jhaveri, 2005). Thus, many projects suffer when the officer is transferred or the project captain moves on to handle newer responsibilities.

Many projects suffer because the stakeholders fail to define the areas of responsibilities among themselves. Importantly, several projects run through joint partnerships or multiple stakeholding. Since there is no set structure of who would take how much responsibility the project invariably suffers. And when the project fails to provide adequate support to the operators or users the parties involved blame each other. The Warana Village Project in Maharashtra, for example, suffered due to the stakeholders' collective failure in providing the village operators adequate support in relation to training and providing proper hardware and software infrastructure. As a result, after the initial phase the project suffered to a great extent. The local people blamed the external stakeholders such as the National Informatics Centre which provided 50 per cent initial financing, computer and communication equipment, software, training, support; and the Directorate of Information Technology, Government of Maharashtra (GoM) which provided 40 per cent initial financing, equipment for village booths, software, administrative and logistical support. The villagers felt these stakeholders should have ensured technical and infrastructural support before their 'exit' (ibid.).

Many researches including Professor Kenneth Kensinton of the Massachusetts Institute of Technology opine that many discourses have taken place at the bureaucratic level about how to digitally connect the villages with the mainstream development but very few of these promises actually matirialize.

One of the biggest problems is lack of proper dissemination about the full range of services provided in the village information centres.

Many villagers don't really know what facilities they can avail of. This lack of information leads to misconception. And this is what exactly has been witnessed in various projects. For example, in the state of Andhra Pradesh many users concluded that computer was meant exclusively for bill paying (APOnline) while in Karnataka, people thought it was for accounting (Bellandur Gram Panchayat Computer System, in Bellandur, Karnataka). In some of the n-Logue Chiraag is the brand name of n-Logue Chiraag Kiosk sites (Tamil Nadu, Maharashtra, Gujarat, Madhya Pradesh) the users thought the machines were toys. Similarly in Gyandoot Samiti project in Dhar district, Madhya Pradesh, many were unaware of the e-governance services. At the same time the target users were not allowed to use the computers. Thus, it potentially distanced the users by denying them the scopes to experiment and acquire knowledge (ibid.).

The centre operators needs to be selected with utmost care as they are the prime agents for revenue generation. They must have basic idea of navigating the internet and make maximum use of the available tools and services. Very importantly, they should be well versed in the services the centre provides to the users. It is imperative that they have good communication and marketing skills, since they are the ones who are directly contacted by the grassroot people for various ICT-based dealings. It was seen in some of the n-Logue Chiraag Kiosks project sites and one Kuppam Community Information Centre (CIC) that the sites with a non-proactive operator always suffered while the others have been successful in making a sizeable positive impact (ibid.).

Several projects discriminate among the local population, in general unintentionally. Projects that aim at serving the farmers preclude the women and the people without land. The e-chaupal and Warana initiatives portray this limitation. The e-chaupals are located in private households. It was observed that in several e-chaupal centres in Madhya Pradesh low caste people were not allowed to enter the households (ibid.). In addition to this problem, the lack of women computer operators a discourages women from using the applications. Such issues make the projects exclusive, further intensifying the socio-economical, cultural and digital divide. Though it is difficult to serve an entire population of a village, projects carried out by the MS Swaminathan Research Foundation (MSSRF) have tried to bridge the divide in the best possible ways. Instead of targeting a particular section of villagers they aim at delivering a rounded package, consisting of employment, enhancement to the existing rural trades like providing adequate information for farming, fishing, etc., health care, education, gender empowerment (www.mssrf.org, 2008) and overall awareness about government and the world outside.

E-governance is one of the most successful initiatives that have been taken up so far by various advocacy groups and state governments. The objective of e-governance in rural areas is to make various economic, social, and fiscal services available to the disconnected villagers. Various documents like marriage certificates, birth and death certificates, paper work for pension plans, caste certificates, tax payment and bill payment are some of the primary features of e-governance. In addition to this, it can work as a potent tool to implement the Right to Information Act by providing people access to various governmental issues. However, this initiative faces various internal problems barring a few exceptions. In most of the cases, though the government takes initiatives the programmes fail to perform as the local governments do not invest a great deal of money into these projects. However, if it's a question of reputation or money as it happened with AP Online the government makes sure that the project runs and lives up to the expectations (Dossani and Jhaveri, 2005).

According to researchers in the field, digitizing governance would demand new technical training for the government officials. Once the governance is digitalized, many government officials and middlemen will have to make do without the bribes they get from the commoners (Kensinton, 2005). Moreover, inter- and intra-departmental political disagreements occur when a project is in its operational stage. All these are enough reasons to sabotage a project.

Often, what is committed by the government officials is not met with during the course of the project. Projects like n-Logue and Kuppam faced big troubles as the support they were promised from the government was not delivered (ibid.). High ranked government officials said that they would digitize all the necessary contents needed to process papers like birth and death certificates, caste certificates, income certificates, and land records. But at the time of delivery none of these promises were fulfilled (ibid.). There was no electronic content available. So, both of these projects had to stop the e-governance facilities.

Apart from these implementation related problems, there are some

TABLE 17.1: STAGES OF GROWTH IN RURAL CAPABILITY ENHANCEMENT

	Urban-based provider's role	Shared roles	Transferred to rural provider	Rural provider's additional roles	Projects
Stage 1	Content, finance, input sourcing, technology, shop-front design and quality control	None	Shop-front capacity and sales	None	HP i-Community e-Chaupal
Stage 2	Technology, input sourcing	Content, finance, and quality control	Shop-front design	None	AP Online Gyandhoot MSSRF n-Logue Warana
Stage 3	Technology, hardware sourcing	Software sourcing, finance, quality control	Content	Add content from other rural providers	Boodikote
Stage 4	Backbone technology	Finance, quality control	All sorucing, access technology	Add content from other urban providers	
State 5	Competitor	None	Backbone technology, finance, quality control	Subcontract to rural providers in other locations	Bellandur

Source: Rafiq Dossani and Roma Jhaveri, 'Enabling ICT for Rural India', Asia-Pacific Research Center, Stanford University, Stanford, November 2005.

instances when there is a question of the practicality of trying to have things done digitally. For example, if someone in a village has a complaint that needs to be addressed, there is no reason to think having the process done digitally (say through email) would actually serve better to solve the problem than meeting the concerned person face to face (ibid.). Moreover, most of the times, the concerned person is often a representative from the village. Naturally, to a villager, it would look more practical to meet him/her in person and explaining things prior to the submission of the complaint in pen and paper.

Another problem is that the cost of deployment is not commensurate with the amount of revenue generated. The money spent on building the technology infrastructure is not redeemed by the incoming money. Despite claims of site managers, even highly successful projects are not able to retrieve the primary cost of deployment. The extent of usage among the customers is simply not enough to make profit. The lack of a practical and financially viable model is a big problem the projects are faced with (ibid.).

In most sites power shortage is a big hurdle. Often there isn't power for more than four hours a day. Back-up systems such as solar power or inverter cannot be accounted for the supply of power required for an entire day. This problem is particularly acute in the e-Chaupal and Gyandoot projects in Madhya Pradesh. It was seen that in most cases the UPS systems were in a state of repairs or lasted only for ten minutes (Dossani and Jhaveri, 2005), making smooth operation impossible. Hardware failure is another major infrastructural problem the projects are confronted with. Specifically in projects in which second-hand computers are used, hardware failure is one of the most prevalent problems. For example, the MSSRF operates through donated second-hand computers. The repair charge incurred is an additional cost that unnecessarily burdens the projects.

The objective of all these projects is to make the rural people directly involved in the process of development. For this, the rural people themselves will have to take part in the ICT-run initiatives. But in most cases, the handing over of responsibilities has not taken place. Various reasons like flaw in the planning of a project or the inability of the villagers to pick-up the responsibilities have barred the projects' envisioned advancement. As a result the aimed empowerment of the rural people has not taken place.

So, there is still not enough proof that spending money on ICT infrastructure is more justified than spending money on providing basic needs such as water, food, medicine and education. None of these projects present any model that has become sustainable and self-supportive (ibid.) though it may be too early to conclude so as it is difficult for any large-scale initiative in a huge country like India to deliver to its fullest potential (Cecchini, 2002). This is especially so when it is targeted to the rural population as the challenges are more than just infrastructural and socio-political. Cultural barriers such low level of education, negative perception of machine, sometimes even fear towards it, play a big negative role. Many people are reluctant to use and experiment with computers as they feel the machine may crash. In such a scenario, making ICT a tool for development seems to be unrealistically ambitious. So, how viable really is this option?

The beauty of ICT lies in its capability to provide unending supplies of information. Increased information gives people access to increased amount of resources and hence, empowering a large number of people who don't have access to both information and resources otherwise. It can weave millions of physically unconnected people in a string by virtually connecting them. Hence, it has the potential to take a very fruitful role in making education, health care and governance available to the unconnected. So far, many initiatives have been taken and these have changed the lives of thousands of people. Let us discuss the successes achieved by the various projects where ICT has been used as a tool for development.

According to a report of the World Bank (ibid.), the computerized milk collection centres in Gujarat is making pro-poor market development through ICT-based calculation process. Previously the milkmen of this locality would collect milk from faraway places and wait for hours in the dairy cooperatives to sell their milk. All the calculations were done manually and they would be paid every ten days. The farmers complained that such long processes was non-conducive for their business and often resulted in miscalculation. But with the emergence of computerized calculation the process has become faster, fairer and more transparent.

ICT can increase access to government services. Since January 2000 Gyandoot—a government-owned computer network—has been making availing of government services easy and less time consuming to the villagers of the under privileged drought-prone Dhar district of Madhya Pradesh (ibid.). They provide various government papers and local important information to the local people, papers like domicile certificate (*mool niwasi*), caste certificate, landholder's passbook of land rights and loans (*bhoo adhikar evam rin pustika*), rural Hindi e-mail, public grievance redressal (*shikayat nivaran*), forms for various government schemes, below poverty line family list, employment news, rural matrimonial (*vivah sambandh*), rural market (*gaon ka bazaar*), rural newspaper (*gram samachar*), advisory module (*salahkar*), e-education general provident fund; and Khasra Nakal application (Avedan) (http://gyandort.nic.in) are provided to the villagers. Apart from providing easy access to various types of documentations, Gyandoot has revolutionized the attitude of the people concerned—that is enabling the villagers to avoid the common practice of bribing the officials (Rama, n.d.).

The kiosks in various projects like ITC e-chaupal and n-Logue has enabled thousands of small farmers to track crop prices. As a result they are no longer gullible enough to be duped by the middlemen or the big traders in the business centres or *mandis*. They can now negotiate crop prices in the wholesale market more confidently. Thus, ICT is resulting in better trades for the grassroot traders. Similar helping bodies have been formed in the other states. Organizations like Simplified and Transparent Administration of Registration (STAR) Chennai and SETU–Integrated Citizen Facilitation Centres of Maharashtra serve the same purpose.

Other organizations like Fast, Reliable, Instant, Efficient Network for Disbursement of services (FRIENDS) (www.apdip.net.) in Kerala and LOKMITRA, Government of Himachal Pradesh's e-governance initiative (http://himachal.nic.in) are readily providing services from government to the citizen and connectivity between the citizen and the government. Such initiatives are generally upgrading the lives of the villagers. E-BillPost and e-Post Services of the Department of Posts are helping people both in rural, urban and suburban areas (Cecchini, 2002). A great deal of effort is being directed in upgrading general standard of life both in rural, urban and semi-urban areas. The fundamental aims are better connectivity, saving time, providing relevant information related to health, education, market economy, and so on. In short, these organizations are working as extensions of the government that cannot physically reach everyone due to the vastness of the country. It is synonymous to expanding the country's democracy.

ICT can be used as an effective tool to expand microfinance (ibid.) Swayam Krishi Sangam (www. sksindia.com), a microfinance institution in the Medak district of Andhra Pradesh has shown impressive result of usage of information technology in their transactions with the farmers. All these transaction happen through Smart Cards. This organization is inspired by the group lending model developed by Bangladesh's Grameen Bank. Initially, the high cost of delivering services to its target clientele was a major problem facing this organization. All cash transactions would occur at the village meeting where each case would be discussed and the decision taken. Once the decision was taken a great deal of time was spent on documentation, discussing loan terms and conditions, and counting money. But with the introduction of Smart Cards, the entire process has become faster and more precise. Each Smart Card holds the history of clients' credit. Thus, it lowers the cost of delivering services by reducing errors and fraud, eliminating unnecessary paper work, and finally speeding up the procedures. Once SKS is in a position to implement the usage of Smart Cards fully, its operational costs could be cut by nearly one-fifth (Cecchini, 2002).

ICT can take a major role in improving health care delivery. Though the implementation of ICT-based tools and services in delivering health care have not been experimented on a wide scale, a few initiatives have so far shown encouraging results. The midwives in Andhra Pradesh use handheld computers which gives them more time to serve the patients in the villages. They used to take care of about 5,000 people—typically across multiple villages and hamlets and had to do a great deal of data entry and paperwork. The computers provided under InfoDev (a development body of the World Bank)-sponsored India Healthcare Delivery Project is freeing them to devote more time to the patients. According to a report by World Bank (ibid.), it has saved them 40 per cent of their service time. Likewise, in Sisu Samrakshak, a joint initiative by the Government of Andhra Pradesh and UNICEF that is based both in Andhra Pradesh and Karnataka, a pilot project is running to make use of ICT for integrated information for Early Childhood Development. Sisu Samrakshak has been able to make positive changes by providing access to rapid, precise and up to date information on issues of child health, maternal care, HIV/AIDS, water supply and sanitation. Moreover, they provide information and vocational training support intermediaries such as Anganwadis, Auxiliary Nursing Maids (ANM), teachers and other workers in health care.

Broadly speaking, ICT can address gender disparity by 'challenging existing social norms, shifts in power relations, an increase in perceived opportunity, and increase in "confidence levels" (ibid.) of the women members as a result of integration of ICT with their professional goals. Significant changes have been observed in a small village called Baduria in West Bengal, since an NGO called Change Initiatives began empowering the women here through various ICT-enabled services conceived in the Nabanna Information Network project. The fundamental concept was to make the local women confident by giving them scope to indulge in creative and interactive activities and helping them learn basic computing skills. They were made to take part in brush painting, learning to use Microsoft Word, writing in Bengali by using I-Leap, and so on. But, above all, such activities gave them a chance to interact with other rural women in a 'non-partisan way' (ibid.). This may not be a big change. But for the marginalized women this exchange of ideas and scope of unleashing their creativity can make a difference and help create mass awareness about the world outside and the possibilities within. Organizations like Sewa in Gujarat and Foundation of Occupational Development in the predominantly Muslim ghetto of Seelampur-Zaffrabad located in the fringes of north-east Delhi are helping under-privileged women gain economic self-sufficiency.

Information technology can also play a big role in spreading mass awareness about AIDS and sex education. Youths of today embrace the use of ICT for entertainment, learning and communication. Even the rural boys and girls can benefit by it if given access and proper orientation to the computers and Internet. The advantage of this media is that it is highly personalized and interactive, qualities which enable people to gain knowledge without hesitation. In recent times, several reports have provided highlights on the use of ICT to combat HIV/AIDS. In November 2001, a consultant for the International Development Research Council (Bloome, 2007) produced a comprehensive report showcasing several pilot project activities in this area.

Looking at these initiatives, it is clear that ICT does make a difference in people's lives. However, achieving this development or change is not easy. There are matters that need to be addressed before we can even think of using ICT as a tool for mass development. So far, we have seen both what is working and what is not. Keeping in mind the negative aspects, there is a need that we focus on how best these challenges could be handled. Providing computers alone would not solve the problem.

Primarily we need to have a clear understanding of the digital divide, so far, the major road block in harnessing ICT for sustainable grassroot development. This is not a problem that has emerged suddenly. The seed of the divide was embedded in our complex socio-economic structure. Since lack of education, different socio-cultural orientation and gender disparity are one of the major reasons behind this divide, the process of bridging the divide has to go hand in hand with providing basic developmental services like education, employment, and the initiatives to include more people in the development. The goal of using ICT with marginalized community is not to overcome a technical divide but rather to further a process of social inclusion (Warschauer, 1993). And to achieve this, it is important to 'focus on the transformation, not the technology' (Jarobe, 2003).

Sharp focus has to be given to factors like content, language, intention of the policy makers, education, literacy and community or social resources.

Applications developed by or in collaboration with local staff are more likely to suit local conditions and thus be sustainable. Outside control and top-down approaches, by contrast, often waste resources. Rajasthan's state-sponsored e-governance programme has failed even though the software was easy to use and delivered in Hindi, because centralized planning did not take account of local conditions (Cecchini, 2002). In addition, content provided through ICT should not be limited to knowledge from outside sources, but extended to draw on knowledge held by under-privileged people. The InfoDev-sponsored Honey Bee Network, based in Gujarat, provides a database of solutions to local agricultural problems and is an excellent example of gathering and disseminating poor people's knowledge.

Applications must be available in local languages to be relevant for the poor. The contents should be visually oriented and use voice interfaces to the possible extent. Illiteracy and knowledge of only the native languages are big hinderances to people's use of ICT (ibid.). For example, the handheld computers used in the India Healthcare Delivery Project use software designed keeping in mind the literacy levels of health care workers. Image-enabled content is required for the less educated or illiterate people.

Since e-governance is the most successful ICT-enabled initiative to include the under-privileged into the process of development, some significant alternatives may be suggested to make such projects successful. To begin with, the projects may be run by the local officials.

It has been seen that projects run better if the local government officials, the panchayats, and the local people are involved. The reason is the operators are more accountable, as the villagers know them personally and can reach them. On the contrary, the government officers operating from their state or divisional headquarters are naturally distant from the villagers and may have gaps in the interaction with the people served (ibid.).

E-governance should be spread in the block and the district levels as well (ibid.). All the government departments work in an interconnected way for various services. The villages need required support in terms of system, content, software, and so on from the district and the block levels. Hence, initiating e-governance only in the village level will not be of much help and thrust should be given to begin e-governance also in the district levels.

There should be a clear and well defined role for the government and the private partners who hold stake in the project. It should be understood by both parties who looks after what. For example, tasks that are routine and standardized and require no decision-making on the part of a government official can be outsourced to private partners (ibid.). Request for the birth certificates will fall into this category. However, digitization of such contents is one primary requirement.

There is another type of documentation that needs discretionary decision making by government officials. Old age pension claims fall into this category. Many steps like digitizing content, system maintenance, analysing the claim against benchmarks, recommending the claim for approval or rejection to the appropriate district official and so on, need to be taken prior to zeroing in on a decision. Private sectors can always take part in this primary information gathering process, but the ultimate decision has to be made by a government official. And both the parties involved need to be aware of their scope of operation.

However, implementation of such ideas is easier said than done. Most of the time, allocation of responsibilities remains a policy challenge to the parties involved.

Training is another important aspect of successful ICT projects. As learning is more effective through practice, innovative and interactive training is more successful. India's Self-Employed Women's Association (SEWA), an Ahmedabad-based NGO, trains poor women to use video cameras and audio-visual equipment to make educational documentaries (ibid.). These women now form teams to produce videos as a tool for learning, education, development, and policy action. It is a well-rounded educational process. The women learn in an innovative way; they make videos that can further educate more people; in the process of making the videos they add to their own knowledge. Training can also reduce the fear of machines a lot of users face. Proper training will also include making people aware of what is useful to them and what is not. Without proper orientation, people may actually spend all their time and money over services (such as various entertainment websites) they cannot benefit from. While the importance of entertainment cannot be looked down upon, it has to be noted that the primary objective of all ICT-enabled projects are to empower people financially, socially and culturally to make them consciously take part in development.

It is also important to raise awareness about the use of information and communications technology. That ICT can actually play a relevant role even in the life of a farmer, a fisherman and a small trader is a big step towards social inclusion of the unconnected people. That is why taking the so-called elitist garb off ICT is so important. This can be done by providing the target users with proper content and useful information. Weather report, news, various educational entertainment programmes can serve this purpose well. According to a report by Marwah (in Pigato, 2001), contents which are not directly linked with the development goals—such as news, matrimonial ads, and entertainment information—can increase the use of internet kiosks. So, whatever ICT-enabled services are provided the basic focus needs to be directed to usability.

It is clear that implementation of ICT to bring about possible change is gaining stronger ground. But even if we put aside the ambitious dreams in regard with the usage of ICT for sustainable development, it can be safely postulated that implementation of ICT will give us a potent network to carry out long-term activity in a more systematic manner than now. That is why ICT is the tool for the future. Negating it would be turning our backs to reality. However, it should be kept in mind that this is just the tool and not the author. The chief responsibility of how a project works has to be shouldered by the ones who make decisions. So, factors like how we use it and for what objective are very important. The stakeholders need to be careful as there is immense scope for experimentation and research. Rigorous monitoring and evaluation are needed to determine if the benefits of ICT projects are worth the projects' costs, especially when they are aimed at social inclusion of the disadvantaged communities.

REFERENCES

Bloome, A. (2002), 'Fighting the Insidious Killer: African Teenagers Battle HIV/AIDS through ICT' , published in http://www1.worldbank.org/devoutreach/spring02/article.asp?id=160

Ceechini, Simone and Giovanna Prennushi (2002), Using Information and Communications Technology to Reduce Poverty in Rural India, 24856, no. 70, The World Bank, Washington D.C., June.

Dossani, R. and Jhaveri R. (2005), 'Enabling ICT for Rural India', Asia-Pacific Research Center, Stanford University, Stanford, November.

Grace, J. et al. (2003), 'Information and Communication Technologies and Broad-Based Development: A Partial Review of the Evidence', The International Bank for Reconstruction and Development, World Bank Working Paper No. 12, Washington, DC 20433, USA, December.

Keniston, K., (2002), 'Grassroots ICT Projects in India: Some Preliminary Hypotheses', *ASCI Journal of Management*, 31(1&2).

McConnaughey, J.W. (2008), 'Falling through the Net ii: New Data on the Digital Divide', National Telecommunications and Information Administration, US. http://www.ntia.doc.gov/ntiahome/net2/falling.html as on 14.2.08.

Rama Rao, T.P.R. (n.d.), 'ICT and e-Governance for Rural Development', Centre for Electronic Governance, Indian Institute of Management, Ahmedabad.

Simpon, G. (2007), 'UK digital divide to deepen? One-third of public has never been online...' , http://management.silicon.com/itdirector/0,39024673,39166402,00.htm

Warschauer, M. (1993), *Technology and Social Inclusion: Rethinking the Digital Divide,* MIT Press.

WEBSITES

http://www.sksindia.com/

http://www.edutopia.org/php/article.php?id=Art_420&key=188 as on 20 February 2007.

http://www.mssrf.org/index.htm as on 12.2.08.

http://gyandoot.nic.in/ as on 12 February 2008.

http://www.apdip.net/resources/case/in08/view as on 2 February 2008.

CHAPTER 18

ICT-Mediated Lifelong Education for Alleviating Marginality in a Knowledge Society

SUTAPA BOSE

OBJECTIVES

This paper intends to highlight the contemporary barriers in the development of an egalitarian knowledge society; define marginality in the context of a knowledge society; deliberate upon the ways to minimize marginalization and elucidate the role of ICT-mediated lifelong education for alleviating marginality.

INTRODUCTION

We are today in the knowldege era, the third wave of human socio-economic development, as said by Charles Savage in his book *Fifth Generation Management*. Today, progress is ensured by the ability to access and use information. Therefore, it has been rightly underlined by Dr. Manmohan Singh (2005), the prime minister of India, that neither military prowess nor economic resources can by themselves ever empower a nation for any length of time. India will be empowered only through the creation of a knowledge society and a knowledge economy within the framework of an open society and an open economy. Therefore, as a part of the globalized knowledge-driven economy, India has to undergo an epistemic shift towards a knowledge society.

A knowledge society, as is known, is characterized by knowledge as the driving force of all the major activities of the society. In this respect it can be argued that even in the past there were activities that were knowledge based. However, the counter-argument is that most of the activities in the past capitalized on land, labour and capital, but now knowledge, an intangible resource rather than these assets, is to be the primary investment. Hence, there would be hardly any activity that can be carried out sans access to information. Also, as envisaged by the renowned management guru, Peter Drucker, a knowledge society has more knowledge workers engaged in knowledge creation and utilization. Access to information, its optimum utilization and sharing are therefore integral to any social activity and also its pre-condition in such a society. Hence, social progress is dependent on the production, utilization and dissemination of information.

The vision of a knowledge society is closely related to Marshall McLuhan's global village wherein Information and Communication Technologies (ICT) lead to the collapse of the barriers of time and space. ICT thus paves the way for free flow of knowledge, its preservation and retrieval. Such flow of knowledge is envisioned to permeate geographical boundaries and reach one and all. In keeping with this, a citizen of a knowledge society, be a farmer, a scientist, a teacher, a medic, a housewife, a student or one pursuing any kind of social activity irrespective of his/her location should be in a position to access, apply and share information. Access to information is thus the leveler of social differences and the architect of an egalitarian society.

A democratic society, be it agrarian or industrial or knowledge society, aims to minimize marginalization. In a knowledge society marginalization itself has a different connotation and certain parameters like access to educational opportunities, access to ICT hardware and key competencies in the form of skills and abilities for accessing and utilizing information, i.e. the software, determine marginality. Unless these pre-conditions are fulfilled, the knowledge society would be far from being egalitarian. The digital skeptics are already critical of the current digital enthusiasm and its creation of new elites. They could be even more vociferous in a society with a sharp digital divide, grappling to accommodate a massive marginalized group. To overcome this problem and also in keeping with the dynamic nature of knowledge, access to information should be on a continuous basis, i.e. there should be provision for lifelong learning.

Accessing the software, i.e. data, and processing it into information requires education and hence education is the key to develop knowledge workers. But providing education to millions and opportunities for lifelong learning is easier said than done. It is now well known that although education is the key to social progress, the conventional system is hardly the recourse. Owing to the several types of constraints of the conventional system, education through the distance mode has to be resorted to, for an inclusive society. Today distance education delivered through ICT is perhaps the only way to reach out to the learners instantly. Hence, even conventional systems are now going for blended mode of education with convergence of face-to-face and distant learning. Informal learning opportunities created through ICT are also important for making people informed. Therefore, those engaged in professions and occupations like farming, fishing, those in rural and remote places and even school-going kids are seeking information over the internet. Thus e-learning opportunities can serve the cause of formal, non-formal and informal education and lead towards a knowledge society.

To become a competitive, dynamic and egalitarian knowledge-based economy capable of sustainable economic growth is a strategic goal for many developed nations today. Hence, to be an equal partner in a globalized economy, India too needs to progress in a similar way and become a knowledge society. But the vision to be a knowledge society would be flawed if it is not an egalitarian one. This requires a missionary approach and its bedrock has to be the steps to eliminate the barriers in the path of an egalitarian knowledge society. In this paper the barriers shall be first deliberated upon. Thereafter the emerging marginalized groups and ways to minimize marginalization shall be discussed at length.

CONTEMPORARY BARRIERS IN THE DEVELOPMENT OF A KNOWLEDGE SOCIETY

Several intimidating impediments are to be eliminated for an egalitarian knowledge society. The major ones can be put under two categories: the first pertaining to education and the second pertaining to access to ICT. Education is the basis for a knowledge society and also lays the foundation for the utilization of ICT. However, access to these two factors is uneven and ridden with certain problems that are as follows:

Problems Associated with Education

Education is indispensable for developing knowledge workers. The quality of education provided determines employability and the quality of the output of those employed. Education and its quality, right from the elementary stage till the level of higher education is therefore crucial. However, in the contemporary Indian society, there are several critical problems associated with education, some of which are the following:

- *Quality of elementary education:* India is still struggling to provide universal elementary education. Although there has been significant gains in the Gross Enrolment Ratio the retention rate is still dismal. The drop-out rate is over 52 per cent by class VIII and regional disparities abound. The Programme of Action (1992) had stressed the need for a substantial improvement in quality of education to achieve essential levels of learning. Bringing about substantial improvement in the quality of education is therefore one of the goals of the ongoing Sarva Siksha Abhiyan (SSA) (a flagship programme of the Government of India with the objective to universalize elementary education in a mission mode). But it is an irony that while the government pumps huge amount of resources into it, the quality of elementary education provided in the government schools remains deplorable (Patnaik, 2006). However, there was at least something to cheer about in the Annual Status of Education Report (ASER) 2007. The report found that enrolment had gone up (98.5 per cent across the country) and that learning levels had improved to some extent. On the other hand, even now nearly 40 per cent of children in Class 5 cannot read a Class 2 textbook (Aiyar, 2008). Such a dismal state of affairs is ascribed mainly to the poor quality of education provided at the elementary level. It had been emphasized long back in the Public Report on Basic Education (PROBE, 1999) that high drop-out rate has more to do with the quality of education than other factors, but this sordid state of affairs continues even today. The Planning Commission has said that the SSA, the flagship programme to universalize elementary education, has failed to provide quality education to a wide cross-section of children.

  Elementary education is the first step in the preparation of the would be citizens of a knowledge society. When we falter at the first step, moving ahead becomes difficult. With the drop-out rate as high as 52 per cent, and in the absence of quality education at this crucial stage, a wobbly foundation is built for further educational efforts.

- *Secondary education:* Secondary education is the largest provider of workforce in all spheres of national productivity. It bridges elementary education with higher education. However, the high drop-out rate (63 per cent between Class I-X) and low gross enrolment ratio (GER) higher education are testimonies to secondary education being infested with serious problems. As per the report of the Central Advisory Board of Education (CABE) Committee (2005), the goal should be to universalize secondary education for building human capital and accelerating growth. A centrally sponsored scheme for universalization of access to secondary education and improvement of its quality will be implemented during the Eleventh Plan period. This is in keeping with the demands of a knowledge society. But the stage is still not set for universalization of secondary education. It has been mentioned by the Ministry of Human Resource Development in its *Compilation on 50 years of Indian Education: 1947-1997* that for several years to come it will not be financially possible for the states to make secondary education universal. This prophecy has proved to be right, as already enrolment has outstripped the available facilities. For the projected enrolment, the needs for infrastructure, human resource and whopping amount of funds (more than Rs. 75 million) for 2019-20 as projected by the CABE Report (2005) have to be mobilized to achieve universalization of secondary education and this appears to be a formidable task.
- *Vocationalization of education:* Many students fail to clear the tenth grade examination. There is also a problem of increase in unemployment amongst the matriculates. If the present trends continue, the gap between the demand and supply of skilled workers needed for the knowledge economy will increase. To cope up with this problem and enhance national productivity it had been emphasized by the Kothari Commission (1966) and thereafter by the National Policy on Education (1968) that at least 50 per cent of the students enrolled should diversify to vocational streams to augment scope for gainful employment later on. The NPE 1986 too reiterated this for economic growth. The scheme advocated by the Kulandaiswami Committee (1985) advocates expansion of vocational education programmes to generate skilled manpower. But so far this scheme has achieved only partial success. Following its review by NCERT in 1998,

it was found that low priority is accorded to it by the states. Of late the National Knowledge Commission (2006) has also stressed the need for vocational studies, as there is growing demand for skilled manpower, which is not met by the existing systems. Creation of a workforce for the knowledge economy demands that vocational education be accorded the status it deserves.

- *Access to higher education*: In order to meet the challenges of the globalized knowledge economy, a strong foundation developed through elementary and secondary education is essential, but to be equal partners and have a firm footing in the globalized economy, universalization of higher education as is being done in the USA and UK is needed. As stated by Kaul (2006) the real challenge is to expand the opportunities for higher education. At the 'World Conference on Higher Education in the 21st Century', held at UNESCO, Paris, in 1998 it was stated that higher education should be a public service as it can ensure social progress. It was expressed that in a knowledge-based society, higher learning and research are essential for cultural, socio-economic and sustainable development. However, the concern was also expressed that higher education itself is confronted with formidable challenges and must undergo radical changes and renewal. The present national-level GER in higher education is only 12.4 per cent in the relevant age group of 18-23 years, whereas China and the Western world are way ahead in this regard. Moreover higher education in India is plagued by a number of problems like inadequate infrastructure, dearth of qualified teachers and resource crunch, that fail to cope up with the ongoing expansion of the system. Besides, the industrial sector has expressed the concern that many of those passing out are unemployable. The grim situation in the area of higher education can be a major barrier to the development of a knowledge economy.

Problems Associated with Access to ICT Facilities

Today there is consensus regarding the potential of ICT in providing opportunities for lifelong education to anyone, anywhere. But this is a function of the access to ICT facilities. The broadcast media—radio and television—have greater penetration than the Internet, but the former are inadequate for providing e-learning opportunities. These media do not make the learner as empowered as the computer and Internet. This is because broadcast timings and their content are fixed and may not precisely match the needs of the learners. Hence, access to ICT basically connotes access to the Internet and the e-learning opportunities created through it. Mainly two types of limitations could hinder access to ICT. They are as follows:

- *Access to physical facilities like a PC and high-speed Internet connection:* This refers to access to hardware and is essential for getting linked to round the clock learning opportunities. The Internet helps in communication and also provides the link to learning resources. But data sharing requires proper networking, the so-called information super highways. A robust cyber networking facility is needed for sharing of resources over the Internet. But as far as network readiness index is concerned, the ranking in 2006-7 put Denmark in the first place and India at the forty-fourth position. But in 2008 India had slipped down to occupy the fiftieth position.
  Internet and Mobile Association of India (IMAI) and IMRB International's I Cube (Internet in India) report 2007 put the number of internet users in India at 46 million while the number of active internet users was 32 million. Therefore, only 4.5 per cent of India can access the Internet. In 2007, India was the fifth highest Internet user, USA occupying the first position and China the second. But the cause of concern in India is that the high number of users are concentrated mainly in the urban areas. The low percentage of active users is thus worsened by the fact that India's Internet penetration percentage is very low, an abysmal 3.7 per cent. The only heartening fact is that in 1998 it was just 0.1 per cent. China is way ahead of us in this matter. The year 2007 had been announced as the 'Year of Broadband' but as far as its penetration is concerned, we still lag behind many Asian countries. India's broadband subscribers are lesser in comparison to many Asian countries. It is estimated to be around 2,520,000, a broadband penetration of just 0.2 per cent is indeed a dismal figure. This is because demand for broadband is primarily conditioned and driven by Internet and PC penetration ('Broadband Policy 2004', DOT, Government of India), which happens to be low. This could be because affording Internet

facilities on a personal basis is not possible for many as the hardware still remains expensive and subscribing to higher bandwidth, is unaffordable for most of the people.

As per NAASCOM estimates nearly 85 per cent of PC-owning households and business establishments have Internet facilities. But this figure is not a matter of pride but rather of concern because it leaves behind the rural areas where majority of the people live. The Internet users are mostly from the metropolises and urban areas. Again for the rural people, Internet usage is mainly limited for occupational purposes rather than as a tool for learning. This is primarily due to the fact that rural India is grappling with the problems of electricity and telephony and is still far from being networked. Hence access to ICT becomes difficult. Many parts go without power for hours together. When it is available, the voltage may be too low for running the hardware. The teledensity, in spite of the ongoing deregulation in the telecommunications sector, is still low. Thus, lack of infrastructure needed for Internet keeps rural India out of the networked world.

- *Access to software*: The hardware even if accessible may remain unused if access to software is hindered. This may be owing to the following reasons:

  - *Low competence in English, the language of the web:* Many cannot access the information on the Internet because of inadequate knowledge of English and this could lead to saturation in the number of Internet users. Content in regional languages have now begun to be available. For instance the services of Google are available in some regional languages; the portal Webdunia is also available in some regional languages; Raftaar, offers information in Hindi. There are also certain local language newspapers that are available online. But more educational portals and search engines providing content in Hindi and regional languages are highly needed. It is expected that computer applications that help in translation between various Indian languages, as well as translate resources in English language on the web into regional languages would soon be available. Till then access will remain limited.
  - *Lack of higher education:* If the information and resources available on the WorldWideWeb are to be utilized, higher

education is needed. But as mentioned earlier, higher education itself needs to be revamped and the gross enrolment ratio has to be hauled up.

- *Digital literacy:* There are many who are educated but lack the skills to operate computers. While literacy rate is about 65 per cent, digital literacy is far behind. Consequent upon the policy decisions of the government, this is being imparted at the school level. The programme Digital Learning India 2008 focuses on: e-education policy and practice, smart classrooms with ICT and other such measures for augmenting digital literacy and e-learning. But again the high drop-out rate at the school level may hinder general education as well as attainment of digital literacy.

These barriers that come in the way of accessing information need to be removed if the society is to be made more inclusive.

MARGINALITY IN THE CONTEXT OF A KNOWLEDGE SOCIETY

The concept of marginality is dynamic. Since the last several decades, there have been more or less unchanging notions about marginality. But in a knowledge society these notions cannot remain fixed and adopting the old view of marginality may not work. It is alleged that in the agrarian and industrial societies the oppressive aristocrats—feudal lords and capitalists respectively—controlled the disinherited proletariat. But in the knowledge society deprivation would be associated with those unable to access and use information. The active users of knowledge resources would be better placed than others. The barriers in accessing information generate a marginalized section constituted by the digital have-nots. Although digital divide is a worldwide phenomenon and is due to the imbalance in physical access to ICT and the skills and resources to use it, but the developed countries are closing the divide and more and more people are getting networked. In India the poor penetration of the Internet and broadband makes the digital divide difficult to bridge. The situation is worsened by low success rates in educational endeavours, which makes access to software difficult. Although there are plans afoot to provide computers at thousands of rural schools across India, the access may still be limited as suitable softwares are not available.

Educational inadequacies, lack of knowledge of English, poor infrastructure, low teledensity, low access to computer, and the non-availability of adequate regional language software are some of the factors that accentuate the digital divide and create a marginalized group. The rural people as mentioned earlier are not in a position to access ICT facilities mainly because of the fact that rural India is still not wired. To compound this problem educational attainments of rural parts do not match that of urban India. Otherwise, the lack of educational opportunities and proper transportation facilities could have been overcome through facilities for telelearning, teleshopping, telemedicine, e-banking, and so on.

Another section constituting the marginalized group is that of women. In the USA the number of women using the Internet is more than men (*Hindustan Times*, 13 December 2007). But in India, female users of ICT are far surpassed by male users. Most of the users of cyber cafes are men. Traditionally women have stayed away from technology (Mehra, 2003). Cultural practices make women less proactive in using any technology including ICT. Also men are privileged because of their educational advantages in comparison to women.

Apart from rural people and women, there are many groups even within urban areas who would get marginalized if they cannot access ICT. It is an irony that a country renowned for its software professionals manning the IT sector of many developed countries has only a small percentage of households with a PC. The pride and euphoria from the success of the IT sector of India therefore has to be accompanied by introspection.

ALLEVIATING MARGINALITY

Marginality as discussed so far is caused by barriers in availing educational opportunities and in accessing the hardware and the software components of ICT. The ways to alleviate the marginality thus emerging could be the following:

WIDENING ACCESS TO ICT FACILITIES

It is a well-known fact that the poor penetration of Internet and broadband is mainly due to the lack of infrastructure. As underlined by Greenspan (2004) during the industrial age, movement of goods and other resources were over waterways. Now, in the information age the movement is of data and it is over networks that could be wired/wireless. The former president of India, Dr. Kalam said India has no dearth of knowledge centres but connectivity is required. A robust network that allows high-speed data transmission is needed to create a knowledge grid. There are proposals that as an option wireless and the Very Small Aperture Terminals (VSAT) technologies have to be tapped for the unreachable parts. It is also being proposed that modern technologies such as Wi-Fi, 3G and WiMAX, may be used to get the rural areas networked. Another promising technology is the mobile Internet which may surpass broadband and PC-based Internet because of the rapidly increasing number of mobile subscribers. Besides the lack of infrastructure, the high prices for procuring the hardware as well as for subscription to broadband limit access. It is being proposed that Voice over Internet Protocol (VoIP), and Wireless-in-Local-Loop (WiLL or WLL) technologies may provide an inexpensive alternative for ensuring rural connectivity. Projects like One Laptop per Child and distributing inexpensive models like simputers have to be undertaken with more seriousness. The ongoing process of setting up Village Knowledge Centres needs to be strengthened and data has to be transformed to information in usable form. At times even the very access to ICT can itself augment computer-related skills through continuous usage. The NIIT experiment in New Delhi's slums has shown that even those with limited education, literacy, or command over English can quickly master some of the computer applications. The responsibility for widening access to the hardware part and the necessary infrastructure lies mainly with the government. However, besides the government, private entrepreneurs and NGOs too have to chip in to close the digital divide.

Alleviating Marginality Through ICT-Mediated Education

As mentioned earlier, education is indispensable for alleviating marginality. While efforts are being made to network the entire country the facilities created would remain unutilized if educational needs remain unfulfilled. Educational background often determines the amount read by a person. Although this is obvious at the divide between literate and illiterate people, a finely graded difference among the fully literate has also been found. People with graduate degrees read more than those with undergraduate degrees, and so forth (Zill and Wingl, 1990, quoted by Griswold and Wright, 2004). Education is thus the prime requirement to access and benefit from the softwares.

However, it is now a well-known fact that the conventional system with face-to-face teaching is hardly the way to provide education to the millions and that too on a lifelong basis. Therefore distance education through ICT is the only way to provide lifelong opportunities for education and training and thus alleviate marginality. Although ICT includes the computer, Internet, broadcast media, and telephony, but as mentioned earlier it is mainly the Internet that provides the scope for e-learning. Mobile phones may also be a possibility in the near future for educational purposes.

ICT-mediated education benefits the individual learner and in turn the society. It has been rightly said that knowledge mediated by ICT has value not only in the academic world but also in financial, societal and governmental environments as it is highly flexible, enables fast-paced activities and has a ubiquitous distributing power (Gayol, Boubsiland and Hoban, 2005). ICT delivers quality education and educational material across vast geographical locations instantly and that too at economic rates and thus expands learning opportunities. ICT-mediated education and training are therefore the only options for providing lifelong education. UNESCO is therefore according high priority to the use of ICT for more equitable and pluralistic development and expanding the knowledge base. In line with this, the UNESCO's 'ICT in Education Policy' aims to promote appropriate policy models and strategies for the integration of ICT into education in the Asia-Pacific region, with special emphasis on developing policies, which utilize ICT to remove barriers to participation in education and enhance its quality.

The first few grades of elementary education require teaching in a face-to-face manner within the classrooms. However, ICT can play an important role in enhancing the quality of education even at this stage. As per the findings of the NGO, Pratham, the dropout rate and the quality of education provided at the government elementary schools have more school-related reasons. As one of the measures to improve the quality and attract children, ICT could be used in the classrooms. As stated by Jenkins (2003), the use of Open and Distance Learning (ODL) at school level is no longer simply an alternative mode of curriculum delivery for out-of-school children and adults wanting to catch up with missed schooling but the scope is much enlarged. The scope for self-learning and interactive learning, viewing animated visuals, scope for simulation through ICT give a new dimension to teaching and learning. In the year 2000, the SSA initiated a programme called 'Headstart' with computer as a teaching-learning tool for elemenatry school children. The main intention was to bridge the digital divide between the urban and rural student population in terms of access to modern technology aids in education. The rationale of this programme was the view that the use of ICT and computer-assisted learning would help in achieving the objectives of SSA like reduction in drop out rate, preventing repetition and making learning joyful. The Azim Premji Foundation too has a Computer Assisted Learning Centre with several objectives, one of which is to attract children to schools. Therefore even at the elementary level ICT can play an important role in improving the quality of education.

Right from the upper primary classes ODL opportunities can take care of those out of the conventional systems through ICT-mediated educational opportunities offered by the Open School systems. In spite of the expansion of educational facilities at the secondary level, all the learners in the concerned age group will not be accommodated in the formal schooling opportunities. This is because far many would be clearing the elementary level than the present facilities can accommodate. Secondly the school hours coincide with the period when many children are engaged in activities for generating incomes. Hence the Open School systems along with centres for vocational education are necessary for providing education at the upper primary, secondary and senior secondary levels. The existing Open Schooling network has to be expanded and strengthened with ICT facilities so that the target group can be reached. Satellite-based video conferencing and DTH facilities through cable network may be helpful in this regard.

In higher education only a small percentage of the aspirants find a place in the conventional system. ODL is recourse for the rest. Today a sizeable proportion of those seeking higher education are enrolled in the ODL system. This is because as stated by Inglis, Ling and Joosten (1999), in the new world of education and training there is a new wisdom about the capacity of digital media to enhance learning or to accommodate learner convenience and preferences. Today ODL has come a long way from the days of correspondence education and its dependence on ICT to deliver instructions is on the rise. Already radio and television are used to deliver instructions and many of these programmes are interactive. The satellite-based and computer network-based teleconferencing can create virtual learning situations with scope for continuous interactions. Today not only education but also training is provided through ICT. Online training programmes are common and provide for professional development without displacing people.

Today ICT is used not only for distance education but also within the classrooms. Even conventional institutions are empowering their learners with instructions delivered through ICT. For instance, Internet, cell phones, etc., are used even by those in the conventional system for teaching and learning. Thus with the advent of new technologies the boundaries between distance and traditional education are getting blurred.

New capabilities of the Internet are constantly being discovered and it is apparent that this point has not yet reached its saturation (Tomei, 2007). Cell phones too may be used in the near future to deliver instructions. Convergence of computer, telecommunication and television technologies allows storage, manipulation, transmission and reproduction of information in any media type. Such facilities for computing, communication, broadcasting data in multiple forms through telecom and IT networks enrich learning experiences and enable communication of data to anyone at any time. Hence, convergence of technologies has been rightly described as the hallmark of present information age by the Department of IT, GOI. Thus access to digitalized information and that too in multiple media through converged technologies is giving a new dimension to distance learning. ICT also enables the content to be presented as multimedia, the technical facility to create, present and control communication or information in a variety of media through an integrated channel (Garson, 2000).

Today ICT aids not only formal and non-formal education but it is also becoming the mainstay for informal education. For instance, information on various aspects is being collected with the help of the Internet. Rather than print-based encyclopedia, dictionaries, and other sources of information, use of information available over the Internet is on the rise.

CONCLUSION

To acquire a central place in the global economy and be a major player in it, there is the need to gear up and shift to a knowledge society. This requires that the members of the society are in a position to access and utilize information to create knowledge and this in turn requires them to be active users of the Internet and e-learning facilities. However, computers and the Internet are still for the elites as they remain expensive, require complicated infrastructure, are difficult to use and require the knowledge of English. Hence, those lacking access to education, ICT, digital literacy and competence in English, constitute the digital have-nots, the marginalized section of a knowledge society.

To keep at bay the problems of marginalization, it is necessary to identify and eliminate the barriers to the creation of an egalitarian knowledge society. Education and that too on a lifelong basis therefore is of primary importance. The quality of education and access to it has to be enhanced right from the primary to the tertiary level. The quality of elementary education determines the foundation on which further vertical growth would occur and ICT can contribute significantly to it. From the secondary stage onwards the conventional system of education will not be able to provide education to all those who need it. Enhancing the GER as envisaged by the UGC too appears to be a distant goal in view of the limitations of the conventional system. However, educational opportunities can be created through ODL and that too through those, which utilize ICT for reaching out. Hence, it would not be an exaggeration to state that education through ODL is the *sine qua non* of a knowledge society. Thereafter, digital literacy and access to ICT facilities are important for alleviating marginality. Digital literacy is again a function of educational attainment. As far as access to ICT is concerned, as stated by the Government of India Working Group on Information Technology for Masses, the government has to play a catalytic and enabling role in enhancing access to it by developing the infrastructure. Suitable policies are also needed to encourage and facilitate the use of ICT by more and more people.

The former president of India, A.P.J. Kalam strongly advocated for a knowledge grid connecting educational institutions, research facilities and industries so that tele-teaching reaches the remotest corners. This could happen by enhancing the bandwidth, the greatest demolisher of imbalances and a great leveler in a knowledge society. Satellite links and under-sea fibre cables could even network the universities of the world. This would benefit rural users as much as the urban ones (One World South Asia, 2005). Hence, it is apparent that for alleviation of marginality in a knowledge society, ICT-mediated lifelong educational opportunities is imperative.

REFERENCES

Garson, G.D. (2000), *Social Dimensions of Information Technology: Issues for the New Millennium,* Hershey, PA: Idea Group Publishing.

Gayol, Y., O. Boubsiland and S. Hoban (2005), 'Information Technology Fluency of Science Teachers in the United States: A Case Study', in S. Garg, S. Panda, C.R.K. Murthy and S. Mishra (eds.), *Open and Distance Education in Global Environment Opportunities for Collaboration*, New Delhi: Viva Books Private Limited.

Greenspan, A. (2004), *India and IT Revolution*, New York: Palgrave Macmillan.

Griswold, W. and N. Wright (2004), 'Wired and Well Read', in P.N. Howard and S. Jones (eds.), *Society Online The Internet Context*, New Delhi: Sage.

Inglis, A., L. Peter and V. Joosten (1999), *Delivering Digitally Managing the Transition to the Knowledge*, London: Kogan Page.

Jenkins, J. (2003), 'Classroom Open Learning: A Case of Old Wine in New Bottles?' in J. Bradley (ed.), *The Open Classroom Distance Learning In and Out of Schools*, London: Kogan Page.

Report of the CABE Committee (set up by the MHRD) on the Universalisation of Secondary Education (2005).

Tomei, L. (2007), *Integrating Information and Communication Technologies*, Hershey: Information Science Publishing.

WEBSITES

Aiyar, Y. (2008), 'A Report Card for India', *Indian Express*, 23 January 2008, http://www.indianexpress.com/printerFriendly/264472.html (retrieved on 12 May 08)

Kaul, S. (2006), *Higher Education in India: Seizing the Opportunity*, Working Paper No. 179, Indian Council for Research on Economic Relations, http://www.icrier.org/pdf/WP_179.pdf (retrieved on 7 December 2007)

Mehra, P. (2003), 'The Day of the Digital Diva', *Business Line*, 15 February http://www.thehindubusinessline.com/canvas/2003/02/15/stories/2003021500120200.htm (retrieved on 15 September 2007)

MHRD, 'Compilation on 50 years of Indian Education: 1947-1997. Towards a Scheme of Learner Evaluation, MHRD, DOE, with National Informatics Center, http://education.nic.in/cd50years/r/2S/99/2S990701.htm (retrieved on 11 October 2007)

One World South Asia (2005), 'Initiative to Provide Education Resources Electronically can Transform Learning (source: *The Hindu*, 12 December 2005), http://southasia.oneworld.net/article/view/123782/1/1893 (retrieved on 25 December 2007).

Patnaik, I. (2006), 'What Arjun should focus on? We Need Qualitative Improvement in Government Schools Not More Quotas', *Indian Express*, 16 May, http://openlib.org/home/ila/MEDIA/2006/ssa.html (retrieved on 15 September 2007)

Singh, Manmohan (2005), India Empowered to Me is Open Democracy and Open Economy', *Indian Express* 15 August, http://www.indiaempowered.com/ (retrieved on 15 September 2007).

'SSA Fails to Provide Quality Education', *Economic Times*, 16 September 2007, http://economictimes.indiatimes.com/News/News_By_Industry/Services/Education/SSA_fails_to_provide_quality_education/articleshow/2373522.cms (Retrieved on 11 October 2007)

Contributors

RENU ADDLAKHA is senior fellow at the Centre for Women's Development Studies, New Delhi.

JAGANNATH AMBAGUDIA teaches Political Science at Rajdhani College, University of Delhi, New Delhi.

P.K. BISWAS is Professor in the faculty area of Sociology and Community Development at the Indian Institute of Forest Management, Bhopal.

SUTAPA BOSE is an Assistant Professor in the School of Education, Indira Gandhi National Open University, New Delhi.

MOUMITA DAS is Assistant Director in the National Centre for Innovations in Distance Education at the Indira Gandhi National Open University, New Delhi.

ALKA DHAMEJA is a Professor with the Faculty of Public Administration, School of Social Sciences, Indira Gandhi National Open University.

SUJATA DUTTA HAZARIKA presently heads the North East Centre for Research and Development (NECRD), a recent initiative taken by IGNOU to create a long-term think-tank and research body dedicated to North East India.

RAJ KUMAR KHOSLA is a Consultant with Planning Commission, Government of India, New Delhi.

RITAMBHARA MALAVIYA is in the Centre for International Politics, Organization and Disarmament, Jawaharlal Nehru University.

O.P. MISHRA is serving presently in Delhi Police as Deputy Commissioner.

S.A.H. MOINUDDIN is a Reader in the Department of Political Science with Administration and Teacher-in-Charge, Department of Sociology, Vidyasagar University, Midnapore, West Bengal.

DAMAYANTI MUKHOPADHYAY is a lecturer in the Department of Sociology, Vidyasagar University, Midnapore, West Bengal.

SILIMA NANDA, is Deputy Director, International Division, IGNOU, New Delhi.

SUDHITI NASKAR is a fellow of Global India Foundation, Kolkata.

T.K. OOMMEN is Professor Emeritus in Jawaharlal Nehru University, New Delhi where he served as Professor of Sociology for more than two and half decades.

SARJERAO SALUNKHE is a Sociologist at Shivaji University, Kolhapur (Maharashtra).

H.A. SHANKARANARAYANA is a Professor and the Director of Dayanada Sagar Business Academy, Banagalore.

S.L. SHARMA is former professor of sociology, dean faculty of arts, Panjab University, Chandigarh.

DEBAL K. SINGHAROY is a Professor of Sociology, in the Faculty of Sociology, School of Social Sciences, Indira Gandhi National Open University, New Delhi.

T.N. SREEDHARA is a professor and the Chairman, Department of Business Administration, Mangalore University, Mangalore.